OBSESSIVE COMPULSIONS

of related interest

Understanding OCD
A Guide for Parents and Professionals
Edited by Adam B. Lewin and Eric A. Storch
ISBN 978 1 84905 783 7
eISBN 978 1 78450 026 9

Touch and Go Joe
An Adolescent's Experience of OCD
Joe Wells
ISBN 978 1 84310 391 2
eISBN 978 1 84642 489 2

The Imprinted Brain
How Genes Set the Balance Between Autism and Psychosis
Christopher Badcock
ISBN 978 1 84905 023 4
eISBN 978 1 84642 950 7

Can't You Hear Them?
The Science and Significance of Hearing Voices
Simon McCarthy-Jones
ISBN 978 1 78592 256 5
eISBN 978 1 78450 541 7

On Being an Introvert or Highly Sensitive Person
A guide to boundaries, joy, and meaning
Ilse Sand
ISBN 978 1 78592 485 9
eISBN 978 1 78450 871 5

OBSESSIVE COMPULSIONS

THE OCD OF EVERYDAY LIFE

C. Thomas Gualtieri, MD

Jessica Kingsley *Publishers*
London and Philadelphia

First published in 2018
by Jessica Kingsley Publishers
73 Collier Street
London N1 9BE, UK
and
400 Market Street, Suite 400
Philadelphia, PA 19106, USA

www.jkp.com

Library of Congress Cataloging in Publication Data
Names: Gualtieri, C. Thomas, author.
Title: Obsessive compulsions : the OCD traits of everyday life / C. Thomas Gualtieri, MD.
Description: London ; Philadelphia : Jessica Kingsley Publishers, 2018.
Identifiers: LCCN 2017060876 | ISBN 9781785928178
Subjects: LCSH: Obsessive-compulsive disorder. | Compulsive behavior.
Classification: LCC RC533 .G83 2018 | DDC 616.85/227--dc23 LC record available at https://lccn.loc.gov/2017060876

British Library Cataloguing in Publication Data
A CIP catalogue record for this book is available from the British Library

ISBN 978 1 78592 817 8
eISBN 978 1 78450 905 7

Printed and bound in the United States

To Frances

Contents

Introduction

The book is about **obsessive compulsiveness** (OC), not **obsessive-compulsive disorder** (OCD). If we limited ourselves to pathological cases, that would prevent us from understanding the idiosyncrasies that make some normal people endearing and others unbearable. What is OC? It's the way a lot of people are. Let me explain.

In Dunedin, a small city in New Zealand, psychologists at the university recruited 1037 newborns—all the babies born in Dunedin in 1972. The goal was to track the children's health and developmental progress. The program went so well that the kids have been tested at regular intervals ever since. When they reached age 32, the study took a new turn. Researchers from London, Barcelona, Sydney and North Carolina joined psychologists from the University of Otago to investigate the symptoms of obsessive-compulsive disorder, or OCD. They discovered that most of the subjects were healthy and free of any mental disorder. However, among normal young adults, no fewer than 42 percent said they were bothered by obsessions, and 45 percent by compulsions (Fullana *et al.*, 2009). They didn't have OCD. They were OC.

OCD is a mental disorder, but being OC—that is, having a few of the symptoms of OCD—isn't a disorder at all. It's the way many people are. In Zurich, several hundred healthy individuals, representative of the general population, were interviewed seven times between the ages of 20 and 50. Twenty-two percent had at least some OCD symptoms, but not OCD (Fineberg *et al.*, 2013). In Cairo, 26 percent of college students had OC traits and 43 percent had OC symptoms (Okasha *et al.*, 2001). The rates were higher in Israel: among 16-year-olds appearing for pre-induction examinations, 72 percent said that they had OC symptoms (Apter *et al.*, 1996). In Toronto, a study of 16,718 children and adolescents reported that 45 percent had at least one OC trait and 31 percent had two or more (Park *et al.*, 2016). In the USA, almost half of all women experience obsessions or compulsions during the postpartum period (Miller, Hoxha, Wisner, and Gossett, 2015). Finally, in two studies of American college students, the rate of obsessions was higher than 80 percent (Muris, Merckelbach, and Clavan, 1997; Rachman and de Silva, 1978; Salkovskis and Harrison, 1984).

OC is the OCD of everyday life. Of all the mental disorders, the symptoms of OCD merge most closely with normal human behavior and cultural traditions (Hollander, Kim, Khanna, and Pallanti, 2007). One prominent OCD expert wrote that "OC experiences occur in 90% of people at one point or another in their lives" (Pallanti, 2008). OC experiences are similar in form and content to those of patients with OCD, but they are less intense, less frequent, and less disabling. Mostly they are innocent foibles, but sometimes they cause problems. When OCs seek help, they are usually misdiagnosed with depression, anxiety, attention deficit disorder (ADD), bipolar disorder or autism (Fullana *et al.*, 2010).

OC is a common trait. My estimate is that 30 percent of us have it, to one degree or another. It is especially common in people who are intelligent and well-educated. There is something about being smart that can make one a bit too self-absorbed, eccentric or controlling, or—as in the case of my friend Miles—all three. Something as pervasive as OC, and as misunderstood, deserves a close look.

OC is the source of many of the problems we make for ourselves, but this isn't a self-help book: *How Not To Be OC*. There are bad OCs, like those angry, controlling men you've probably encountered along the way. They need help, but more than they can get from a book. There are unhappy OCs, too, people riven by anxiety and fears, and those who are so occupied with getting it right that they never get it at all. There are OCs who are convinced they have attention deficit disorder: they often take medications that make their attention worse—*and* their OC. Most OCs, however, are happy, productive individuals; they're just a little weird, sometimes.

Nor is this book about an epidemic of OC. *We need to arrest it before it corrupts the human race and some other species will evolve and take our place.* As it happens, there *is* an epidemic of OC, but I'm not an alarmist because it's mostly "good" OC. So, we shall meet a man whose obsession with venomous snakes has saved hundreds of lives, and another fellow who assembled the largest collection in the world devoted to any one fruit. Where would we be if it weren't for such men, or for other like-minded souls—the fussy men and women, the Great Detectives and other Great Minds who have walked among us, the Ditzy Blondes, and children with such active minds that they seem to be evolving before our very eyes. If you take such a child to a "mental health professional," he's likely to be diagnosed with ADD or else as "on the spectrum."

We shall meet some other characters, too, whose frailties are best understood when one understands OC. The SAs, people with the traits of social anxiety, don't have social anxiety disorder but are exquisitely sensitive to the unpredictable and irrational nature of social intercourse. Most SAs have OC traits. OC and SA tend to cluster in families, along with Aspergerism, which is a not-quite-pathological variant of autism. SAs are given to flights of fantasy and Aspergerites can do wonders with mathematical formulae and computer programs. Where would we be without them? Narcissists are here, too, and I shall try my best to say something good about them. You don't have to be a narcissist, though, to be obsessively self-absorbed.

OC explains so many mysteries of the human condition that it's possible it explains nothing at all. That is the risk an author takes when he introduces a new theory. But this book isn't about a theory; it is only about observations of the human condition.

A critical reader might suggest that the author is obsessed with OC, but I don't think so. However, even Sherlock Holmes, the Great Detective, admitted, "Perhaps, when a man has special knowledge and special powers like my own, it rather encourages him to seek a complex explanation when a simpler one is at hand."[1]

I don't have special powers as Sherlock had, but I am a neuropsychiatrist and my patients have brain-based disorders— learning disabilities, autism, dementia and brain injuries. My colleagues and I also see patients with unusual or hard-to-diagnose psychiatric conditions. Many are OC or SA, or both, and their traits have often been overlooked by other clinicians. Since I don't have the Great Detective's gifts of clarity and intuition, I worry that my explanations may be turgid, at times. After all, I shall be giving you Brain Science—and the latest news from Brain Science, too— although it's only to complement my observations. OC provides a window into how the mind works, and the brain. So, this is a brain-book, I suppose. It's not one of those books that drubs you with how complex the brain is, yet its circuits are less complicated than the wiring diagram of my daughter's Volkswagen (which I am trying to fix). No, this is a brain-book with *humility*. My premise is that brains are as naive and simple-hearted as people are themselves. Nevertheless, there is something about our brains that makes a good number of us fussy, perfectionistic, eccentric, worrisome, hypochondriacal, uptight, rigid, angry or controlling. Something in our brains can tangle us up in our own cogitations; something else can confer meaning to the most ordinary things we do. There are also mysterious regions in the brain and neural processes that we don't understand very well. In such cases, I shall make something up.

What, then, is OC? It's a lot of things, depending on the per-spective one takes or the neural processes one wants to highlight. Stripped to its essentials, OC is an excess of mental energy that finds

1 Arthur Conan Doyle, "The Adventure of the Abbey Grange" (*The Return of Sherlock Holmes*).

its outlet in thoughts and actions. They can be weird or hilarious, disturbing or comforting, avoidant or exuberant, enervating or highly productive. It depends, I suppose, on those forks in one's neural pathways, whether the oscillations in one part of brain overwhelm the others, or whether one's disposition is, at heart, riven with anxiety or good cheer. Wherever your OC traits may carry you, they are the expressions of a complex brain and an active mind. I wonder if that qualifies as a theory. If it does, remember that "The theories which I have expressed there, and which appear to you to be so chimerical, are really extremely practical—so practical that I depend upon them for my bread and cheese."[2]

---

2   Arthur Conan Doyle, *A Study in Scarlet*.

1
The Great Detectives

It's not a good sign when a brain-injury patient describes a symptom one has oneself. Let me be frank. *My* brain-injury patient, a new one who came to see me last week, has a quirk that *I* also have. He has the habit of responding to questions by saying the precise opposite of what is true. His mother might say, "Are you drawing, Jack?" And he says, "No," although there he is, drawing away. If he waves his hand in class and the teacher asks him, "Do you want to go to the bathroom, Jack?," he says, "No, of course not." But then he gets up and goes to the bathroom. Everyone thinks that Jack is autistic. I know better, because I do the same thing. I don't think of it as a *symptom*, though. It is one of my endearing traits.

I'm on my way to work, my briefcase and lunch-bag in hand, I'm wearing a tie, and it's eight-thirty in the morning. I meet one of my colleagues in the parking-lot. He asks, "Are you on your way to work, Tom?" This is what I say: "No. What makes you think I'm on my way to work?" If my daughters and I are in the kitchen at night eating ice-cream, my wife invariably comes in and says, "Aha! So you're all eating ice-cream, I see." I could say, "That's why I love you, darling, for your keen powers of observation," but she knows I won't say that. She knows that I will say, "No, Frances, what makes you think we're eating ice-cream?" Such clever ripostes contribute to the good humor that suffuses our household.

These days, the girls are older. It is hard to believe that Geni is in college. But they learned at a young age not to ask questions like "Are you and Mom going out tonight?" when we're dressed and ready to go out the door, or "Are you going into the library now to smoke your pipe and work on that stupid book?" They know what I would say if they did, but they don't think the joke is funny anymore. They're at the age when their father's jokes are, necessarily, unfunny.

To me, it's a joke, and some jokes get funnier with repeated telling, at least to me. It's similar to what Jack, my patient, does. He has a tic. It's a verbal tic, a phrase, word or sound he repeats over and over. It's a complex tic, to be sure, that makes him turn "yes" to "no" and "up" to "down." Another psychiatrist might call it a compulsion. Another would say that it's avoidant behavior, a way to keep people at bay—at least the kind of people who ask redundant questions. I know better; it's just a verbal tic, a mannerism, that Jack does for no good reason. Jack, for all his supposed disabilities, has a mischievous sense of humor. He is also a bit OC.

* * *

I consider myself, most of the time, the model of balance and equanimity. I can be a bit fussy sometimes, but I am not a certifiable case of OCD and I certainly am not a wrathful, controlling man, as long as people do right. Nevertheless, I wonder sometimes if I am *obsessed* with OC. I find it everywhere. Maybe that's because it *is* everywhere. Jack, for example. He hadn't really had a brain injury as such, but he was born with an encephalocele, a portion of his right frontal lobe protruding out from the front of his cranium. It's not the kind of thing a neurosurgeon can just put back in as if it were a hernia. He did have surgery and it was successful, but it cost the boy a chunk of frontal lobe. Fortunately, when an event like that occurs in a very young child, the rest of the brain can take over for the missing part, more or less. So Jack was a more or less normal boy, although he had a few awkward traits. He tended to be inattentive, but he was also obsessed with videogames and hated to be disturbed when he was playing. He was a loner and didn't care much for other children—or adults, for that matter. That's why people thought he was autistic. His social skills, however, were quite sound, and he was perfectly able to interact socially when he was so inclined. That wasn't often, though, because society was annoying to him. It made him anxious and obsessive and compulsive. And when someone asked him a question, he knew exactly what he would say.

As it happened, the day before I met Jack, I saw two new patients who were OC. One was a graduate student who was frantic over his comprehensive exams and dissertation and everything he had to do to get ready for them. There was no reason to think that this brilliant fellow wouldn't do well, but he had worked himself into a frenzy. He was so obsessed with the amount of material he had to master that he couldn't think clearly. He made notes and outlines and checked them so often his memory got clogged. He felt utterly muddled. He came to me because someone told him that he had ADD—attention deficit disorder.[1] Of course, his academic career had been nothing but stellar from grade school on. He already had two Masters degrees and was attending one of the most prestigious graduate programs in the country. But he was convinced he had ADD. As it happened, he also had the habit of checking his doors and windows at night and his stove a couple of times before he left for school. He also described a thought that intruded, quite frequently, into his conscious mind: *You're not very smart—you know that, don't you?* As intrusive thoughts go, it was a clever one. Does one answer, *Yes, I knew that* or *No, I didn't?*

The very next patient was a medical student whose neurologist had told her that her tremor was "psychosomatic." She was a lovely girl, smart as could be. Her parents were immigrants, but her brother was in dental school and her sister was working on her PhD. The student did have a tremor, a benign positional tremor. It might compromise her career if she wanted to be a micro-surgeon, but her ambition was only to be a neurologist. The tremor got worse when she was nervous, but then most tremors do, and if it bothered her she would do well enough with a small dose of propranolol. She was also a counter and a checker. She was a sweet girl but she was

---

1   Officially, Attention Deficit/*Hyperactivity* Disorder, but in these pages, ADD.

wound up very tight. Benign tremors are just that: benign. But she was obsessed with the thing.

The weekend came, and Frances and I had precious moments in the garden while our daughters went off in their respective directions. At least, *I* had precious moments in the garden, because F was at her restaurant preparing for the usual weekend events. I took a break from the weeding and fetched the newspapers from the week before from the special place where I keep them. I could catch up on the world at last. The Friday paper first; one should read them in reverse chronological order. One may not get to all of them, so the ones missed, from Wednesday, Tuesday and Monday, are old news anyway. It's good to have a system if you want to keep up with the world.

OMG, I said, *there it is again. I must have OC on the brain.* There she was, on page 8, "The Phantom of Fifth Avenue," a debutante who had inherited untold millions of dollars.[2] She had estates in California and Connecticut and an apartment on Fifth Avenue, but she had spent the last twenty years of her life living in a hospital room with the shades drawn. She was in perfect health but she decided to move into a room in a hospital and stay there. Shades of Howard Hughes, right? Except HH didn't collect dolls, and the Phantom did. She commissioned fashion houses to design dresses for her dolls and spent thousands of dollars on their dollhouses. Before she became a recluse, she used to take a doll with her on social outings. A different one every time or an old one with a new designer outfit.

Then, on the facing page: a new biography of the pop singer who spent millions on his fabulous ranch and exotic zoo.[3] He was a shopaholic and a dysmorphophobic, and he had a loathsome habit that had got him into trouble with the law more than once.

Turn the page: on page 11, an IT guy who predicts that before

2   *Wall Street Journal*, June 1, 2014. Book review: "Empty Mansions" by Bill Dedman and Paul Clark Newell Jr.; and "The Phantom of Fifth Avenue" by Meryl Gordon. Walter Vatter.

3   *Wall Street Journal*, June 1, 2014. Book review: "Michael Jackson, Inc." by Zack O'Malley Greenburg. Edward Kosner.

very long "man and machine will be one." He believes that living forever is within one's grasp. To that end, he consumes "120 vitamins and supplements every day, takes nutrients intravenously (so that his body can absorb them better), drinks green tea and exercises regularly."[4]

I skipped back to page 3, an encomium to math prodigies,[5] lost my nerve and turned to the Friday paper.

On the first page! Keith ("Superfan") Franklin, a former dope-addict and burglar, was banned from baseball games at the University of California at Irvine, despite his extraordinary dedication to the team. He'd come to the games decked out in "a full get-up of UC-Irvine gear—including fingernails painted with the team's signature blue and gold colors."[6] He was devoted to the "Anteaters," as the team were called, shouting maniacally for nine innings, accompanying them on road trips, and helping the ground crew roll out the tarpaulin when it rained. When more temperate fans complained that he was loud, boorish and annoying, the school administration banned him from home games. The administration ruled that he had "stretched the rules of normal fan behavior."[7]

I set the paper down and went back outside. Thursday, Wednesday, Tuesday and Monday would never get read. Newspapers are good to set down among one's flowers to control the weeds. Then you cover them up with a bit of mulch.

The Great Detectives

Perhaps I am a bit OC, but then many of us are, and almost all of us have had an OC experience or behavior at some point during

---

4   *Wall Street Journal*, June 1, 2014. "Weekend Confidential: Ray Kurzweil." Alexandra Wolfe.

5   *Wall Street Journal*, June 1, 2014. "The Wrong Way to Treat Child Geniuses." Jordan Ellenberg.

6   *Wall Street Journal*, June 4, 2014. "UC Irvine Gives Anteaters 'Superfan' the Boot." Erica E. Phillips and Ben Cohen.

7   Ibid.

our lives. It isn't obsessive to be concerned about OC, either. OC is something that pops up all over, if you know what to look for. For example, F and I both like detective stories. Is every Great Detective OC (who isn't a degraded alcoholic)?

For several years there was a TV series about a detective named Monk, who was played by Tony Shalhoub. Monk was germ-phobic and afraid of milk, ladybugs, and food touching on his plate. He was also quite clever and his attention to detail helped him solve cases that stumped the police. Monk, though, was not the only fictional detective who walked on the OC side. Hercule Poirot was fastidious about his waxed mustache and his patent-leather shoes, he was punctual to a fault, and he was uncomfortable if his bank balance wasn't exactly 444 pounds, 4 shillings and 4 pence. He was also a hypochondriac, preoccupied with his digestion and prone to sea-sickness and air-sickness. Poirot, too, solved baffling crimes with his penetrating intellect and his keen powers of observation.

Monk and Poirot were OC, we assume, because they were born that way; OC is, after all, a heritable trait. Batman, on the other hand, was obsessed with bats because he had been frightened by bats when he was a little boy, in a cave.

Being OC isn't a *requirement* for fictional detectives. Miss Marple, Judge Dee and Adam Dalgliesh were just fussy; and being fussy is simply a comedic flaw, much preferable to being a tortured alcoholic like Kurt Wallander, Henry Hole and John Rebus, or to being like Lord Peter Wimsey, who was not only fussy but also had PTSD.

Lord Peter's library was one of the most delightful bachelor rooms in London. Its scheme was black and primrose; its walls were lined with rare editions, and its chairs and Chesterfield sofa suggested the embraces of the houris. In one corner stood a black baby grand, a wood fire leaped on a wide old-fashioned hearth, and the Sèvres vases on the chimneypiece were filled with ruddy and gold chrysanthemums.[8]

---

8   Dorothy Sayers, *Whose Body?*

That a fictional detective must be vulnerable, eccentric or borderline certifiable is a literary cliché we owe to Arthur Conan Doyle, who was a Scottish physician and an odd duck in his own right. Doyle endured a hostile-dependent relationship with Sherlock Holmes and kept trying to kill him off so that he could pursue his true interest, which was spiritualism. Doyle believed in fairies. Whether he was obsessed with fairies I can't say, but Holmes was certainly OC; a hoarder, for one thing. He may also have had an eating disorder and was addicted to tobacco and cocaine. In light of his diffident social manner and hyper-rationality, his modern diagnosis would be Asperger's syndrome, a condition that is very close to OC. "I was never a very sociable fellow," he once said, "Always rather fond of moping in my rooms and working out my own little methods of thought."[9] As we shall learn, Asperger's syndrome, a form of autism, is closely linked to OC.

Whatever the appropriate diagnosis, Holmes's perceptual abilities were astonishing and the power of his intellect was superhuman, although narrowly confined. Smart as he was, he seemed not to understand (and nor did Doyle) the difference between *deductive* and *inductive* reasoning.

OC fiction is not always so incisive. Sometimes, it can be wrongheaded, if hilarious. There was a movie in 1997 about a misanthropic fellow who wrote steamy romance novels. The character, Melvin Udall, was played by Jack Nicholson. If he weren't such a good actor, one would think he was acting from life. Udall had a few odd characteristics; for example, he required several bars of Neutrogena soap to wash his hands. He even announced to his psychiatrist that he was OCD, as if the shrink couldn't guess. He has a memorable line that occurs when he is accosted by a fan, Zoe, who wants to know how he is so sensitive to the inner workings of her heart and mind. He tells her that he thinks of a man and takes away reason and accountability.

---

9   Arthur Conan Doyle, "The Adventure of the *Gloria Scott*" (*The Memoirs of Sherlock Holmes*).

The movie is about Melvin's redemption, so to speak, as he defies his inclinations and rescues his gay neighbor, Simon (played by Greg Kinnear), his regular waitress, Carol, and her little son, who had a respiratory ailment. This being a Hollywood movie with Carol played by Helen Hunt, Melvin fell in love and Carol did, too. The movie fades as Melvin, redeemed by true love, deliberately steps on a crack in the sidewalk, something he had always assiduously avoided.

Melvin probably had the obsessive-compulsive personality disorder, not OCD. He had many OCD symptoms, but he was also an angry, controlling man who was homophobic, misogynistic and intolerant of fools. Hollywood knows how to solve such problems: I wish I did. One of my patients had been married to a controlling man and it had taken her years to get rid of him. When she saw the movie, she shouted out to Helen Hunt, "Don't do it, girl."

When a good OC pops up in the world's literature, it isn't long before he appears on the silver screen. There have been more than 250 Sherlock movies. There is also a series of books that were turned into movies about a cultured man—a psycho-analyst, in fact—who was multilingual and also a gourmand. He had odd tastes, though. It was the compulsion to eat human parts, sometimes raw, but more often prepared in creative ways. Did you know, for example, that human liver is best served with fava beans and chianti? He even ate one of his patients, something that these days would get you in trouble with the Medical Board. The analyst, Hannibal Lecter, was a serial killer. It is probably true that most serial killers are driven by bizarre obsessions and compulsions, but I can assure you that hardly any psycho-analysts are cannibals. Nevertheless, the idea that OC individuals are inordinately intelligent is a stereotype that authors and movie producers alike find appealing.

There have been six movies, at my count, about a sea-captain who was obsessed with an albino marine mammal who had bitten off one of his legs. The book *Moby Dick* was written by Herman Melville in 1851, and he referred to the sea-captain's problem as "monomania." That, presumably, is because the sea-captain was obsessed with only one particular thing, although it was a big thing, for sure. The story is silent on the point, but one assumes that the whale ate the rest of Captain Ahab in the end.

> But, as in his narrow-flowing monomania, not one jot of Ahab's broad madness had been left behind; so in that broad madness, not one jot of his great natural intellect had perished. ...so that far from having lost his strength, Ahab, to that one end, did now possess a thousand-fold more potency than ever he had sanely brought to bear upon any reasonable object.[10]

There have been more than six movies about a Danish prince, Hamlet, who was tortured by what Coleridge said was "disproportionate mental exertion" and whose exertions reflected the inconsistency of his character.

> Hence we see a great, an almost enormous, intellectual activity, and a proportionate aversion to real action consequent upon it, with all its symptoms and accompanying qualities. This character Shakespeare places in circumstances, under which it is obliged to act on the spur of the moment: Hamlet is brave and careless of death; but he vacillates from sensibility, and procrastinates from thought, and loses the power of action in the energy of resolve.[11]

Hamlet didn't have overt symptoms of OCD, unlike Adrian Monk and Hercule Poirot, or, if he did, they aren't explicit in the play. He wasn't fussy, like Lord Peter Wimsey. He wasn't a controlling man, like Melvin Udall. His powers of observation weren't particularly acute; he didn't even notice Polonius hiding behind the "arras" until the poor fellow gave himself away by yelping "What, ho!" At

---

10 Herman Melville, *Moby Dick*, Chapter 41, paragraph 20.

11 Samuel Taylor Coleridge, "Lectures and Notes on Shakespeare and Other English Poets." Lecture given in 1818. (Lectures collected by T. Ashe. First published in 1883.)

that point, as you know, Hamlet ran him through, right through the "arras."

Hamlet showed subtle signs of OC, but they are closer to the germ of the condition. He could act impulsively, "obliged to act on the spur of the moment," and impulsivity is an OC trait; but he also had the OC trait of procrastination—"he vacillates from sensibility"—seemingly the opposite of impulsiveness. In real life, OCs are full of paradoxes like that.

Hamlet had the perfect chance to dispatch his uncle in Act III, but he demurred. He had to kill him at just the right time. So he waited until the last scene of Act V to kill him, and during the ensuing mêlée everyone else managed to get killed as well. Shakespeare has been criticized for the bloody ending of his greatest play, but he captured exactly the kind of schemozzle an OC can get himself into, and everyone else, too. To the OC, the perfect is the enemy of the good. Pursuing the perfect, he makes a hash of everything.

Most of the characters in the play thought that Hamlet was addled, but he wasn't. He did have visions and what psychiatrists call "command hallucinations," but it was his *girlfriend* who went insane. It's possible the poor girl became unbalanced because Hamlet killed her father behind the "arras," but he also didn't help much by making so many stupid puns. OCs, as it happens, love puns. Hardly anyone likes puns except OCs.

Hamlet was not OC in a caricaturish way. He had what I think is the essence of an OC: his analytical mind was so active that it would tangle and thwart clear vision and proper action.

> Thus conscience doth make cowards of us all;
> And thus the native hue of resolution
> Is sicklied o'er with the pale cast of thought,
> And enterprises of great pith and moment
> With this regard their currents turn awry,
> And lose the name of action.

* * *

"OC" describes obsessive and compulsive traits and behaviors that occur in about a third of the population. That means that if you're not OC yourself, there's a 50:50 chance the next person you meet will be. "OC" also comprises obsessive thoughts and compulsive behaviors, which are virtually universal.

It's a disservice to say that OC is a *mental disorder*. OC is the way many people are most of the time and most of us are some of the time. Almost everyone has had an OC experience at one time or another. If we were to confine ourselves to pathological cases, that would prevent us from understanding the irrepressible teases, ardent fans, unhappy graduate students and clever detectives in our midst; not to mention the man you live with who walks around the house at night turning off every light that doesn't have a person reading directly underneath it, or the woman who insists you take a clothespin to your socks before you throw them in the laundry-basket. (For Christmas, F gave me a set of plastic gadgets *designed* to hold socks together. I misplaced them. Socks must be allowed to pursue their destiny.)

I have discovered OC traits in the daily newspaper, in comic books and detective stories, among my friends, acquaintances and, unhappily, in my own family. Our second daughter, for example, has a phobia of escalators. My wife thinks she got it from me. Riding on an escalator with the little children—in airports, usually, because there aren't any escalators in Chapel Hill—I always think it is hilarious to say, "Did I ever tell you about the time I was trapped on an escalator and it took six hours for the men to get us off?" The other two girls learned to ignore this when they were young, but Nora was always a serious girl, even when she was little, and she would say, "But why didn't you just walk off the escalator?" To which I would reply, "I know! That's why it was so frightening!" I can picture poor Nora in thirty years trying to explain to her analyst why she has an antipathy to escalators. Or, more likely, to silly men.

How to proceed

If we confined our researches to the personalities of fictional detectives, comic-book heroes and villains, public figures and plutocrats, that would be a shallow exercise. Such exertions only reveal the prejudices of the analyzer.

We would be at a loss without brain science. We can find important facts in what it has to say about OC, or at least about OCD. OCs have reverberating, self-referential loops of useless worry, in case you didn't know. They also have some molecules that are out of balance. There are OC genes, too, and they must be quite numerous, those genes, and potent in effect.

Mind science is another matter, but I have a way of doing it. I like to examine the lives of ordinary men and women and the events that abrade them. That's why I left a promising if obscure career in neuroscience to return to medical practice. Don't expect me to dazzle the reader with the complexity of brain, how it has more neurons than there are stars in the universe or more synapses than there are grains of sand on the beach. If the brain were as complex as most brain-writers would have you believe, it would be even more difficult to get up in the morning, put on your shoes and get to work, not to mention getting home at the end of the day and explaining to your wife why you forgot to pick up her dress at the cleaner's. Nor am I one for brain models based on hydraulic systems, clocks, telephone switchboards, digital or quantum computers or rain forests. No, I am one who thinks that the only cogent model for brain, mind and the way they work is *people*. Yes, people, some more complicated than others, at least on the surface, but "In most cases, people, even the wicked, are more naive and simple-hearted than we generally assume. And so are we."[12]

Minds, like people, are simpler than we generally assume, and so are brains. Of course, that is my bias because I am a physician, and the problems of ordinary men and women fill my days. So do

---

12   Fyodor Dostoevsky, *The Brothers Karamazov.*

the solutions: helpful suggestions like "Stop doing that" and "Don't worry about it" are remarkably effective if accompanied by the right medication. Of course, you have to know what *that* and *it* are, and OC accounts for a good number of the *its* and *thats* people have.

Many of my patients are OC. Their problems are usually transient and easy to fix. Sometimes, though, the problems are debilitating, and I have known a couple who were monsters. Is it possible that they all arise from the same source? If that is so, evolution, having constructed our analytical minds, has some explaining to do.

> This is what I propose. Let me run over the principal steps. We shall approach with an absolutely blank mind, which is always an advantage. We shall form no theories. We are simply here to observe and to draw inferences from our observations.[13]

---

13 Arthur Conan Doyle, "The Adventure of the Cardboard Box" (*His Last Bow*).

2
What, If Anything, Is OC?

OC is OC behaviors and traits. OC behaviors are similar in form and content to the symptoms of obsessive-compulsive disorder, and OC traits are like the characteristics of the obsessive-compulsive personality disorder. OC is not so intense, disturbing or debilitating, but it does have certain characteristics in common. One is *disproportionate mental exertion*. That is, OCs think too much. That can be good or bad.

Obsessive-compulsive disorder (OCD) and the **obsessive-compulsive personality disorder** (OCPD) are categories in the DSM, the *Diagnostic and Statistical Manual* of the American Psychiatric Association. OCD is a *mental disorder* because (1) it inflicts distress on the bearer and/or (2) it disables him from doing more important things. OCPD is a *personality disorder*, because the bearer just *is* that way. If there is any distress involved, it is what he inflicts on the people around him. Such distinctions may seem arbitrary, even trifling, but "To a great mind, nothing is little."[1]

Some psychiatrists call OC behaviors and traits "subclinical OCD," but if that is so, a good many of us are subclinical. The implication is that we have the germ of a debilitating mental illness that's just waiting to pop out. I hope that's not true.

---

1   Arthur Conan Doyle, *A Study in Scarlet*.

OC behaviors are like OCD

OC behaviors are **obsessions** and **compulsions**, *intrusive thoughts*, *brooding* and *ruminative worry*, and *repetitive behaviors* like *fidgets, rituals, touching, tics* and *nervous mannerisms. But*, you say, *everybody does that! It's automatic.* You're right, of course, except not everybody. Besides, there may be more to so-called automatic behavior than you think.

Obsessions are "persistent ideas, thoughts, impulses, or images that are experienced as inappropriate or intrusive and that cause anxiety and distress. The content of the obsession is often perceived as alien and not under the person's control" (APA, 2013). A familiar obsession is when one is obsessed with a new lover. That's how distracting an obsession can be. Another one, equally distracting but more painful, is after a lover has dumped you. Clearly, he's a cad, but you can't get him out of your mind. "He's just not into you," your best friend says. "Get over it." Or she might say, "There's lots of good fish in the sea." Such good advice doesn't assuage one's lacerating memories of the stupid clod. Not only are they intrusive, but they give rise to this ill-advised impulse: *I just want to talk to him.* As it happens, there are loops in one's brain, tiny circuits within which thoughts go around endlessly. The loops can reverberate with an alien thought that is not under one's control. At this very moment, it may be vibrating with an irretrievably dumb idea, such as *Blaine just doesn't realize how happy he would be with me. I shall call upon him at home...* You need to know about those loops.

I daresay that many if not most of the obsessions that 80 percent of college students experience are about someone who is or isn't into them, but most obsessions are not nearly so distracting or painful. For example, one might have a strong preference for symmetry. A common example is arranging the furnishings of a room in perfect symmetry, or perhaps the tchotchkes on the mantle or plantings in the garden. It's not a pathological obsession by any means. Since it doesn't cause anxiety or distress, it's not really an obsession at all. But it is OC. It may not be a problem, but it's sure not *feng shui*.

Here are some common obsessions: *germ phobia*, that is, an antipathy to filth; *misophonia*, hating certain sounds, such as someone chewing; *superstition*, the fear that something awful will happen if you do or don't do something to prevent it; *forbidden thoughts*, especially about sex; and *special numbers*. OCs have the same obsessions as patients with OCD, only not so intense or disturbing.

A recent patient of mine seemed to be a perfectly normal fellow and he was, more or less. However, he had an unusual and excessive degree of concern with the odometer reading in his car. He could never stop driving if his odometer reading ended in a nine. If it was likely to do so, he would drive around until it flipped to zero. I tried to help the poor fellow. I told him that it is more convenient to confine one's obsession to the numbers of the volume setting, which, as you know, ought always to be set to an even number.

Intrusive (or forced) thoughts are another form of obsession. Like this one: *You're not very smart—you know that, don't you?* Or this one: *I could kill myself if I drove my car really fast into that abutment.* That's another nasty one, but not so uncommon. New mothers are horrified by the intrusive thought of doing harm to their infant. Postpartum obsessions of this kind are remarkably frequent, almost 50 percent in one study (Miller *et al.*, 2015). Intrusive thoughts that are less disturbing are like a fabulous new joke one can't help but share, even in the least appropriate places. This happens a lot: *I can't get that song out of my mind.* Don't worry. Sooner or later, you will.

* * *

Compulsions are "repetitive behaviors or mental acts that are carried out to reduce or prevent anxiety or distress and are perceived to prevent a dreaded event or situation" (APA, 2013). If you check the doors at night to "prevent...a dreaded event," that's not a compulsion. If you check them seven times, it is.

The germ of a compulsion is this: *repetitive behaviors or mental acts*. Thus, tics, fidgets and nervous mannerisms are related to compulsions, and whether one does them to relieve anxiety or just to discharge some extra mental energy, they are cuts of the same cloth. Perhaps you find yourself clearing your throat every time you walk into your boss's office or the principal's or your wife's. That's probably a nervous tic. Compulsive teasing, on the other hand, has nothing to do with anxiety. I knew a man who felt compelled to speak sign language to his wife whenever they rode together in an elevator. Much to her annoyance, I should add, because neither he nor she was deaf and the signs were wholly made up. He thought it was hilarious but she didn't. Another fellow tells the same stupid joke when he rides with his daughters on an *escalator*. (OC traits are heritable.)

Yet higher on the OC scale is the man who has the compulsion to sleep upside-down in imitation of bats. I don't know if Batman has OCD or if he is just on the OCD "spectrum," but he does sleep *upside-down*. He has some other well-known OC traits: he is a techie and works out compulsively. He wears the same outfit every day. Also, he never seems to have got up with a woman or a man. Sexual inhibition, as it happens, is an OC trait. Paradoxically, OCs may also have sexual compulsions.

Obsessions and compulsions are more common around eating than they are about sex. I know a woman who eats her dinner circumferentially, working in a spiral around the perimeter of her plate. I have met more than one individual who eats only one thing at a time—first the peas, then the mashed potatoes, and then the meat loaf; alternatively, the kale first, then the quinoa, and only when the quinoa is dispatched, the butternut squash. Then there's this one: today, a young woman told me, "There's no excuse for letting your food touch on the plate." You know the expression, *You are what you eat*. I think it should go like this: *You are how you eat*.[2]

Here are some common compulsions: *counting*; *checking*;

---

2   When I mention a patient I saw "today," as I often do, it isn't because today was a particularly busy day in the clinic. "Today" is the day I happened to be writing a particular chapter.

oniomania, or *compulsive shopping*; *hoarding*; *writing and re-writing* (uh-oh); *ritualized eating behaviors*; *list-making*; *ordering*; and *arranging*. OCs have the same compulsions as patients with OCD do, only not so intense or disturbing.

At this point, a dubious reader might say: "It appears, Dr. Gualtieri, that you classify every human idiosyncrasy and foible as OC." That question is no less than the compulsion to doubt. Chapter 9 will illuminate the point to the reader's satisfaction, unless he or she has a *very* strong compulsion to doubt, of course. Is it OC to follow a ritual as one prepares for the day, to eat the same breakfast, to load the dishwasher just so, to assure a proper and consistent distance between hangers in the closet? Is it OC to say one's prayers in the same way every night? You're not going to pin me down with questions like that. Besides, I've already warned you that I may be obsessed with OC. I've also told you that of all the mental disorders, the symptoms of OCD merge most closely with normal human behavior and cultural traditions. Perhaps you haven't been paying attention. OC may well be about trifles, but "There is nothing so important as trifles."[3]

OC traits are like the OC personality disorder

OC is also a personality trait. An OC may be fussy, perfectionistic, eccentric, hypochondriacal, uptight, rigid, angry or controlling. The same traits occur in the OC personality disorder, but are less intense and less disabling in OCs. Whether they are less annoying to the people who have to live with the OC is another matter.

A personality disorder is an "enduring pattern of inner experience and behavior in the way one thinks, feels, behaves or relates to others" (APA, 2000). An individual with the OC personality disorder is preoccupied with orderliness and mental

---

3   Arthur Conan Doyle, "The Man with the Twisted Lip" (*The Adventures of Sherlock Holmes*).

and interpersonal control at the expense of flexibility, openness, efficiency and empathy.

In 1989, two prominent psychiatrists described individuals with obsessional personality traits. They (the individuals, not the two prominent psychiatrists) prefer to exercise control over both themselves and their environment. They are "cautious, deliberate, thoughtful and rational in their approach to life and its problems." They emphasize reason and logic at the expense of feeling and intuition, and "they do their best to be objective and to avoid being carried away by subjective enthusiasms." They may seem sober and emotionally distant, but also possess great steadiness of purpose, reliability and conscientiousness. "What they lack in flexibility, imagination, and inventiveness, they make up for in a conservative cautiousness about change that provides for a healthy balance to the transient but violent enthusiasms of others" (Uhde and Nemiah, 1989).

It is a clue to the authors' proclivities that they characterize the "enthusiasms" of non-OCs as "violent," but they are right on when they note that the frequency of OC is higher in "upper class persons and in those with higher intelligence levels." On the other hand, just because you're OC that doesn't necessarily mean you're smart.

The most troubling OC trait is a preoccupation with control, as in: "He's a real control freak." OC personalities seek to exercise control, "both upon themselves but also on their environment." Their environment, indeed. It means *you*.

Psychiatrists have studied OCD rather energetically, and much of the science I shall inflict on you is based on research done in patients with OCD and the OC personality disorder. Although they are extreme forms of the behaviors and traits that many of us have, they provide useful points of comparison and often illustrate cogently the points I make. The curious reader can find the current DSM definitions of OCD and OCPD on the internet, as well as the Y-BOCS, a test that psychiatrists use in their research. Print out the Y-BOCS and take it yourself, or give it to someone you know. If your boyfriend scores high enough on the Y-BOCS, you can refer him to the National Institute of Mental Health. A better idea is to look for another boyfriend.

Theories

There are a lot of these theories of OCD. A venerable psychiatric theory is that obsessions and compulsions are attempts to control or "bind" anxiety; alternatively, that obsessions are the expression of anxiety and compulsions a way to work it out. The idea was that patients with OCD experience intolerable anxiety as a consequence of hidden psychological conflicts. A patient might have feelings of rage and aggression deep inside, feelings that he is unable to acknowledge because they are addressed to some perfectly innocent person, like one of his parents, his girlfriend's personal trainer, or Mr Kim at the fruit store who sold him mealy peaches. Thus conflicted, the obsessional patient experiences anxiety. He displaces it in a symbolic direction, engaging thoughts and behaviors that are repetitive and meaningless but at least safe. According to the theory, what lie at the root of OCD are unacceptable aggressive impulses and anxiety that can only be expressed indirectly.

The theory is not so outlandish as it seems to the more than 30 percent or so of us who have OC traits and know very well that we are as gentle as sheep. It's just backwards. Anxiety is certainly an element in the life of OC people, and aggression is a trait of controlling people. However, they are not the *cause* of OC behavior, but the *consequence*.

Psychologists have proven that this is so. In one famous experiment, they gave normal subjects an opportunity to behave as if they were OC. It made them quite anxious. Two groups of healthy subjects were given a gas stove to check, to make sure it was turned off. One group was told to check and re-check the gas stove multiple times, as if they were OCDs with what is called a "checking ritual." The other group simply checked the stove and then went off to do something else.

The test was what the subjects remembered about the gas stove, which contained a number of the usual appurtenances. What transpired was surprising, or, as scientists say, "counter-intuitive." The subjects who had checked the stove just once had much more vivid and detailed memories of what else was on the gas stove than the subjects who had checked it repeatedly. You would expect just the opposite to be so. If one had to go back again and again to examine the stove, that ought to reinforce one's memory, right? But no, the act of checking actually *reduced* the confidence of the checkers in their own memories (van den Hout and Kindt, 2003). Checking didn't make them *more* secure about the gas stove: it made them *less* secure. This, I think, is precisely what happens in OC patients: their self-absorption and doubt contribute to inaccurate perceptions. They don't trust their own perceptions, or their memory. This can make one nervous.

Obsessions and compulsions have also been described as "harm-avoidance strategies," which may explain why some OCs are germ-phobic and wash their hands so frequently. The theory doesn't account for people who like to add up the numbers on the license plates of cars they pass or keep their volume-control knob on an even number. Another theory has it that OC behaviors evolved because they "have the potential to be beneficial to society." Aside from the fact that virtually everything has the *potential* to be beneficial, it's not likely that checking one's work so many times that it never gets done, or collecting old newspapers and egg-cartons in a spare bedroom, is beneficial to anybody, let alone to society.

It is customary, these days, to ascribe human frailties to the persistence of traits that arose during the evolution of our hominid ancestors. We are presumed to have inherited only their nasty traits. In that vein, evolutionary theorists have pictured proto-humans tramping around the savannah. It would serve them well, the theory suggests, to have hoarded food in preparation for times when supplies were scarce. A bright idea, but one that attributes to the proto-humans a level of food-preservation technology that I don't think they possessed.

* * *

Fortunately, there are theories of OCD that have empirical support. They also make sense and they are relevant to the wider problem of OC. The first is that OCD is a "thinking disorder." The "pale cast of thought" is the function of one component of psyche, the **analytical-theoretical mind**. One expects it to guide action by reason, but in OC reason just tangles things up.

The analytical mind resides in the neocortex, the gray matter. It is brain's outermost layer. It is the largest part of brain and consumes the most energy. It is said to have undergone "disproportionate expansion in recent evolution," which means that it may have got a bit ahead of itself (Semendeferi *et al.*, 2001).

The neocortex has two advantages over all the rest of brain: it can generate ideas, which are things we humans value, even when they are stupid; and it can express ideas as language, which we also like, even if we seldom remember what other people or we ourselves have said. Nevertheless, the analytical-theoretical mind, newly evolved and armed with size, energy, ideas and language, has the habit of intruding on the activity of brain parts that govern feeling, intuition and habit. It ought to do that, we are taught, because reason should govern our passions, our soma (see below) and our instincts; as in, "There is nothing higher than reason" (Kant) and "Whatever is contrary to reason is absurd" (Spinoza). We are never taught that reason can gum things up. The neocortex, we are told, is the most highly evolved part of the brain, although my suspicion is that it is still in the beta-testing stage.

* * *

There may be nothing higher than reason and that is true, anatomically at least, but there are other "minds" in one's head. They have minds of their own, even if those don't express themselves in words or ideas. Technically, our multiple minds are **complex integrated functional systems**, and brain has several. They are neural networks that reside in the lower parts of the **cerebral cortex** and also in **subcortical** regions. Think of them as parallel processors. Three such systems are sufficiently important and autonomous to warrant referring to them as "minds" in their own right. Because they occupy more or less discrete anatomical regions, we can take the liberty of calling them "brains."

Those complex functional systems—our multiple minds—operate independently. One is the *social brain*, a mental system that is occupied with who we are and why, and who other people are and why, and how we both happened to get into the fix we are in. How one feels about it is a function of one's *emotional brain*. The latter is the source of passion and is usually thought to be a mischief-maker, but that is just wishful thinking. As it happens, the social and emotional brains are close together and largely overlap, so we shall refer to them as one, the **social/emotional brain**. It is the seat of our *empathic mind*. There is also a **somatic brain** that occupies itself with information that burbles up from one's *soma*, the body, one's physical self.[4] It integrates its data with all the other complex neural systems and tells the soma what to do. It is probably the source of intuition and has no small role in the experience of feelings. Finally, there is a **habit system**, a network that sees to getting things done quickly and without thinking about it. It does things on automatic, as if it had a mind of its own.

The social/emotional brain, the somatic brain and the habit system reside in the basal ganglia, the thalamus, the cingulum, the insula and a few slim layers of lower cerebral cortex. Mammals and birds do perfectly well, thank you, with just these regions, which I take the liberty of calling the "subcortex." Because they are lower parts of the brain, parts we share with animals, we tend to think of them as inferior or less worthy of respect. That is a mistake that OCs make. The subcortical brain may be ancient, but its parts are tried and true, reliable and endowed with great strength. In comparison to those lower parts, the neocortex is an *arriviste*. As far as I'm concerned, it has yet to prove itself.

* * *

---

4   *Soma* is used throughout these pages to refer to all parts of the body that are not the central or peripheral nervous system. I don't mean to be pretentious by using a Latinism: there simply isn't another word that refers to all of the body parts that are not the nervous system.

WHAT, IF ANYTHING, IS OC?

We may have multiple minds, but we sometimes give priority to one or another. Perhaps you are subject to your social/emotional brain and your life is governed by passions. Perhaps it is your somatic brain and you are a slave to signals from your body. Or you may be a creature of habit; days pass as if you're on automatic. If your analytical mind exerts undue influence, you may give priority to ideas over feelings, intuition and habit. In OC, the analytical mind behaves like a tyrant. Not only does it generate thought and behavior, but it is content to do so even when that thought and behavior is devoid of meaning.

That's not the way we are meant to be. We aren't designed to be controlled by one or another of several minds. None should have primacy. The parallel processors in our brain should operate with parallel constraint satisfaction. When they do—when our multiple minds operate in balance and harmony—we experience fleeting moments of equanimity. What makes such moments evanescent is that one or another of the several minds is usually acting up. It is just in the nature of things for one part of brain or another to oscillate its networks in a way that doesn't synchronize very well with the other parts. Most people have minds that are balanced some of the time, and some people have balance most of the time, but no one, save the Saints and the High Lamas perhaps, have minds that are balanced all the time.

We are taught that the likeliest mind to go out of balance is one's emotional brain, which only exists to be restrained by the powers of reason. There are certainly people who fall into that category and they deserve to be restrained, if not by reason then by the authorities. For most of us, the emotional brain is a docile fellow, like a hedgehog who prefers living in the undergrowth and hides most of the day in his small burrow. He may give you a bite if provoked, but rolling up into a ball is his usual *modus operandi*. The lesson of OC is that among humans more threats to equanimity arise from the analytical mind, with its endless ruminations and apprehensions. The analytical mind inflicts its anxieties on mental systems that prefer to behave as *pares inter pares*, equal participants in the great game. The purpose of that game, for brain-as-a-whole, is equipoise. To the analytical mind, however, it is *control*.

I don't have to list the entanglements to which the analytical mind disposes, but they extend beyond the acrimonious disputes of academics, the corruption of Art by excess of intellectualizing, and the inability of thought-ridden young men like Hamlet to commit themselves to sweet, endearing lovers like Ophelia. They include most of the great wars and rivalries among religious sects. The most violent conflicts in history, you may have noticed, have been driven by *ideas*. Even science, the critical manipulation of ideas and knowledge, is prone to excess. In science, for example, we are told that "Any mingling of knowledge with values is unlawful, forbidden" (Monod, 1971). Values and meaning are the domain of the social/ emotional brain and the somatic brain—*I feel it in my gut* or *My heart tells me it is so*. To the analytical mind, values and meaning can be petty annoyances.

OC is the result of one's analytical mind being so active that it gets tangled up and thwarts clear vision and proper action.

   ...enterprises of great pith and moment
   With this regard their currents turn awry,
   And lose the name of action.

* * *

There are other brain parts relevant to OC. One is the **cingulum**, which resides at the intersection of our multiple minds. It is, quite literally, an inborn error detector. Its function is to identify "conflicts" that arise among competing processors. When it does, it emits this signal—*Something is wrong here*. Closely linked to the cingulum is the **insula**, a component of the somatic brain. It is a receptive organ, the only place in brain where nervous signals from all five senses converge. In patients with OCD, the cingulum and insula are hyperactive. This accounts for their perceptual sensitivity, and their perennial suspicion that something is wrong.

It's safe to assume that OC is the product of multiple brain parts operating together, although not necessarily in synch. Assuming that is so, neuroscience has examined the way brain parts are connected. Brain **connectivity** refers to the short and long nerve fibers that connect neurons to one another, and that connect the different parts of brain. In OCD patients, the short connections that serve high intelligence and the analytical mind are especially robust, but there is an imbalance between short- and long-range connections that favors a particular way of thinking. Patients with autism and social anxiety have similar patterns of connectivity, which is only one of many things they have in common with OCs. People with only a touch of autism are the Aspergerites, or "Aspies," as they like to call themselves, and people with mild forms of social anxiety I refer to in these pages as SAs.

Abstract thinking may be dry, impersonal and analytical. It may also be lively and imaginative, given to leaps of creativity and fantasy. An active mind need not be nefarious—it seldom is—but most of us are cautious when we encounter one. The eccentricities to which it is drawn make people uncomfortable. That's probably why, whenever a character is identified as a Great Brain, the author makes him an eccentric. The analytical mind is a thing of incisiveness and clarity, but there is a common assumption that, left to its own devices, it will do something odd or nocuous. To most of us this is only common sense: "I would rather be governed by the first two thousand people in the Boston telephone directory than by the two thousand people on the faculty of Harvard University."[5] It is a commonplace that high intelligence is laden with idiosyncrasies. Fiction and common prejudice lead one to believe it's freakish, if not a *bad thing* altogether. "I am a brain, Watson. The rest of me is a mere appendix."[6]

It's not only the Great Detectives who are OC and highly intelligent. Hollywood and the comic books, as well as children's stories, present great villains in similar wise. Think of any number of wicked witches, the Mekon, Moriarity, Blofeld, LeMaire,

---

5   William Buckley, *Meet the Press*, 1965.
6   Arthur Conan Doyle, "The Adventure of the Mazarin Stone" (*The Case-Book of Sherlock Holmes*).

Rastapopoulos and Hannibal Lecter. They are controlling, unempathic and self-absorbed, and, by the way, *real smart*.

That a high intellect must be vulnerable, eccentric or borderline certifiable is a literary cliché we owe to Shakespeare himself. Coleridge could have been talking about OC when he said that it is "a common oppression on minds cast in the Hamlet mold and is caused by disproportionate mental exertion."[7] Hamlet was tortured by intellectual vacillation. He was the exemplar of how tangled one can be by one's own thoughts. Hamlet captured something essential about the way some of us are.

OC is the way a mind organizes itself when its various parts are connected in a particular way. What makes that happen? I am not about to theorize until we have more data, but *I have observed* that the analytical mind is at least as prone to excess as one's emotional mind can be, or one's somatic mind. The power of reason tames one's emotions and instincts, and that is supposed to be a *good thing*. That the power of reason is equally prone to stray beyond the boundaries of common sense or simple humanity is not something they teach you in college. You have to learn it from movies and comic books.

---

7   Samuel Taylor Coleridge, "Lectures and Notes on Shakespeare and Other English Poets." Lecture given in 1818. (Lectures collected by T. Ashe. First published in 1883.)

3

The Problem with Types

OC traits and behaviors are found in a lot of people—as many as 90 percent of us, according to experts. My opinion is that OC is a trait that about 30 percent of us have. Whether 30 percent or 90, it's much more common than the OC personality disorder (3–8 percent) or OCD (1–3 percent).

OC is a spectrum of traits that arise from the way one's brain is organized. If one has an overactive analytical mind, a hyperactive cingulum, a hypersensitive insula, or basal ganglia incited by noisome thoughts, the varieties of experience that can arise are virtually infinite, and we haven't even got around to the problem of reverberating loops. None of those qualities are categorical; they are dimensional. All of the brain parts in question may be *hyper-* or *hypo-*, a lot or a little, and one can only hope that most of one's own are somewhere in between. The combinations and permutations are virtually infinite, and for that reason OC is manifest in many different ways; in more ways than just OCD or the OC personality disorder. Among the characters we have met so far, Monk is a certifiable OCD. He manages to get the job done, but there is no denying how disabled he is. Melvin Udall had the OCPD. Hollywood redeemed him, but notice that there hasn't been a sequel. The others—Hamlet, Captain Ahab, Lord Peter Wimsey? Well, not all our friends fall neatly into DSM categories.

Some of them, like Sherlock, fall into a new psychiatric category, the **obsessive-compulsive spectrum**.[1] Officially, it includes hoarding, skin-picking, hair-pulling (trichotillomania) and "body dysmorphic disorder," the obsession that something about one's body is repulsive. OCD specialists, however, also include eating disorders like anorexia nervosa, as well as Tourette's syndrome, pathological gambling, kleptomania, Asperger's syndrome and autism (Allen, King, and Hollander, 2003). The "spectrum" idea reflects the suspicion that mental disorders that appear different may in fact be the consequence of a common problem in brain circuitry.

A spectrum, however, is misnamed if it's simply the accumulation of categories. The word "spectrum" implies continuous, not discrete, variables. There are seven colors in the rainbow, but you may have noticed that they blend gently one into another. Rainbows, like human beings, are analog, not digital. Our personalities comprise multiple traits, each occurring somewhere on a continuum. Most of us are somewhere between very short and very tall, very dull and very bright, drop-dead gorgeous and butt-ugly. We spend our lives taking advantage of our salutary traits and compensating for—or hiding—those that may be undesirable. One could say that Hercule Poirot was "on the OCD spectrum," but that doesn't tell us very much. Did he have an eating disorder? No, he was gourmand. Hair pulling? No, although he did twiddle his mustache. Better to say that he had some OC traits, some of them irksome and others comical. You could consign him to the category of "fussy men," were there such a category in the DSM, but it is more informative to say that he was towards the fussy end of a dimension that stretches from perfectionists to slobs.

OC traits are much wider than the OCD spectrum. Physicians have noted OC traits in patients with social anxiety and autism, and also in people with ADD, bipolar disorder, schizophrenia, alcoholism and substance abuse; and also in mysterious medical

---

1   In the clumsy prose that characterizes DSM-5, the category is "Obsessive-compulsive and related disorders."

conditions like migraine, irritable bowel syndrome, chronic fatigue and fibromyalgia. OC traits are also met with in patients with traumatic brain injuries, toxic brain exposure, Parkinson's disease and Alzheimer's disease, and all the other dementias. We encounter them in patients with intellectual disability and with neurogenetic syndromes such as the Lesch-Nyhan and Cornelia de Lange syndromes. It's no surprise that OC traits and behaviors are so common in patients with mental illness; they're just as common in the general population. Mental patients are just less able to control them, or to hide them.

Some psychiatrists believe that OCD and the OC personality disorder are not only different but also distinct. I don't think that's true. Individuals with the OC personality disorder are also prone to obsessions and compulsions; they are just reluctant to disclose them. Patients with OCD may be fussy, perfectionistic, eccentric, hypochondriacal, uptight or rigid, but they are not usually angry or controlling. There is a great deal of overlap between the two conditions. By the same token, OCs may have OC behaviors as well as OC traits. At heart, OCD, the OC personality and OC are probably just different manifestations of the same thing. That thing is the circuitry and activity of brain, which is dimensional, not categorical, and infinitely variable.

The problem with categories

Diagnostic categories, especially the personality disorders, imply the existence of *types*. Speaking of "types" is appropriate in certain circumstances; for example, there are 246 types of French cheese. I remember that because Charles de Gaulle said, "How is it possible to govern a nation that has 246 kinds of cheese?" It's one of those non-sequiturs that sticks in one's mind. I later discovered that there are more than a thousand kinds of cheese in France, and they fall into eight categories. Anyway, it may be appropriate to speak of "types" now and then, but you gotta get the facts straight. We can't even get cheese right, yet we describe *types* and *categories* of human beings, as if we knew.

I have an antipathy to types, at least when it comes to human beings. Types are static; I prefer to think that we exist in dimensions. A good many dimensions, in fact. How tall we are, how much we weigh, the size and shape of our nose—we're all somewhere on each of those dimensions, and our position on the spectrum may change from time to time, as you may have noticed. So also our position on the "agreeableness" spectrum, and all the other dimensions of our personality, like how energetic one is, how curious, how smart, etc. Picture one of those starburst chandeliers made of a hundred lighted tubes that meet in the center and then radiate in every direction. The dimensions of our personality are like that, except that we twinkle, as the light within each tube turns on or off, shines bright or dim, and moves outwards or inwards or across the middle into the opposite arm.

For that reason, you can't accuse me of trying to invent a new type. Furthermore, discovering new types—that's for a different breed of biologist. A naturalist, for example, is the kind of fellow who potters around in the garden looking for insects. His ambition is to discover a new species of beetle, and when he does he will name it after his girlfriend. "Here, Charlene, is a new and heretofore undiscovered variety of weevil! I have named it after you." Physicians belong in the naturalist camp, and psychiatrists do, too, because we like to think in terms of types and categories. So also this psychiatrist, at least sometimes, although I have no interest in discovering a new type of mental illness. If I did I wouldn't name it after Frances. "Look, darling, my new paper has been published. I have described a new syndrome characterized by unpredictable outbursts of irrational rage, and I have named it after you." Entomologists can get credit for such gestures, but not psychiatrists.

* * *

It's not fair to blame psychiatrists for their attachment to types—that is, to diagnostic categories. They're just being good naturalists. They are employing a method common to naturalists since Aristotle, and that is *to understand the natural world by describing its categories*. It is the essence of naturalism. All of the animals and plants can be classified, a process that the Philosopher himself began. Animals that swim in the sea, according to Aristotle, were in the category of fish. It was a sound abstraction, based on the information that was available to him at the time. Aristotle knew nothing of penguins, for example, and he assumed that whales and dolphins were fish because they swam in the sea and looked like fish.

In the 18th century, the Swedish naturalist, Linnaeus, elaborated the categories of Nature for all time. All the known animals and plants belonged in a category, an inverted pyramid of *kingdom, phylum, class, order, family, genus* and *species*. The Linnaean system was so good we still use it, and new plants and animals are being discovered and added to it even as you sit reading this. Humans, to Linnaeus, were all in the category *Homo sapiens*. Nevertheless, it has always been a temptation to sub-divide *H. sapiens* into categories or types. Now, I don't know anybody who likes to be considered a *type*, and one doesn't refer to types in polite society, but we use them in psychiatry on the assumption that typology is foundational to the study of living things, and even rocks.

An individual may qualify as a type if something about him is typical of a particular category. One can talk about types of squirrels, or types of arboreal mammals, or types of bothersome varmints that devour one's tulip bulbs. Analyzing the world in terms of categories is an efficient and effective way to understand it and deal with it. Even little animals can do it. *Something big moving in my direction* is a sufficient categorization to mobilize an effective action step in a mouse, a bird or a housefly.

Human beings have a more sophisticated perceptual apparatus than mice do, or birds or houseflies, and it is integrated with a complex analytical mind that likes abstractions. The categories with which we address the natural world are correspondingly advanced. The squirrels that attack my wife's bird-feeders, for example, are in her category of friendly rivals. They are the occasion of kindly bemusement as well as a war of minds, as she buys ever more advanced squirrel-proof feeders and the squirrels evolve ever more highly developed acrobatic skills. She won't let me deal with them, but when she saw a rat clinging to her bird-feeder one day, she was quick to call the exterminators. Thus, one's capacity for loving kindness and oneness with the natural world can be restricted by categories. Or, as we shall see, the analytical mind has the power to confine the empathic mind.

One should resist the temptation to define categories of human beings, and for good reason. Our history is replete with examples of kindness withheld from certain of those categories. Humanity is a sufficient category for all of us, as far as I am concerned, and if another level of abstraction is necessary, *individuals* are categories unto themselves. Beyond that, nothing more should guide one's empathy and compassion. One's deliberations, though, are another matter. We know, for example, that certain genes occur with different frequency in the nations, that men and women metabolize certain drugs at different rates, and that diseases occur with different frequencies in different races. Appreciating proclivities in such regard among the nations, sexes and races should never restrict one's respect or affection, but it can guide intelligent, empathic actions.

Behavioral proclivities do not defy categorization, but one must be careful. *That fellow is angry* is a discernible event. *He is an angry man*, however, describes two possibilities: one, that he is angry; and two, that he is an angry type of man. The second possibility may be true or it may be an unfair generalization. It is possible that he is a kindly and helpful mate who is angry because he dropped his wife's expensive new bird-feeder from the ladder as he was trying to fasten it to the eaves and smashed the thing to pieces. It is also possible that his emotional expressions represent not anger but only dismay over his wife's inevitable disappointment. In men, virtually every untoward emotional expression makes him look like an angry type, but maybe that's an unfair generalization.

It is easier to type the animals and plants, even animals that swim in the sea and the green sea slug, which lives in the ocean but doesn't swim. It's easier to type animals and plants than human beings, anyway, and humans are less amenable to collection by naturalists for display in natural history museums.

4
The Banana-Man

It may come as a surprise to learn that people may be governed by ideas or that reason itself can lend a measure of automaticity to what we do, but there you are. If one of our minds is the habit system, isn't that the source of automatic behavior? In fact, the habit brain is a marvel of flexibility. It is *ideas* that may be obdurate and inflexible. The essence of OCD is unwanted thoughts that arise repetitively, as if the mind were on automatic. It's a disorder of too much thinking, and it clogs the loops in one's brain. The essence of OC is thought, not necessarily unwanted, that governs behavior in repetitious or persistent ways; it may be fertile or unproductive. Whichever, thinking uses up a lot of juice, so if that's your style, you need to stay in shape. If not, it will make you physically ill, or worrisome, enervated or irritable.

Thinking *a little too much* may make one fussy, but think of what the world would be like if there weren't fussy people to neaten it up a bit. It may also make one creative, imaginative, fantastical and wildly amusing, if perhaps a bit ditzy or muddle-headed. To illustrate, there is the Banana-Man.

* * *

The Banana-Man was a fellow named Ken Bannister who spent more than thirty years and $150,000 assembling "the world's largest collection devoted to any one fruit" at the International Banana

Club and Museum in Hesperia, California. Hesperia is in the High Desert northeast of Los Angeles. His preoccupation with bananas began innocently enough; someone gave him a roll of Chiquita Banana stickers when he was at a convention and he had a good time distributing the stickers to the conventioneers. A different kind of psychiatrist might suggest that perhaps he had been traumatized by a banana when he was a boy, perhaps in a cave, but I prefer to take the Banana-Man at his word. Besides, whenever I eat a banana, I like to take the sticker and recycle it by sticking to the arm or shirt of one of our daughters. You can imagine the hilarious good times we have around our home, but you can't say that I am preoccupied with bananas. I do the same with the stickers that come on apples, pears and other fruit.

The Banana-Man was certainly preoccupied with bananas, if not obsessed. Before he was done he had collected no fewer than 17,000 banana-related items. This, it seemed, was his limit and now he says that he is "done with bananas." His obsession just ran its course, although his decision may have been influenced by the Hesperia Recreation and Park District, which evicted him and his bananas from the space it had lent him because it wanted to rotate the exhibits. One only wonders what exhibits they had to equal the impact and potential social benefit of 17,000 banana-themed items.

The Banana-Man occupies a happy corner of the OC space. His OC trait was leavened by his positive energy, good humor and love for mankind. One could call his preoccupations an obsession, in a careless kind of way, just as one might say a man is depressed because he is down in the dumps or that a girl's father is crazy because he loves to play tricks with the stickers he peels off fruit. Bannister's fascination may or may not have been an obsession. It is better to think of it as an eccentric hobby, harmless if expensive and time-consuming.

In his prime, Bannister called himself "Bananaster," which was probably redundant, according to research done by Brett Pelham, Matthew Mirenberg and John Jones, psychologists in Buffalo, New York. They observed that the first few letters of one's name are statistically related to one's occupation and where one lives, and presumably also to one's preoccupation, as in *Bannister* and *Bananas*. Women named *Mildred*, for example, are more likely to live in *Milwaukee* and men named *Phil* in *Philadelphia*. People named *Denise, Dena, Denice, Denna, Dennis, Denis, Denny* or *Denver* are more likely to be *dentists* and names like *Laura, Lauren, Laurie, Laverne, Lawrence, Larry, Lance* and *Laurence* predispose their bearers to the practice of *law*. This the psychologists attributed to their own theory of "implicit egotism," but they acknowledge it may just be due to "priming." **Priming** refers to subliminal suggestion. For example, college students who had been primed to think about old people walked more slowly than usual when they left the psychology lab and they also tended to drool (Pelham, Mirenberg, and Jones, 2002). As it happens, OCs are remarkably susceptible to suggestion. Thus, OC men named *Newbold* are likelier to live in *New York* or *New Jersey*. If your boyfriend's name is *Newbold* and he lives in *Newark, New Jersey* or *Newburgh, New York*, chances are he's an OC. Whether he's just a fussy guy or a control freak is another matter.

* * *

Hypnotic suggestion is a good illustration of the strength an idea may have. The clever hypnotist suggests that his subject will bark like a dog when he mentions the word dog-biscuit. Such exhibitions invariably reduce the audience to a state of helpless mirth when the fellow barks, although I may be showing my age. What the clever hypnotist has done is to induce a state of **dissociation**. He has planted an idea: *I will bark like a dog when I hear "dog-biscuit."* He has isolated the idea from two parts of brain that would ordinarily prevent someone from barking like a dog in a theatre: the orbito-frontal lobe and the cingulum, one a component of the social/emotional brain, the other an inborn error detector (Gruzelier, 2006). The compulsion to bark is dissociated from one's sense of propriety and fear of embarrassment. Hypnosis is an interesting example of what happens when one's mind operates on the basis of an idea unrestrained by good sense. It is an illustration of one's mind going on automatic, as if life were just a series of equations to solve or algorithms to write.

Suggestibility is a trait that frequently co-occurs with OC. One fellow I knew had a habit that was not only expensive but got him into trouble. He had a compulsion to travel. Not the compulsion that old people have after they've retired and believe that they've missed out on a lot in life. They make up for it by taking a river cruise on the Danube, where they meet a lot of other old people who have been similarly deprived. My patient was a young man, but he didn't deprive himself. The mere suggestion of a foreign place like a picture in a magazine or a story on TV aroused an obsession with the place and a compulsion to visit. What placed him beyond the pale, though, was his idea of a visit. He would have done better taking a river cruise with old people. My patient would fly somewhere, say Marrakech, on Friday night, spend a night at the airport hotel and then fly back in time to go to work on Monday. If the connections were inconvenient, he might have to take a comp day. It cost him a bundle, though he probably accumulated a lot of frequent-flier miles. The problem was his name. It was Mohammed Al-Aziz, and before long Homeland Security took notice of his peregrinations, for which he could give no satisfactory explanation. I had to write a letter on his behalf.

* * *

Not only is it possible for a person to be governed by an idea, but the idea may come from no place. One doesn't expect a roll of Chiquita Banana stickers to exert such effects. Yet the Banana-Man was seized by an idea. *I shall assemble*, we must imagine him saying to himself, or perhaps to his wife, *the largest collection in the world devoted to any one fruit*. He was suffused with extraordinary energy and a drive to share his epiphany with all humanity, or at least those who happened on the International Banana Club and Museum in Hesperia, Calif. The idea put him on automatic, just as Mortimer from Mauritania is, inevitably, a mortician. Or a mortgage-broker.

It is possible that Bananaster's obsession with banana-related objects was the consequence of a suggestion that overrode his normal good sense and any conceivable sense of proportion. It may have been the power of suggestion that focused his attention and mental energy in a way that nothing else ever had. It may have given him an *idée fixe* or even a transient episode of monomania.

That may be what happened to the Banana-Man, but there is probably more to it. Why don't we all fall into similar engrossments? I never knew the man, but I would guess he is an extravert, a high-energy guy with an interesting sense of humor. I wonder, though, if he didn't have an OC disposition.

An OC disposition

The OC trait that overrides all others is the primacy of thinking—that is, abstract thinking divorced from meaning and context. Most other OC traits develop from there. Suggestion takes an idea and removes it from context. It was an energizing experience for the Banana-Man. Hamlet's OC trait was rumination. He chewed over the same idea for five acts; it was the opposite of energizing. Captain Ahab, on the other hand, followed his governing idea with a slow, solemn purpose. The idea was vengeance and his trait was a controlling disposition. The whale had threatened his integrity, quite literally. You and I, having been bitten by a giant whale and losing no more than the lower part of our leg, would probably breathe a sigh a relief that we had gotten off so easily. It made Ahab seethe.

Abstract thinking divorced from meaning and context can be a fertile exercise; the tallest trees have their heads in the clouds. Transient excursions into what seems meaningless, far from the context of day-to-day assumptions, is what the best human minds are good at. But it's always necessary to keep one's feet on the ground, and deep roots are good, too. A happier mind may seethe at some unforgivable insult or it may say, *Hey, that's what sperm whales do. They bite.* Then it will look for a more fruitful and less mutilatory field of endeavor. It just wouldn't make for a good story.

OC traits are manifest in different forms at different stages of one's life and at different levels of intensity. They are heritable—that is, genetic in origin—but they are also changeable. They may originate in DNA, but they aren't one's life-plan. Controlling ideas are for OCDs. OCs are content with guidelines.

What is a trait?

Traits are something we are born with, or grow into. Personality traits are readily observed in children; as they grow up, they learn to amend them. They hide or suppress the traits that aren't helpful, that their friends laugh at or that get them into trouble. Some childish traits disappear or at least go underground. Others grow stronger. Special talents can be cultivated by events in one's life or they can be forgotten. Traits are determined by one's genes, but what one does with them isn't.

Psychology no longer concerns itself with personality "types," which are static and stereotypical, but rather with traits. Considering traits rather than types describes individual differences as they really are: that is, **dimensional** rather than **categorical**. This is as true of personality traits as it is of physical traits. The difference between "dimensional" and "categorical" is like the difference between "analog" and "digital." Height, for example, is a dimensional trait. Some people fall into the category of "short" and others in the category of "tall," but a great deal of information is lost by describing everyone as either tall or short. Pregnancy, on the other hand, is categorical; either one is or one isn't. Pregnancy is digital, although there are better ways to get that way.

Modern psychologists think that *personality* is composed of traits. Psychiatrists think that personality *disorders* are an assemblage of untoward traits. So, what *is* a trait?

A **trait** is a stable, definable characteristic. Ideally, it is measurable. One's height is a trait. Weight is not; it's measurable but not stable. The color of one's eyes and hair and the size of one's nose are physical traits. The resilience of one's joints, the stability of one's pulse and blood pressure, and the reactivity of one's GI system are also physical traits. They are also known as somatic or visceral traits. People have social and emotional traits; and they have different ways of thinking, that is, cognitive traits. The way one's physical, social, emotional and cognitive traits come together results in what we call *personality*.

The word "trait" conveys *drawing forth* or *pulling* an element from the whole and making it knowable. Hence, one *draws* a portrait. "Trait" and "portrait" are both from the Latin word *tractus*, whence also *tractor*. When one draws a portrait, the goal is to draw forth the salient traits of a person in order to produce a coherent image. The choice of which traits to draw and how to assemble them, however, is not a neutral act, because it depends on the perspective and intentions of the person doing the drawing-forth. The drawing-forth may result in something satisfactory to one's analytical-theoretical mind, but its meaning might be obscure. This has been the perennial problem in psychology, which has always been about pulling forth elements of the human mind using different tractors.

17,953 adjectives

If we had to assign the psychology of traits to one person, we would assign them to Gordon Allport, a kindly and common-sense man from Indiana who was a psychologist at Harvard. His project was to study personality in a theoretically neutral way. To do so, he used a neutral, atheoretical instrument: the 1925 edition of Webster's *New International Dictionary*. Allport discovered that there were 17,953 adjectives in the dictionary that described human characteristics (Allport and Odbert, 1936). Honing the list down a bit, and submitting them to a panel of judges who had no idea what he was up to, Allport found that the words described different aspects of personality. "Cardinal traits" were one's "ruling passions": for example, *greedy, narcissistic, altruistic.* "Central traits" were the building blocks of one's personality: *loyal, kind, agreeable, friendly, shy, sneaky, wild, grouchy.* "Secondary traits" were attitudes and preferences, which are changeable and situation-specific, such as laughing at one's boyfriend's lame jokes but only scowling when one's father does something really hilarious.

The honing down left Allport with 4500 traits. This is probably about right, but it was an unwieldy number. The list was shrunk further by a British psychologist, Raymond Cattell, who worked at several American universities, including the University of Illinois, which happened to have a computer. In 1952, it was the only American university that did, at least for purposes such as this. Cattell needed a computer to make sense of the enormous amounts of data he could generate by asking people about the 171 traits he had culled from Allport's 4500. The method he used was **factor analysis**, a devilishly clever statistical method he had studied with its inventor, Charles Spearman, in London. Elements in a data set that are correlated are "rotated" in various ways, generating linear models that speak to underlying, latent variables, or "factors." So, from 171 traits Cattell derived 16 factors, or dimensions of personality.

Factor analysis is one of those tractors and the outcome depends on who's driving it. It is a creative exercise, because the data can be rotated until the psychologist discovers latent variables that make sense to him. The endeavor is permissive of a good deal of flexibility. In subsequent studies of personality traits, therefore, psychologists determined that personality was composed of two dimensions, three, five, seven or fourteen. Finally, modern psychologists arrived at a consensus. Having collected data from women and men in all the corners of Earth and applying the cleverest statistical manipulations, they reduced the number of relevant adjectives to ten, which, in an uncharacteristic burst of colloquialism, they call the Big Five:

Conscientious, as opposed to **careless**.

Agreeable, as opposed to **surly**.

Neurotic, as opposed to **secure**.

Open to experience, as opposed to **narrow-minded**.

Extraverted, as opposed to **introverted**.[1]

The Big Five are the five dimensions of personality: five continua or spectra. All of us fall somewhere between the two poles of each dimension and some of us may even be at the tips. Theoretically, the Big Five contain the basic traits from which every personality is constructed. All those 17,953 adjectives are somewhere in there, because each dimension is subject to shadings or gradations. The combinations and permutations among the five dimensions and all their gradations are virtually infinite, which is about right. Individuals are different, you may have noticed, one from another, and some of us are more different than others. There was a girl I knew when I was in college. She had way more than five traits and most were manifest during the course of an evening. Then there was a guy I bumped into in a bar in New Mexico who had just two: he was big and mean. I wouldn't be talking to you now if I hadn't got away from them both.

Are traits stable?

Knowing that a child has a controlling disposition, a fastidious nature or a tendency to avoid confrontation is helpful for parents and therapists. They can understand why the child is given to angry outbursts, to loneliness or failure at school. When the kid is older and he gets Ds and Fs in his second semester in college, it's nice to know what's behind it. Psychological treatments, including drugs, are not very effective unless one knows what one is treating.

Knowing that a child has OC traits does not, however, predict his or her future. How is that? Traits are characteristics that are

---

1   The mnemonic is CANOE.

both measurable and stable. Their origin is in one's genes; they are, in fact, heritable. One advantage of the careful study of human traits is that they can be associated with confidence to biological parameters. Thus, behavioral geneticists have established that the Big Five have a heritability coefficient around 0.5, the same as IQ[2] (Bouchard and McGue, 2003).

Certain genes seem to be related to personality traits. The gene *5-HTTLPR*, for example, expresses a protein that influences metabolism of the neurotransmitter serotonin. The SSRI antidepressants (selective serotonin reuptake inhibitors) target this particular protein. The *5-HTTLPR* gene comes in two different forms, or **alleles**: *s*, with 14 repeats, and *l*, with 16. A number of studies have shown an association, albeit a small one, between the *s* allele and anxiety-proneness or neuroticism (Munafò, Clark, and Flint, 2004; Sen, Burmeister, and Ghosh, 2004). Theoretically, if you have the *s* allele, you ought to take medicine.

There are two genes, *DRD2* and *DRD4*, that affect the structure and sensitivity of the dopamine receptor. Dopamine is one of the governing neurotransmitters in brain, and is often cited in pop-brain books as one that you need more of, or less, depending on the point the author is trying to make. *DRD2* is associated with a weakness for drink. It also has behavioral manifestations that are apparent long before alcoholism is apparent, like novelty-seeking and impetuosity (Fowler, Settle, and Christakis, 2011). Another dopamine receptor gene, *DRD4*, is said to be associated with sexual behavior. One form of the gene is associated with the age at which a person first has sexual intercourse and the number of sexual partners he or she has during the course of a lifetime.

DRD4 has three common alleles, *D4.2*, *D4.4* and *D4.7*. The *D4.4* allele is the most common, especially among Asians, and it is said to be associated with altruistic and prosocial behavior. The *D4.7* allele is less common, although Europeans have more than Asians do, and

---

2   The **heritability coefficient** is a measure of the genetic contribution to a particular trait, and it ranges from 0.0 (no correlation) to 1.0 (perfect correlation). A heritability coefficient of 0.5 means that 50 percent of the variance in the trait in question is attributable to genes. In behavioral genetics, 50 percent is an impressive result.

American Indians have the most of anyone. *D4.7* people have fewer dopamine receptors and they are prone to sensation-seeking—not, however, drug addiction or compulsive behavior, but other forms of "novelty-seeking." These include aggression, financial risk-taking and disinhibited sexual behavior. The *D4.7* allele is also found more frequently in populations who have been on the move, like the American Indians, and also in people with mixed racial ancestry. This, to geneticists, indicates a measure of adventuresomeness, referred to in genetic quarters as "penile readiness," clearly a useful trait for someone to have if he moves around a lot (Garcia *et al.*, 2010; Zion *et al.*, 2006). One might think of penile readiness as an element of extraversion, openness to experience or agreeableness, depending on one's point of view.

If traits are our genetic endowment, they ought to be stable; the fact that only two genes, thus far, have been associated with particular traits may just be because the field of behavioral genetics is still very young. Or it may be that traits are not so stable as we think.

* * *

It's a common belief that personality traits are stable and that one's "personality" is something one is born with. Psychologists differ, however, on the point at which personality traits become fixed. The psycho-analytically-inclined aver that it occurs by age five. William James claimed that personality was "set like plaster" at age 30 (Costa and McCrae, 1994). Be that as it may, the case for stability has probably been overstated. Although personality traits are mostly stable—most people have similar personality traits when they are young, middle-aged and old—they aren't fixed or immutable. Data have been accumulating that show that personality traits are prone to change—in some individuals, at least (Allemand, Zimprich, and Martin, 2008; Bleidorn *et al.*, 2009; Rantanen *et al.*, 2007; Small *et al.*, 2003). As my grandmother used to say, "People change or they don't."

If our traits do happen to change, research indicates that they do so in a predictable way. The definitive study in 2003 studied personality traits in no fewer than 132,515 adults from ages 21 to 60; a sample size that was at least a hundred times bigger than most of the studies done in this field. The results were fascinating: conscientiousness improves as people get older, and so does agreeableness, although people tend to get a bit grumpy after age 50, probably because their hair has started to fall out and their joints have begun to hurt. Openness to experience tends to decline slightly as people age, which may not be such a good thing but is understandable. On average, neuroticism gets better in women but not in men, a factoid that might inform your decision about the appropriate action step if you have (1) a neurotic wife or (2) a neurotic husband. Extraversion goes down a little as women age, but extraverted men are as annoying at age 60 as they are at age 21 (Srivastava, John, Gosling, and Potter, 2003). Personality traits are kind of stable, then, more or less. They also change, especially if one's personality gets on the right drug.

That all the traits that comprise all people can be reduced to five dimensions is an exercise in statistical creativity; reductionistic, perhaps, but probably all right as far as it goes. However, such theories run the risk of confining our observations.

Everett

Last week I saw a young man, Everett, who was said to have Asperger's syndrome. I asked him, "What's your favorite number?"

"Four."

I asked him, "Why?"

"Because every number can be reduced to four."

"Really? What about seven?"

"Seven is five. Five is four."

It took me a while to figure it out. "What about twenty-three?"

"Twenty-three is eleven. Eleven is six. Six is three. Three is five and five is four."

I said, "But in French, four is quatre, which is six." He was not impressed.

Cinq is four

Trait theory is atheoretical as long as one accepts the premise that reducing the human psyche to a few dimensions is a meaningful exercise. And as long as one isn't bothered by excluding temperamental traits like altruism, perseverance, reward dependence, harm avoidance, novelty-seeking, and so on; or cognitive traits, like attention, memory, processing speed and intelligence; or physical traits, like strength, energy, activity, good health and stamina. Trait theory is also mathematically sound as long as one accepts that the relations among the dimensions of personality are linear, rather than nonlinear. I don't want to be a spoilsport, but if that were true, human personality would be unique among all the complex systems, in which the relations among the component parts are nonlinear.

The Big Five are meant to be inclusive; in a feat of reductionism no less than heroic, 17,953 adjectives were reduced to ten. Like every exercise in over-simplification, the limitations are evident when they are applied to practical matters. A good illustration, something that really matters, is marital satisfaction.

Partners with similar personality traits have higher levels of marital satisfaction and lower levels of conflict, at least when they are young. After people have been married for a while, however, "greater overall personality similarity predicted more negative slopes in marital satisfaction trajectories" (Gaunt, 2006). In other words, the more similar people are, the more they come to hate each other. Hell is other people, it seems, especially if they are just like you.

Conscientiousness and extraversion are healthy traits, but they are predictive of marital dissatisfaction in middle-aged people. The idea is that conscientious people get more rigid as they get older. Two people who are used to their own way must run into conflict during their golden years when they are stuck at home together. Conscientious people tend to get on each other's nerves.

Extraverted couples have higher marital satisfaction when they are young. If, however, one partner is extraverted and the other is not, divorce is more likely. One presumes that the extraverted partner is out having too much fun (O'Rourke *et al.*, 2011; Shiota and Levenson, 2007).

Neuroticism and agreeableness are consistently related to the quality of a marriage, albeit in opposite directions (Cundiff, Smith, and Frandsen, 2012). Neuroticism measured at the beginning of a relationship is a strong predictor of future marital discord, although if you wait a bit your wife is likely to calm down. Your husband won't, though.

Nevertheless, the five dimensions of personality are not irrelevant to the subject at hand. Some things about OC can be mapped onto the Big Five. OCs are, as a group, more conscientious, which implies organization, thoroughness and reliability. They are more open to experience: that is, imaginative, curious and creative. They can also be neurotic (anxious, depressed, tense, moody, hypochondriacal, guilty, low in self-esteem and lacking autonomy). They also tend to be introverts. On the "agreeableness" spectrum, however, they can be anywhere. Some are rigid, uptight and surly, while others are pleasant and compliant, especially when they are on the right dose of an antidepressant or mood-stabilizing drug.

The OC trait

OC is not a trait I discovered by making a reduction of Webster's *Dictionary*. Like the Great Detective himself, I have *induced* the existence of such a trait from my work in the clinic and my experiences in the world. If I had to define it, I might say that it is a propensity to *disproportionate mental exertions*. It is a tendency for oppressive thoughts to occupy a mind that would be better occupied doing something else.

OC is a trait that more than 30 percent of us normal people carry about. The proportion is probably higher among people who read books about OC. Not to worry, reader, because the OC trait expresses itself in many different ways. It's not so bad being an OC; it can be the driver of high achievement. The great savants like Einstein and Newton had OC traits. OC traits are associated with high intelligence and deep thought, with undivided concentration and single-minded pursuit of worthy goals. That is why we find these traits credibly attached to great writers, scientists and clever detectives. OC traits are also associated with highly desirable personality characteristics, like conscientiousness, loyalty, perseverance, self-sacrifice, endurance, honesty and fidelity; and also with the highest goal of spiritual exercise and industrial engineering alike, *continuous quality improvement*. On the basis of brain science and keen observation, we know that OC traits are characteristics of the analytical mind; they contribute to what makes it effective.

By itself, the OC trait is neutral. However, it can manifest itself in different, even orthogonal, ways. Individuals with OC traits tend to have high moral standards; rotate the standard by 90 degrees and the OC is moralistic and hypocritical. Rotate the axis 180 degrees and you find monsters: fanatics of every stripe, serial killers, pedophiles and sexual predators. The mass murderers of the 20th century were evil, controlling men.

Is it possible that so many human events, felicitous and infelicitous alike, are explicable in terms of OC? Not only all the good traits listed above, but also alcoholism, addiction, eating disorders, outbursts of rage, excessive neatness, mass murder, uncontrollable teasing, vulnerability to suggestion, all-consuming hobbies, and a controlling disposition? Or, going back to earlier chapters, procrastination leading to paralysis of action, intellectualizing, vacillation and ambivalence, cannibalism, homophobia and misogyny, a preoccupation with certain numbers, a fussy nature, fear of ladybugs, and a monomania for whales? Such a trait, poised to explain everything, may only account for nothing.

OC includes many different traits and they are often opposites. Just as an OC disposition may be sweet, ditzy and a bit fussy, it can also be wrathful and controlling. Rationality, for example, is an OC trait. OCs are thinkers and tend to be more intelligent and better educated than the population as a whole. So, it is not surprising that they pride themselves on their critical thinking. On the other hand, even scientists can behave towards a prevailing theory or a fashionable line of research like heathens towards an eclipse of the sun. We are taught that ideas have power, and that may be true, so long as they aren't subjected to critical judgment. The most balanced and rational among us can be carried away by an idea. Think of the Banana-Man.

Paradoxes and inconsistencies

> ...it is moreover, striking that in this condition the opposite-values (polarities) pervading mental life appear to be exceptionally sharply differentiated.[3]

Traits may be stable, more or less, but how they are expressed may change with the vagaries of life. Having spent my career working with patients who had learning disabilities or brain injuries, I know that human beings, like their brains, are flexible, adaptable and capable of continuous improvement. But then, some aren't. "People change or they don't."

There is something about OC that makes predictions about stability unreliable. It is this: the inconsistencies and paradoxes that characterize the lives of OCs. While all of us are prone to contradictions, OCs are virtual chimeras.

It is remarkable how OCs can be one way and the other at the same time. For example, *sobriety*. Seriousness and humorlessness are said to characterize OC people. They are also compulsive jokesters. They love puns and teasing and practical jokes. There is no more solemn and serious tribe than the psycho-analysts, devoted as they are to finding dark secrets in every corner of day-to-day life.

---

3   Sigmund Freud, *Introductory Lectures on Psycho-analysis*, 1925.

But what do they do, these dour psycho-analysts, at their annual get-togethers? They tell jokes! They love to tell jokes. They even write *books* about jokes.

This is the kind of paradox that exists in the psychology of the OC. It makes diagnosis a bit tricky. "Is he very neat?" you ask. "Neat! Heavens, no. His office is an utter mess with clutter." It is, but if you happen to move one small thing in the room, one crumpled old magazine, or if you borrow his staple-gun, buried beneath a stack of papers, he will notice and fly into a rage.

Below are some more dark secrets about the OCs and their psychological contradictions. An individual OC may be one way or the other. Sometimes, both ways.

- *Dubitation.* This is such an old word I don't even think it exists. Neither does *dubiety*, except in dictionaries. If it did, it would refer to doubt. OCs are notorious doubters. They check their work over and over because of persistent fear that something is wrong. On a personal level, they are sure of their own rectitude, and given to righteous indignation. At the same time, they may be afflicted by gnawing self-doubt. Their chronic lack of self-confidence is reflected in their attitude towards others. For example, they may idolize their doctors, and treat them with great deference. At the same time, they are deeply skeptical about what the doctors say, and especially treatments. "I still feel bad, Doc." "Oh, that medicine didn't work then?" "No, I didn't take it. I read the side effects on the internet."

- *Deprecation.* Much as they are attached to their routines and idiosyncratic ways of doing things, OCs are nagged by doubt about their value. They may achieve some milestone, at extraordinary cost in time and effort, and then lose interest in what they have done. Groucho Marx said he would never join a club that would have him as a member. In that spirit, OC people are given to degrading their accomplishments, the rewards they have achieved and especially the people who love them. They alternate between idealizing and contempt.

- *Rectitude.* A sober attitude is usually associated with a preoccupation with righteousness, an abiding sense of certainty about the correctness of one's beliefs, sometimes manifest as religiosity, political correctness, health-awareness or attachment to abstract views (like theosophy) or eccentric interests (organic gardening, earth shoes). But OCs are also given to "superego lacunae"—that is, Swiss-cheese holes in their conscience. So, you will also see kleptomania, pornography addiction, coprolalia, pedophilia, necrophilia and all manner of nasty bad habits.

- *Proper speech.* A compulsive person will correct your English when you say "Her and me are goin' out coon huntin' tonaht." He will correct you if you say "normally" when you should say "ordinarily" or "usually"; or "optics" when you mean "appearance"; or if you over-use the words "nuance" or "narrative." But compulsives are also notorious cussers. Coprolalia is a symptom of Tourette's syndrome, a condition that is related to OCD. It is also a clue to OC. The fastidious writers at *The Economist* and *The New Yorker* must experience a *frisson* when they can quote some foul-mouthed celebrity in scatological detail.

- *Scrupulosity.* This, of course, is a form of fastidiousness. One is preoccupied with holding to the letter of some concocted code of behavior. Like fastidiousness, its setting will be the tendency to neglect one's real duties. Scrupulosity is a technical term from the medieval Church, and it refers to a rigid adherence to the externals of religious practice, usually to the exclusion of Christian charity. Controlling people are often drawn to organized religions where they can indulge their love of rituals, display their rectitude and deprecate unbelievers. The lacunae in their conscience are well-known.

- *Control.* OCs insist on controlling their immediate environments, and especially their families. They have difficulty delegating authority, they tend to micro-manage and they get bogged down in details. They are infuriated by resistance to their intrusions. On the other hand, OCs are usually highly suggestible and pathologically docile towards authority themselves. In certain circumstances, they are remarkably passive.

- *Rumination.* Things stick in their craw. Anxieties and angry thoughts, typically, almost invariably about trivial things that they think to death. Then they will do something very important, on impulse, without thinking about it at all.

- *Slowness.* Naturally, if you have to check things over and over, or ruminate over every little thing, doing stuff is going to take longer. But it is not so simple. OCs have prolonged processing speed even on simple, abstract tasks that have no importance whatever. But they are also capable of rushing through things, responding impulsively and carelessly, especially to important events. If something is really important, they may ignore it entirely.

- *Avoidance.* Introverts as most of them are, OCs may prefer to avoid confrontation and risk. Others, however, turn the most innocent interaction into the occasion of argument, opposition or antipathy. OCs can be gentle and retiring or intense and hateful.

- *Emotional restriction.* Anxiety and anger are the characteristic emotions of OC individuals. They have difficulty experiencing a more nuanced emotional life. Paradoxically, when they marry, it is usually to someone who is emotionally overactive. Or they marry someone just as controlling as they are, and you can imagine what their issue will be like.

- *Self-absorption.* One who is attached to his rectitude and way of doing things, who thinks more critically and incisively than everyone else, who deprecates those closest to him and who tries to control every aspect of their lives, has to be an egoist of the first order. OCs can also be wildly generous, self-sacrificing and devoted to people, especially to those less advantaged than they. That's why there are so many of them in the medical professions.

Defining a condition as A *and* non-A is an old trick for psychiatrists. If patients accept that they are *neurotic*, then they are. If they resist the idea, that simply evidences their *resistance*. "Are you excessively neat?" the psychiatrist asks. "Heavens, no. I'm as messy as can be." "Does it annoy you if your food touches on the plate?" "No, I like to mix it all up in a swirl." Just two occasions for that *Aha!* moment, and diametric opposites at that. The diagnosis is clear, at least to a psychiatrist who has OC on the brain.

A condition defined by a trait and by its opposite creates certain difficulties for those of us who would prefer to take a scientific approach to OC. To that end, I resolved to approach this problem with a blank mind, forming no theories but only observing and drawing inferences from my observations. *I have observed*, therefore, that a certain tribe of human beings are given to *disproportionate mental exertions*. Their thoughts and impulses occupy their minds in ways that exclude more beneficent endeavors. If that characteristic—call it a trait—is the root of the tree, then it likely does run in many different directions.

The inference one draws from the paradoxes and inconsistencies of an OC life is that it is hard, if not impossible, to maintain a consistently analytical approach to life, if only because life itself is, if not irrational, nevertheless utterly mysterious. The analytical-theoretical mind is an agent of extraordinary power and concision, but it functions best in short bursts of intense activity. Asking it to account for or amend all the petty failures that surround us, the inconsistencies and silliness, the surprises and disappointments, the surges and falls—it's asking too much. The analytical mind gets tired, poor thing, it gets cranky or over-heated. Contending with mysteries and irrationalities, the analytical parts of brain do well to rely on other parts, especially the eternally flexible social/emotional brain. The OC mind is hesitant to do that.

Contending with mysteries and irrationalities as we shall do, we shall remain atheoretical. Like Holmes, we shall be astute observers of the human condition but not theoreticians. It is my *observation* that our introductory cast of characters have something in common. I call it OC because it resembles the signs and symptoms of OCD and the OC personality disorder. It's my observation and that of other neuroscientists that the analytical mind participates to an unwholesome degree in the activities of an OC. I have also observed that OC traits are very common, not only in patients but also in their families and in everybody else, too.

If you don't believe me, you can play this interesting game. During an idle moment, ask someone if she or anyone in her family has an odd quirk or an idiosyncrasy. This is what my hairdresser told me last week: her husband, after a shower, dries himself with the hair-blower.

Ah yes, the old hair-blower ploy. A trivial quirk, of course. But he is fixed on it, an invariant pattern, and if there isn't a hair-blower available, he doesn't shower. He may be a nice enough fellow, but one must agree that he has a thing about hair-blowers. Or towels, maybe.

Our method will be founded upon the observation of such trifles.[4] We are not quite ready to promulgate a theory of OC, let alone predictions about the future of the race, although we shall get to both before the end. "It is a capital mistake to theorize before one has data. Insensibly one begins to twist facts to suit theories, instead of theories to suit facts."[5]

---

4   Arthur Conan Doyle, "The Boscombe Valley Mystery" (*The Adventures of Sherlock Holmes*).

5   Arthur Conan Doyle, "A Scandal in Bohemia" (*The Adventures of Sherlock Holmes*).

5
The Count

Count von Count is a character on *Sesame Street* whose penchant for counting is the opportunity to teach numbers to little children. In case you've missed the show, he wears a cape, has slicked-back hair and two vampiric teeth. Vampires, the producers must have known, like to count, and one way to keep a vampire at bay is to scatter pebbles or raisins around the room. An intruding vampire will become preoccupied with counting them while you make your getaway.

OCs, too, like to count. The motto of the OCD association is "Every member counts!" Sherlock Holmes was also a counter:

> "Quite so," he answered, lighting a cigarette, and throwing himself down into an arm-chair. "You see, but you do not observe. The distinction is clear. For example you have frequently seen the steps which lead up from the hall to this room."
>
> "Frequently."
>
> "Then how many are there?"
>
> "How many? I don't know."
>
> "Quite so! You have not observed. And yet you have seen. That is just my point. Now, I know that there are seventeen steps, because I have both seen and observed."[1]

---

1   Arthur Conan Doyle, "A Scandal in Bohemia" (*The Adventures of Sherlock Holmes*).

What's so bad about counting? Do *you* know many steps there are between the first and second floors of your house? While climbing the stairs, isn't it natural to turn the mundane task into an exercise of sorts, and exercise almost invariably involves counting. "I try to bike at least 50 miles every weekend," said one of my patients. The rituals of sport are simply festooned with magical numbers, like 26.4 miles for a marathon, not to mention *Love, 20, 30, 40, Game*. Baseball has nine men on a team and nine innings, three strikes for an out and three outs for an inning, four bases and four balls for a base on balls.

Psychiatrists have determined that counting *compulsions* fall into the broad category of "rituals and superstitions." That may be true, but I believe that numbers are a splendid example of the power of abstraction. If numbers do excite abstraction, it is because they crystallize the power of an idea, especially an idea unrestrained by meaning. Galileo said that the book of the universe is written in the language of mathematics, but I prefer the movie.

The power of number

One's prayers have to recited in a particular order and a particular number of times. The priest walks around the altar three times with a censer holding incense, swinging it precisely three times on each of three sides. Number obsessions and counting compulsions are fairly common, and they are sometimes associated with fears of exacting harm. *If I look away from the clock at 1:57, my family will die; if I look away at 2:05, I will go blind.* There are magic numbers and lucky numbers and numbers that speak to the grand anthropic principle of the universe.

What is it about numbers that excites superstition? Whatever it is defies the idea that OC arose during prehistoric times, because human beings haven't been counting that long. The crow, it seems, has numerosity surpassing that of primitive humans, many of whom have not even achieved the stage of finger-counting. The proof is from Tobias Danzig, who told of a "squire" who was determined to kill a crow that had made its nest in the watch-tower of his estate. He tried to surprise the bird, but failed. Even the most surreptitious approach would induce the crow to fly away. It would wait in a tree until the squire left the watch-tower. He finally had a bright idea— the squire, not the crow. He went to the tower with a companion; one left, one stayed behind. The crow stayed in its tree. Then he went with two companions and two left. Then four men went to the tower, and three left. The bird was undeceived. Finally, five men went to the tower and four left. At this point, the crow lost count. It flew back, and was summarily shot. It was concluded that crows, or at least one particular crow, can count to four but not five.

Edward Curr, who made a study of such things, reported that few Australian aborigines were able to discern four, and the Bushmen of South Africa had no number words beyond "one," "two" and "many" (Curr, 1887). Small children, like many animals less clever than the crow, can readily distinguish one, two or three objects; those numbers seem to be basic perceptual qualities that our brains can process without counting. Therefore, all the world languages, even those of primitive tribes, have counting words for one, two and three, although three may stand for "many," "several" or "a lot" (Hurford, 1999). "Three," in fact, is a residual form: "troppo" in Italian means "too much," as does "trop" in French, resembling *tre* and *trois*, their words for "three" (Ardila and Rosselli, 2002). Three's a crowd, right?

Numerosity is the ability to count beyond three or four, the numerical boundaries of simple perception, and it has acquired a special place in the domain of critical intelligence. When Pythagoras discovered that music was, at its root, an exercise in mathematical relationships, he was inclined to consign transcendent qualities to both: *the harmony of all creation, the music of the spheres*. The reader is not likely to assign transcendent qualities to any of my assertions, for example, when I say that *The commonest mental problems associated with early sensory integration disorder are OC, social anxiety and autism*. But if I express this in numerical terms, the dubious reader will be impressed:

Post-hoc tests revealed that OCD subjects had significantly lower percent prepulse inhibition than healthy controls at all PP intensities: 74dB ($t(42)$=2.43; p<0.019); 78dB ($t(42)$=2.15; p<0.038); 86dB ($t(42)$=2.17; p<0.036). The consolidated PPI measure also demonstrated that OCD patients had significantly lower PPI than healthy controls (mean±SEM: healthy controls=45.4±4.2; OCD=30.1±4.3; $t(42)$=6.48; p<0.015). (Ahmari, Risbrough, Geyer, and Simpson, 2012)

(Prepulse inhibition of the acoustic startle response reflects abnormalities in processing and integrating sensory data.)

* * *

Human beings have advanced considerably since the days when the number "4" was high-tech, and that might not have been too long ago. Although there are still tribes of wild men and women who haven't yet got to "4," Stone Age artifacts from Europe include ordered notches on bone and antler, as if something were being counted. Written numbers, though, didn't appear until about 3000 years BC, among the Sumerians, who were the first to make systematic marks on the floor or on a clay tablet, rather than using their fingers, pebbles or knots (Childe, 1936). They were using numbers to keep track of commercial transactions well before they had written language (d'Errico *et al.*, 1998).

Counting developed comparatively recently in human history, just as it develops relatively late in child development. In both instances, it begins with finger-counting, or finger- and toe-counting (as in "digit"). That accounts for the decimal system (numbers to the base ten), which appeared in Sumer, Egypt, India and Crete at about the same time. The Sumerians also had a sexagesimal system, based on the number 60, which persists for contemporary measures of minutes and seconds, but not tennis. Twelve (as in a dozen) may be a remnant of that system, although it may also be related to the number of lunar months in a year. The base 20 (the total number of one's *dedo's*) was used by the Mayans and is captured in the French *quatre-vingts*, or eighty. There used to be 20 shillings in a pound and 12 pence to a shilling. Or was it the other way around?

Recognition of individual marks up to 3 is easy: it is an immediate perception. Beyond 3, the number of marks (strokes or dots) has to be counted and errors can occur. For that reason, number symbols past 3 have no ideographic meaning but are purely abstract. In our Arabic notation system, "1" is a vertical line, whereas 2 and 3 were originally horizontal lines that became tied together when handwritten. In China, the numbers one, two and three are still written as shown in Figure 5.1.

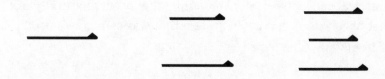

Figure 5.1 Chinese numbers: one, two and three

The counting brain

The same brain regions that mediate finger-counting, the left and right parietal cortex, are areas that participate in body awareness. Children who are poor in arithmetic skills also misrepresent fingers when they draw a person. The **Gerstmann syndrome** is difficulty with arithmetic, difficulty in identifying fingers (finger agnosia), difficulty in writing, and right–left confusion; as in, *Is this my right hand or is it this one?*

Body awareness is present in most animals, and the brain regions that do it in humans seem to have pre-adapted for the acquisition of numerosity, a skill that is only a few thousand years old. That means there was something about the evolving brain that was ready to receive numbers greater than three as soon as someone came up with the idea. That something was a newly expanded neocortex, the analytical mind, with hosts of little modules ("mini-columns") that were ideal for local computations, like adding 1 to 2 to make 3, and then adding 1 to 3 to make 4, and so on.

Math is not a natural skill and, as you know, the development of numerical concepts is a painstaking learning process. Adding and subtracting numerical quantities and using computational principles begins for children in the first and second grades, but kids can't manipulate the principles of multiplying and dividing until they have endured a long and arduous training period. That many children have arithmetic disabilities is not nearly so surprising as the fact that so many don't. Numerosity—the ability to count beyond 3 and the ability to understand and manipulate numerical concepts—is not something that occurs naturally. Yet it must have arisen in a brain system that was somehow hospitable, or "pre-adapted."

* * *

The left and right parietal lobes are the likely candidates, because that is where one's sense of oneself in space resides, and mathematics is fundamentally an exercise in spatial reasoning. The parietal lobes, however, only contain the precursor to primitive numerosity, the function present in human babies and most animals. Primitive numerosity, what preschoolers have, is an innate sense of *approximate* numerical quantities. It is accurate for perceiving and estimating one, two or three objects, but is grossly inaccurate for judging large numbers. It is perfectly suitable for evaluating continuous qualities, like duration, length, area, volume, density, rate, intensity, and so on. It is a system of mental magnitudes, a numerosity system that is approximate and compressed and situated towards the back of the brain in the left and right parietal lobes. Babies have it, as well as crows, and it is preverbal.

By the age of five, most children have cultivated intuitions about the meaning of number and numerical operations based on their native, approximate system. How good a child is at making estimates—*Which is bigger?*—is actually a predictor of success in math later on (Halberda, Mazzocco, and Feigenson, 2008). However, even in adults, approximation ability is much more accurate than math. Try this: at the next boring party you attend, ask your date to observe a group of people chatting together. Ask her to rank them in terms of size, say their height. She will rank them correctly. Then ask her to guess their heights. She will likely get it wrong.

As one moves beyond primitive numerosity based on relative dimensions, numeric symbols are acquired. This doesn't happen because symbols are superimposed on that core parietal-lobe system for approximation. Rather, it entails profound changes in other parts of brain. As a child grows up in school, he or she begins to refine the representation of numerical symbols in the left hemisphere (Piazza and Izard, 2009). Bushmen, babies, primates and crows possess the ability to make approximate quantitative distinctions. The ability to map symbols—that is, numbers—onto those distinctions, and then to manipulate them in lawful ways, is a cultural acquisition that involves brain regions that are close to and that overlap the language areas of the left hemisphere.

The abilities to perceive and to understand continuous quantities like duration, length, area, volume, density, rate, intensity and the like are our natural endowment. How basic they are can be illustrated by what happens at the end of a presentation made by a quant,[2] using slides festooned with arcane symbols and inscrutable formulae. One of the senior executives, one who is well past feeling ashamed, will inevitabily ask, *What's the bottom line, Chao-wen?* He doesn't want symbols: he wants the meaningful information that is no less than the primitive foundation of numerical reasoning. One may count the ways, therefore, but to render the sum meaningful it has to be translated from digital to analog:

> How do I love thee? Let me count the ways.
> I love thee to the depth and breadth and height
> My soul can reach, when feeling out of sight
> For the ends of being and ideal grace.[3]

* * *

---

2   Wall Street jargon for a mathematician.

3   Elizabeth Barrett Browning, *Sonnet 43*.

Mathematical skill is built upon a phylogenetically ancient system that is operative when a monkey decides that tree A has more fruit hanging from its boughs than tree B, or when a fox decides to carry off the fat goose, not the skinny one. Approximate arithmetic does not depend on linguistic representations, but instead relies on "a quantity representation implemented in visual-spatial networks of the left and right parietal lobes" (Dehaene *et al.*, 1999). Mathematical skill, however, relies upon the discrete character of language. Solutions to exact arithmetic problems rely "on language-specific representations and…on a left inferior frontal circuit also used for generating associations between words" (Dehaene *et al.*, 1999). Math is language, except it's made-up, like Esperanto.

Math and the abstract mind

Mathematics is the abstract science of numbers, quantity, and space. The basic methodology of mathematics is abstraction and symbolic inference… (Wang, 2012)

It's not abstractions that make math hard. In case you haven't noticed, we deal with abstractions all the time. Words are abstractions. There is nothing about the phoneme assembly "brown" to suggest the color brown or "dog" to suggest a type of canid, but we accept that they do because we learned it long ago, and so did all the other English-speakers we hang around with. "Brown dog" may refer, specifically, to the canid rolling around right now on the rug in my library. He does that sometimes when he needs a scratch. Alternatively, it may mean that F needs to take him to the vet. It shows how facile we humans are at associating abstractions like "brown" and "dog" with real-world events. Syntax is a higher order of abstraction, the ability to manipulate words to form meaningful ideas. A sentence is the statement of an idea, and a paragraph is the elaboration of the idea. The idea I just elaborated is that our lives are not only suffused with words but with abstractions and, hopefully, with devoted pets as well.

We don't mind abstractions because we are intelligent, and intelligent in a particular way. We humans have a special kind of intelligence. Our ape ancestors were certainly intelligent, in their way, and so are dogs, cats and birds. The sea slug, we are told, has remarkable capacity for learning. Plants, too, have plant intelligence. "Plants continuously screen at least 15 different environmental variables with remarkable sensitivity—a footprint on the soil or a local stone, for example, are perceived and acted upon... The flow of information is continuous. Integrated responses are constructed after reference to the bank of internal information that specifies the plant's ecological niche" (Trewavas, 2002).

The intelligence of the analytical mind, however, is not something we share with plants, slugs, or even dolphins, elephants or chimpanzees. We don't even share it with our remote human ancestors. Abstract intelligence—the ability to manipulate concepts in a useful way—was first detected about 50,000 years ago; the first real evidence is the extraordinary cave paintings at Lescaux, Chauvet and El Castillo. There is evidence of decoration by hominids long before, but in the cave paintings humans first produced something *transcendent*—images that were not only beautiful but meaningful. Meaningful, because they captured not only the image of the beasts but something of their essence.

Language and intelligence probably evolved together among the hominids. They both involve the manipulation of abstractions and we use them both so often we hardly think about it. We start doing so in the second or third year of life. At that point, a child begins to apprehend language and responds not just to coos and pleasant sounds but to the semantic meaning of those sounds. At this point in life, just as it did at some point during evolution, the brain encounters "a benevolent, octopus-like parasite whose tentacles invaded the brain" (Paivio, 2007). The metaphor is feverish but apt. It refers to language, an octopus-like parasite, arising in the left hemisphere. During development, language has a transformative influence and allows children to endow experience with a language-based organization (Gainotti, 2014). Language confers upon children, just as it did among the early humans, the capacity for analytical thinking in a verbal format. For example, the future tense. We tend to take it for granted, but at some point a band of humans stumbled upon it and discovered it was a good thing. Not only could they think about what might happen in the future, but they could communicate that information to their conspecifics. It's hard to plan for the future if one doesn't have a future tense. Food-preservation technology is helpful, too.

The evolving primate brain endowed hominids with language that was richer, more flexible and more efficient than the various modes of animal and plant communication. Language endowed the humans with a conceptual or analytical brain, "the ability to construct conceptual models of the human universe" (Donald, 1991). It is a far advance from mimicry, which is supposed to have preceded language in the course of hominid development. Mimicry is a powerful tool but not very efficient, and the quality of the mental concepts it conveys is limited. Try to act out *The Critique of Pure Reason* in charades. Language is a much more efficient way to transmit information of this sort:

> Human reason begins with principles, which cannot be dispensed with in the field of experience, and the truth and sufficiency of which are, at the same time, insured by experience. With these principles it rises, in obedience to the laws of its own nature, to ever higher and more remote conditions. But it quickly discovers that, in this way, its labors must remain ever incomplete, because new questions never cease to present themselves.[4]

* * *

The analytical-theoretical mind doesn't perceive it to be a problem, that *its labors must remain ever incomplete, because new questions never cease to present themselves*. It isn't intimidated by such challenges and always seems to rise to the occasion. It likes the

---

4   Immanuel Kant, *The Critique of Pure Reason*, 1781.

challenge of unanswered questions. It doesn't bother the mind one little bit if the questions it poses may occupy levels of abstraction remote by orders of magnitude from human experience. It likes to bathe in the waters of self-absorption, the endless river of ideas and invention.

The analytical mind—the agent of abstract intelligence—is an organ of surpassing power. It occupies the vast domain of the neocortex, with six layers of neurons unique to humans and 60,000 miles of connecting fibers that mostly connect within. It is a distributed cortical function, involving all the cortical lobes of the cortex, but especially the frontal and parietal lobes, which also happen to be the two most recently evolved cortical regions. The structural correlates of analytical intelligence are increased cortical volume, density and connectivity. Its functional correlates are plasticity, stability, speed and resilience. Its operations are characterized by its efficiency and its ability to form new functional networks as the need arises. The intelligent brain reacts quickly and consistently, mobilizes a greater mass of neuronal tissue and, at the same time, utilizes less energy.

Intelligence speaks to something essential to human adaptation. A good definition of intelligence is that it is *the ability to deal with complex cognitive problems*, and people have recognized its importance for thousands of years. It is why Odysseus, not Achilles, is the survivor of Homer's epics, and it is probably why God preferred Jacob to Esau. Intelligence is an innate ability of the brain. Its functional components include working memory and attention, coordination of goal-directed cognitive processes, and inhibition of goal-irrelevant processes. Central to these psychological functions is the ability to control the thrust of all mental activity.

The social/emotional brain, the somatic brain and the habit system generate a different kind of intelligence. Their operations are feelings, intuitions and habits; mental activities, to be sure, and they can even be said to be intelligent, in the colloquial, imprecise meaning of the word, synonymous with *effective* or *successful*. They even have a psychology. But feelings, intuitions and habits do not have a language until they are processed by the left hemisphere of one's analytical mind. Nor do they generate abstractions.

They do, however, generate the *thrust* of mental activity; that is, who we are, what we are about and why, how to do it and with whom, and whether it hurts when we do. Those rather prosaic elements are no less than what we know as *meaning*. The analytical mind evolved to enrich those activities and to put them into words and, sometimes, numbers. It may be "higher" in terms of brain anatomy and it is newer in terms of evolution and phylogenesis, but the lesson of OC is that it does not work very well by itself. Even the most circumscribed activities, like mathematics, philosophy and theoretical science, are governed by intuition as much as by abstract thought. The analytical mind may *direct* the thrust of mental activity but it doesn't *control* it—and the thrust itself, one's sense of meaning, comes from below. Below is the full quote from Allan Paivio. He was writing about language, but the principle is the same for abstract intelligence:

> Language never worked its magic alone and it cannot do so now. Instead, it always depended on a silent partner that provides it with something to talk about... I see language as a benevolent, octopus-like parasite whose tentacles invaded the brain and was empowered by it to survive and thrive to the point where it could contribute something useful to its host. (Paivio, 2007)

* * *

The analytical mind stumbles if it tries to assert itself upon such ambiguous events as meaning. It is designed to make local computations and can make fine distinctions, but its goal, if we can say it has a single goal, is something like certainty. To that end, it learned to make logical operations and invented mathematics, a form of logic. From those sources it was enabled to make the finest distinctions within the broadest range of topics. It has contributed not a few things that are useful to its hosts. Yet the analytical mind has limitations. It was built for a certain kind of work and it is readily frustrated by events that work with a logic of their own. The analytical mind has difficulty with common sense, which it finds parochial, and with intuition, which arises from one's psyche as feeling. It can't be broken down or analyzed. The analytical mind hates ambiguity, for the same reason. It struggles, in particular, with meaning:

> The more the universe seems comprehensible, the more it also seems pointless. (Weinberg, 1994)

Analytical intelligence is endowed with the qualities one might attribute to a central executive: the ability to integrate data from diverse sources and to recruit the resources it needs to solve problems efficiently. It also strives for a power that every central executive would like to have: the ability to control its underlings. That may not be such a good thing. Peter Drucker said, "So much of what we call management consists of making it difficult for people to work" (Drucker, 1995).

Every member counts

Abstract intelligence, the analytical-theoretical mind, finds an agreeable resting place in the manipulation of abstractions—the more pointless and the less value-laden, the better. And if one can count them, all the better. Counting is an exercise devoid of ambiguity. It is exact measurement, beloved by vampires and OCs, by the Great Detective himself as well as by his arch-enemy, Professor Moriarty:

> His career has been an extraordinary one. He is a man of good birth and excellent education, endowed by nature with a phenomenal mathematical faculty. At the age of twenty-one he wrote a treatise upon the Binomial Theorem, which has had a European vogue. On the strength of it he won the

Mathematical Chair at one of our smaller universities, and had, to all appearance, a most brilliant career before him. But the man had hereditary tendencies of the most diabolical kind... He is the Napoleon of crime, Watson. He is a genius, a philosopher, an abstract thinker.[5]

* * *

Exactitude appeals to OCs, who like regularity and precision, and can find it in no better place than in numbers. By their very nature, numbers are ordered and behave predictably. They can be arranged symmetrically, and even their asymmetries are rule-bound. The operations that can be undertaken using them are limited in number and guarded by immutable rules, but the operations can be exercised in ways beyond number. Such paradoxes appeal to the OC. So does the symbolic, disembodied nature of numbers, divorced from the ambiguities of real life. Irrational numbers are subject to reason, and imaginary numbers are as real as real ones. Random numbers aren't really random at all. Finally, the relationships among numbers can be established, not by experience or common sense, but by deductive reasoning.

The origin of written numbers was prosaic: to keep track of commercial transactions. Yet, before very long, humans began to assign them transcendent if not magical powers: "All things that can be known have number; for it is not possible that without number anything can be either conceived or known."[6] Since Pythagoras, 2500 years ago, numbers have been the agent of control.

Control, but not meaning. *What's the bottom line, Chao-wen?* Yet OCs down through history have tried to endow them with meaning, and the belief that numbers have mystical significance is still with us. Sigmund Freud dabbled in numerology and Isaac Newton was committed to it. His rainbow contained seven colors (red, orange, yellow, green, blue, indigo and violet), and in antiquity there were

5   Arthur Conan Doyle, "The Final Problem" (*The Memoirs of Sherlock Holmes*).
6   Philolaos of Tarentum (ca. 475 BC).

seven planets, or non-fixed objects, in the sky (the Sun and Moon, Mercury, Mars, Jupiter, Venus and Saturn), which also happen to be the days of the week. The Hebrew Bible is replete with direct or obscure references to the number seven.

The superstition persists, and to the man or woman equipped with numerosity we still attribute the most fabulous powers of insight, analysis and prediction, often in defiance of experience and common sense. The idea, from Pythagoras and perhaps the Babylonians before him, was that numbers were reflections of the Divine, perhaps because, in all Creation, only numbers behave with regularity. They do, of course; although I'm not sure that Divinity does.

6

The Habit System, Oppressed

Repetitive behaviors and rituals make it seem as if OCs are creatures of habit. Going to the store, an OC might follow the same route every time, first around the perimeter, and then along the rows, from the outermost in. When eating, eat in pairs: two chips, two raisins, two asparagus spears, and so on. Pancakes should be eaten circumferentially and clockwise, starting at six o'clock. Rituals for eating are particularly common. Anthropologists have written books about them. If there is a habit system in one's brain, isn't that the source of automatic behavior? That is a superficial construction. It consigns the considered behavior of OCs to the level of a simple reflex. OCs have perfectly good reasons for doing what they do and the way they do it. Having thought through a matter to which we philistines are oblivious, they have learned how to do it right. If their behavior seems habitual, it's just because they've been doing it so long, it's become second nature.

The habit brain is a marvel of flexibility and efficiency. It can take the stupidest idea in the world and turn it into an action step requiring only one or two more synapses than a reflex arc. The fault, however, is not in the basal ganglia. It is *ideas* that are wrongheaded. And also obdurate and inflexible.

OC and anxiety

I told you that obsessions and compulsions are supposed to be attempts to control or "bind" anxiety; obsessions were the expression of anxiety and compulsions were a way to work it out. I also said that this was an erroneous conclusion. Anxiety may not be the cause of OC behavior, but the *consequence*. I shall illustrate my argument with a vignette from the life of a famous ethologist.

> I once suddenly realized that when driving a car in Vienna I regularly used two different routes when approaching and when leaving a certain place in the city... Rebelling against the creature of habit in myself, I tried using my customary return route for the outward journey and vice versa... The astonishing result of this experiment was an undeniable feeling of anxiety so unpleasant that when I came to return I reverted to the habitual route. (Lorenz, 1966)

According to conventional theory, Konrad Lorenz was "binding" anxiety by driving to and from Vienna in a symmetrical way. Theoretically, there was something about driving to Vienna that roused deep feelings of rage and/or anxiety in the poor man. But, as usual, the old psychiatric theories got it backwards. In Lorenz's case, it wasn't anxiety that made him take one road to Vienna and another road back home. It was just one of his little habits. Anxiety arose when he tried to change it. According to the old theory, the compulsion to drive symmetrically was "binding" his anxiety. When he changed his habit, anxiety spewed forth. It's more likely that he was used to doing it one way and trying to break the habit made him nervous.

The habit system

Since OC people aren't creatures of habit but, rather, the generators of habit, this is an appropriate time to talk about habits and what they have to do with OC. **Habit** means different things in different contexts, but the word always refers to something one does frequently, if not all the time, and without thinking about it very much.

The original sense of the word refers to the habits of living things, the behavioral characteristics of a plant or an animal. It is the way something lives: a small plant may have a dwarf habit, a squirrel has an arboreal habit. A related word is "habitat," the ecological niche in which an animal or plant exercises its habits. Human beings have a number of such habits. For example, we have a habit of *pairing off* and raising young ones together. It's the way we are, an **enduring orientation** that we have. Another habit we have is *getting along*; we humans occupy a social habitat, and that makes some problems, like the wrathful, controlling man, a bit hard to explain, let alone abide.

Another kind of habit is the **nervous habit**: tics, stereotypies and nervous mannerisms. They are repetitive behaviors that occur, in minor forms, in just about everybody—fidgeting, for example, biting one's fingernails, or brushing back one's hair with one's fingers or a shake of the head. Habits of this sort occur in rather dramatic form in patients with Tourette's syndrome, autism, dementia, certain forms of schizophrenia, and severe brain injuries. They also occur in caged animals: what is called "zoo behavior," a form of self-stimulation in which the animal has to engage, I suppose, to keep its sanity.

A "bad habit" like tapping one's teeth at table with a knife is a nervous mannerism—a form of zoo behavior. A bad habit like watching porn or internet sex is more like an enduring orientation; addictions are enduring orientations, too. They occupy one's interest and attention at the expense of other courses of action, which is not a good thing because just about any course of action is better than porn or cyber-sex.

To a brain scientist, habit has a third meaning. It is behavior that is "overlearned" and virtually automatic. Brushing one's hair, shaving, driving a car and keyboarding are overlearned skills. They are not unconscious but they don't have to occupy one's attention; while executing the behavior one can do something else at the same time. Habits in this sense have been learned by repetition and are the product of one's **procedural memory**. They are also known as "species-specific motor patterns" that reside in the **basal ganglia** (BG) of the brain.[1] When one is engaged in a habitual behavior, like folding the laundry, the habit system in one's BG is active in directing one's behavior; this leaves one's mind open to do something else at the same time, like listening to music or pondering the mystery of where socks disappear to and why they always seem to journey there by themselves.

"Habit," therefore, has several meanings: what is common to all of them is that one does them frequently without thinking about them very much. They may serve a purpose, but they do so at a level that is not usually conscious.

Fast and slow operators

Habits speak to the way brain works; brain likes less-than-conscious activities because they are quick and efficient and they don't eat up much mental energy. They are how the mind does things automatically. When a behavioral pattern is overlearned, one's mind consigns it to the habit system, the basal ganglia, which can express the pattern whenever it needs to, automatically and without expending too much energy.

At some point, we may have the opportunity to learn the distinction between procedural and declarative memory. The first is the memory of *how*, like how to ride a bicycle, and the second is the memory of *what*, like that fellow you met whose name didn't come immediately to mind. They are only two of the many kinds of

---

1   Brushing one's hair and shaving are in the brain-science category of "grooming behavior"; driving a car is in the neuropharmacological category of "locomotion"; keyboarding is, well, "typing."

memory we have, but they are relevant to two mental systems that are central to OC because they govern different kinds of learning and behavior.

The two mental systems are called the **fast operator** and the **slow operator**. The fast operator is a **habit system** that guides behavior automatically and effortlessly, and the slow operator is sometimes called the **mnemonic system**. "Mnemonic system" is another term for the analytical mind. It is extremely efficient, considering all that it has to do, and its short-range connections are very fast; but, compared to the habit system, it operates slowly, especially in OCs. Their active minds attach discursive computations to the simplest problem, and this tends to slow things down. But even in non-OCs, the neocortex burns much more mental energy with its computations.

This is how they work, these two mental systems:

- In order for the mind to operate efficiently, it is necessary to consign certain actions, thoughts and feelings to a fast system that behaves virtually automatically. It is not really automatic, like the pumping of one's heart muscle or reflexes like an eye blink. The habit system is *kind of* automatic, in the sense of something that is overlearned, something that one has done or seen or felt so many times that one doesn't have to think about it anymore. The efficient operation of the brain requires a fast operator like the habit system to deal with overlearned tasks (e.g., walking, brushing hair, driving a car). The mnemonic system is a slow operator. It is responsible for more complex operations (e.g., learning to walk after you've had a stroke, writing a college essay, or explaining to your wife that No, you're not lost, you're just taking a short-cut, and you're not going to stop to ask for directions).
- Driving a car, brushing one's hair and eating with chopsticks aren't really automatic behaviors, like a reflex, but they are overlearned, they require very little mental energy, and one is perfectly able to do other things, like talking to someone or

listening to the radio, at the same time. They aren't mediated by the "unconscious mind" because we know quite well what we are up to. It's just that we don't have to think about them. We tend to say that habits are automatic or unconscious, although they really aren't. The mnemonic system, on the other hand, isn't automatic at all, but entails "cogitation": thinking and critical analysis, pulling up relevant items from one's memory banks and making a decision, coming up with theories to explain what happened or to predict what is going to happen. All of this takes time and energy, which is why the mnemonic system is a slow operator.

- The habit system resides in the basal ganglia and it is phylogenetically ancient: that is, it is the mental system that drives animals, even reptiles and fish. It is a bit more complex than a simple reflex, which means more nerve cells participate in the things the habit system does, but it is almost as fast as a reflex. Habits form naturally on the basis of repetition. The analytical mind, on the other hand, resides in the cortical regions of the brain, the neocortical areas that are "higher" and phylogenetically quite new. It evolved much later than the habit system; it is only operative in higher mammals and some really clever birds, like parrots, and it can do all manner of clever things.

- The habit system operates on the basis of instinct and repetitive experience. The analytical mind operates on the basis of learning and theory. One's habit system might kill out of fear or self-defense. One's analytical mind could kill on the basis of a theoretical disagreement.

- One's habit system prefers to do things in the same old way. The mnemonic system prefers to tinker with things, and not just for the hell of it. It *believes* it can make things better. Sometimes it can.

- The habit system remains intact in the face of cortical diseases like Alzheimer's. Thus, patients with Alzheimer's disease retain their learned skills and are capable of driving a car, much to the dismay of their family. Alzheimer's patients don't lose their ability to drive a car or to play a musical instrument until the disease is well advanced. Their habit system—knowing *how*—remains intact long after their mnemonic system—knowing *what*—is long gone. In contrast, patients with diseases of the basal ganglia like Parkinson's disease lose their ability to perform overlearned activities even while their memory and judgment remains intact.

Although these two systems, the habit system and the mnemonic system, can be differentiated quite neatly, they are not entirely separate. They work closely together—or at least they do in a healthy mind. The mnemonic system evolved out of the habit system, and it relies upon it to get stuff done. I shall explain how they work together with this pithy vignette about two sisters who are taking a road trip. We shall make this personal: you and your sister are taking a road trip.

A trip to Potomac, Maryland

You and your sister are off to visit your cousin Leo who lives in Potomac, Maryland. You've never been to Potomac, Maryland, but you've been to DC, right next door, lots of times. So you set your Nav system to Leo's address and, as is her wont because she is a bit fussy, your sister codes the destination into her iPhone. Then you both forget all about the directions because you know perfectly well how to get to Washington, and you cheerfully drive four hours on one Interstate and then another, chatting all the way, listening to music, eating almonds and dried apples, even brushing your hair. Then you get to the River Road exit on the Capital Beltway. You get off and head west.

At this point, you go from habit mode into mnemonic mode. You've never been on the River Road before and, as in most of the Washington suburbs, there is a lot of traffic. You're going to have to make a right turn somewhere and then some more turns to get to Leo's house. Your sister is listening to her iPhone and you are keeping an eye on the Nav system. Of course, the directions never quite match, but that's another story. Your sister turns off the radio but you hardly notice.

When you finally get to Leo's house, he is in the front yard, waiting for you. He asks you, "How was the trip?" It was an effortless trip, wasn't it, aside from the few harsh words you had with your sister over the directions. The reason it was such a leisurely trip was: you only had to think about it after you got to River Road. The first part of the trip was, well, automatic. You didn't have to think about your foot on the accelerator or your hands on the wheel, you didn't have to think about depressing the clutch pedal every time you changed gears, you didn't even have to think about how to get to Washington. It was all habit. On the other hand, everything that happened on the River Road was considered behavior, consuming vast amounts of cortical metabolism, and leaving you with precious little patience for your sister when she told you to turn right on Hall Road and your Nav system said wait until you get to Highway 189. The trip to Washington was your habit system and the drive along the River Road occupied your mnemonic system. The whole trip represented an easy alternation between two mental systems that know how to work together. Your sister, though, is a pain in the neck sometimes.

This is the way the mind works, and people, too. We rely on fast operators for most of the things we do. Interspersed among those fast operations, a little bit of the mnemonic system intrudes, but only when it has to.

* * *

One's brain is said to consume 25 percent of one's blood supply and 33 percent of metabolism, but it doesn't *mean* to be an energy hog. Efficiency is a constant concern. When it can't do efficiently what it ordinarily does do efficiently, it lets one know by generating unpleasant feelings of fatigue, irritability or anxiety. Such events probably reflect persistent disequilibria in one's oscillating neural assemblies, or something like that.

At a party, we automatically gravitate to people with whom we have shared interests. Think of how enervating it would be to address considered attention to every guest at a party. Social intercourse is leavened by things that we do automatically. By the same token, if your car exuded ugly grinding noises and a foul smell of burning clutch all the way to Potomac, Maryland, you'd hardly have the mental energy to brush your hair or eat kale chips. Your mind would be consumed with concern over the stupid car, and when your sister said "I told you we should have taken my car," you might have said something regrettable. We rely on our machines to operate efficiently, just as they rely on us to press the right buttons and always to depress the clutch pedal when we change gears. In such wise, we rely on the smooth, integrated operation of our mnemonic and habit systems.

So, poor Konrad, sensitive soul as he was, was in the habit of going to Vienna one way and driving home by another route. It was the way he did it every time. But then he decided to inflict his mnemonic system on what his habit system had been doing perfectly well all along. So what happened? He had an anxiety attack. For no good reason, he had decided to interfere with a perfectly comfortable routine and one that even makes sense to a fussy man; he can keep up with what's going on in *two* parts of Vienna and its suburbs. His habit system was quite happy getting to Vienna and back in its own particular way, leaving his cogitations free to wander, as was his wont, on the curious habits of gallinaceous birds. Then, for no good reason, his cogitation decided to take over the whole shebang. It made him feel anxious. What did he expect?

The two mental systems are like a husband and wife whose life has settled into a comfortable routine. They get along perfectly well until one of them tries to do something different. "Tonight, darling, we're having tofu and steamed vegetables instead of meat loaf," or,

"Tonight, sweetheart, let me have the handcuffs." Such deviations from routine often lead to friction and are not recommended.

Habits of an OC

It's natural to think that our OC friends have an overactive habit system. There is a theory to that effect. It is based on the observation that repetitive behaviors are generated from motor patterns in the habit system of the basal ganglia (BG). They must be subcortical in origin, because they arise spontaneously in patients who have lost cortical function (the demented, stroke patients, and patients with brain injuries), and because they are so frequent in patients with cortical hypoplasia (people with an intellectual disability) or cortical immaturity (infants and young children) and in lower animals (e.g., rats) who don't have much of a cerebral cortex at all. Children are very prone to tics, repetitive motor or phonic behaviors, the same kind of tics that occur in Tourette's syndrome. Abnormal, compulsive movements as well as obsessions are typical symptoms of BG pathology. The idea is that OC arises when the BG are not under control by inhibitory projections from the frontal cortex. OCD, therefore, is a "disturbance of the BG" (Kandel, Schwartz, and Jessell, 2000).

That is a theory, all right, but it is a bit off. OC individuals are not creatures of habit. What really happens in the brains of people with OCD is quite different, but it is similar to the trick Konrad Lorenz tried to pull off. In OCD patients, activities that are appropriately dealt with by the habit system are driven by an intrusive analytical mind. OC people use slow operators to do what fast operators can do better. This accounts for a notorious problem that OC people have—**obsessive slowness**. Every single step of an action sequence has to be evaluated, appraised, considered and checked. It is a very expensive way to do things, using a system that burns a lot of fuel to do a task that can be done more efficiently by a less complex, less cumbersome mental system. When the brain burns too much mental energy, it gets tired; a tired brain, like a tired child, gets cranky and irritable. That is why OC patients are often given to emotional outbursts of one sort or another. They are prone to anxiety, depression and angry explosions. Poor things, their brains get tired.

* * *

Neuroscientists have shown that this is exactly what happens in OCD. Behavioral operations that justly belong to the fast operators of the habit system are slowed down by the intrusive activity of the mnemonic system. One can look at PET scans of OCD patients during a simple procedural learning task—that is, learning how to do something new. When most people learn how to do something, they activate their basal ganglia. They let their habit system learn the new procedure. When OCD patients try to learn a procedure, they activate areas of the neocortex instead. They keep the procedure in their analytical system, rather than putting it in a system where it can operate automatically and without effortful awareness. Thus, in OC patients, cortical intrusions contaminate the execution of automatic behaviors. Their central executive continually interferes with the efficient activity of the habit system (Rauch *et al.*, 1997).

When one brain system tries to do what another does better, it's like grinding the clutch. Friction occurs, the gears get hot, and the foul smell of burning rubber pervades the inside of one's head. In some individuals, such events are experienced as anxiety; in others as irritability or anger.

A controlling man is not controlling because he is struggling to control his inner anxiety. Rather, he is someone who is trying to keep all of the operations of his day-to-day life actively engaged in his controlling analytical mind. Because it is very hard to do that, he feels cranky and irritable. It's simply exhausting when all of the simple transactions that comprise a relationship and that are better left in the realm of the routine are subjected to critical analysis. For example: some nights A loads the dishwasher, some nights B loads the dishwasher. Everyone, as you've noticed, loads dishwashers in a different way. But B gets anxious when A loads the dishwasher, *because she doesn't load it in an optimal way.* Another example: A turns the lights on, B turns them off. If B were just a fussy man, he would just turn off the light, as long as there weren't someone reading directly beneath, and go about his business. Since B is a controlling, compulsive man, however, he also gets angry at A for leaving the lights on.

It's not easy to live with a person who subjects all of life's routine, day-to-day activities to critical analysis and then gets mad about it. But take a moment to think about it from his point of view. How hard his brain has to work all the time! How exhausting it must be to keep up with all the things that other people do wrong. It's such an effort; he gets cross. What he really needs is a little lie-down. One of the most controlling men I have ever known used to come into my office at regular intervals, sit in the most comfortable chair, sigh and say, "I'm tired. I'm so tired. I'm so tired of having to take care of all this s—."

Lessons from the basal ganglia

The dwelling-place of our habit system is in the basal ganglia. "Ganglia" are plural; the singular is "ganglion." They—that is, the BG—are composed of several nuclei, including the corpus striatum (the caudate nucleus and the putamen), the globus pallidus and several others. For a long time, neurology assumed that the BG were only responsible for movement control. That is because the prototypical diseases of the BG are movement disorders.

We know the basal ganglia are important because we know what happens when they don't act right. We will take a careful look at that tangled nest of subcortical nuclei when they get sick. We shall also look at what they do when they're particularly influential, in the lives of children who haven't yet endured puberty.

* * *

Two diseases disturb the BG: **Parkinson's disease** (PD), the shaking palsy, and **Huntington's disease** (HD), Woody Guthrie's disease. They are polar opposites, contraries one to the other, although as they progress the outcome is the same: severe motor impairment, dementia and death.[2] PD is a hypokinetic disorder (motor activity is reduced, except for tremor) and HD is a hyperkinetic movement disorder (it causes excessive and abnormal movements).

Parkinson's disease is caused by degeneration of neurons in the basal ganglia. It was the first brain disorder to be related to a specific neurotransmitter, **dopamine**. About 80 percent of the dopamine in brain is found in the BG, and in the 1960s Parkinsonian patients were discovered to be deficient in BG dopamine. Soon afterwards, L-DOPA, a drug that mimics the effects of dopamine, was used to good effect in patients with PD. The event was captured by Oliver Sacks in his memoir, *Awakenings*. In 1966, Sacks was consulting at a chronic-care facility in the Bronx, where there were survivors of the *encephalitis lethargica* epidemic of the 1920s. Encephalitis lethargica, or Von Economo's encephalitis, was a viral illness that attacked the brain and led, years later, to Parkinsonism. My Uncle Delmore had that disease, although he never made it into the book.

My uncle's case involved his prefrontal cortex, but Sacks' patients had damaged the basal ganglia. They were unable to move on their own for years. You may know what happened after they were treated with L-DOPA, from the movie, if not the book. If you don't, I don't want to spoil it.

In contrast to Parkinson's disease, Huntington's is a disorder of dopamine excess, and the abnormal movements of HD patients can be alleviated by drugs that block dopamine, like Haldol®. The abnormal movements of an HD patient are chorea (dancelike, broken movements, from Terpsichore, the Muse of dance), athetosis (slow, writhing movements) and ballismus (throwing movements, as in ballistic missile).

The basal ganglia are, in fact, occupied with the control of

---

2   Dementia is inevitable in HD, and is common but not inevitable in PD.

movement, but they have many other functions as well. They are the repository of overlearned behavioral programs, instincts and "species-specific behaviors." They are also involved in cognition, emotion and perception; thus, patients with either Parkinson's or Huntington's disease commonly have unusual thoughts and behaviors, including obsessions and compulsions. Dementia occurs during the late stages of both diseases, but early on subtle cognitive deficits can be detected. Mood symptoms and behavioral disinhibition also occur early in both diseases. The cognitive deficits occur in attention, memory, executive function and processing speed; mood problems include apathy, depression, anxiety, irritability and hypochondriasis. It is remarkable that, although the motor symptoms are so different and the chemical changes are polar opposites, the cognitive, mood and behavioral symptoms of both conditions are similar.

Parkinson's disease is the equivalent of a chronic overdose of Haldol®, and Huntington's disease can be compared to a chronic overdose of amphetamine; consistent with that chemical profile, one is hypokinetic and the other hyperkinetic. One would expect the cognitive, emotional and behavioral symptoms to be quite different. The PD patient should be withdrawn and apathetic and the HD patient manic and disinhibited. That is often the case. Disinhibition is a cardinal symptom of early HD; the first signs of Woody Guthrie's disease were the salacious letters he sent to an old girlfriend. He and his old girlfriend were married at the time, but to other people.

It doesn't always happen that way. Both PD and HD patients can be impulsive and disinhibited. Impulse control problems affect up to one in seven people with Parkinson's disease and are sometimes worsened by the dopaminergic drugs that are used to treat them. They are called **impulsive-compulsive behaviors** and include pathological gambling, compulsive shopping, hypersexuality, binge eating, hoarding, kleptomania, impulsive smoking, compulsive medication use and "punding" and "hobbyism," which are well worth looking up. Men suffer more frequently from pathologic gambling and compulsive sexual behavior, while women tend toward compulsive buying and binge eating (Evans *et al.*, 2014).

Here we confront the first of many paradoxes associated with the basal ganglia: something that is both A and not-A. In this instance, both the conditions and their outcomes are polar opposites. A is impulsive behavior that we associate with people who are *wide-open*; not-A is compulsive behavior, typical of people who are *wound up tight*. Such paradoxes arise more and more frequently as one observes the human condition. One might have hoped that brain science could resolve things like this for once and all, but as it happens we have no more than hypotheses.

The basal ganglia are composed of several nuclei. They are different in structure, but tightly interconnected, and they are connected as well to the entire neocortex and to many other parts of brain. Within the various nuclei, there are different kinds of neurons, with connections that are direct and indirect: this has the consequence that a nervous signal arriving there might be enhanced or inhibited. Think of it as forks in the road. A signal may take the fork that leads to enhancement or the one that leads to inhibition, the direct or the indirect way. It is possible that dopamine plays a role in balancing the flow of traffic, and prevents either too much enhancement, which might lead to abnormal, hyperkinetic movements and impulsive, disinhibited behavior, or too much inhibition, which would result in a paucity of movements, apathy and depression. It's also possible that some individuals always take the wrong fork. Some may be prone to amplification, leading to repetitive behaviors, or diminution of the signal, making them a bit inert. Theories have been built around the tendency of some people to be augmenters and others to be reducers. We don't need a theory to know that.

7

Fussy Men and Women

They say that OC is the tyranny of the analytical mind. An intrusive neocortex, however, is not the only brain part that contributes to OC. In this chapter we shall meet another. It's the cingulum, an inborn error detector. It's something we all need, some of us more than others.

The cingulum is a rather large expanse of cortical tissue that surrounds the corpus callosum. The corpus callosum is the huge fiber bundle that connects the right and left hemispheres, so we only have one of it, but we have two cingula, one on each side. Some of us might do better with only one, perhaps, because in patients with OCD the cingulum is positively robust, if not muscle-bound. A hyperactive cingulum is the brain basis for this OC trait: the perennial feeling that *Something is wrong here*. The cingulum occupies a central location on the inside, lower part of the frontal and temporal lobes, wrapping around the corpus callosum like a belt; hence the name. It is well positioned to monitor things that are going on, and to look for mistakes.

What emerges on one's behavioral surface by virtue of an aggressive cingulum is variable. It may make one go back and do another count, or check the stove one more time, or wait until Act V to dispatch the King of Denmark. The heat generated by hyperactive cingula may be manifest as anxiety or rage. Or, it may just be a small, still voice that makes one fussy.

* * *

Fussy is the dark side of conscientious. Fussy men and women are meddlesome and irritating, nagging old crones, unquiet, dithering, exercised over trifles. Well, you know how I feel about trifles and I don't even have to Sherlock you again. Besides, I think that fussy men and women have got a bum rap. They may be worry-warts but most are kind and generous, understanding and tolerant. In that respect they differ from controlling men who are also meddlesome and irritating but also selfish, sour, self-absorbed and, well, controlling. One shouldn't confuse the two, although controlling women may be hard to detect. Controlling men are usually angry, which makes them easy to identify, but controlling women usually get their way.

Fussy men and women are not controlling. They have OC traits but they use them for the benefit of mankind, or, at least, on behalf of people in their immediate vicinity. Their hyperactive error detector has taught them how to do things right. You may think they are fussing but they just want to share the knowledge with you. When two fussy people get together, they have the most interesting conversations about things you probably think are inane. Poor you.

The fussy man may be a bit compulsive about it, but he is useful to have around. He is well-organized and he likes things to be orderly. He always knows where you can find the needle-nosed pliers or the duct tape or the cumin seeds. When any of those useful items aren't where they're supposed to be, he sighs, resigned to the imperfections of the world but not angry about it. Besides, it gives him something to do. He runs off to the hardware store (knowing full well that the needle-nosed pliers are irretrievably lost) and buys *two* pairs, one of which he will place in its usual, correct place. The other he will put in a special, secret place that only he knows, anticipating that the first pair will be irretrievably lost before very long. Of course, his clever albeit scattered wife will have discovered that secret place before long; and if there are children around, they know all of his secret hiding places even when he's forgotten where they are or what's in them. Another trip to the hardware store, then, and as he goes he reflects that life is like a river, an endless flow of little chores to be done and problems to be solved; imperfect people who get trapped in the eddies and snags and have to be nudged gently into the softly flowing stream. It is a cheerful reflection. He isn't Sisyphus, pushing the rock up the hill only to watch it crashing back down. He isn't really a perfectionist either, because he accepts that life is imperfect—even *he* loses the wretched needle-nosed pliers sometimes. To the fussy man, doing things right is a blessing, an act of accord with the harmony of the universe.

There are probably more fussy women than men, probably because most women know how to do things right and they are generous in sharing the knowledge with their less-than-fussy husbands. Also because the traits of kindness and generosity tend to concentrate in females of most species.[1] Have you ever wondered why your mother never complained when she had to pick up after you or your father, and when she did, it was in a gentle, good-humored way? Well, I hope your mother was like that, because fussy women make very good mothers. Fussy men make good Dads, too.

Fussy people usually have a few OC traits, but they are harmless ones, like checking the doors at night or keeping the items in their drawers neat and tidy. Mostly, they are *conscientious*, which is a thoroughly *good trait*. Fussiness is a good illustration of how personality traits work. In case you haven't noticed, there are dimensions to everyone's personality. For example, the OC dimension:

NOT OC AT ALL ⟷ VERY OC

Fussy men and women are towards the right, right? Now, some other dimensions:

KIND AND GENEROUS ⟷ SELFISH, SELF-CENTERED

SWEET ⟷ SOUR

---

1   Hyenas are the exception that proves the rule.

FM&W are on the left side of those two. What about this one?

TOLERANT ⟷ CONTROLLING

Right again, on the left side of the spectrum. Fussy people try to help you to do things right. They seldom force the issue. They know this:

CAREFULNESS IS LOVE

LOVE IS CAREFULNESS

And also this:

FUSSINESS IS ITS OWN REWARD[2]

People who are more towards the selfish, self-absorbed, sour and controlling side may be OC to the same degree as the average fussy man or woman, but you shouldn't call them fussy. They are selfish, self-absorbed, sour and controlling.

Fussy men and women have a hyperactive error detector, but it is fueled by a sensitive perceptual apparatus. They are towards the *right* side of this dimension:

CLUELESS ⟷ PERCEPTIVE

* * *

The Great Detectives are known for exquisite attention to details that bumbling policemen always miss. "It has long been an axiom of mine that the little things are infinitely the most important."[3] They have a keen perceptual apparatus, presumably because they have another hypertrophied brain part, intimately connected to the cingulum, that processes sensory information. That is the **insula**, which we shall meet soon enough. The combination of an unusually

---

2   L. Rust Hills (1993) *How To Do Things Right*. Boston: Godine. If you want to know how to be a properly fussy man, this is essential reading.

3   Arthur Conan Doyle, "A Case of Identity" (*The Adventures of Sherlock Holmes*).

perceptive insula and a hyperactive cingulum is characteristic of patients with OCD, and, so we assume, of the OCs as well, and the Great Detectives too. It serves the latter well, of course, even if they only exist in fiction. Among the OCs it may cause only vexation, as one notices things, flecks and motes, that are better left unnoticed. This may be distracting, or it may cause dismay or anxiety. The accumulation of errors detected, faults unmasked and dangers anticipated can clog one's brain and cause foul internal backwashes.

Even Sherlock knew that. "It is of the highest importance in the art of detection to be able to recognize, out of a number of facts, which are incidental and which vital. Otherwise, your energy and attention must be dissipated instead of being concentrated."[4]

The cingulum

The hominid brain hasn't had a lot of time to integrate the behavior of its subcortical structures with the vast expanse of neocortex. It has to integrate slow processors in the analytical mind with fast processors in the habit system, as well as other inputs from the social/emotional brain, the somatic brain and other sources. In the case of an individual trying to execute a motivated behavior—that is, when we try to do something—each of those parallel processors presents a different perspective on what is proposed. In order for behavior to emerge smoothly from this tangle, all of these competing viewpoints have to be resolved. Inevitably, when different points of view come together, there is "conflict," as the brain scientists like to say, although I prefer "disagreement." F and I, for example, rarely experience conflict, at least with each other. When we do happen to disagree, it is usually because one of us (F, more often) is operating on the basis of erroneous data. She often tells me how grateful she is to have married her own in-house error detector.

It is interesting that brain evolution reflects the events that

---

4   Arthur Conan Doyle, "The Reigate Puzzle" [or "The Reigate Squire"] (*The Memoirs of Sherlock Holmes*).

typify the normal, happy family. In order to rectify errors and reconcile different perspectives, the brain has evolved a cingulum. The **cingulum** resides at the intersection of our multiple minds. It is an inborn error detector. Its function is to identify "conflicts" that arise among competing processors—*Something is wrong here.*

It's not entirely clear how the cingulum manages to do that, but it processes the most basic mental events, like movement control, reward and pain. Take the first, motor control. The movement is raising one's hands and twiddling one's fingers in greeting to a good friend. The motor sequence is generated in the motor cortex, which generates an **efferent signal**. The signal is modified appropriately in the basal ganglia and cerebellum and then executed by the spinal nerves that innervate the muscles of one's arm and hand. But how does one know that one is doing it right? The cortex knows, because it also generates an **efference copy** of finger-twiddling. An efference copy is a mental representation of the movement that is maintained for a few moments in the premotor cortex. The cingulum can compare it to what is actually happening in one's fingers; *the actual movement is compared to the desired movement.* Thus, one knows one is doing it right.

Doing it right or wrong are necessarily associated with two other mental processes, the systems that govern reward and punishment and those that mediate pain and avoidance. The cingulum participates in both systems, in its midsection, a region that is stimulated by the neurotransmitter, dopamine. It is connected to the thalamus and the insula, naturally, because that's where sensations are processed, and also to the amygdala, which conveys intensity to one's emotional response to what is going on. The complexity of this arrangement, the different kinds of neurons involved and the different neurotransmitters that may exist in quantity, or not, is probably what accounts for the responses one makes when an error is perceived. The fussy man or woman finds it rewarding; it is one more opportunity to neaten up. The controlling man, however, likely finds it painful, because he typically reacts with fear and anger (Modirrousta and Fellows, 2008; Vogt, 2016).

* * *

OCs, like all the rest of us, have cingula that are wired in their own particular ways. It's all part of life's rich pageant, I suppose, and it gives natural selection something to work with. Patients with OCD have cingula that are not only robust but also hyperactive. That means they spend more time and energy reconciling internal conflicts; the heat thus generated is not good for them. One source of potential conflict arises between the slow operations of the analytical mind and the fast operations of the habit system. Brain scans have indicated that OCD patients have cingula that have more gray and white matter than most of us have in ours, even those of us who are fussy. PET scans have shown high levels of metabolic activity in the cingula, as if they were always working overtime, which they are. In patients with OCD, the error detector has a very low threshold. It is an essential part of their psychology; they have a very low threshold for generating an error message. It may be that the OC is born with a hyperactive error detector, or perhaps his error detector has been so exercised by dealing with inappropriate inputs that it got bigger to meet the challenge. Whatever the explanation, the cingulum represents an additional bottleneck in the execution of effective action. A hyperactive cingulum can generate exaggerated or false error signals. It triggers the feeling that things are "not just right" even when no actual error exists (Maltby *et al.*, 2005). Not only is the cingulum of OCD patients robust and hyperactive, but its microstructure is all awry and it likely connects to parts of the brain that it shouldn't. It's not only a bottleneck, it can create a world-class traffic jam that will tie you up and then lead you away from the Holland tunnel and back onto the Pulaski skyway.

* * *

Endowed with such important roles and typified by extraordinary diversity, the cingulum seems to have a mind of his own. Think of him as a *homunculus* (a little man), a word biologists use to describe the ghost in the machine. He is an inborn error detector, a region of brain that can appraise the synchrony of oscillating signals and send them back into the loop until they are properly synchronized.

He is active in the proper integration of signals from different sources and monitors the activity of the various loops that connect the cortex with the subcortex. One of his jobs is to make all the inputs into the loops work smoothly together.

The cingulum integrates information from the various sources that comprise critical judgment—the nature of an event, its emotional and motivational importance and how it relates to one's prior experiences, the likely responses that one may make, the anticipated outcome of that response and whether it will hurt. Those psychological elements are carried by neural assemblies oscillating at different frequencies. Ultimately, they find themselves in a loop that reconciles inputs from the higher and lower parts of brain (see Chapter 16 for more about the OC loop). In that loop, they gradually become synchronized. When they are, a coherent signal is generated and a behavioral output is emitted. If not, back they go into the loop and make it work that much harder.

As this is going on, one's cingulum is operating as a constraint, an *error detector*. It evaluates the nature of an event (your boss says he has to leave early and would you mind dropping the report at his apartment after work?), its emotional and motivational importance (*This is weird*), how it relates to one's prior experiences (*The last time something like this happened I was filled with remorse*), and the appropriate action step ([a] *Oh, what the hell* or [b] *I'll ask Doreen to come with me*). The cingulum is one of those slow operators, so all this cogitation takes a while—say, a second or two, which is a long time for neural tissue. Then it (your cingulum) will either give the all-clear signal (*OK, boss*) or an error message (*Me and Doreen will bring it by*). All the rest, as you know, is fairly automatic, though not necessarily unconscious.

It is a useful little fellow to have around, an inborn error detector that can access data from a number of little computers in one's frontal and temporal lobes, evaluate it critically and generate a message, *Something is wrong here.* We all have a pair of these cingula, and most of us give them both a good workout. Most of us have cingula that are tolerant of a degree of uncertainty, that know what it means to give a prospective action the benefit of the doubt. One wouldn't like to have a built-in error detector that was so intrusive that it went off at the slightest provocation, like a smoke detector that went off when you blew out candles on a birthday cake. No, one wouldn't, but some people do, and you can guess who they are.

8

Dirt Is Good for You

The **insula** is the oldest part of the cerebral cortex and the first to form during embryonic life. It is a receptive organ, the only place in brain where nervous signals from all five senses converge, along with signals from all the nerves within the body. In OCD and related conditions, the insula is also hypertrophied and excessively active. This accounts for another variant of the OC disposition: OCs with a keen and sensitive perceptual apparatus. It serves them well in certain circumstances but it's usually just a pain. Fussy men and women notice things that ordinary people don't. The insula informs the cingulum, which is quick to decide that something is wrong.

What are the consequences of a hypersensitive sensory apparatus? They may be clinical symptoms—for example, **cacosmia**. The patient perceives a fetid stink where none exists. **Hyperacusia** and **phonophobia** are pathological sensitivities to sounds, and **misophonia** occurs when specific sounds generate feelings of anger, hatred or disgust. There is a symptom, **macropsia**, where what one sees seems much larger than it really is. Lemuel Gulliver described what it feels like when he visited Brobdingnag:

> That which gave me most uneasiness among these maids of honour (when my nurse carried me to visit them) was, to see them use me without any manner of ceremony, like a creature who had no sort of consequence: for they would strip themselves

to the skin, and put on their smocks in my presence, while I was placed on their toilet, directly before their naked bodies, which I am sure to me was very far from being a tempting sight, or from giving me any other emotions than those of horror and disgust: their skins appeared so coarse and uneven, so variously coloured, when I saw them near, with a mole here and there as broad as a trencher, and hairs hanging from it thicker than packthreads, to say nothing farther concerning the rest of their persons. Neither did they at all scruple, while I was by, to discharge what they had drank, to the quantity of at least two hogsheads, in a vessel that held above three tuns. The handsomest among these maids of honour, a pleasant, frolicsome girl of sixteen, would sometimes set me astride upon one of her nipples, with many other tricks, wherein the reader will excuse me for not being over particular. But I was so much displeased, that I entreated Glumdalclitch to contrive some excuse for not seeing that young lady any more.[1]

To most of us, the neurobehavioral syndromes are as remote and fantastical as Brobdingnag. If our senses are keen, we may just feel dirty.

One of the questions I ask a patient is whether he or she flushes a public toilet with his or her foot. A related question is whether he or she opens the rest-room door with his or her elbow. Such behavior used to be deemed an OC trait, but apparently no longer. Yesterday, in fact, when I posed the question to a patient, she, her mother and the student who was with us looked at me as if I were an atavistic throwback. They all remarked to this effect: "Aren't you supposed to? Doesn't everybody? Don't you?"

"What's so bad about OC?" you say. Do I really have to tell you?

OC may be only a small island in the ocean of madness but, some days, it looks like a continent. You can challenge me on that. You say, "Cleanliness is next to godliness." Within limits, I say.

---

1 Jonathan Swift, "A Voyage to Brobdingnag," *Gulliver's Travels*, 1726.

Cleanliness is next to godliness

The action of oxytocin upon the brain in the large doses expressed during pregnancy is associated with the cultivation of pro-social and altruistic behavior. Less well known is that it also leads to reorganization of the language centers of the left hemisphere. Certain stereotyped messages are cultivated that a maternal conspecific can utter not only with authority but with circadian regularity. The neuro-psycho-linguists refer to these as "motherisms,"[2] but I think they are the endearing qualities of a fussy Mom. They are usually conveyed in the common tongue, but among some tribes the emitting organism may employ her language of origin, most commonly Yiddish or Italian, but seldom Oxbridge English or Esperanto. Examples are:

> "Don't scratch like that."
> "Don't chew with your mouth open."
> "You're not wearing that to _____ [school, Temple, Grandpa's wake, etc.]."
> "I'm not angry, child, I'm disappointed, that's all."
> "Your Aunt [aunt's name] will take good care of you when your father and I are away."
> "Here. Let *me* do that."
> "Did you wash your hands?"

The last one appears to have had an enduring effect on the psychology of many youngsters, not to mention the public-health authorities, the restaurant industry and most OCs. Nothing, to them, feels quite so good as a nice, clean pair of hands. If a sink isn't readily available, for example, after one has pressed the button on an elevator, one can buy a small bottle of hand-sanitizer with a plastic hook to hold it on one's belt, bra strap or whatever. "What's wrong with cleanliness?" you ask.

---

2   In fact, Jean Shepherd did.

Only this: it exposes one to the risk of chronic disease.

The epidemic of cleanliness that has swept the land has only recently been evaluated in terms of its ecological impact on what is called the "biome," the universe of all living things, including germs. The latter may be low on the food chain but they possess more biodiversity and more genes than all the other organisms put together. If they are there, there must be a reason, and excluding them from one's life may not be a good idea.

The dubious reader is referred to the **hygiene hypothesis**, an idea that originated with an English epidemiologist, David Strachan, who reminded readers that hay fever was a "post-industrial revolution epidemic," its prevalence increasing with every passing decade in modern societies. He based his theory on data from more than 17,000 British children born in 1958; he discovered an inverse correlation between hay fever and the number of older siblings they grew up with. Strachan suggested that allergic diseases were prevented if a child had frequent infections, which were likely to be transmitted by unhygienic contact with older siblings or acquired prenatally by a mother infected by contact with her children (Strachan, 1989).

In 1998, about one in five children in industrialized countries suffered from allergic diseases such as asthma, allergic rhinitis or atopic dermatitis. This proportion has increased over the last 10 years.

The prevalence of atopic dermatitis has doubled or tripled in industrialized countries during the past three decades, affecting 15–30% of children and 2–10% of adults. In parallel, there is also an increase in the prevalence of autoimmune diseases such as type one diabetes, which now occurs earlier in life than in the past, becoming a serious public health problem in some European countries. The incidence of inflammatory bowel diseases such as Crohn's disease or ulcerative colitis and primary biliary cirrhosis is also rising.

Public health measures were taken after the industrial

revolution by western countries to limit the spread of infections…
Interestingly, several countries that have eradicated common
infections have seen the emergence of allergic and autoimmune
diseases… (Okada, Kuhn, Feillet, and Bach, 2010)

Early childhood exposure to dirt in general and to germs in
particular exercises one's immune system, just as early exposure
to speech exercises one's brain. Germs, therefore, are good for
you—within reason, of course. As we have learned from recent,
deadly epidemics, it's not a good idea to eat bats or to have sex with
monkeys, and one anticipates that before very long such wholesome
advice will join the lexicon of motherisms.

"Who ate the bat?"
"I never want to see you having sex with that monkey again!"

Eating can be dangerous

Is it possible that unexplained somatic syndromes like chronic
fatigue and fibromyalgia are the results of Modern Society and its
War Against Germs? ("Aren't you glad you use Dial? Don't you wish
everybody did?") For example, the *Daily Mail* reported the story
of Samantha Brown, a 27-year-old English artist, who suffered
from fibromyalgia. Her condition, apparently, made her unduly
concerned about the food she ate. Her weight fell to 77 pounds
because she thought food was going to poison her. (Samantha was
5' 8" tall.)

I began dictating to myself what I could and couldn't eat. As
my behaviour developed, it became an OCD, where I thought
practically everything was poison. It was all rooted in my desire
for control. I didn't want to be thin. I wasn't avoiding eating to
stay skinny. Instead, I was convinced that unless I restricted
myself to the foods I had decided were OK, I would poison

myself. I drew up an "allowed" list and a "forbidden" list. Before long, the "allowed" list had just three things—Coco Pops, salt and vinegar crisps, and thin-crust pizza. Eventually, all I could manage was Coco Pops. My mum became really concerned. She would try to tempt me with new foods like macaroni cheese [sic], but all I could do was sob into the plate, pleading with her and warning her that it would kill me.[3]

The article informs readers that Ms. Brown was "eventually diagnosed with an unusual form of obsessive compulsive disorder." However, there is reason to believe that conditions like fibromyalgia and chronic fatigue are related to an imbalance in one's intestinal flora. *What's so bad about OC?* If Ms. Brown had been less cautious about what she took in, she mightn't have had fibromyalgia and chronic fatigue to begin with.

* * *

The fear of contamination is frequently concerned with germs as if they were some kind of poison, instead of our little animalcular friends. The OCs have known that for a long time, or at least some of them have. The OC stereotype is that Neutrogena soap thing, but it only shows the peril of trying to fit people into categories. There are OCs who answer to the opposite persuasion. "Did you wash your hands?" Mother asks. "Good. Tonight for dinner we are having a nice bit of dirt."

Mother is not likely to say any such thing, because geophagists—dirt eaters—tend to do so in secret, abashed by the sanitary engineers who equate dirt with germs or, worse, poison. Soil contaminated with human waste can be the source of parasitic infestation; nevertheless, in undeveloped societies people routinely eat dirt, especially clay, for its medicinal qualities.

---

3   Anna Hodgekiss, "Woman's weight plunged to just 5st 7lb after rare form of OCD made her believe everything she sate was POISON (apart from Coco Pops, crisps and pizza)," *The Daily Mail*, November 12, 2013.

Geophagy is common among the animals. Bats visit "mineral licks"—mud, that is—to supplement their diets with calcium and to protect themselves from fruit toxins. Parrots do, too, and tapirs. Chimpanzees are said to eat dirt to protect against malaria (Voigt *et al.*, 2008). Among humans, dirt-eating occurs in children and pregnant women; especially kaolinite clay, which subdues nausea and decreases hunger without fear of morning sickness. Kaolin used to be an ingredient in Kaopectate, an anti-diarrheal. Mahatma Gandhi believed that eating clay could detoxify the body and assist in avoiding constipation. In Haiti, people eat *bon bon des terres* made from water, salt, sugar, vegetable oil and clay-based mud, consumed to fill empty stomachs although it has little nutritional value. A report I discovered somewhere—there was no reference attached—asserted that people worldwide eat up to 50 grams of dirt every day. One of those *Speak for yourself, Jack* factoids, I think.

Nevertheless, there is a chef in Tokyo (where else?) who serves dirt in his Tokyo restaurant; a six-course meal that includes dirt soup, dirt risotto, dirt mint tea, dirt sorbet, and a dirt-covered potato ball with a truffle center that he calls "dirt surprise."

The psychiatrists have a name for such behavior. They call it **pica**, after the Latin word for *magpie*, birds that are supposed to eat anything, though what they really do is carry stuff away to their nests. Magpies are hoarders, not geophagists. Nevertheless, according to the DSM, individuals with pica consume an eclectic variety of substances, including mud, pottery and clay; and laundry starch, paper, tissues, wood, plastic straws, soap, cloth, carpet, hair, string, wool, paint, gum, metal, pebbles, chalk, charcoal, coal, cigarette butts and ash. Persistent consumption of ice does not satisfy pica criteria, "since ice is a food," but consuming freezer frost, "if not regarded as food within local norms," meets the criteria for pica (Hartmann, Becker, Hampton, and Bryant-Waugh, 2012). Thank God for the DSM.

Pica is an ugly habit, a condition ordinarily met with in patients with chronic mental illness or intellectual disability, but mild forms are really quite common, like swallowing pieces of skin or nail that one bites off while grooming. Chewing things like pencils or small pieces of plastic is also common. The appropriate observation is that *People will eat things they would never serve their guests.*

The converse is also true: *What you serve your guests might be poisonous.*

> I've suffered from harm obsessions for as long as I can remember. For a long time it was fear of choking someone, but after getting married it morphed into a fear of poisoning someone. I stopped cooking and baking and avoided the kitchen and touching food as much as possible. I've gotten a little better with that now, but it's still not easy. I started going to therapy last October and it was traditional talk therapy, which helped me very little. Now I'm doing Exposure and Response Therapy with a new therapist.
>
> With my other therapist who I was doing the talk therapy with, she just exacerbated my anxiety. She mentioned "short of putting rat poison in someone's food you wouldn't go to jail"… and that's when my obsession with insecticides and rat poison began. I was so upset with her for mentioning it. Now I'm so afraid of finding particles of it loose on the ground or on a shelf and putting it in my pocket and bringing it home and sprinkling it on food. Then having to go to jail for hurting someone. I'm constantly seeking reassurance from my dad. Asking if I'd go to jail for specific scenarios I create in my mind…for example, "would I go to jail if I found some loose pieces of rat poison on the ground and were to sprinkle on someone's food and they got hurt?"…and it just goes on and on. My brain gets into an endless loop.[4]

Thank Heaven that "talk therapist" didn't tell her patient that some countries, like the United States, permit arsenic-based additives and drugs in animal feed for chickens, pigs and turkeys. Arsenicals (roxarsone, carbarsone, arsanilic acid, and the like) improve growth,

---

4   Brittany, Pure-O/Harm Obsessions.net (no longer active).

feed efficiency, pigmentation and disease prevention in poultry and swine.

The therapist might also have mentioned the Styrian arsenic eaters, Austrian peasants in the southeast of the country, who in the old days consumed 400 milligrams of arsenic trioxide every 2–3 days without side effects. Lethal doses of arsenic trioxide are 70–300 milligrams, but the Styrians had apparently built up an immunity to the poison. They defended the practice by pointing out that arsenic enhanced female beauty, made one's hair black and sleek, increased potency, improved breathing at elevated altitudes, acted as a prophylactic against infectious disease, increased courage and was an effective digestive aid. Their habits were reported in 1851 and subsequently arsenical health and beauty products were widely used in Britain and America. (In his psychiatric textbook, published in 1895, Henry Maudsley recommended opium to OCD patients three times a day. He suggested that adding low doses of arsenic could be helpful.)

Someone who is too clean is not only OC but also vulnerable to hay fever, asthma, atopic dermatitis, inflammatory bowel disease, biliary cirrhosis, diabetes and multiple sclerosis. Individuals with the compulsion to eat dirt, on the other hand, are prone to hepatitis, childhood diarrhea, filariasis, onchocerciasis, schistosomiasis and other soil-based helminthiases. They are a bit OC, too, I imagine, especially the Tokyoites who are regular diners at that restaurant. How often have *you* had the occasion to say, "This is the best dirt soup I ever had."

The epidemic of poliomyelitis was the second-to-last great epidemic to have afflicted the United States and Canada. It was particularly troubling because it preferentially affected middle-class children, whose mothers were wont to say, "Did you wash your hands?" Dirty children were more likely to have immunized themselves against the disease because they had been exposed to the wild-type polio virus. I told that to my student, after we had left the room, to make this point: the first responsibility of a physician is not to the individual patient but to public health. In the interest of public health, therefore, I advise my readers not to be overly concerned with germs. On the other hand, I don't recommend eating any more dirt than you have to.

How to deal with dirt

So, if you or someone you know and love has a thing about dirt, you may find these suggestions helpful. First, dirt is neither good nor bad. Alternatively, it is both good and bad. Dirt has no meaning, save what one chooses to give it. I wouldn't spend too much time on it, though. Here is a fellow who did:

> I open my hands, I want to let go of the slimy, and it sticks to me, it draws me, it sucks at me. Its mode of being is neither the reassuring inertia of the solid nor a dynamism like that in water. It is a soft, yielding action, a moist and feminine sucking... Slime is the revenge of the in-itself. If I sink in the slimy, I feel that I am going to be lost in it. (Sartre, 1969)

I can't say that Jean-Paul Sartre was OCD or even OC, although he did consume massive amounts of tobacco, alcohol and amphetamines, had a controlling disposition and was intolerant of fools. He certainly seems to have had strong feelings about dirt, slimy dirt at least. Ruminations such as his are only likely to get one into trouble, especially with one's girlfriend.

Dirt is not something to bother about. In the words of Mary Douglas, dirt is just "matter out of place" (Douglas, 1966). If, then, you happen to have tracked some into the house, or someone you know and love has, do as a fussy person does: sweep it up and carry it out to the compost heap. Be thankful that it will join that conurbation of bacteria, fungi and nematodes, none of whom seek to do us harm. A fussy man or woman takes on life's innumerable burdens with good humor and gratitude. He or she likes to make small contributions to the proper order of the universe.

Second, give yourself credit. You have an active mind and a sensitive perceptual apparatus. That is why you notice things that pass the rest of us by. But you're not one to go overboard or fall over the cliff's edge. You have your faults, as all of us do. Perhaps you like to mix metaphors. But you are not mentally ill.

Third, appreciate what you are doing. Knowing that *sensu strictu* you are not a head-case, you should muster the confidence to master your weakness. You think too much about things that are hardly worth a thought. Your incisive, OC mind is prone to hyper-focus, and that's a good thing. It's only bad when you hyper-focus on the wrong things. It could be about something filthy on the floor of your lovely kitchen. It may be a sound out of place, like the noise of someone chewing or clicking a ball-point pen during a lecture. It might be a smell, like the girl in the cubicle next to yours who wears patchouli. There are so many things that violate one's sphere of equanimity. There are people whose opinions pollute the body politic, and others whose customs contaminate one's sense of moral hygiene. If you can't master your intolerance with an act of will, then up your dose of escitalopram.

Fourth: elevate your game. When you narrow the focus of your mind, it should be to get something done. Otherwise, you are just brooding. The slings and arrows of everyday life are neither outrageous nor thought-worthy; they are inevitable. Widen your vision, as if you were looking down on yourself from above. Think of the Ghosts of Christmas Past, Present and Yet to Come. They gave Scrooge the proper perspective. *There you are, A, unduly exercised because B, someone you know and love, has pooped in the kitchen.* The ghost lets A listen to her own harsh words. Then he shows her B, cowering in fear and self-loathing. Does a small quantity of dog-doo merit bringing despondency to one of God's creatures?

Finally, deep understanding. If you find it difficult to raise your consciousness to a higher plane, it may be because your remarkably sensitive sensory apparatus is imbued with a high level of **disgust sensitivity**.

Disgust sensitivity...really?

Yes, there is such a thing; psychologists have written about it. They have even written *books* about disgust. Can you imagine? Your little girl comes into the library and asks, "Whacha doin', Daddy?" And you say, "I'm writing a book about disgust, sweetie." One can only imagine the demons Daddy is trying to expunge, but at least he has elevated his game. His book written, greeted with fanfare and short-listed for a literary prize, he has made a small contribution to the proper order of the universe.

The world is laden with dangers, pollutants, slime and corruption. It is enough to have to deal with it. Thinking too much about it contaminates the mind. It can lead to an obsession with **contamination**, one of the "main OCD dimensions."[5] The emotion attached to it is disgust. *Touch that handle? Disgusting!*

Disgust is a normal reaction to *something revolting, primarily in relation to the sense of taste.*[6] It is one of the six primary emotions, and an odd one at that.[7] Of all the primary emotions, it is the latest to develop. Suppose you tell your daughter, "I'm writing a book about disgust, sweetie. Did you know that every human culture finds these things disgusting? Feces, vomit, sweat, spittle, blood, pus, sexual fluids, nail clippings, cut hair, intestines, and dead bodies; rats, snakes, worms, lice, cockroaches, maggots, and flies; and spoiled food, especially meat and fish" (Curtis, 2007). Depending on how old she is, she may respond, "Yuk." If she does, she is closer to seven, and if not, she is only two or three.

Disgust is also unique, I have read, because animals don't exhibit disgust. People who believe that, I think, have never lived with a cat. You have to be careful what you read about disgust.

---

5   Depending on whom you believe, there are three, four or five OCD dimensions: (1) contamination and cleaning; (2) doubt and harm; (3) superstitions and rituals, including counting; (4) taboo symptoms (religious, sexual and aggressive obsessions); and (5) hoarding and symmetry, including perfectionism.

6   Charles Darwin, *The Expression of the Emotions in Man and Animals*, 1872.

7   The others, as you know, are happy and sad, fear, anger and surprise.

Whether animals *experience* disgust is another matter, of course. They do, however, exhibit *avoidance behavior* towards things that are potentially harmful. For example, I have read that ants are hygienic: they groom themselves to remove fungi and dispose of diseased and dead ants. Bees remove dead and diseased brood, they defecate away from the nest and employ antibacterial compounds to keep nests free of parasites. Caribbean spiny lobsters avoid lobsters with viral infections. Tadpoles avoid other tadpoles with signs of candidiasis, and whitefish have evolved the ability to avoid *Pseudomonas fluorescens*, a virulent egg parasite. Bats groom to remove ectoparasites, as do most other mammals, fish and birds. Birds and mammals keep their nests free of fecal material, while racoons, badgers, lemurs and tapirs use latrine sites. Sheep avoid grazing near fecal remains, and one reason that reindeer and caribou migrate is to avoid fields they have dunged. Some chimpanzees have been seen engaged in penile hygiene after mating, and mother chimps have been observed wiping the behinds of their infants after they have defecated (Curtis, 2007). It is also said that cockroaches spend more time cleaning themselves than people do.

Cleanliness, therefore, is older than subphylum *Vertebrata*, but none of the above exhibit the facial expression characteristic of disgust in humans: furrowing the eyebrows, closing the eyes, wrinkling the nose, retracting one's upper lip, moving the lip and chin upwards and drawing the corners of the mouth down and back (Olatunji and Sawchuk, 2005; Rozin and Fallon, 1987). Nor do any of the animals exhibit the disgust that humans feel in the face of torture, incest, cannibalism and other gross violations of our moral code, and which, by the way, elicit the same facial expressions.

* * *

Animals, even insects and worms, exhibit avoidance behavior towards things that are likely to make them sick, and so do humans. The appropriate avoidance behavior that humans exhibit after they flush a toilet—public or private—is to wash one's hands. But some of us conjure in our minds a sticky, slimy feeling that can't be assuaged by the nearness of soap and water. Even talking about it is, well, *disgusting*.

Hypersensitivity

What is slime to one man is a Calistoga mud-bath to F and me.

I promise not to dwell any longer on the subject of disgust sensitivity. We should move beyond its narrow confines and consider the more general problem of hypersensitivity. Some human beings, especially OCs, are extremely sensitive to sounds, tastes, smells and textures. Not only do they sense them, the very thought of them sets off a reverberating loop in their minds.

Mom teaches a baby that *The world is a loving place* without using any words at all, but when she says, "Don't cry. That's only your Aunt Filomena," the baby is understandably dubious. Even children have minds endowed with dubiety: *She could be Mother Theresa as far as I'm concerned, I'm not letting her touch me*, the baby would say, if she had words.

The little snuggie Aunt Filomena brought by for the new baby is the softest cotton and even the colors are gentle. Babies have such sensitive skin. It's a long time before they are inured to the rough feels, loud noises and strong tastes of the real world. Brain-injury patients are the same way, during the unstable period when they are emerging from coma. One has to be quiet and gentle when working with them because the merest noise makes them agitated. Some mentally handicapped patients retain their infantile preference for soft textures and familiar smells or the familiar feeling of a hand or a finger in their mouths. They retain their sensitive sensory detectors all their lives. So do some OCs.

As a child she had been wild and high-spirited, and in the course of the last few years had changed, without any visible cause, into a neurotic... We will not concern ourselves much with her complicated illness, which called for at least two diagnoses—agoraphobia and obsessional neurosis—but will dwell only on the fact that she also developed a sleep-ceremonial, with which she tormented her parents... Our present patient put forward as a pretext for her nightly precautions that she needed quiet in order to sleep and must exclude every source of noise. With that end in view she did two kinds of things. The big clock in her room was stopped, all the other clocks or watches in the room were removed, and her tiny wrist-watch was not allowed even to be inside her bedside table. (Freud, 1955)

Children are sometimes diagnosed with something called **sensory integration disorder**. Such kids tend to respond quite sharply to sensory events, like the sound of a ticking clock, the feel of certain fabrics, their hair being brushed or even being touched by one of their parents. They don't like it at all. The idea is that such children *process* sensory data in an unusual way; what ought to feel nice makes them uncomfortable. Think of it as a connectivity problem: sensations that ordinarily excite pleasure centers in brain are routed, instead, to centers that excite pain or fear. Some kids react sharply to loud noises or to the hubbub in a crowded room. Others are very picky eaters. The odor of a car's interior, plastic or leathery, can be offensive to some children.

The theory of Lockean sensationalism is that one's psychology is formed by the accretion of sensory data. The mind at birth, according to John Locke, is a *tabula rasa*, a blank slate. The theory is no longer widely held; we have since learned that many mental operations are innate, like language, social bonding and good hygiene. Nevertheless, no one can deny that the accumulation of sensory data is irrelevant to one's sense of self. A substantial chunk of our psychology is the assimilation of what we have seen and heard, smelled, tasted and touched.

Consider, therefore, what may happen to children who have strong and unusual reactions to certain sensations, reactions that those closest to them can't understand. Well, what happens is that most kids get over it. Sensory peculiarities are just one more example of mild developmental pathologies that almost always get better, whether you cart the kid to an Occupational Therapist for sensory integration therapy or not.

Suppose one's sensory apparatus is designed to react to a sensory event, such as broccoli, in precisely the way one's mother says it shouldn't. "Eat your broccoli, dear. It's good for you." Suppose the forms of stimulation that satisfy your misconnected nervous system are behaviors of which your mother disapproves: "Don't scratch like that." "Don't take such long showers." "Don't chew on that plastic thing, you may swallow it." Now, I am not about to attribute OC, social anxiety and autism to a fatal mismatch between one's mother's good advice and the data one takes in from one's own senses, but imagine the dilemma of an individual who is endowed, from the very beginning, with a slightly different way of perceiving and appraising those data.

Sooner or later, most of us learn that broccoli is good for you and that chewing little plastic things will disgust your boyfriend. One learns that if it is necessary to scratch like that, it ought to be done in the privacy of one's dressing-room. Childhood is replete with minor sensory peculiarities that ultimately abate and allow us to enjoy oysters on the half-shell, a single malt and a good cigar. Or kissing with *tongues*. Yuk.

What happens to children who have strong and unusual reactions to certain sensations if they *don't* get over it? Will the accumulation of distorted experiences make them subject to mental aberrations in later life? A substantial chunk of their psychology has built up around sensations that few others have shared—perhaps no one else, in fact. Some of their perceptions are unpleasant or even threatening. What psychology might thus arise? We know that the adult mental problems most strongly associated with sensory hyper-reactivity in childhood are OCD, social anxiety and autism. What happens is a particular flaw: patients with OCD don't trust their own senses.

The Island of Reil

> In many animal species, individuals differ consistently in suites
> of correlated behaviors, comparable with human personalities.
> Increasing evidence suggests that one of the fundamental
> factors structuring personality differences is the responsiveness
> of individuals to environmental stimuli. (Wolf, van Doorn, and
> Weissing, 2008)

There happens to be a part of brain that governs the responsiveness
of individuals to environmental stimuli—that is, how we react
to what we see, hear, taste, smell and touch. The five senses are
exteroceptors. The same part also processes data from our
interoceptors, the nerves within the body that convey the state of
our muscles and bones, the blood vessels, glands and all the organs.
It is the insula, the "Island of Reil," located in the deepest and
most ancient convergence of the frontal and temporal lobes. It was
named for Johann Christian Reil, who first described it in 1796.[8]

Reil had no idea what his insula did. He didn't know, for example,
that it is the first region of the cortex to form during embryonic life.
He never would have guessed that modern insulophiles call it "the
fifth lobe of the brain." Living in a time and place where personal
hygiene was a less-well-developed art, he couldn't have known that
the insula informs the cingulum in ways that are relevant to the
obsession with contamination, with disgust in particular and with
sensory hyper-reactivity in general.

The insula is connected—reciprocally, as if with loops—with the
cingulum and also with the frontal, parietal and temporal lobes;
and with subcortical structures such as the amygdala, brain stem,
thalamus and basal ganglia (Flynn, 1999). Its strongest connections
are to nerves within the body; as such, it is a component of the

---

8   Reil was a pioneering anatomist and also a psychiatrist—in fact, he coined the word.
    Like Pinel, Reil waged a crusade for the humane treatment of mental patients. He
    was also Goethe's physician. He died of typhus while tending to the troops at the
    Battle of Leipzig (1813).

somatic brain. Stimulating one part of the insula, for example, induces nausea and vomiting. Stimulation also causes the feeling of disgust, by virtue of its connections to the limbic system; it generates the facial expression of revulsion, because it is connected to the habit system, and also the typical verbal expression "Yuk" or "Eugh." It also stimulates the formation of memories that are the origin of avoidance behavior.

If anything, the insula illustrates the primacy of the somatic brain in so much of our psychology, a topic we shall address later. The insula is central to just about everything that happens on the sensory side of brain activity. It may be the only part of brain where input from all the senses converge. It processes all the sensory data from without and within and engenders distinct feelings of pain, temperature, itch, touch, hunger, thirst, air hunger, exercise, muscular and visceral sensations, vasomotor activity, music and (in sommeliers) wine-tasting (Craig, 2003). It integrates the data, synchronizing nervous impulses and connecting them to brain regions that govern learning, memory, and behavioral and emotional response.

Together with the cingulum, the insula forms a "subjective representation of the body," as it monitors the environment and one's body in relation to it (Taylor, Seminowicz, and Davis, 2009). They are central to one's experience of "the material self as a feeling (sentient) entity, that is, emotional awareness" (Craig, 2003).

* * *

When the insula is damaged, individuals lose their ability to experience basic sensations and have difficulty mounting appropriate behavioral or emotional responses. This happens in patients with neurodegenerative diseases like Alzheimer's, Huntington's, Parkinson's and frontal-temporal dementia. Patients lose weight because they don't feel hungry, or they may eat things that would normally be revolting. They lose their sense of hygiene— they don't feel dirty as you and I do. Nor are they deterred from behaviors that most of us would regard with moral disgust.

The "dirty old man" is aptly named. The insula is also central to emotional awareness. Patients lose the ability to respond to events in emotionally appropriate ways. They can't read the emotions of other people or even their own. Patients with autism, for example, tend to have lower insular activity (Gu, Hof, Friston, and Fan, 2013).

In contrast, abnormal activation of the insula is associated with greater awareness of or sensitivity to the inner and outer environment in general—that is, sensory hyper-reactivity (Aron, Aron, and Jagiellowicz, 2012). Its closest confederate is the cingulum, and a hyperactive insula makes the cingulum hyper-aware. When the cingulum decides that "something is wrong here," it is likely responding to information from the insula—current data, or learned experiences. For example, the insula is where taste aversion occurs—almost everyone has had a childhood experience of taste aversion, something they ate at age six or so that made them sick. For years after, one avoids that particular taste. It shouldn't be surprising, therefore, that high insular activity is associated with avoidant behavior in patients with social anxiety, for example, and also with OCD (Terasawa, Shibata, Moriguchi, and Umeda, 2013; Woolley *et al.*, 2015).

The insula, it seems, is not only occupied with how we feel, or with whether we react sharply to a sensation or not at all, but also with how we think. It is amply connected to higher regions of the cerebral cortex, the analytical brain. Thus, the intensity of one's sensations can bias one's thoughts, judgments and behavior. Since the connections are reciprocal, however, one's thoughts may also bias one's feelings. *My hands feel sticky.*

The insula is especially active when dealing with ambiguity or uncertainty. In such circumstances, the insula processes data from multiple sensory domains. It is part of the somatic brain, so the decision may come from within: *I have a gut feeling* (Gu *et al.*, 2013; Woolley *et al.*, 2015). Your gut feeling may be a reliable guide—as long as you don't have a high level of disgust sensitivity.

9

How to Avoid Death
by Poisoning

Eating dirt may or may not detoxify one's body, but consuming small quantities of poison on a regular basis can protect you from poisoning at some later date, if that is something you are afraid might happen. The exemplar of this practice was no less than Mithridates VI of Pontus (132–63 BC). Pontus is an area of Anatolia on the Black Sea. M6 had reason to fear assassination by poison, since his father, M5, had been killed in just that way, perhaps by his wife, M6's mother. Assuming the throne, M6 had his mother and brother killed, perhaps by poisoning, but he made up for it by marrying his sister.

M6 was known to amuse his guests at banquets by demonstrating his immunity to poison plots, inviting the guests to sprinkle his food and drink with deadly substances which were, apparently, readily available in Pontus at the time. Dio Cassius (*Roman History 37.13*) reports that M6 protected himself by taking a secret "antidote" every day. He should have known, in the face of capture by the Romans, that an alternative exit strategy was advisable.

Mithridates "mixed" the poison and shared the dose with his two young daughters, then swallowed the rest. The two girls died immediately, but Mithridates only became weak. The composition of this suicide poison is unknown... He had shared

the single dose with his two daughters and the remaining amount
was sublethal, also due to his tolerance. (Valle *et al*., 2012)

The way Mithridates protected himself was by means of a "universal
antidote," called Mithridatium. During the Renaissance, when the
Borgias and other unsavory characters also were given to poisoning
each other, it was very much in demand. Much to the frustration
of the Borgias, the recipe for Mithridatium has been lost. We have
since learned that M6 manufactured it from the blood of Pontic
ducks, who had the habit of eating poisonous plants. There were
other noxious ingredients in Mithridatium, about fifty in all.

Mithridates may or may not have been OC. His preoccupation
with poison may have been reasonable, considering the
circumstances, especially when compared to Samantha Brown's
and Brittany's. Is someone OC, therefore, because she is afraid of
poisoning her close friends and relations or is he OC if he poisons
most of his first-degree relatives and can think of nothing better to
do at a dinner-party than sprinkle poison on the entrée?

What about the herpetologist Bill Haast, who was known to
inject doses of snake venom into his body, thus protecting himself
from the many snake bites he received during his long career. When
he was young and began working with venomous reptiles, Haast
began injecting himself with minute amounts of venom at regular
intervals. Having been bitten by venomous reptiles on 173 separate
instances and legally pronounced dead twice, the practice saved
his life on numerous occasions. At age 97, he no longer handled
snakes because of the nerve and tissue damage to his hands
from snakebites, but he continued injecting venom until he died
at age 100. Many lives have been saved by transfusions of Haast's
blood to snakebite victims.

If you find your personal weaknesses portrayed unfairly in these
pages, therefore, reflect on the paradox of OC: you have an evolved
harm-avoidance strategy that carries the potential for harm in
whichever direction you choose to pursue it. It shows just how
tangled we can get if we think too much: *N is poison! N* might be

broccoli, wide-mouth fish, genetically modified food, gluten, Coco-Pops or the dinner you are about to serve your guests. Who knows?

A simple kiss with an infinitesimal exchange of saliva

> In addition to compulsions of both positive and negative character, doubt appears in the intellectual sphere, gradually spreading until it gnaws even at what is usually held to be certain.[1]

The fear of harming someone with poison, for example, or with a sharp knife that happens to be lying there on the counter, falls in the general OC category of **doubts**. Psychiatrists have found that the obsessive fear that one may harm oneself or someone else is statistically related to obsessive doubting (*I'm not sure that doctor is right when he recommends eating an occasional dirt-ball*) and checking (*Did I remember to wash the salad?*).

Just because your irrational fear of poisoning your loved ones over dinner is irrational doesn't mean it mightn't happen. If I were a mystery-writer, I might concoct just such a plot. Samantha feeds her husband nothing but Coco-Pops for fear that anything else will poison the poor fellow. The murderer, who seeks revenge against S's husband for a former slight, knows this. (*How?*, you wonder. Maybe he read about her in the *Daily Mail*.) So, the blackguard puts 300 milligrams of arsenic trioxide in the Coco-Pops. It is the perfect crime because S confesses right off.

In my opinion, none of the Great Detectives are equipped to deal with such an event. Except Lord Peter Wimsey, of course.

> "Then how is it," asked Wimsey, coolly, but with something menacing in his rigidly controlled voice, "how is it that you have this evening consumed, without apparent effect, a dose

---

1   Sigmund Freud, *Introductory Lectures on Psycho-analysis*, 1922.

of arsenic sufficient to kill two or three ordinary people? That disgusting sweetmeat on which you have been gorging yourself in, I may say, a manner wholly unsuited to your age and position, is smothered in white arsenic. You ate it, God forgive you, an hour and a half ago. If arsenic can harm you, you should have been rolling about in agonies for the last hour."[2]

You have to admit that Dorothy Sayers knew all about Mithridatism and even the Styrian peasants. She liked poison: "Ask your boyfriend with the title if he likes arsenic in his soup."[3]

A better story involved the ancient Indian practice of selecting beautiful girls and feeding them poison in small amounts until they grew up. They were called **vishakanyas** (*visha* = poison, *kanya* = maiden). Making love with a vishakanya will result in the death of their partners. They were thus employed to kill enemies.

Chanakya had personally supervised the creation of an entire army of such maidens. His secret service would identify young and nubile girls whose horoscopes foretold of widowhood. These beautiful damsels would be sequestered at an early age and fed a variety of poisons in graduated doses, making them immune to their ruinous effects. By the time each of Chanakya's vishkanyas reached puberty, they were utterly toxic. A simple kiss with an infinitesimal exchange of saliva was lethal enough to kill the strongest bull of a man.[4]

The history of constipation

Most of us are content to believe that neither the lips of that nubile maiden nor the sweetmeats we are served at dinner are laden

---

2   Dorothy Sayers, *Strong Poison*.

3   Dorothy Sayers, *Gaudy Night*.

4   Ashwin Singh, *Chanakya's Chant*.

with poison. Judging from the novels just cited, we are probably
overconfident. Psychologists have proven that people, as a rule, are
afflicted by an excess of certainty when they are asked to evaluate
what they believe.

> Overconfidence was found in a wide range of tasks, including
> general knowledge questions, semantic and episodic memory
> and predictions of future events, in laypersons and experts alike.
> (Dar, 2004)

Someday, I would like to meet one of those "experts in predicting
future events," but that's beside the point. Overconfidence, I think,
is too strong a word. Most people are satisfied with *perceived
confidence*. One is reasonably confident that the sun will come
up tomorrow morning, that the house will be there when we get
home at night, that one's mate is faithful and that the cat will be as
annoying tomorrow as she was yesterday. Heraclitus said, "There
is nothing permanent except change," and who am I to argue with
Heraclitus, but I think sometimes he overstated the case. *Plus ça
change, plus c'est la même chose* makes more sense to me. Perceived
confidence is the confidence of the heart, and its basis is no more
than the routines one has experienced for a long time. It's all the
confidence we need to make it from point A to point B.

Most of us are content with perceived certainty, as in *I think I'm
sure*, except for that tribe of OCs who are smitten with doubt. And
what is most likely to make them suspicious is food. Their gut, it
seems, and what they put into it hold the secret to a long and happy
life. Alternatively, the food they eat is likely poison. "The gastro-
intestinal tract," one physician wrote, "is the primary battleground
for conflicts between psyche and soma" (Whorton, 2000).

What one should or shouldn't stuff into one's pie-hole has been
at issue for a rather long time, and at this point most learned
disquisitions describe the dietary restrictions of the various sects.
Having met Mithridates and Heraclitus already, the reader probably
has little taste for more ancient history. There have been more than

enough dietary injunctions in our own day. For example, should one eat less fat and more carbs, as in *Calories Don't Count*? Or fewer carbs and more fat, as in *Grain Brain*? Are beans likely to promote longevity, or are they poisonous? Eat more fish, they say. When we did a study of retired executives living in South Florida, men rich enough to devour fish two or three times a week, we found they had mercury levels in their blood and mild cognitive impairment as a consequence (Masley, Masley, and Gualtieri, 2012). Are genetically modified (GM) foods good for the environment or an ecological catastrophe? Eat egg whites or whole eggs? Is low cholesterol bad for one's brain? Do food additives make children hyperactive? Or autistic? Shouldn't we all eat as our primate ancestors did? That one I find troubling, because our closest primate relations, the chimpanzees, are occasional cannibals.

Beyond discouraging cannibalism, I am reluctant to take a public stance on any of these issues. I have observed, however, that we human beings are an omnivorous lot, we seem to have evolved well enough in spite of it, and, at the beginning of the third millennium, we are living longer than ever. When patients ask me about foods that will strengthen their brain, my usual advice is to eat a bit less of just about everything. Not fresh fruits, vegetables or nuts, of course. And green tea. The Mediterranean diet? Well, yeah, but a Neapolitan diet is Mediterranean enough for me.

Food fads have always left me cold. They remind me of the constipation wars that were waged a century ago, with residua that lasted well into my own childhood, and good parenting inevitably involved enemas. "Daily evacuation of the bowels is of the utmost importance to the maintenance of health. Without this the entire system will become deranged and corrupted…a diseased stomach, bad breath, sallow complexion, enlarged and diseased liver, rush of blood to the head, loss of memory, headache, heart disease…" and so on, and so on. Psychologists have proven that people who are outgoing, energetic and optimistic defecate "at an optimal level" and constipated individuals tend to be anxious or depressed or both (Whorton, 2000). Which is the cause and which the effect they don't tell us, but the theory is that a costive colon is the locus for the "absorption of toxic substances." That is "auto-intoxication," and you certainly don't want that (Gant, 1916). What I suggest is, eat dirt. It detoxifies the body and assists in preventing constipation.

Eating, you have to admit, is something human beings are good at. Good food, I have observed, is *really good*. But there are OCs who doubt that it is. They think it's poison.

Uncertainty intolerance

How do you know the food isn't poisonous? Or your languid intestinal tract? If the thought even occurs to you, you will find yourself caught between Scylla and Charybdis. You could make a type 1 error—the food isn't poisonous and you think that it is. Or, a type 2 error: it is poisonous, and you think it's not. The consequences of a type 2 error are catastrophic, while the first, well, Coco-Pops are *really delicious*.

Type 1 and type 2 errors are terms from medical statistics. A medical screening test might generate a lot of false positives; the patient doesn't have cancer but the test suggests he does. Another test has a high rate of false negatives and misses patients who really do have cancer. The first test is problematic—it causes distress to patients and leads to expensive and sometimes invasive diagnostic procedures. The second test, on the other hand, is dangerous.

The challenge of type 1 and type 2 errors is pervasive. Should you drive at the speed limit because there may be cops around (type 1) or speed and trust there aren't (type 2)? Should you save old newspapers because you may want to read them someday (1) or consign them to the rubbish bin (2)? Then there is Pascal's wager, where type 1 is a good bet: If you have faith but there really isn't a Providential God and an afterlife in paradise, what have you lost? Salvation is a false positive but you haven't lost anything, save perhaps the few coins you drop in the collection basket on Sunday morning. If you *don't* believe and that turns out to be a type 2 error, you've won eternal damnation and all that comes with it—weeping, gnashing of teeth, and the like. Blackstone, on the other hand, advised against type 1 errors: "It is better that ten guilty persons escape than that one innocent suffer" (Blackstone, 1765–1769). Stalin never read Blackstone, apparently, because he flipped the ratio. He didn't mind false positives. He just wanted to be sure he got all the true positives.

In medicine, we try to evaluate the sensitivity and specificity of a screening test and to use them appropriately. Nevertheless, not even statistics may convince physicians or their patients that an annual pelvic examination is unnecessary, or a PSA test.[5] We like harm-avoidance strategies whether they are effective or not. *Perceived* harm avoidance is good enough for most of us.

One expects modern medicine to have settled questions like cancer screening with scientific certainty, but if one reads the relevant papers, this is what one finds: *probability estimates*. René Descartes wrote *The Method of Rightly Conducting One's Reason and Searching for Truth in Science*[6] in 1637, but after 380 or so years of searching for truth, the best Science has achieved, at least with respect to things that matter, are *pretty good estimates*.

How do we know what we know? A satisfactory answer, absent ideological divagations, is that we know stuff on the basis of our observations and experience. The problem, as we just learned, is that individuals vary in the nature and quality of their perceptions and some of us—autists, OCs and SAs—perceive certain things in reliably wrongheaded ways. Perhaps that accounts for OCs who mistrust their perceptions. *Did I really hear the door click when I closed it?* As it happens, our tribe of dubious OCs also mistrust their memory, like the students whose memory failed when they had to check and re-check the gas stove. Psychologists have tested "checkers"—real checkers and not college students pretending to be.

---

5   Prostate Specific Antigen, a test for prostate cancer of dubious value as a screening
     measure.
6   The full title of the *Discourse on Method*.

Their performance on memory tests was quite normal; they just didn't trust that their answers were correct. OCs also mistrust their attention, which explains the large number who believe they have ADD. Shapiro wrote that they have an "inability to experience a sense of conviction, and doubt not only in their cognitions but also in other internal states" (Shapiro, 1965). Judith Rapoport described patients as "disbelieving their senses" and thus "needing continuous reaffirmation" (Rapoport, 1991). Pierre Janet, a great French psychiatrist in the 19th century, said that obsessives have an "exaggerated need for precision and perfection in perceptions and actions." He thought it was to "compensate for a lack of certainty" (Mayo, 1952).

It is a paradox. Patients with OCD and many OCs are *uncertainty-intolerant*. They seek certainty but the very act of searching leads them to doubt the accuracy of their mental processes. The need to be certain increases their doubts. They are tormented because certainty is never achievable. Most of us, thank goodness, are content with *perceived* certainty.

In all obsessional states of mind there is a predominance of a tormenting, compulsive quality of thinking; but the obsessional need to hold on to certainty and the torments of obsessional doubt are extremely different, in fact diametrically opposed states. One is dominated by inflexibility, rigidity, and immobility, as if one tyrannical thought is constantly keeping out all other points of view: doubt is forbidden. In the other, dominated by constant oscillations, it is as if the mind is constantly thrown from side to side by opposing thoughts: no certainty can be achieved. (Sodre, 1994)

Deduction and induction

Ms. Brown's dubiety is the occasion of good-natured fun in the morning newspaper. Hardly any of us think that all food, save

Coco-Pops, is poison. But how do we know? The question may be trivial but the answer is not.

How we know what we know is a logical problem as well as a perceptual problem. The latter is *What are the facts?*, and the former concerns how facts are put together to generate what we think is the truth. Suppose your girlfriend, Margo, tells you that your boyfriend is playing around.

"How do you know?" you say. Suppose your friend said, "By deduction, Sheila." What does that mean? "All men play around. Todd (your boyfriend) is a man. Therefore, he is playing around." If that were her argument, you wouldn't pay much heed, even if deduction is the essence of logic and philosophy. Deduction is the logical exercise of drawing out the implications of known principles. One deduces that Todd is cheating (conclusion) because the premise, that all men cheat, is a known principle.

Your friend is more likely to report an observation: "I seen him and Charlene driving into the Bostic Motel yesterday at lunchtime. They wasn't there for the meatloaf." An observation such as this is more likely to stimulate your suspicions, unless, of course, Margo is one of those people who has the habit of seeing things that aren't really there, as some people do. Before you confront your boyfriend, however, you want additional evidence. While Todd is sleeping, you discover a number of calls on his phone to Charlene's number. There is also a text affirming an assignation with Charlene at 12 noon. In the pocket of his jacket, you find a receipt from the Bostic Motel. In at noon, out at 1 pm. As he sleeps, you hear him say "Charlene, oh, Charlene" several times. The method you have employed is "Baconian empiricism." This time you have arrived at what is probably the correct conclusion on the basis of **induction**.

Inductive reasoning arrives at a conclusion (Todd is fooling around with Charlene) on the basis of several premises, which are independent pieces of evidence (Margo's sighting, the phone calls, the text, the receipt from the Bostic Motel and Todd's somniloquy). Induction is the scientific method: evidence accrues from many different sources and a conclusion is surmised on that basis. Now she knows, right? No, because the evidence confers nothing more than **inductive probability**. Induction is never more than *probable*. Sheila's mother, who has always liked Todd, points out that he works as an inspector for the Health Department, Charlene is his intern and the Bostic Motel was put in quarantine the day after their supposed assignation.

> Our aim as scientists is objective truth; more truth, more interesting truth, more intelligible truth. We cannot reasonably aim at certainty. Once we realize that human knowledge is fallible, we realize also that we can never be completely certain that we have not made a mistake. (Popper, 1996)

Inductive reasoning is associated with the physical sciences and also detective work, but its premise is not a known principle, such as *I think therefore I am*. Its premises are pieces of scattered evidence— accumulated systematically, we like to think, but usually more or less at random. Unlike deduction, the conclusions one draws are necessarily tentative. The essence of the scientific method is to accumulate evidence and to draw tentative conclusions on that basis. The conclusions, though, are never more than new hypotheses which demand nothing less than further testing.

> Whenever a theory appears to you as the only possible one, take this as a sign that you have neither understood the theory nor the problem which it was intended to solve. (Popper, 1996)

The scientific method, properly done, is an exercise in perpetual doubt. A scientist always doubts the conclusions drawn from a body of evidence. If she is a good scientist, she may doubt the accuracy of the evidence itself. Induction is only as good as the evidence. Deduction is similarly limited by the soundness of the known principle from which its conclusions are drawn. A good scientist, therefore, is OC; she disbelieves her perceptions and the conclusions drawn from them. She seeks continuous reaffirmation.

* * *

In fact, good science is not OC at all. A theory is not acceptable or "scientific" because it is certain or because it can't be falsified. A proper scientist arrives at a new conclusion—a new theory— but only if it seems to be a better explanation of empirical data than previous theories; only if it leads to the discovery of new information; and only if predictions based on the new theory seem to be correct. Good science is not about certainty or truth but rather the further accumulation of probabilities. It devises "new conjectures which have more empirical content than their predecessors" (Popper, 1996).

Operating on the basis of probabilities, scientists and detectives draw conclusions on the basis of evidence, strong or weak, and sometimes they are right. Psychologists draw dimensions from factor analysis, and sometimes they get it right, too. Sheila also came to a conclusion, but was she right? Several days after she kicked Todd out, she discovered that he had moved in with Charlene. Her mother, who always thought the world of Todd, asks how she knew.

> "Ah, that is good luck. I could only say what was the balance of probability. I did not at all expect to be so accurate."
> "But it was not mere guesswork?"
> "No, no: I never guess. It is a shocking habit—destructive to the logical faculty. What seems strange to you is only so because you do not follow my train of thought or observe the small facts upon which large inferences may depend."[7]

Both Sheila and the Great Detective give proper homage to good luck, and every good scientist does the same. But they never guess. Something in their train of thought, their intuition, allows them to make the proper inferences.

---

7   Arthur Conan Doyle, *The Sign of Four*.

Abduction

The art of making proper inferences is what allows most of us to be overconfident in our perceived certainty. As it happens, it has a name; it's even a logical operation. The American philosopher Charles Sanders Peirce, named it **abduction**. It is similar to induction, but more likely to be followed in day-to-day life because it is more likely to arrive at the right conclusion. Abduction is the process of forming an explanatory hypothesis. It is Occam's razor; on the basis of evidence, strong or weak, one selects the simplest and most likely explanation.

Our perceptions can't be understood independently of how we observe and understand them. Even without realizing it, we make sense of what we have observed (Carson, 2009). Peirce said it was the way "to give us an expeditious riddance of all ideas essentially unclear" (Peirce, 1931). The word for it is *intuition*. It is a "humble argument," the "innermost of the nest," "the one that instinct suggests, that must be preferred; for the reason that unless man have a natural bent in accordance with nature's, he has no chance of understanding nature at all." In a familiar vein, Peirce likened it to what the Great Detectives do. His exemplar, however, was C. Auguste Dupin, Edgar Allen Poe's detective.

> Problems that at first blush appear utterly insoluble receive, in that very circumstance, as Edgar Poe remarked in his *The Murders in the Rue Morgue*, their smoothly-fitting keys. This particularly adapts them to the Play of Musement.(Peirce, 1931)

* * *

The "Play of Musement" is an interesting term to describe intuition because it antedates what we now know is the **default mode** of brain activity, of which more later. The idea was taken up by Peirce's contemporary and fellow professor at Harvard, William James, who suggested that reasoning occupies two distinct processing systems: one that is quick, effortless, associative and intuitive, and another that is slow, effortful, analytic and deliberate. (You know that already, don't you?) Intuition is an unconscious process. Intuitions can't be explained in terms of logical operations or expressed very well with language. They are feelings, but not like emotions; rather, they are a *sense* that something is true. They are something we sense in our bodies—*I know it in my heart, It took my breath away, A gut feeling, It made my skin crawl.* They arise, not from analysis or deduction, but from the accumulated experiences of a lifetime, from our habits of thinking, feeling and behaving. It is the source of our perceived certainty and most of the time we get it right.

Intuition is not a product of the analytical mind. Imaging studies have located intuition in the lower cortical regions and the subcortical structures that comprise the social/emotional and somatic brains and the habit system (Volz and von Cramon, 2006). Intuition is one's natural psychology, common sense, the way we draw the most important inferences of our day-to-day lives: whether one should wait for the bus or take an Uber. One intuits the behavior of other people, their goals and intentions, and if you didn't get it right most of the time I don't think you would be here right now. Even chimpanzees understand the goals, intentions, perceptions and knowledge of their fellow chimps. Babies are able to do it before they are two years old (Poulin-Dubois, Brooker, and Chow, 2009).

Intuition entails a leap of faith, a measure of confidence in one's inner nest as well as one's perceptions, memory and attention. It is the ability to judge events on the basis of memories that are not consciously retrieved (Bolte and Goschke, 2005). It is a function of the subcortex, which is neither verbal nor preoccupied with consciousness. The poor OC has difficulty enough judging his or her conscious memories, let alone ones of which he isn't even aware. For that reason, OCs are prone to obsessive self-monitoring (Nestadt *et al.*, 2016). Mental processes are not to be trusted; they have to be analyzed. *Isn't something wrong here? Does this new conjecture really have more empirical content than the others?*

Sheila was confronted with three alternatives: Margo's construction of a suspicious event, her mother's vindication of the stupid clod, and Todd's own prevarications. "Charlene? You mean that girl who works at my office? Are you serious, Sheila?" If Sheila were OC, Todd's ostensible sincerity would make her reconsider her decision-making process. But she has confidence in her perceptions, her memory and especially her common sense. She *abduced* that Todd was a certified no-goodnik.

* * *

Most of us are happy in our Play of Musement, but some OCs aren't. They mistrust their intuitions as much as every other mental operation. It is necessary to monitor one's mental processes, obsessively, because *something may be wrong*. The tribe of dubious OCs doubt the strength of accumulated probabilities that experience has conferred. The idea that truth is only one more layer of conjecture supplanting prior ones is intolerable to someone who is uncertainty-intolerant.

One of the early names for OCD was the *folie à doute*, the doubting disorder. William James called it the "questioning mania," a pathological excess of doubt. Think of the consequences of having left one's door unlocked or the gas stove on, let alone the liability exposure attendant on serving poisoned food to one's guests. The risk of a type 2 error is catastrophic. Better be safe than sorry.

The social/emotional brain accepts that confidence is really just hope; that the unpredictable and unwelcome are inevitable and that life itself is uncertain, but one will likely muddle through, with a little help, of course. It knows there are more than two types of errors one can make: (1) we think something is true when it's not; (2) we think something is not true when it is; (3) we're not sure and are afraid to ask; and (4) we forget what the question is. Most errors are stupid, of course, at least in retrospect, but that's OK because we are, too. If the social/emotional brain is certain of anything, it is uncertainty. It knows its limitations.

Is it really true that certainty is never achievable? Once, during a long and onerous deposition, the attorney asked me, "Doctor, can you say you believe that with absolute certainty?" I told him that I knew only three things with *absolute* certainty: that Jesus, my wife and my dog love me more than I deserve. Soon after, he gave up.

10
Controlling Men

Among all the OC traits, an obsession with control is the nastiest one. It is usually linked to other infelicitous traits like anxiety, narcissism, catastrophizing and wrath. Like every obsession, control feeds on itself, and can take a malignant course. It is one of those psychological cancers that absorbs one's normal psychology and grows until there is nothing else left. *They are so stupid, it is up to me get it right. It makes me mad when other people are so stupid.* If this is what a man thinks, one can only imagine what a horrible burden it must be and how scary. There is only one thing to do, he thinks. An additional increment of control. *I must get them to do right in spite of themselves.*

People with a controlling disposition can be difficult to work with, as you've probably noticed. They tend to micro-manage—that is, they impose their high intellect and critical judgment upon tasks that are better left to underlings. It doesn't matter that neither their experience nor their judgment is suited to deal with said tasks. Nor does it occur to them that by intruding into other people's business they neglect their own responsibilities.

Controlling people are even more annoying to live with. The bitter emotions of a controlling man are governed by this heuristic: *Something is wrong here.* If he simply left it there, and patiently set things to right, he and everyone in his circle would be the better for it, but he can't. That reverberating circuit, *Something is wrong here*, picks up more and more emotional valence as it goes round and round in his head. It emerges as something ugly and riven with generalizations: "Why can't you ever do anything right?," "You always disappoint me," "You are stupid," "You are bad." His analytical mind has a hyperactive error detector, especially for your errors. His obsession with control is a preventive measure, in its warped, unhappy way: *If she is allowed to load the dishwasher improperly the machine will not operate in an optimal way!* This he fears will violate the proper order of things. It is important to do things right. It is no less than dangerous if his wife doesn't. One of them told me once, "When he cleans, he doesn't clean with me. He cleans at me."

Control is nasty because it is often associated with a nasty emotion, wrath, a form of anger that is fueled by righteous indignation: that is, *I'm not angry. I have a right to be angry, because I'm right.* The wrath of men thus disposed may be beastly, but it is an animal expression only on the surface. It originates in his analytical mind. Psychologists who have studied this sort of thing call it a "moral" emotion, occurring as "the result of an appraisal of some deliberate, negligent, or at least avoidable, slight or wrongdoing... most usually directed at another person," and directed towards "punishment for, or correction of, the wrong that has been carried out" (Power and Dalgleish, 1997). In defense of the Proper Order of Things, therefore, wrath is not only condoned but a moral obligation. Be that as it may, if one's wrath is stirred every time a conspecific commits a deliberate, negligent or avoidable slight or wrongdoing, one will hardly have time for anything else, and such is often the case (Averill, 1983; Ortony, Clore, and Collins, 1988; Power and Dalgleish, 1997).

Meeting such a man, I am reminded of the neurobehavioral syndromes: cacosmia, misophonia and the others. Such disorders of perception usually arise when the sensory apparatus is infected or when the cranial nerves are damaged, or they can arise in the company of abnormal brain states like epilepsy, depression or psychosis. To some controlling men, the gentle stirring of the social breeze carries a fetid stink; a gentle "Good morning, I'm Dr. Gualtieri" generates feelings of anger, hatred or disgust. Such men must perceive the "moles" on one's personality, "as broad as a trencher, and hairs hanging from it thicker than packthreads." Their perceptions thus besmirched, they must make a special effort to control their antipathy. When men like that visit our clinic, it is usually because their wife sent them. It usually means that they haven't risen to the effort.

* * *

Not every controller is wrathful, or a man, for that matter; nor is every wrathful person a controller. There are men whose anger is esthetic: your Italian husband, for example, explodes if the linguini is not *al dente*. But he will settle down before very long and defer, as all good Italian men do, to *la mia moglie*. Some angry controllers just seethe, and seething may be hard to detect. It is a subtle sign of a man or woman awaiting the proper moment to exact retribution, as in *Revenge is a sweet dish best served cold*. Seethers, thinking they are clever, contrive to hide their fury. They do so by not saying anything, sometimes for days at a time. One has to be alert to such subtle signs.

There is another tribe whose seething has become perpetual and has invaded their personality. They are identified by a sign that can't be hidden but it's hard to put your finger on it. It is *intensity*. There is a sharpness to their gaze and an edge to their voice, even when they say "Good morning." They seem to be waiting for an opportunity to pounce, except perhaps when they are asleep, but even then you have to be careful. If you want to be a critical student of the human condition, you have to learn to recognize this pre-pounce position. You have to feel the vibrations emanating from the tension in their bodies.

Another group are petulant because *bad things* happen; life, to them, is an irritation to their pure, analytical minds. The human condition is hopeless because it doesn't unfold in an orderly, predictable fashion. Other people are arrant fools, and they are intolerant of fools. The Universe is meaningless and perhaps they are intolerant of that, too. "It's all a mess," they say. "And it's only going to get worse unless we embrace the most decisive actions."

Some arrive at this position: they are the champions of the Earth, which would be better off if most people didn't exist. *There are too many damn people on the poor Earth.* One is reluctant to ask how they propose to solve the problem, and one wonders whether Earth will know She is better off. Some controlling people are moralistic. OCs are said to mistrust their perceptions; some can compensate by attaching too much value to their opinions.

"I eat nothing but fruit and nuts and milk," one says. "Nothing that involves killing an organism, even a shaft of wheat." My niece, in that same vein, eats nothing that has a face, but judging from her sturdy, abundant frame, she's putting down enough sweet-potato enchiladas to feed a Bangladeshi village. Not every OC believes that food is a poison; some think it is a moral outrage. "Do you know how they treat those factory-farmed chickens?" she says. Yes, we do, but when my Nora goes to the store, she looks for the chicken that is on sale.

Others are champions of humanity, who devote their lives in service to a benighted group. You may have noticed that such champions are almost always from social, ethnic or economic groups that are orthogonal to the oppressed class they propose to serve. I have known many such people, having worked in some benighted regions of the world myself. Some, indeed, are Saints. Others, though, are riven with hate for the very group that whelped them, brought them up and sent them to expensive colleges. They identify with the alienation they presume their adopted clients experience. The latter are usually no more alienated than I am, and are just trying, like everybody else, to make it from point A to that elusive point B. The goal of the self-anointed champion of humanity, however, is to enlighten the poor souls to just how oppressed they really are, as if that might be good for them. In such individuals, the membrane in their brain that separates philanthropy from hatred is full of lacunae, if it exists at all.

There are many other controlling types, men and women, boys and girls. Controlling people who are anxious are said to be "uptight." Some controlling people are depressives, and like to suck your mental energy and make you depressed, too, or at least guilty. They are known as "energy vampires." Some controlling people make you feel guilty by being kind and others by being lonely or sick or oppressed. Controlling people who have heart attacks are "Type As." There are so many controlling types, there may not be a single underlying psychology behind the compulsion to be in control. I may have to make one up.

Theory of control

Alternatively, we could limit our investigation to angry, controlling men. Why, then, are some men obsessed with controlling everything, while most of us are content with a modicum of perceived control over some of the events in our lives?

Psychology takes a positive view of control, as in self-control, autonomy, self-determination, competence and mastery. Everybody wants a modicum of perceived control over some of the events in their lives.

> An underlying assumption of all control theories is the idea that humans desire to produce behavior-event contingencies and thus exert primary control over the environment. (Heckhausen and Schulz, 1995)

Our lives are full of behavior-event contingencies. If one drops an egg, it is expected to splat upon the floor. If it just hovered beneath your hand or hit the floor and bounced right up, the events would defy your expectations of gravity and/or the true nature of eggs. When you drop a token into the turnstile, you expect to hear a *thunk* that signals that the thing will turn when you push against its arms. The inanimate world is governed by lawful connections between behavior and event, cause and effect. The lawful order of the inanimate universe is the foundation of all science. It renders at least some aspects of our lives predictable.

I shall concede, for the sake of argument, that there are forces in the Universe that control the behavior of things. The animate world, however, is less amenable to such forces. People, in particular, usually defy prediction, let alone control. Life itself, like Love, the destiny of our children and the fate of the bulbs we planted last autumn, is not controllable. It is a stochastic process that is intrinsically unpredictable.

We all know that, of course, and in response we humans have cultivated what psychologists call **perceived control**, the sense that there is at least a probabilistic relation between our behavior and events, and if not, well, we'll just have to make do. Content with perceived control, we are not discountenanced when things turn out in unexpected ways. As long as most things go as expected, or some things at least, we're OK, and if nothing happens according to plan, well, there's always plan B.

A sense of perceived control is one of those illusions that makes it possible for people to put up with their lives. Perceived control is important to one's psychology. It is essential to what psychologists call **self-efficacy**. It is normal human psychology, "a person's *estimate* that a given behavior will lead to certain outcomes" (Bandura, 1977). Its biological basis is adaptation. We can change our circumstances—outer-directed, or primary control—or we can change ourselves—inner-directed, or secondary control, "to fit in with the world and to flow with the current" (Rothbaum, Weisz, and Snyder, 1982). We all exercise primary and secondary control to different degrees in different circumstances. Too much secondary control typifies a submissive individual, too much primary control characterizes the controlling man. Having a sense of perceived control is associated with good health, achievement, optimism, persistence, motivation, coping, self-esteem, personal adjustment and success in a variety of life domains. In contrast, the sense that one is not in control is the feeling of helplessness. It has untoward consequences on one's health and emotions and one's relations with other people (Skinner, 1996).

The irony of the controlling man is that he perceives that he is *not* in control. He is too rigid to change himself and too clumsy to induce others to change. What, then, is to be done? An additional increment of top-down control, that's what, seasoned with a surly expression, threats and a harsh, demeaning tone. He has to do it because otherwise he just feels helpless. *Why can't the animate world behave with the orderliness of a well-tuned machine?*

There is a theory that such individuals express an exaggeration of natural psychology. Control, it is said, is "an extreme on a continuum of evolved harm-avoidance strategies" (Brune, 2006).

> To manage such risks, a special motivational system evolved, which we term the security motivation system...this system is designed to detect subtle indicators of potential threat, to probe the environment for further information about these possible dangers, and to motivate engagement in precautionary behaviors. (Woody and Szechtman, 2011)

The controlling man is poised to detect subtle indicators of potential threat. *I am simply being conscientious*, he must think; and some psychologists agree, although they acknowledge that it is carrying conscientiousness to the extreme. The controlling man is also determined that everyone should be as conscientious as he is. He is obsessed with the dangers that may accrue if his superstitions are violated. His universe is ordered just so, and he is afraid of the consequences of disorder.

The theory fails because the universe of the controlling man is not well-ordered but precisely the opposite. He thinks he is conscientious but he deceives himself. He is preoccupied with wrongs that occur all the time, slights and wrongdoings that should be avoidable but they never are. His perceptions are biased towards mistakes. Perhaps, then, the controlling man has a perceptual disorder. Perhaps his sensory mechanisms are the site of fungal eruptions that inject toxins into his nerve endings; some OCs believe that just that sort of thing is happening to them. OCs as a group are perceptive, but only a small number experience their perceptions as a fetid stink. Perhaps it arises from a toxin or a virus, or perhaps from anxieties deep in their soul. However it arises, it drives their *Vorstellung*, an overplus of nocuous thoughts. You can't blame the angry, controlling man; he can't stop.

If we were so inclined, we could blame his insula. Or perhaps his cingulum. Psychologists at Carnegie-Mellon have found that the cingulum responds to the perception of error by calling down an *additional increment of top-down control* from the cerebral cortex (Botvinick *et al.*, 2001).

1. Information processing is controlled top-down from the frontal cortex which helps to prevent the occurrence of error.
2. When errors do occur, the conflict monitoring system in the cingulum is engaged.
3. Activation of the error monitoring system triggers an intensification in top-down control by the cerebral cortex.

The intensification of top-down control explains *how* someone happens to be controlling. But what *makes* him wrathful? Perhaps it is his amygdala.

You can load the dishwasher any way you want

An additional increment of top-down control may prevent the occurrence of error, but consider the cost. It's replacing a fast, efficient operator that makes occasional mistakes with a slow, ponderous operator that may also make mistakes. Complex systems, like organisms, brains and dishwashers, are designed to be fast and efficient and to accommodate an occasional mistake. Mistakes? That's what organisms, brains and dishwashers are made for. In that regard, I agree with Tolstoy:

Properly loaded dishwashers are all alike; every improperly loaded dishwasher is improperly loaded in its own way.

However, it is also true that it doesn't much matter how you load the dishwasher—within reason, of course—because the modern American dishwasher is a miracle of engineering and will get dishes clean no matter how you load it. You don't even have to rinse the crumbs off the plates before you put them in. The dishwasher is designed to take care of that too. You might say that it is over-engineered; not quite to the degree a jetliner is, or a nuclear submarine, but sufficiently over-engineered to compensate for the vast numbers of people who rush through the job of loading the dishwasher and aren't particularly fussy.

Human beings are also over-engineered and do quite well, thank you, even when they rush through things. As a group, we humans do a good job of compensating for weaknesses and making up for mistakes. We are a disorderly group, too, and hardly ever say our prayers the precise number of times. Taboos simply make us curious about what's on the other side of the taboo. Aches and pains and minor lapses in attention are things that most of us put up with without submitting to medical tests or ill-advised treatments. When our cingulate gyrus sends us an error message, we pay as little heed as we do to speed-limit signs. There is a reason, I think, that the number *pi* is ultimately incalculable. Imprecision and uncertainty are simply in the nature of things, and for most of us, that's OK. The controlling man seethes with anger at the very idea. He seems to be angry because the order of the Universe is violated when you mis-load the dishwasher or leave the lights burning. Down deep inside, behind his angry shell, he is afraid of the disorder that pervades the Universe.

Complex biological systems, like human beings, operate successfully, not in an orderly way, but in a coherent way. Individual components of the system function in their autonomous ways. They respond to the exigencies of the moment, sometimes correctly, sometimes in the wrong direction. Sometimes they overshoot the mark, sometimes they fall short. There is constant crosstalk among all the components, though, and the direction of response can be changed and its magnitude adjusted. The process accommodates the variability in all of the component parts. No single element in the system is indispensable. Every element in the system can play more than one role, which they must do, compensating for weakness or failures in other elements. The system as a whole is not orderly but it has integrity. It is what is known in biology as **homeostasis**. Another word for it is **coherence**. We could also call it harmony or balance or even happiness.

Coherence is an essential element for any complex biological system to function successfully, whether it is a large organization, a society, an ecosystem or a brain. Order is not. A successful system appears to be orderly, when viewed from a distance or from the outside, but when it is examined closely one finds unpredictability, tolerance for mistakes, and corrective actions undertaken cheerfully.

11
Amygdalomania

Whenever the subject at hand is rage, or fear, or just about any baneful experience, brain-writers turn to the **amygdala**. For a brain part the size and shape of an almond, it has attained such prominence in the annals of human suffering that if it didn't exist, neuroscience would have to invent it.

> The amygdala appears capable of not only triggering and steering hypothalamic activity but acting on higher level neocortical processes so that individuals form emotional ideas. Indeed, the amygdala is able to overwhelm the neocortex and the rest of the brain so that the person not only forms emotional ideas but responds to them, sometimes with vicious, horrifying results. A famous example of this is Charles Whitman, who in 1966 climbed a tower at the University of Texas and began to indiscriminately kill people with a rifle.[1]

Charles Whitman's autopsy did reveal a brain tumor, a glioblastoma multiforme, in the temporal-occipital white matter. The tumor was

---

1   Rhawn Joseph, "Charles Whitman: the amygdala and mass murder" (blog), brainmind.com/Case5.html. An autopsy of Whitman's brain revealed a glioblastoma multiforme tumor compressing the amygdaloid nucleus ("Charles J. Whitman Catastrophe, Medical Aspects. Report to Governor, 9/8/66"). Tumors invading the amygdala have been reported to trigger rage attacks.

originally said to be the size of a nickel, but in subsequent accounts it had grown larger, impacting the hypothalamus, extending into the temporal lobe and compressing the amygdala. "One is informed that Whitman's intuition about himself—that something in his brain was changing his behavior—was spot-on," a critic wrote.[2] That Whitman also had a father who was prone to murderous rage and had tried to kill his son at least once, and that he consumed amphetamines "like popcorn," are seldom mentioned in such accounts.

I agree that compressing the amygdala is not strictly advisable, but that amygdalar compression by itself can turn a devoted son and husband into a murderous monster is a bit of a stretch. The amygdala plays a role in simple forms of emotional learning and memory, like fear conditioning in rats. Events like murderous rage usually have more than one cause. The people who blame the poor little amygdala for it are direct intellectual descendants of those who blamed rejecting mothers for infantile "complexes" in the 1950s and who continue to blame "Modern Society" for everything else.

Amygdalomania may have begun in 1970 with a neurosurgeon-psychiatrist pair at Harvard, Vernon Mark and Frank Ervin, who were creative if injudicious and thoroughly deaf to the tenor of the times. Mark and Ervin had the idea that angry, aggressive behavior in human beings could be corrected simply by ablating the amygdala, which is part of the **limbic system**, the emotional brain. Scientists had known for years that stimulating the amygdala in cats would induce heightened emotionality, rage and targeted aggression against whoever or whatever was close by. If stimulating the amygdala made cats so angry, they reasoned, then it was obviously the place where rage came from. So, why not destroy the amygdala in human beings who were intractably aggressive?

The first time we were able to demonstrate that system in the limbic brain that both starts and stops attack behavior was with

---

2   David Eagleman, "The brain on trial," *The Atlantic*, July/August 2011.

patient Thomas R... Thomas' chief problem was his violent rage. He often felt that people were gratuitously insulting to him; when he was driving to work in the morning, for instance, and another car cut in front of him, he would take it as a personal affront. Nor was he willing to let any such affront go unpunished. He would speed up after the other driver, weaving in and out of the traffic, threatening pedestrians, and going through stop signs until he finally caught up with the driver and forced him to the side of the road. If the other driver were a man, Thomas would hit him; if it were a woman, he would insult her... [He] picked up his wife and on numerous occasions threw her against the wall, even when she was pregnant. (Mark and Ervin, 1970)

The guy, clearly, needed help. Dr. Mark convinced Thomas R to submit to the destruction of a small region in both of his amygdalae (there is one in each hemisphere). This took some doing, but finally he agreed. It is said that Thomas R's wife threatened to divorce him if he didn't consent to the procedure. What happened after the surgery depends on whom you believe. The surgeon wrote that:

Four years have passed since the operation during which time Thomas has not had a single episode of rage. He continues, however, to have an occasional epileptic seizure with periods of confusion and disordered thinking.

Not everyone agreed that the surgical results were beneficial. A second version has it that Thomas R was totally disabled, chronically hospitalized, and subject to fears that he "will be caught and operated on again at the Massachusetts General Hospital" (Breggin, 1974). In 1971 an attendant is said to have found him with a wastebasket over his head to "stop the microwaves" (Breggin, 1974). A sympathetic doctor at Boston's VA hospital, where he was transferred, ordered "a large sheet of aluminum foil so he may fashion a protective helmet for himself" (Breggin, 1974). The VA doctors, apparently, were never told that he had been treated with brain electrodes, and wrote him off as a delusional paranoiac. His wife divorced him anyway.

Mark and Ervin were on the wrong side of history during the 1960s when they were accused of collaborating with secret government agencies for all manner of nefarious ends involving psychosurgery. They were on the right side of science, though, at least for a while; the prevailing wisdom was "localizationism"— that is, that psychological functions were **localized** to specific brain centers. As we know now, some functions are localized and others are not. Anger is not, but Mark and Ervin didn't know that. The experience and expression of all the emotions, including anger, entail the participation of numerous brain regions. For that reason alone, this writer hesitates to recommend amygdalotomy for one's exploding husband.

"Amygdala" is the Greek word for "almond"

The amygdala resides on the inside surface of the temporal lobes and we have one on each side. It is one of several temporal lobe nuclei that process and integrate information from the sensory apparatus. The amygdala is special, though, because it has to do with the "emotional processing of sensory stimuli." It has a role in mediating the emotional quality of one's engagement with the world. Its emanations have been assigned the role of endowing responses to external events with emotional intensity. Neuroscience calls this **valence**, just like the charge on an ion. The amygdala is sensitive to the quality of an event, and its sensitivity generates valence. When a perception is endowed with valence, it has a charge, or energy, which might be positive (we like it) or negative (we don't). Valence, thus applied, is a term from chemistry; we don't really think that feelings have electrical charges as hydrogen and chloride ions do. Our mental activities do consist of some kind of electrochemical energy, but valence may mean something less value-laden. As far as the amygdala is concerned, valence may just mean intense (important!) or not (ho-hum). More of the neurons in the amygdala are equipped to process intense stimuli than innocuous ones.

The amygdala is usually said to be the fear center or, alternatively, the anger center. Studies in animals and humans also associate activity in the amygdala with feelings of anxiety or disgust. Conversely, the activity of the amygdala can be decreased by exposure to pleasant stimuli like happy faces or "chill" music, whatever that is. The extent of the decrease is directly related to how pleasant or "chill" the stimulus happens to be. Men have larger amygdalae than women do, although individual differences in the size of the amygdala are more impressive than gender differences. There is a theory that some mental illnesses are related to a very small or feeble amygdala and others to a large, robust one (Zald, 2003).

As the amygdala appraises the emotional salience of a sensory event, it generates some kind of emotional energy which it proceeds to send down the line—to the hypothalamus, for example, where the energy is transformed into physiological changes in the autonomic nervous system and the elaboration of the relevant stress hormones. It also directs its energy up the line, into the **prefrontal cortex** (PFC), where the emotional event is subjected to the usual scrutiny. It is at this point that heuristics and rational decision theory come into play, and hopefully moderate the emotional energy (fear or anger) the little amygdala is thrusting forth. This theory, with anger bubbling up from the amygdala but held back by the PFC, has led to a mechanistic view of the neurobiology of wrath:

> Aggression emerges when the "drive" of limbic-mediated affective prefrontal response to anger producing or provocative stimuli is insufficiently constrained by inhibition and is channeled into violent behavior. Excessive reactivity in the amygdala, coupled with inadequate prefrontal regulation, serves to increase the likelihood of aggressive behavior. (Siever, 2008)

To illustrate, I shall give you a pithy tale from an old mountain-man in Alaska. He was in the forest, just wandering about, when he stumbled upon a clearing. There he saw an enormous brown bear who happened to be in a foul mood. The bear saw the mountain man first and proceeded to charge, with nothing but mayhem on his mind. The sensory stimulus that presented itself to the mountain man, therefore, was a charging bear. At the sight, sound and smell of the bear, the mountain man's sensory processing units activated his amygdala which responded with a predictable degree of emotional valence. You could say it was quite exercised.

Now, at this level of neural activity, words are not generated, except perhaps an expletive. One may infer from the circumstances that the mountain man was scared stiff. His autonomic nervous system was making his heart beat fast, his palms were sweating and his mouth was dry, and the hairs all over his body—he probably had a lot of them—were standing up. But then something marvelous happened. His prefrontal cortex kicked in. This level of neural activity is quite verbal, and this is what it said to the mountain man: *We are going to die. And the last thing we shall ever see in this life is the spectacle of a charging bear, as big as a pick-up truck. Here, let's climb onto this rock, and get a good view of an extraordinary event.* And so the man did. He stood on the rock, calm and attentive, concentrating on the fearsome beauty of the charging bear.

The bear was so thoroughly nonplussed by the man's behavior and his calm, commanding presence that he stopped in his tracks, gave the man a searching look, turned and ran off into the forest.[3] I don't think this sort of thing happens very often—that is, charging bears and all—but it does illustrate how intense emotions can be constrained by prefrontal inhibition, and how at least one such case had sanguine results.

* * *

Another scary tale: a dark and lonely night in a cabin in the country, where one's sister lets out a scream and says, "I have seen

---

3   This agreeable story was told to me by Fisher, a medical school classmate, who had heard it from the old mountain man himself. Fisher was a good friend, but he would believe anything.

the disembodied head of Claude Heckman at the window!" The appearance of such an apparition would ordinarily evoke wild feelings of dread or panic, if the prefrontal cortex didn't announce to the rest of brain that his sister is an unreconstructed psycho and all too prone to hysterical perceptions such as Claude Heckman's disembodied head.

In fact, my older sister did see just such an apparition when she was babysitting for me and my little cousins at our cabin in the mountains, and, unfortunately, our cortical regions were not yet sufficient to the task of dealing with her visions. Children, you see, don't have very well-developed frontal cortices, and their capacity for considered judgment is correspondingly deficient. That is why they are so given to fears and anxieties, and why tantrums are such a problem in children. Some kids, of course, more than others, and they are probably the ones with really big amygdalae. If the amygdala is just spewing forth intense emotions like fear and anger, one needs something to keep the lid on, or perhaps to transform all that emotional energy to a useful purpose. Thus, patients with brain injuries are prone to rage attacks, and so are patients with certain forms of dementia that afflict the frontal lobes, or strokes that do the same. One might say, then, that one's angry, explosive mate has a congenitally weak cortex or, alternatively, an especially robust and hyperactive amygdala.

This, of course, is what our friends Mark and Ervin were talking about. There is a "bad guy" in the sub-human brain (the *id*, or your bad angel) who has to be restrained by the good guy in the prefrontal cortex (*superego*, good angel). That doesn't mean the theory is outlandish; rather, it explains its appeal. It is like a primal myth, the forces of good versus the forces of evil.

A salience detector

The neurons in the amygdala have been identified with fear and wrath, but such interpretations may be overwrought. The amygdala probably functions as something like a **salience detector**; responding selectively to signals that may be important to the life of the organism. In the amygdala, depending on how big it is, I suppose, such signals are incubated or extinguished, amplified or degraded. The signals are events that are rousing: social events, rewards or ambiguous or novel stimuli that require further investigation (Adolphs, 2010). Threats to one's safety certainly fall into the category of salient events and therefore involve the amygdala. It processes them and participates in the generation of the appropriate feelings; that is why it is said to be an "emotional processor." That it processes events, however, is less interesting than *how* it does it. At every stage of emotional processing, it demonstrates innumerable opportunities for individual differences and pathology as well.

Different people must have amygdalae that are likely to assign negative energy to most events, while others confer positive charge on just about anything. Social critics and journalists are in the first category and cheap dates are in the second. There are also people who rarely attach emotional energy to anything. My cousin Angelo, for example, was a hulking brute who hardly noticed the most horrific tricks my sister played on him at our summer home, while I, a delicate child, was usually stricken with fear as soon as she walked into the room. One may attribute to the amygdala the fact that different people react differently to events. We assume it is an inborn quality, because such temperamental differences are evident in newborn babies. Even now, sixty years after my sister played tricks on (i.e., tortured) Angelo and me, I can't tell you whether it is better to have a sensitive amygdala, like mine, or a sluggish one, like Angelo's.

Like everything else in one's brain, the sensitivity and reactivity of one's amygdala can be altered by experience. We know that even a calm, optimistic amygdala can be conditioned—by chill music, for example. It can grow more sensitive through the experience of repeated traumatic events, especially when one is young and impressionable. It is interesting that the amygdala can also be conditioned and can grow more sensitive through the utter absence of untoward events.

* * *

The sensitive and reactive amygdala can direct immediate responses on the basis of emotional importance—the salience, or valence—of an event. This accounts for a well-known event: one pulls back one's hand from a hot stove well before one is consciously aware of what has happened. One says, *Oh, drat. I burned my hand*, and not, *I burned my hand. Oh, drat.*

Our friend the amygdala does more than just respond to an immediate occurrence. It can *learn*. Having experienced a hot burner, one learns never to touch one again. The amygdala, therefore, is an agent of memory and, in the case of a hot burner, of very strong and enduring memories. It sits in the medial temporal cortex right next to the hippocampus, and both are involved in the consolidation of long-term memory.

The way the amygdala processes experiences is governed by its sensitivity, reactivity and capacity for forming memories. As it does all this, it changes the mental representation of an event. The event is directed one way or another, assigned valence or not, amplified or inhibited, remembered or quickly forgotten (as Angelo must have done). Then, as the event is transformed, and passed on to other parts of brain, it is subject to extinction or incubation. Over the long term, it may gradually diminish or it may grow stronger.

So, a little boy learns about geese when a goose bites him on the leg. There is something about his amygdala and its connections that determine how strong his emotional reaction is and there is another process that determines whether the fear will be incubated or suppressed. The little boy is an example of the latter; he was mortified by the event but he wasn't stricken with fear by the subsequent sight or sound of a goose. Nor did he develop a phobia or an obsession. I assure you, though, that he still doesn't *like* geese. In this way, your author, having been bitten by said goose when he was five, is different from the Batman.

* * *

The fate of an untoward event involves more than the emotional processors in one's amygdala. The amygdala has numerous connections to other parts of brain and they participate in the subsequent amplification or inhibition of an emotional event. The circuit that connects the amygdala to the prefrontal cortex is of particular importance. Like most of the circuits that connect the cerebral cortex to lower structures, it's a loop, and I shall call it, for convenience's sake, the **A/P loop**. The loop doesn't turn on and off; neural energy is always coursing through its veins in gentle oscillations. It has a *basal state* and, in most of us, its basal energy level is gentle oscillations. In some people the basal state of the A/P loop is low and strives to go higher; in others, it is high and causes mischief when it goes higher.

The loop responds to the emotional processing of an event. If the event generates valence, the A/P loop reverberates energetically and recruits other parts of brain to deal with the problem. Think of it as an alarm system. Its role is to determine whether a stimulus deserves further consideration or even an action step or two.

The action step, in the face of a noxious event, is the **biological stress response**. The sight or sound of a goose, or of popcorn, or of a cave full of angry bats, activates the amygdala and the prefrontal cortex more or less at the same time, and the A/P loop vibrates with intensity. The noxious event is being processed, not in two places, but in a reverberating loop. This reverberation is no less than the brain's experience of the event; experiences, to brain, are oscillating cell assemblies.

More forks in the road

The sensitivity, reactivity and persistence of this reverberating loop determines whether one's emotional response to an event is amplified or inhibited, extinguished or incubated. Within the subcortical organs, like the amygdala, neural tracts are bifurcated. They have forks in the road. A signal can go one way or the other.

One way leads to **aversive amplification**, which occurs in individuals who are prone to anxiety disorders, like phobias and

PTSD, and also in people who tend to get cross. If the process is initiated too readily or if it persists too long, it can cause sustained attentional bias for threat. The attentional bias, if not restrained, can become generalized. More and varied cues are added to the individual's repertoire of dangerous things and he begins to perceive the world as a dangerous place.

It is a feed-forward process. The accumulation of incubated fears makes one more attentive and more sensitive to new fears. There have been studies with functional brain imaging that show such individuals have amygdalae that are no less than beefy from incubating so much negativity (Bishop, Duncan, and Lawrence, 2004).

The other fork is the one your neural impulses should take. Following this path leads to **aversive inhibition**. It is the path taken by individuals who are less prone to anxiety or wrath. This one is a feed-back process. Activity in the amygdala around a novel or fearful event is addressed by the reverberating loop, and then it is suppressed (Pickens *et al.*, 2009; Quirk, 2004). Events can be dealt with by expressing a gentle sigh, a barely perceptible shake of the head, and then the gentle application of appropriate correctives.

One's proneness towards aversive amplification and inhibition is usually balanced, because too much of one or the other isn't good for you. The disproportionate reaction to events among individuals who are prone to aversive amplification drives the angry, controlling man. Most of us, thank goodness, are on the aversive-inhibition side. A pleasant disposition, even if it is a bit fussy sometimes, is the best harm-avoidance strategy I know.

The future of the amygdala

Drs. Mark and Ervin are probably best remembered for a letter they wrote to the *Journal of the American Medical Association* in 1967. They suggested that at least some of the more violent urban rioters of the time were actually victims of "brain dysfunction" and that efforts should be made to "pinpoint, diagnose, and treat those people with low violence thresholds before they contribute to further tragedies" (Mark and Ervin, 1967). "We need to develop an 'early warning test' of limbic brain function to detect those humans who have a low threshold for impulsive violence, and we need better and more effective methods of treating them once we have found out who they are" (Mark and Ervin, 1970). The treatment they were referring to, of course, was brain surgery—that is, amygdalotomy. In a later chapter, "Theory of Autism," we shall learn why that may not be a good idea.

Amygdalomania is not entirely in our past, but the model of a roiling center of fear and rage held down, only just, by the mature counsel of the prefrontal cortex is a bit fabulous, like the serpent who gnaws at the tree of life and will bring Asgard crashing down. Leave it to the spoilsports of modern neuroscience to ruin a perfectly agreeable theory. They point to the complexity of the amygdala, small as it is but extensively connected with many other cortical and subcortical structures, continuously updating and deploying representations "of stimulus value" (Murray, 2007). They tell us that the amygdala is not one thing at all, but rather a collection of thirteen centers with "a bewildering variety of neuronal response types" (Swanson and Petrovitch, 1998). In fact, it is probably not a "center" at all (Swanson and Petrovich, 1998). At one point, the amygdala was thought to be specialized for fear processing, but it comes into play whenever stimuli are unpredictable or ambiguous. Because we have a negative bias in the face of uncertainty (i.e., we don't like it), the consequence is a net negative valence which may be expressed as fear or anger. So, the amygdala is not a simple organ of anger and fear at all. It just generates arousal in the face of the need to gather additional information from the environment (Adolphs, 2010). Since gathering that information is an effortful process, it entails the participation of the prefrontal cortex, the cingulum and other parts of the brain.

We have the habit, when something breaks down, of assigning the failure to one of its parts. It is appropriate to a car that breaks down, or a dishwasher, but not to an organism. The amygdala probably does participate in the wrathful expressions of a controlling man, frustrated and fearful as he is. The emotional evaluation of events is too important to be left to one small nucleus, or even thirteen subnuclei. The emotional processing system has many channels, and they are not segregated into positive and negative poles. If they were, it would limit the flexibility of the human psyche in the face of uncertainty. Individuals have distinctive activation patterns in the face of uncertain stimuli and those can only emerge from a system that is much more complex and widely dispersed.

On a practical level, in your appraisal of a potential life-mate, an investment adviser or a candidate for local office, it would be nice to have an early-warning test of limbic brain dysfunction. In your dealings with an explosive husband, it would be nice to have better and more effective methods, but neither test nor treatment should be concentrated on his amygdala.

12

Brain Control

The controlling man is not hard to understand if we assume that brain has a **central executive** that directs the flow of information and activity. He must have a big one. Since the executive powers of brain control are in the frontal lobes, we may also expect him to have a prominent brow, like a Klingon.

There is, in fact, something in brain that psychologists call the central executive; parts there mediate the **executive functions**. The latter are things we rarely do: planning, critical judgment, foresight and problem-solving. Cognitive flexibility is another, the ability to shift between multiple tasks or mental sets. Inhibition is the ability to restrain automatic or ongoing mental processes when it is necessary to do so. Without it, one is at the mercy of impulses, habits or irrelevant stimuli, which is the way some people like it.

The assumption that brain control resides in the neocortex, and in the prefrontal cortex in particular, is based on a hierarchical model of brain organization. It's a cogent model; brain evolved by layering, it is suggested, one structure forming atop another, each new structure assuming some of the functions of the older ones and elaborating upon them. The ensuing arrangement is a progression of more potent and complex computational units superimposed on older ones. The **higher cortical functions**, therefore, have evolved to govern, or so the thinking goes. Since the lateral surfaces of the PFC and the parietal lobes are the newest and most complex computational unit in the brain, that is where the central executive must be. It is a brain model modeled after a bureaucracy.

Neural networks are hierarchical, but we tend to forget what that means in the case of a complex biological system. In effective hierarchies, there is always a balance between top-down and distributed control; it is as true of biological systems as it is of successful societies. The Pope doesn't really control his bishops, and the Emperor of China never controlled his Mandarins, and still doesn't.

Every component in a hierarchical system has controllers and regulators, but they operate both from the top down and from the bottom up. The organism itself is regulated from the top *and* from the bottom. Functions occur in modules or networks, which are influenced by other networks and modules. Every element in a complex system is ignorant of the behavior of the system as a whole: it responds only to information that is available to it locally. In that respect, every component is expected to act autonomously. At every level of a biological system, parts behave in relation to controllers, regulators and influences from within and without. However, all the components and subsystems behave in a manner that is true to their nature, their strengths and weaknesses, their history and their inclination at a moment in time.

Brain, like the organism itself, tries to find a balance between **hierarchical control** and **distributed control**, modularity and integration, organization and autonomy, but it is a dynamic balance that changes in response to a host of influences, including the time of day. Regulation occurs in organisms, as it does in brains, by means of **feedback loops**, which allow networks to regulate themselves. Brains are recurrent systems, and most neural circuits are loops. Activity moving in one direction stimulates activity to move in the other direction. A simple loop is from A to B to A to B, and so on. Most neural circuits have more than two nodes, each node contributing to the signal going around the circuit, and each node modulating the signal in its own preferred way, depending, of course, on the exigencies of the moment. Feedback in neural networks is positive (enhancing, stimulating) or negative (detracting, inhibiting). Virtually all networks are capable of both, and whether feedback will be positive or negative at a given point in time is difficult to predict (Cilliers, 1998).

Within brain, what we think of as controllers are really *limiters*, constraints that set the boundaries within which mental activities occur. One's thoughts and behavior and all of the physiological functions are governed, whether one is hypervigilant, alert, somnolent or inert. Parts of brain are differentially affected by constituents in the blood and by molecules floating free in the intracellular space. Processing speed is another governor; the speed with which one's networks can connect and synchronize determines how much they can do, how effortful it is to do it, and whether one ought to bother at all. Finally, every complex system in brain responds to constraints imposed by other systems. What governs brain activity is a system of checks and balances—in computerese, **parallel constraint satisfaction**. Regulation in brain, in all organisms and in complex systems in general, is a cyclic process that relies on feedback loops.

Biological systems like brains and people are not built for control, but for resilience, robustness and flexibility. They are designed for adaptability, not control. They are governed by a "Universe without a master but neither sterile nor futile."[1]

The analytical mind has controllers

Nevertheless, we have control over at least some of our actions, if not our thoughts or feelings. The lives of human beings are more than a perpetual volley between stimulus and response. Neither are the decisions we make determined by secret events deep in brain, whether they are infantile complexes, repressed memories or neural loops that aren't sure if they want to augment or inhibit,

---

1   Albert Camus, *L'étranger.*

to feed back positive or negative. We make choices; brain, like soma, simply lends constraints to the choices we can choose.

We know that that is true because we have conscious **awareness** and at least some of the time we know what we're doing. As it happens, awareness resides in one's central executive. One's active awareness of the moment is called **working memory** or **immediate attention**. It's special for many reasons, and one is how small it is.

Active awareness is a limited space, only about 6–8 bits long, and for that reason access to it must be guarded jealously. To that end, there is **selective attention**, which gives entrée only to small fragments of one's perceptions, memories, feelings and thoughts. Attention and working memory may be thought of as controllers; not only that, they are a biological and psychological bottleneck. At any given moment, even when we are asleep, the processors in brain are generating many more than 8 bits of data—more than 8 billion bits, I venture to guess. The massive flow of mental activity is not gratuitous. It must be up to something, but only the smallest part of it makes it into the narrow confines of active awareness. When psychologists speak of a *central executive*, therefore, they mean something that limits access to conscious awareness.

The observation that *we make choices* is fundamental to one's self-concept, the marriage industry, the entire structure of jurisprudence, and entry, or not, to eternal salvation. Active awareness is a good candidate to be one's internal choice-maker and hence the brain controller. But its capacity is so limited, it's hard to think it's capable even of *perceived* control.

Default mode

Neuroscientists have known for more than a century that the brain is active even when one is at rest; daydreamers have known it longer than that. When Hans Berger invented the **electroencephalograph** (EEG) in 1924, he noticed that the brain expressed electrical activity even when the subject was resting (alpha waves) or in deep sleep (delta). The brain was quiet but not silent; it never stopped. The importance of the discovery wasn't appreciated for a long time, except by the psycho-analysts, who always suspected that brain was up to something we didn't know about.

Critical studies of the state of relaxed mental awareness didn't begin until fifty years later, when David Lund, a Swedish physician, began to study regional blood flow in brain using radioactive isotopes—the precursor of PET and SPECT scanning. Studies of cortical blood-flow patterns showed a hyper-frontal pattern in awake healthy subjects in the resting state: that is, high regional blood flow in the prefrontal cortex. Lund surmised that the PFC was generating a state of conscious awareness (Ingvar, 1979). It occurred, however, when the individual and his or her brain was in a **resting state**. Since it occurred when the individual wasn't doing anything but quietly resting, it was said to be the brain's **default mode**.

The idea that the brain might have a default mode, a state of activity when it isn't doing anything that engages its attention, struck many as absurd. When an organism isn't doing anything in particular, the activity of its brain is of no interest; or so it must have seemed to busy people who don't pay attention to things that just lie about not doing anything. Lying about in a state of idle reflection, however, is perhaps the most productive thing a brain can do. Think of Newton sitting under the apple tree, Descartes lying in bed, or your brother-in-law in his ice-fishing hut.

As studies of brain activity became more sophisticated, neuroscientists realized they had been overly focused on brain activity during specific tasks. It was a productive approach, but ignored the possibility that brain functions that are mainly *intrinsic*—that is, *not directed*—might be more interesting than brain functions that were **task-positive**. Intrinsic, non-directed activity is the resting state; one isn't doing anything at all, daydreaming perhaps. As one is just sitting there, one's brain is not only active but is doing something. It seems to be engaged in information-processing. Without something to do, something that requires attention, we all have the experience of the mind wandering from one passing thought to the next. It seems like woolgathering, but it is meaningful, as we muse about past events and try to understand them, ponder what may happen in the future, or imagine worlds that are far from our immediate surroundings. One is in brain's default mode; therein dwell fantasy, imagination, daydreams and deep thought (Buckner, Andrews-Hanna, and Schacter, 2008; Raichle, 2010).

The brain's default mode occupies the default mode network. It is in the medial prefrontal cortex, the medial temporal lobe including the hippocampus, and parts of the cingulum and inferior parietal lobe—locations, as it happens, that are also components of the social/emotional brain.

The default mode elaborates experience. It is active during quiet moments when the only external information to process are leaves rustling in the trees or clouds floating by. Brain is not about to let such idle moments pass by staying idle itself. It capitalizes on them, consolidating past experience in ways that will prepare it for future events. Think of your laptop. You've turned off all your programs and it goes into sleep mode, but what it's really doing is thinking about itself. The little computer is looking after herself, backing up files, inserting patches into programs and updating her security (Buckner *et al.*, 2008).

Brain's default mode is events essential to oneself, and to others one is close to. It occupies itself like a pianist doing her scales, exercising an important function, reminding us who we are, where we stand with respect to others and why. It is scrapbooking, you could say, contemplating events in light of one's memories, sorting and arranging them according to their emotional valence, and trying to anticipate what might come of it all. The default mode almost always has someone else in there with you, or several others. Yet, curiously, it is also the seat of one's deepest thoughts and insights. Picture Socrates "standing all day in the market place lost in thought and oblivious of the external world," with his head in the clouds (Buckner *et al.*, 2008).

The default mode is not only a normal state but essential to health; apparently, we all ought to spend more time doing nothing. Patients whose default mode network is impaired are gravely disabled: patients with Alzheimer's disease and schizophrenia, for example (Broyd *et al.*, 2009). Connections within the default mode network, particularly with the medial prefrontal cortex, are weak in patients with OCD, social anxiety and autism (Hou *et al.*, 2013; Peterson, Thome, Frewen, and Lanius, 2014; Yerys *et al.*, 2015).

In normal circumstances, the only way to modulate the activity of the default mode is to turn it off, and that happens automatically when one is involved in goal-directed activity. One wonders, then, if too much task-positive behavior can weaken one's default mode; or if a weak default mode network forces one to keep busy. In either event, a weak default mode undermines the foundations of who we are, what we do and why we do it. Socrates, his head not always in the clouds, said *Beware the barrenness of a busy life.*

The dorsal attention network

The default mode network has a reciprocal relation with the central executive, which means they take turns. Good thing, too, because the central executive can hold 6–8 bits in one's immediate span of attention. Good grief. If that were true, it would mean our active awareness of *now*, of life and love, truth and beauty, the flag and apple pie, are no longer than eight bits. Perhaps you have known someone of whom that is true.

Goal-directed behavior—task-positivity—is a function of one's central executive, in particular the **dorsal attention network** (DAN). The DAN is the agent of active awareness and extends along the surface of the prefrontal cortex back to the parietal lobes. Put your palm in the middle of your head, with the heel above your eyebrows. No, not the heel of your foot, the heel of your hand. That's better. Now your palm is over the dorsal-lateral surfaces of the PFC and your fingertips are right on top of the dorsal-lateral parietal lobes, at least if you have long fingers. This is the DAN, one's central executive, the analytical mind at work in the dorsal-lateral surfaces of the hemispheres. It is on the top of the neocortex, more or less parallel to the default mode network, which is on the bottom of the cortex.

How the dorsal attention network interacts with the default mode network is a matter of no little importance. Consider T, a middle-aged man of modest means, engaged in a simple cognitive task. Let's say he is trying to rebuild an old car—a 1973 MGB-GT, say. As he ventures forth to the workshop, his DAN is active. It is active whenever behavior is initiated or when errors arise during its execution, which happens not infrequently to T, especially when he tries his hand at welding.

Like most of us, our friend also has a **posterior attention network** (PAN) that extends from the parietal lobes as far back as the cerebellum, which is just above the nape of the neck. The PAN is active during the maintenance of a task (Dosenbach *et al.*, 2007). In other words, there is a cognitive controller for starting something and another for finishing it up. T must have a problem with his PAN because he has been working on the stupid car for a long time. He allowed me to use him as an example in this book so long as I didn't disclose how long.

Patients with prefrontal lesions have problems with their dorsal attention network, that is, with behavioral initiation (initiative) and changing sets when the behavior is unproductive or counter-productive. They perseverate, however, because the posterior network is intact and maintains the behavior. That is why my Uncle Delmore would turn the taps on and off, interminably, until my mother or one of his brothers made him stop. I have no neuroanatomic explanation, however, for why, in his later years, Uncle Delmore would walk up to Bath Avenue and, on his own initiative, direct traffic. It was not, in those days, a heavily trafficked byway and the police didn't seem to mind.

Both the dorsal and the posterior attentional networks are top-down controllers; there are also bottom-up controllers. **Arousal**, for example, is a form of attention that can turn a mind that is thoroughly engrossed in the direction of a loud noise, a sudden burst of light or the arrival of an unexpected intruder. For example, one may be concentrating on the problem of how the activity of multiple mental systems are controlled, if they are at all, when two Chinese girls come into the library and say, "Daddy, we're going out now. Can we borrow your credit card?" Decidedly, a First World problem. The example more frequently given for bottom-up control of attention is a loud noise or a sudden burst of light that interrupts one's directed attention. My little girls are far too polite to allow such events to occur, but their intrusion is equally determinant. The train of their father's task-positivity has been interrupted.

A welcome intrusion, at that. I sit back in my chair and reflect on our good fortune. F and I are only thankful to have the resources to satisfy the girls' needs, and especially thankful to have them with us at all. Thankful, too, that they are good Chinese, clever shoppers and temperate in their desires. They are going out, each for a pair of shoes. The ones they wear to school every day have holes in the bottom. Have they shown me those same holey shoes before? That they will return with more than two pairs is immaterial to my resting state, because they never buy anything that's not on sale.

As I sit back, my mind wanders into a resting state, its **default mode**. It is the Play of Musement, gentle reflections on one's autobiographical self and the biographical selves of the persons close to one's heart. It is where the brain resides when it is freed from directed attention and goal-driven activity. If anything, though, it is where one's goals come from, one's motivations, and the meaning of one's life. Does that make sense? One's mind is controlled *by default*.

* * *

The default mode network (DMN) is active during the brain's **resting state** and that is, by definition, uncontrolled. It occurs when executive attention is turned off. But what does the DMN have to do with control?

The default mode network is distinct from the dorsal attention network, but they happen to have a reciprocal relation. The DMN is active when no goal-directed activity is happening; it is quiescent when one's attention is focused on a particular task. The relation between the DMN and executive attention is said to be "antithetical," "anti-correlated," or "competitive." Such descriptors imply that the two systems are rivals, but that would be a dumb way for brain to be. The relationship between the dorsal attention network and the DMN is not master–slave, but reciprocal, a descriptor that conveys mutuality.

It is true that action towards a particular goal deactivates the default mode network, but as soon as the goal is achieved, or the action is set aside, it becomes active again; at which point, it updates one's autobiography in the appropriate way. Think of a High School senior preparing her college application. *There, I am finished with my common app, except for one thing. I still have to write an essay.* At some point, the girl will return to the essay; during the interval, her DMN is culling and reorganizing data about her autobiographical self, occasionally sending an idea to her attentional eye, even when she is asleep. Finally, she returns to the essay and, as she writes, her attention is directed. Then she pauses, and reflects.

I was born in a dirty suburb outside of Zhenjiang, China and spent the first year of my life in an orphanage funded by the Chinese government. On August 4, 1997, the day after my first birthday, I was adopted by a man and a woman from North Carolina. I can now proudly call these people my parents. I have grown up an American, but I was born in a country on the other side of the world. Throughout my childhood, I have always wondered where I came from. During the summer of 2012, I got the opportunity to find out...

The dorsal attention network is also called the *top-down control network*. There are individuals whose lives are spent in these remote, lateral reaches of the hemispheres; the Aspergerites, for example, and a good number of OCs, too. Most of us, however, spend our days *hovering* between moments of directed attention and reflective resting states. As a young lady writes her college essay, her mind moves back and forth between two mental systems, the DAN and the default mode.

The dorsal attention network is a component of the analytical brain, and the default mode network is coterminous with the social/ emotional brain. The two systems have a reciprocal arrangement; it might be competitive, anti-correlated or antithetical, but that depends on how OC one's world-view is. But mutual is better. Hovering between a state of personal reflection and directed attention is not only what we do but also why.

Hovering

I'm not being a mysterian. Something lies between the controller and the default and it does hover. What is it?

This question occurred to Nathan Spreng and a group of psychologists at Harvard who had probably just met with their retirement adviser. They wondered which network is active when one is planning for one's personal future, an activity that entails both inner-focused reflection (the default mode network) and goal-directed cognition (the dorsal attention network). Having had as little luck with their retirement fund as I have—or you, I bet—they wanted to resolve the problem.

They conducted a series of experiments involving, naturally, a scanning machine and a number of marginally willing undergraduates. They administered tests designed to engage their subjects' central executives and an individualized psychological test that could measure their personal goals. The elements of that test were simple action steps like *studying hard*, *getting married*, *doing drugs* and *dropping out of school*. The test was to assemble items that would allow them to achieve their goals and to subtract items that were potential obstacles. The test measured their anticipated autobiography—that is, their default mode.

As expected, imagining personal future events engaged the

subjects' default network. Tests of executive function engaged their dorsal attention network. However, both tests engaged yet another network, the **frontoparietal control network**. It coupled its activity with the default network during autobiographical planning and with the dorsal attention network during an EF task (Spreng *et al.*, 2010).

Now there is a third controller that lies between the dorsal attention network and the default mode network, a frontoparietal control network, and it facilitates the interplay between the two. When the DAN is active, it is active, too. It is also active when the DMN is active. This in-between network occupies a vast expanse of cerebral cortex, extending from the PFC to the parietal lobe, more or less in parallel with the DAN and the DMN and right in between. One of its components is our friend the cingulum. The network *hovers* between the DAN and the DMN. It is a mental system that facilitates crosstalk and reciprocity. A girl writing her college essay is hovering in that intermediate network, deactivating her DAN as she dips into her autobiographical self for a new, meaningful idea, and then activating it back up again as she writes. All the time, the frontoparietal network is facilitating the exchange.

* * *

As we look for what controls brain, we discover yet another convergence zone that integrates the activity of two or more networks and that keeps the traffic moving smoothly, as my Uncle Delmore used to do on Bath Avenue. Functionally, it resembles the A/P loop, and also the OC loop we shall visit in Chapter 16. It reminds us of Charles Spencer Peirce, who noted that "Perceptions can't be understood independent of how we observe and understand them. Even without realizing it, we make sense of what we have observed" (Peirce, 1931).

What controls brain is the reciprocity among multiple processors, or minds or little brains inside the brain. The so-called controllers in the cerebral cortex are engaged in continual crosstalk with other mental systems, especially the default network—that is, the social/emotional brain. They are parallel: cognitive control in the dorsal surfaces of the cortex and social/self-awareness on the medial surface. Nor does the analytical mind properly regard the social/emotional mind as an atavistic throwback; although some of the Aspergerites do, and many OCs. Rather, it recognizes its components as thoroughly up to date. We update them all the time.

The default mode enlivens the motivational processes of the neocortex. The social and emotional life of an individual resides in the prefrontal cortex. It discharges gently during one's resting state, harmonizing multiple voices into a single theme: *This is who I am and why I am doing whatever dull, boring task I happen to be engaged in at the moment.* The why of it usually has something to do with one's closest and most intimate friends. Maybe they are the ones you will be going home to this evening, or maybe they are the emanations of close and intimate friends long gone. Whichever it is, "We live in a social arena; virtually all of our actions are directed toward or are responses to others" (Batson, 1990).

* * *

OC illustrates that the analytical mind is exceptional. The OC has so much task-positive activity to keep up with. There is so much directed attention to direct. The world is an executive task, with rules that change without warning, overlearned behaviors that have to be unlearned, and ever more information that has to be held in an active, quickly retrievable state and shielded from distraction. One sympathizes with a fellow who is only vexed during his occasional visits to the Play of Musement. OCs who are obsessed with control are too impatient even to *hover*. Their minds, wandering into the peaceful reflections of their personal mind, only get distracted. *By gad, there is something wrong here,* they say to themselves. *I must be ADD.*

Another tribe of OCs have a resting state that is suffused with anxiety. When their minds fall into what ought to be a state of quiet reflection, it seems unstable, as if the floor were moving. Hovering only seems risky. Better to be task-positive. One can always count.

Or take a shower, check the stove-top, or go for a nice long ride on one's titanium bicycle.

What normally controls one's brain is pretty much what controls a person; something outside of itself, reflected and contained in the social/emotional brain. The brain's controllers, like yours and mine, have names and faces. They are our long line of intimates. They are present in the resting state of the social/emotional brain. Their voices continue to resonate there long after they are gone. As one's mind wanders for a moment away from directed tasks, one's efforts are nourished by the memories of their names and faces, of what they said and what they would likely say if they were in the room with us now. Their words and gestures transcend the flow of time and give meaning to who we are, what we are doing and why.

The social arena is as close to a controller as any of us is likely to have. Control, however, prefers order, and order appeals only to the dorsal side of one's psychology. The other side, its default mode, is more attracted to harmony, balance and happiness. The social arena gives us more negative feedback than we like, usually, but a lot of feed-forward control, which most of us need. The social arena has redundancy. Even those devastated by grief find backup components to restore balance in their lives.

13
Controlling Children

I'm sure you knew all about controlling men before you read the previous chapters. You may not know that there are controlling *children*, too.

Colin

Kathy, an intelligent and well-educated woman, brought her son for a consultation. He had been having outbursts of rage for several years and they were getting worse.

The boy was Colin, he was ten years old, healthy and quite bright. He was a handsome child, dressed more neatly than most ten-year-old boys, and his short, fair hair was done back with gel. He was sitting next to his mother in the examining-room, engrossed in a game on her mobile.

Kathy had taken Colin to a lot of different doctors, but he was as surly as ever when someone annoyed him, which happened most of the time. *People are fools*, he was probably thinking, *and this one is likely a bigger fool than the rest of them.* How did I know? Having observed children and their ways for longer than I care to disclose, one knows. He wasn't playing the game in a placid, contented way, as Jack did, but in a belligerent way. When a child is engrossed, his or her emanations say, *Don't bother me, please* or *Don't bother me, you moron.*

Kathy had taken her son to several therapists and she had had him tested several times. One of the psychologists thought he might be autistic. "Not really autistic, you know, but 'on the spectrum.'" She and her husband had taken him to a pediatric neurologist who did the obligate MRI and an EEG. He wasn't having seizures—the child, that is, not the neurologist—but "Why not try an anticonvulsant for his rage attacks? He may have a temporal lobe syndrome. His amygdala, you know." So the boy was on Tegretol® for a while. His anger attacks got worse. "Some seizures actually get worse on Tegretol®," said the neurologist, so he tried Keppra®, another anticonvulsant. On that particular drug, the child started to hallucinate and was admitted to a psychiatric hospital.

There, a psychiatrist told Kathy and her husband that the boy was "bipolar." He prescribed Abilify® and Seroquel XR®. The two drugs cost $1400 per month, but at least the boy didn't have so many rage attacks. At the cost of sleeping all the time, and he gained 15 pounds in four weeks.

Kathy had already seen a pediatrician, who treated him for ADD, to no particular effect; then another pediatrician, who was an expert in ADD. Kathy had taken her son to several psychologists, an occupational therapist and a couple of other psychiatrists. One psychiatrist recommended BuSpar® for his anxiety and another, Prozac® for his mood disorder.

One of Kathy's friends told her she needed to take her son to a *neuropsychiatrist*. Nothing had worked very well, of course. So why not a neuropsychiatrist? They are the ones, after all, who understand brain *and* behavior.

I'm not sure that the *neuro-* prefix on one's shingle by itself confers deep understanding of brain *or* behavior. In my career I have met neuro-chiropractors, neuro-optometrists and at least one neuro-lawyer. If I live long enough, I'll probably meet a neuro-neurologist. But I did know what the matter was with Colin.

Colin was ten years old, but had already consumed more mental health services than most of us do in a lifetime. That's because he was impulsive, unpredictable, willful and stubborn. He was prone to smacking another kid, usually his little brother, in response to any perceived offense, which usually was just being there. He was also prone to explosions of anger, banging doors and running around the house screaming and throwing things. The tantrums might go on for an hour. Afterwards, it was as if nothing had happened.

He was a healthy child and had a keen mind. He didn't have any developmental problems, although when he was a baby he was colicky and then he was resistant to new foods his mother tried to introduce. He never liked to take naps. At Day Care, he was bossy with other kids and they didn't like to play with him, but he didn't mind as long as he got the toy he wanted to play with. That was usually a toy that some other kid was playing with. Even when he was very young, he was good company when it was just him and one of his parents doing something that he liked to do, but he hated to be denied. Once, Kathy and her husband had to rush home when the babysitter called. Colin told his mother he was going to spray her eyes with acid. He was seven years old at the time.

* * *

The evaluations we do in the Neuropsychiatry Clinics are a bit different from most other psychiatrists and neurologists. While Kathy and I were talking, Colin was ignoring us furiously, playing his i-game and listening to every word we said. While we talked, I sent him out to take some of our computer tests—you can give them to your own child, or your husband, at www.atonc.com. The tests showed that he was a smart kid, but if he found a test boring he would give up on it. This pattern is presumably what led his teachers to conclude that he was ADD. On tests that he liked, though, he did well above average.

Then the examination, which is like a neurological exam, but there's plenty of room for talking and interacting in all manner of interesting ways. He complied with the exam. It helps if the physician is six feet tall and weighs thirteen stone. But you have to keep a step ahead of such children if you want to keep them engaged. Joking doesn't help, because they are usually humorless, but asking inane questions—"How many fingers do you have on your right hand?"—keeps them off balance for a while, especially if you ask the question while they are trying to oppose their thumb to each finger in rapid succession or walk a straight line with the heel of one foot touching the toe of another. Colin enjoyed being the center of attention for five minutes, and then he was back to Kathy's iPhone.

I asked Kathy: "Is anybody in the family a perfectionist? Which of you, you or your husband, tends to be on the controlling side?" Colin was a controlling child, but neither his mother nor his father were that way. His paternal grandfather, however, was a retired colonel and a rigid, controlling man. Kathy hated to visit, not because her father-in-law behaved incorrectly but because of how cowed and demoralized her mother-in-law was. She was a nervous, timid woman, kind to Kathy and the children, but always with an eye on her husband as if she expected him to erupt at any moment. Which he used to do a lot, but not so often anymore because his wife knew how to accommodate his aggravations. Their son hardly went to visit his parents, although he was their only child. He was an IT guy, somewhat shy, and he preferred to stay away from everybody. He took Ritalin® for his ADD.

Kathy herself was kind, sweet, open and natural, in spite of the persecutions she endured. She was on just the right dose of Zoloft® for her depression, and she wasn't nearly so depressed as her mother, who had had at least one course of ECT (electroconvulsive therapy), or her sister, who had had an eating disorder when she was young. Kathy didn't know much about her father, who was a degraded alcoholic from a long line of alcoholics. When I asked, "Does Colin eat one thing at a time?," she said he didn't; "But when I was young, I used to do that. I never liked it if my food touched, either."

Randy was their younger son. He liked to be in his room playing by himself. He avoided his brother as much as he could. Kathy said, "Randy thinks his brother is a monster."

* * *

There, on an average day in our Clinic and in just one family, were several variants of OC. Colin had a special one. There had never been a child like Colin in the family, although one of Kathy's nephews was autistic. Colin was unique, just as all of us are unique, but he carried the signature of his family's OC genotype.

"He seems to have gotten it from both sides," I said, and Kathy knew what I was talking about. *What is the matter with the child?* was an easy question to answer. Colin had obsessive-compulsive traits and a controlling disposition. His temperamental behavior arose in that context. His attention deficit was, in fact, impatience. He couldn't stand to be bored, and what bored him was anything he didn't want to do.

What is the diagnosis? sounds like the same question, but it isn't. It's problematic to assign a psychiatric diagnosis to a ten-year-old, a diagnosis that will stick to his name in cyberspace forever and probably deprive him of the opportunity ever to buy insurance or join the Navy Seals. One prefers not to hang a grown-up diagnosis on a child when one knows that emotional and behavioral problems in childhood are not very good predictors of mental disorders in adult life. Colin did carry an OC genotype, so "What will he be like in ten years?" His mother asked me that. I don't know the answer. It's tempting to predict that Colin will be a controlling, wrathful OC man, but that isn't the way it happens. Colin inherited a strong dose of OC traits, but there are many OC outcomes.

I have seen too many children like Colin over the years. I've seen them again after they've grown up, and I've even met their issue. "You know me, Dr. Gualtieri. I saw you when I was seventeen. I was Tiffany Roberts. Now I'm Tiffany Jones. This is Hannah and I brought her to see you, too." Such events are flattering—as long as I forget the deterioration thirty years have wrought on my frame, if not my mind—but they aren't predictive. Hannah probably has some of Tiffany's traits, but her problems will be different.

* * *

The problem that doctors have with children like Colin is that they understand OCD to be a discrete diagnosis and "He doesn't meet the diagnostic criteria." Child psychiatrists have been trained to think in terms of categories, and the categories are defined in terms of a patient's overt symptoms. These, in turn, are based on what the patient *says* his symptoms are, or what his parents say, or his teachers, his guardians or the people who work at his group home. It's important, of course, to glean such information, but that's not all there is to a medical examination, even in psychiatry. In the fifteen minutes doctors have in which to take a history and examine a new patient, it's the best they can do, but the diagnosis will be superficial if not wrongheaded.

So, if a child is said to have difficulty paying attention in school he must have Attention Deficit Disorder. It doesn't register that he is inattentive at school because he is intolerant of fools (e.g., the teacher) and easily bored (the curriculum). If a child is oppositional and defiant, he has Oppositional-Defiant Disorder. That he is disrespectful and obnoxious because he is controlling doesn't register on the diagnostic criteria. If a child is prone to explosions of rage he has Mood Dysregulation Disorder, and if his moods are subject to ups and downs he is bipolar. And so on. Too often, psychiatrists fail to appreciate the salience of an underlying trait even though the trait is what is behind the overt symptoms. Traits are more likely to speak to the origins of the problem than overt symptoms are. The doctors who saw Colin didn't understand how different kinds of problems can be the consequence of OC traits.

I see four or five new patients in the Clinic every day, but we aren't under the thumb of corporate medicine, so we can spend as much time with a new patient as the circumstances require. Children like Colin aren't all that common—only about one a week—but children and adults with OC traits, well, we see a new one every day. Some days more than one, and I say to myself, *OMG—I must have OC on the brain.*

The problem with children

My original credentials were in Child Psychiatry. It's customary for pediatric specialists to hand off their patients at age 18, but I didn't want to lose my autistic and intellectually disabled patients just because they were at the age to vote, buy porn and smoke cigarettes. Besides, my purpose in studying children was to learn the origins of personality and mental illness, or at least their adumbrations. How to do that, if one didn't hang around long enough to see what was being adumbrated? We packed up our little clinic and set up on our own. Having done so, we have had the unusual opportunity to treat patients across the span of ages, which has conferred depth and breadth to my superficial observations. They are deep and broad superficial observations. I have been rewarded with deep insights. For example, *Children are more annoying and intrusive when they are grown than when they are small.*

When a prominent child psychiatrist, Judy Rapoport, published a book about OCD in children in 1991, it caused a stir (Rapoport, 1991). Since then, studies have shown that OCD is more prevalent among children and adolescents (2–4 percent) than adults (1–3 percent). Parents and teachers have known for a long time that children are prone to "normal" obsessions and compulsions. Little children insist on the same bedtime book every night, and bedtime rituals are universal. Little kids play the same ritualized games endlessly. Children watch the same show over and over again, and adolescents listen to the same awful music. Children are prone to OC behaviors, like eating rituals, lining up their toys, obsessive fears and strange preoccupations, and motor and phonic tics; and also OC traits, as in Colin, the controlling child. Children are suggestible, too. You may rant and harangue a child to do this or that but to no effect. Let her see one other child wearing a top in just a certain way, however, and her dressing habits will change overnight.

Many children are exquisitely sensitive to the feel of certain fabrics or to certain smells or sounds. "The Princess and the Pea" isn't a fairy tale. My Nora has such an exquisite sense of smell it amounts to a disease. When she rides in my car she wraps her face with a bandana and puts on dark glasses (?) so she doesn't have to smell the leather seats.

Children are ardent collectors. They hoard the oddest stuff in their rooms and hate to throw things out. I had three whose junk piles became so formidable that I used to arrive in their room with one of those enormous black plastic bags one uses for garden refuse. As the little darlings slept away on Saturday morning, I would announce that he (she) could sleep in while I just neatened up. It was a good way to get them out of bed.

Children become addicted to videogames and social media. They also develop phobias, which are nasty little obsessions. The monster in the closet is a childhood obsession that made millions for Disney, as if he needed it.

Children are also prone to behaviors that fall into the OC "spectrum." These are symptoms of serious neuropsychiatric conditions in adults but are utterly harmless in a seven-year-old. Some are picky eaters and hate to try anything new. There are more than a few children who will eat nothing but chicken tenders and chips. Self-injurious behaviors, like picking at one's cuticles or at scabs or warts, are also common in children. The bad habit of making superficial cuts on one's forearms is not uncommon in teenage girls, but it has little relation, if any, to the serious self-destructive behaviors of mentally ill adults. Children, especially boys, are given to motor tics, repetitive, jerky movements or phonic tics, like snorts, sniffs or shouts. Tics occur in 10–20 percent of normal children and a good number of these tics are so severe that they require treatment. Hardly any of my young patients go on to develop Tourette's syndrome (TS), which is comparatively rare.

Even children with OCD or Tourette's syndrome diagnosed by

the standard criteria are not like the OCD and TS adult patients we occasionally see. The childhood conditions are mild and easily treated with conventional medications or therapies, and they usually don't persist into adult life. Severe, disabling cases of OCD and TS usually begin in late adolescence. The kids I've seen with OCD or TS have mostly grown up to be OCs. Usually, good ones.

The theory is that OC and TS symptoms are more common in children compared to adults, because as the immature cortex matures it doesn't control the lower orders very well. As one grows up, one learns to control certain traits and behaviors, or at least to hide them better. The theory would be half true if OC behaviors were less common in adults, but the data indicate they're not. It also fails because post-adolescent brain maturation is not confined to the neocortex. Or rather, it is—but only if one uses myelination as the index of brain development. **Myelin** is the insulative sheath that surrounds the axons and dendrites of neurons and helps then conduct signals faster. The prefrontal cortex isn't completely myelinated until about age 50, while the subcortex is completely myelinated by the time one is an adolescent. Myelination, however, is only one measure of maturation. There are others, among them the pruning away of disused neurons, the birth and development of new ones, the growth of spines on dendrites, and the reinforcement of neural networks in the service of efficient processing. These are processes that continue throughout life, at least until one comes down with a neurodegenerative disease. I don't think that brain is fully mature until age 50 or so, by which time, of course, the whole of the rest of one's body is falling apart.

Children and adolescents tend to be less inhibited in their actions and emotional expressions, which may be a function of brain maturation in general, or it may just speak to the fact that they spend their lives among familiars, and all of us are less inhibited among our intimates. Their OC traits are duly noted by concerned parents and busybody teachers, although they usually don't know that it's OC that they are seeing. So they truck the little darlings off to someone like me.

I tell them that OC traits and behaviors are similar in form and content to those of OCD as it exists in adult patients, but that OC is not OCD. I tell them that 30 percent of adults have at least some OC traits. Most children who are diagnosed with OCD elsewhere are only having transient explosions, like germ-phobia, that will pass in time; then they will resume their baseline OC. Many OC adults are the same way. At one time or another they will have an episode of disabling OC symptoms, sometimes just out of the blue and sometimes in reaction to an unusually stressful event. Then they will calm down and carry on like the good or bad OCs they are. In contrast, there are patients whose OCD is severe and persistent, even in the face of treatment; such patients are among the most disabled of all psychiatric patients. If you're a good OC reading this, or even a bad one, don't worry. You're not likely to fall over the cliff. OC is different from OCD.

As mentioned earlier, Colin's mother asked me, "What will he be like in ten years?" I told her I didn't know. He may become a prominent academician, a trauma surgeon or an ambitious attorney general, hopefully in some other state. He probably won't be a debased alcoholic or spend his life living under a bridge. Children with OC traits and controlling children usually get better as they grow into adolescence, and even those who are compulsive drug-users usually grow out of it. Their overt symptoms go underground for a while. The mental energy they exert pursuing idiosyncrasies or maintaining aloofness can be channeled to more useful ends. Their anxieties subside. Most of the kids are smart, they come from good families, and they learn to get what they want in more socially appropriate ways. But they will always be a bit OC.

I tell her not to worry. The most difficult time for such individuals is when they are young. It's not that they grow out of it but that they pursue their obsessions and compulsions in less disagreeable ways. I could mention Dr. Johnson, who was fastidious in many ways— he avoided cracks in the pavement—but his personal habits were slovenly. One day, a lady said to him, "Dr. Johnson, you smell." He said, "No, Madam. You smell. I stink" (Freeman, 2009). His OC traits were accompanied by motor and phonic tics and a lively, mischievous sense of humor. It's a frequent concatenation of weaknesses among the OCs. He also composed the first scholarly dictionary of the English language and did it all by himself. He didn't have a Boswell at the time to scurry about checking references. It took Dr. Johnson nine years and he illustrated his definitions with quotations from the great writers, citing the first known use of each word. The *Oxford English Dictionary* still does that. Dr. Johnson said that lexicographers were "harmless drudges." I would like to update his entry. They are good OCs.

Siblings

In our clinics, if other children come along with the patient and his or her parents, we see them all together for a while.

Hope and Ainsley

Hope and Ainsley, two sisters who visited the clinic together, had a number of traits in common. They were beautiful brown-haired little girls and quite intelligent, like their parents, both of whom had had professional educations. Hope, the younger girl, was the patient. Ainsley was along for the ride. When two siblings come together, even if only one is the patient, I ask them both to hop onto the examining table. Kids love to have their deep tendon reflexes checked. They both take the computerized tests, too. It gives them something to do while I talk to the parents.

Hope was a controlling child, like Colin, and had the same problem with losing control and getting angry. Both she and her sister had soft signs of OC. Hope had misophonia; small, innocuous sounds would drive her mad, like the sound of her sister chewing food at the table. She couldn't stand how some fabrics felt against her skin and hated to wear T-shirts that had labels. She couldn't stand T-shirts that had labels printed on, either, so her mother had to buy T-shirts *with* labels and then cut them off. Then she had to pull out the tiny threads that remained with tweezers.

Ainsley, on the other hand, never got mad. She was sweet all the time and was happy most of the time, even when her sister complained that she was chewing too loudly. She, too, was sensitive, but on an emotional plane, not a tactile one. The walls of her room were covered with pictures of cute little kittens. She loved kittens, but she was allergic, so the family didn't have pets.

They both did well at school, although Hope didn't have many friends because she was so controlling and got mad a lot. Ainsley was probably the smarter of the two but she never liked to speak up in class. When she was asked a question directly she wouldn't say anything. When she had to make a presentation her charts were beautiful, but all she could do was face the chart, away from the class, and read it. By mid-September her teachers would usually realize what her phobia was about and never called on her to present again. Her written work was perfect and she always made the highest grades.

Hope was ten and Ainsley was eight. Their forebears included the usual suspects; suffice it to say that H and A got it from both sides. Their Aunt Martha was especially interesting. She had also been very shy as a girl and lived a quiet, unassuming life alone with her cats. She had been a brilliant student but went to community college and took most of her courses online. She worked as a pharmacy tech on the late shift.

On several occasions so far we have met social anxiety or SA, which relates to social anxiety *disorder* as OC relates to OCD. As it happens, the two are very close; most people with SA traits have OC traits and/or behaviors, and many OCs have SA traits. Both conditions have a connection to autism. Patients with one of those problems usually have relatives who have one of the others.

Asperger's syndrome is a subclinical form of autism and many OCs and SAs are misdiagnosed as Aspergerites or, worse, "on the autism spectrum." As we move along, we shall learn why the three conditions are so similar. One explanation is the tug of the familiar. On the level of the organism, there is something called **homeostasis**, a biological process that maintains physiological functions within circumscribed limits. On the level of psychology, one can call it **equanimity**, or balance. It conveys order to one's existence and the sense that one is in control. An SA preserves balance through avoidance, but his or her avoidance can take many unusual and even paradoxical forms. The OC, also, tries to maintain his or her balance in unusual and paradoxical ways, sometimes by compulsive, repetitive behaviors, sometimes by trying to be in control. In both, life is better as long as it is ordered just so.

14
The Art of Detection

In 1882, a short novel was published by the Brazilian writer Joachim Machado de Assis, called *The Psychiatrist*. The psychiatrist was Bacamarte, a man of science and one of the most prominent physicians in Europe. In spite of the entreaties of the King himself, Bacamarte returned to his home town in Brazil, Itaguaí. There he resolved to devote himself to the study of mental disease.

Bacamarte, with the soul of a true man of science, was exact in every corner of his life. He chose Evarista to be his wife; she was homely, but he determined, scientifically, that she would be fit to bear his children. His expectations were disappointed because they never had children. Chastened, he doubled his efforts on the study of insanity.

In Itaguaí, he opened an asylum, the Green House, for people who were insane. An asylum of this sort represented all that was modern and good in medical science, and Bacamarte had studied with the masters in Coimbre and Padua. His assiduity at discovering mental conditions quickly populated the asylum until it held the larger part of the population of the town, including his wife, Dona Evarista, the priest, Father Lopes, and his best friend, the pharmacist, Soares.

Till now, madness has been thought a small island in an ocean of sanity. I am beginning to suspect that it is not an island at all but a continent.[1]

Before long, civil disorder broke out in the town. The uprising was led by the town barber, Porfirio, who said: "I know nothing about science, but if so many men whom we considered sane are locked up as madmen, how do we know that the real madman is not the psychiatrist himself?"

> ...this led people to say that the psychiatrist's concept of madness included practically everybody.

Bacamarte concluded that if the majority of people seemed to be mentally ill, then he ought to revise his method. It must be the remaining citizens of Itaguaí, the ones who seemed to be balanced, temperate and lucid, who were the insane.

> The psychiatrist informed the Council, first, that he had checked the statistics and had found that four-fifths of the population of Itaguai were in the Green House; second, that this disproportionately large number of patients had led him to reexamine his fundamental theory of mental illness, a theory that classified as sick all people who were mentally unbalanced; third, that as a consequence of the reexamination in the light of the statistics, he had concluded not only that his theory was unsound but also that the exactly contrary doctrine was true— that is, that normality lay in a lack of equilibrium and that the abnormal, the really sick, were the well balanced, the thoroughly rational...

To wide celebration, he released all the inmates of the Green House, and resolved to commit the others. Yet, applying his new criterion,

---

1   Joachim Machado de Assis, *The Psychiatrist and Other Stories*, English edition, 1963. The quotes that follow are also from this edition.

he couldn't find anyone suitably rational and well-balanced to commit and study. He decided there was only one man in Itaguaí who was well-balanced and perfectly rational.

> He entered the Green House, shut the door behind him, and set about the business of curing himself. The chroniclers state, however, that he died seventeen months later, as insane as ever.

* * *

Think of me as the Bacamarte of OC; I see it everywhere. In the clinics where I work, we have a new one come to visit every day. They come in because they think they are ADD, or because they're depressed, or they think their bodies are infected by yeast or toxic mold. "Ever since I had my brain injury, Dr. Gualtieri, I haven't been the same." The brain injury in question was a bump on the head three years ago.

The clinics are busy places, and we see many new patients every day. OC traits are so common among them, though, I've stopped asking after them. *It must be the others who are really insane.* Today, for example, there was a fellow who worked as a political consultant; he ran campaigns for senatorial and gubernatorial candidates all over the country. He was as ADD as the day is long, but he thrived in the brouhaha of campaigning, keeping up with ten things at once, meeting the inexorable deadlines and working in a war-room with five TVs, each tuned to a different station. He had been ADD when he was in school; he wasn't one of those professorial types who complains "But I always had to work harder than everybody else" when I point out that a High School GPA of 4.6 is not typical of an ADD kid. We tested him, and his cognitive profile was typically ADD.

His only problem was a desire for a Master's degree, which he felt would bolster his credentials and convince more aspiring Senators and Governors to contract his services. In contrast to his day job, getting a Master's was dull, boring work, and he just couldn't get it done. Likely, with a small dose of Ritalin® or Adderall® he would find the Master's requirements, if not less dull or boring, at least more do-able. In our clinics, we give prospective ADD patients a "test dose" of Ritalin® or Adderall® to see how the drug might change their cognitive profile. We gave him a test dose, and his cognitive profile normalized.

It was all pretty straightforward and I was giving him directions about how to compare a couple of different medications over the next month. Then he laid it on me:

> I want to ask you something. When I was young I used to do this. If there was something wrong in my room, something out of place, I would go to school with the feeling that it was going to be a bad day and something awful was going to happen. It still happens. I was at a meeting and there was a wrapper on the floor. It was right under one of the interns and I couldn't just reach down under her and pick it up. But the whole meeting I couldn't get it out of my mind. I couldn't concentrate on what was going on. The wrapper just stayed with me the whole time.

I looked at the student who was there with us and she looked at me. We both rolled our eyes. She knew what to say:

> About half of the patients who come to clinics for ADD are, in fact, a bit OC. Sometimes we treat their ADD with a stimulant and their ADD gets better. Sometimes we treat their OC with Zoloft® or Lexapro® and their ADD gets better. At one time or another, you will get a chance to try both. It doesn't matter where we start but how well we communicate and how well we can evaluate how the drugs affect you, objectively.

I couldn't have said it better.

* * *

Yes, I do see OC everywhere, but I don't make a fuss about it. I just drink it all in and try to make sense of it later. *What does it all mean?* I run home, kiss F and pet the dog, and look for the girls.

"How was school?" "Fine." "Did you learn anything?… Did anything interesting happen today?" (Scowl.) It is the stupid-question-stupid-man-scowl that every girl acquires at around the age of six and that I have been dealing with since before I was six. I learned by age fifteen that it meant that I am dismissed. This day it is relief from domestic obligations. An ounce of shag, sanctuary in the library, and back to this stupid book. *What does it all mean?*

I am haunted by Bacamarte. I think, *A theory that accounts for everything explains nothing.* But then I think of Sherlock Holmes, and am encouraged to forge ahead. He said, "One's ideas must be as broad as Nature if they are to interpret Nature."[2]

Today I had a sudden revelation that resolved the dilemma without having to cultivate an idea as broad as Nature. It was a normal day in the clinic and there was a variety of new patients to share with the students. Here is A, and he has social anxiety disorder. B had a bad concussion after a dog ran into his car, head on!—when does a dog ever do that?—and his car rolled several times down the embankment. And C, the poor fellow, who left school for a while, worked in a bar and started doing drugs. D brought her husband back to see us after a week; he was getting better from his conversion disorder, which began when he woke up in the morning and discovered he couldn't talk.

Ah, the variety of the flowers that bloom in the garden, I thought. But before I could escape, every one of them, even D, the patient's wife, wanted to tell me about a symptom they had. "You know, Doc, I always thought I was a little OCD." A liked to count to 100. B would chew his food ten times on the left and ten times on the right. C used a hand sanitizer after he touched a doorknob or a button on the elevator. D was convinced she had narcolepsy. I hadn't got out soon enough, I told the student.

Then my sudden revelation. An epiphany, a sudden burst of insight. It was *me*!

I told the student that what was wrong was this: I was dead,

---

2   Arthur Conan Doyle, *A Study in Scarlet.*

and my Purgatory was to work in a clinic where *every patient* was OC. It was my punishment for intellectual presumption, or maybe for having been, in my youth, a controlling, wrathful man, before my conversion, my semi-annual weekends at drumming circle and massive doses of antidepressant and mood-stabilizing drugs. I shared my insight with the student, then with my wife and the girls, but none were impressed. If I were, in fact, in Purgatory, where were they? So I resolved to re-examine the theory. An ounce of shag, sanctuary in the library, and back to this stupid book. Maybe *this* is Purgatory.

Fuzzy theories

Think of these idle thoughts as my Play of Musement. Our perceptions can't be understood as independent of how we observe and understand them; we try to make sense of what we observe. However, they illustrate a point: reason defers to how we observe things, how we perceive and understand them. Western Man—that is, you and I—tends to understand things in a way that Aristotle invented. It is *the law of the excluded middle*; everything is either A or not-A, on or off, zero or one. A logical operation is correct or not. A fish belongs to the kingdom *Animalia*, or not. OC is in the Diagnostic Manual or it isn't. Binary logic is a force that guides the most powerful computing devices, but it's been around longer than that.

The dolphin is a fish. No, it's not, it's a mammal. It may be a mammal, but it looks like a fish and it lives in the sea, where hardly any other mammals do. You go to an aquarium to see dolphins, or to the beach, not to a zoo. "Such imprecisely defined 'classes' play an important role in human thinking, particularly in the domains of pattern recognition, communication of information, and abstraction" (Zadeh, 1965).

The law of the excluded middle is not wholly successful when called upon to address ideas as broad as Nature. Not everything is either A or not-A. Some categories are *fuzzy*. If not dolphins, then how about the green sea slug, a mollusk that lives in tidal marshes on the East coast of North America. The small green mollusks are hermaphrodites, but that's not nearly so fuzzy as their habit of generating energy directly from the sun by means of photosynthesis. They are green because they are laden with chloroplasts, which they obtain from the algae they eat. The chloroplasts survive and function in the green sea slug as if they were in a plant, because the slug has incorporated algal DNA into its chromosomes. So, is the slug an animal or a plant or both? You could say that it is an animal with some of the characteristics of a plant, but that's pretty fuzzy. It also happens to be true of some of my nearest relations.

Here is a better way to understand the green sea slug. It is an organism that resides 80 percent in the set of animals and 20 percent in the set of plants. The sets, or categories, of "plant" and "animal" are both fuzzy. So also are the categories with which we try to understand complex systems and behavioral events. The behavior of complex systems is better organized by fuzzy logic.

Fuzzy logic was invented by an Azerbaijani-American electrical engineer with a penchant for mathematics, Lofti Zadeh. His penchant was applying mathematical principles to the study of biological systems and also to artificial intelligence. He appreciated that complex systems may be a bit A and a bit not-A. "Such objects as starfish, bacteria, etc. have an ambiguous status with respect to the class of animals." He might have mentioned dolphins, who are 90 percent in the set of mammals but 10 percent in the set of fish.

> "The class of beautiful women," or "the class of tall men," do not constitute classes or sets in the usual mathematical sense of these terms. Yet, the fact remains that such imprecisely defined "classes" play an important role in human thinking, particularly in the domains of pattern recognition, communication of information, and abstraction. (Zadeh, 1965)

Fuzzy set theory allows something to be partly a member of one set and partly a member of another. A **fuzzy set** is a class "with a continuum of grades of membership." The term "fuzzy" refers to the fact that the logic involved can deal with concepts that cannot be expressed as "true" or "false" but rather as "partially true." It is not simply a theoretical exercise. Applications of fuzzy set theory allow computers to run complex systems (like climate-control systems in large buildings or mass transportation networks) with a high degree of precision.

Zadeh's rule for dealing with complexity was to *simplify*. Not all available information needs to be used and a certain amount of uncertainty is accepted in order to create robust summary concepts. When a digital computer is programmed to operate by fuzzy logic, it uses an algorithm known as **centroid averaging**. The relative importance of a host of dimensional inputs is computed and translated into an intelligent action step. The process is repeated until the desired result is attained. This is precisely the way neural circuits operate, as loops incorporate data from multiple sources, iterating and reiterating by feedback from one's memory banks and new perceptions until a coherent signal emerges. Neural circuits are fuzzy sets, and the brain fields they generate are fuzzy, too. So also are one's personality and also one's mind: centroid averagers of a host of multi-dimensional inputs. They may be a bit fuzzy, but they gets things done, even when the air-conditioners are out of order or the mass transportation network is on strike.

The rules of fuzzy logic are clearly applicable to the study of the central nervous system (CNS), a system of inordinate complexity, and where structure-function interactions are obscure, to say the least. In the CNS, the idea of organization by serial and hierarchical control modules has been abandoned in favor of the idea of functional assemblies or syncytia of cells, whose aggregate behavior may vary in nature and intensity in response to a host of internal and external constraints. Cells in one assembly are associated with cells in other assemblies; under certain circumstances, they have a partial association with one behavioral action, and in other circumstances have different amounts of association with other behavioral actions. The boundaries of structures within the CNS are imprecise because they participate, to varying degrees, in many behavioral programs. Cell assemblies in the CNS are not well insulated one from another. They leak.

The neuron, too, is a centroid averager, processing input from synapses and extrasynaptic receptors, from glia and the extracellular fluid. Cell assemblies are centroid averagers, processing input from other cell assemblies with which they are associated in different ways. Complex functional systems compute dimensional inputs from multiple sources, and the organism itself is the final or ultimate centroid averager.

OC is a fuzzy set

OC is a fuzzy set. The method of assigning membership to the set is fuzzy, too. Our method, as per Lofti Zadeh, has been to *simplify*. Not all of the available information is used and a certain amount of ambiguity must be accepted in order to create robust summary concepts. Thus advised, your author simplifies the study of brain by studying people who *are much more naive and simple-hearted than we generally assume*.

I said earlier that you might want to test your boyfriend for OCD. Perhaps you have, with the Y-BOCS. That's a clinical rating scale, though. It will give you only the gross symptoms that find their way into the *Daily Mail*, and if he has them, you probably know it already. Clinical scales, however, ask about problems. "Do you have a problem with counting?" "No, I don't," your friend responds. "I do it all the time." Q: "Do you have a problem with drugs?" A: "No, not at all. I can get them anytime I want."

If your loved one is OCD, you probably know it already. What you are looking for are the soft signs that typify OC. Ask him:

"Are you a picky eater?"
"Do you eat one thing at a time?"
"Does it bother you if your food touches?"
"Does it bother you if someone touches your food?"

"Or drinks from your glass?"

"Do you keep food in your room?"

"Is it hard to throw things out?"

"Sometimes, do you throw *everything* out?"

"Do you sort things with the labels right-side up, facing out?"

"Do you neaten your desk before you begin to work?"

"Do you have to do things in special ways?"

"What is your favorite number?"

"Do you like to count?"

"How many stairs are there to the upstairs in your house?"

"Do you flush with your foot?"

"Do you open the rest-room door with your elbows?"

You can devise any number of simple questions like these, but the answers don't really matter, because the questions usually stimulate an OC to say something like, "No, but I used to" or "No, but I do this..." Then he will tell you that he sprays Lysol on the bottom of his shoes before he walks into the house or surreptitiously uses hand sanitizer after he shakes hands with someone. You can also ask questions about first-degree relatives:

"Is anyone in your family a perfectionist?"

"Is anyone in your family controlling?"

Don't forget to ask about shyness, because SA and OC are closely related:

"Is anyone in your family very shy?"

"Is anyone in the family a hermit?"

"Does anyone in your family still live with his mother?"

"Is anyone in your family a *writer*?"

The point of such exercises is not to generate answers and count them up. It is to get the person talking. People, I have observed, will elaborate on just about any question you ask, as long as it's not creepy, if you (1) seem sincerely interested, (2) seem non-judgmental, and (3) have the kind of face people want to talk to. I must have that kind of face, because strangers tell me anything, even in the checkout line at the supermarket. It used to happen to my mother, too. It's not a face that resembles a basset hound physically, but it exudes the same languid curiosity and an *I-know-I've-been-through-it-too* disposition. You may have to encourage a diffident subject by telling him your aunt had to cover the wall sockets for fear the electricity was leaking out. With a bit of encouragement and a basset-hound expression on your face, almost everyone will disclose an idiosyncrasy, an odd bit of eccentric behavior or a close relation who was certifiable. "You know what my sister used to do? She was a real psycho..."

The point of such exercises is not to establish that your target is or isn't OC. Nor does it mean that almost everyone is OC. OC is a fuzzy set with *a continuum of grades of membership*. The logic involved is a concept that can't be expressed as "true" or "false," but as "partially false" or "mostly true." Endowed with the correct physiognomy and my tricks of the trade, your domains of pattern recognition, communication of information, and abstraction will only be enhanced.

Don't think of OC as if it were a category or even a noun. The fuzzy set of nouns includes a good many adjectives that pose as nouns; so also, OC. In these pages, you may have noted that I say "the OC," as one might also say "the free" or "the brave" or "the fussy."

Detecting OC

Whether someone is OC, and to what degress he or she is a member of the OC set, can be surmised by what they tell you about themselves. They may do so by confiding a peculiarity they may have, a ritual or an odd fear, concerning for example the electricity that drips out of disused sockets or the inadvisability of drying oneself if a hair drier is not available. The skills thus acquired will allow you to make informed decisions about really important things like choosing a life partner. The problem is that bad OCs are not quite so willing to disclose their quirks or mental twists. In the case of a potential boyfriend, you may have to infer that he must have some when you tell him about your aunt. If he looks at you as if you were mad for even disclosing such a thing, then you know. *Everybody* has a crazy aunt. If he looks pained when you reach over and spear an asparagus from his plate, his membership grade in the OC set is getting higher. Such ploys don't always work. You take a swig from his Mountain Dew and he says, *You can finish it*. Maybe he's just generous.

How unlikely that is you can surmise from his emanations. Humans are very good at expressing their thoughts and feelings, and sometimes they even do it with words. We are even better at perceiving what someone *else* is thinking and feeling, and we do this not from their words but from their manner, their tone of voice, the small expressions on their face, their stance and position, the tension and electricity they emit. Thoughts and feelings in the brain are electrical fields; those fields effuse from one's body. My friend Jordana said, "When I am with him, it is electric." She didn't know the half of it.

Humans can't help but communicate. The prime emitting device is not the language center of the left hemisphere but the social/emotional brain. The receiver is there, too. It is ironic that the most important thing that any of us do—emitting and receiving signals with another person—is only occasionally verbal; and even when it *is* verbal, it is hardly ever conceptual. For example, consider how men and women converse. Women converse with other women, not with facts but with expressions of support and understanding; men converse with other men with expressions of competition and dominance. Men usually converse with women by grunting, or saying, "Oh, really?" The words that accompany such events are usually unimportant. What is conveyed are feelings. What he is really saying is, *I love you, darling, now please shut up*. The exception that proves the rule is when a woman tries to communicate with a man, using words that, for a change, carry content. She usually has to repeat herself, because he's not listening. A woman's silence, on the other hand, will usually get his attention. The relevant term is *a pregnant silence* because it induces the same feeling of unease.

A complicating element of the human condition is a disconnect between the signals we emit and receive and our ability to appreciate them in terms of language and abstract concepts. *He asked me for dinner. Does he want to feed me or eat me?* The answer to important questions like that are hard to verbalize. They arise as feelings. Were they words, they would be, "Oh, what the hell" or "He gives me the creeps." The lives of humans are no less than *governed* by intuition. We shouldn't discount it, although the OC does.

The way a good psychiatrist appreciates something like OC is not a novel exercise in anthropometrics but rather by attaching words and concepts to the intuitions generated during an interaction with a patient. There is an inherent danger in such exercises, as we know from the outlandish theories famous psychiatrists have attached to their intuitions. Nevertheless, when properly applied, the clinical method addresses subjectivity in a disinterested, objective way. We try to apply a new vocabulary to what one's natural psychology already knows.

It may not be appropriate to compare the critical judgment of gallinaceous birds and the courtship behavior of young humans to the hypothesis-testing method that physicians have cultivated over years of study and experience. It may not be *in*appropriate, but it is certainly oblique.

To illustrate: the clarity of one's mating decisions are obscured by the vapors of the heart. It is easily deceived by the protective coloration with which a suitor adorns himself. He is inclined to put forth his most attractive qualities and to suppress, insofar as he can, his disagreeable attributes. Youth has special energy that sends one's less likely attributes underground for a few years, at least until after one has bagged a mate. As a child he was controlling and temperamental, but now he is an energetic and dynamic young man; his OC genes have retreated into his chromosomes. They will re-emerge later in the form of a controlling and temperamental husband, but that's not apparent when he is in his larval, stud-muffin phase.

One may suspect that one's prospective mate is OC if he uses a hand sanitizer whenever he handles money; if he tells you there are exactly 256 black tiles on the floor of the pizzeria but only 254 white tiles, and if, when he leaves, he steps only on the black tiles; or if he's late because he had to drive back home to check the stove. If he gets angry when you're late to the restaurant, and he texts you every minute or so while you're standing in the rain on 47th and Lexington, trying to hail a taxicab at 7:30, that's not a good sign. If he makes subtle remarks to suggest you ought to change something about yourself—wear your hair differently, use a different scent, not laugh so loud, or "Don't eat off my plate, darling, please"—well, if he's like that at 25, just think what he's going to be like at 50.

Those, however, are the overt signs of OCD, the signs one sees in stories on TV. Remember, the fellow is going to be on his best behavior, at least until he's managed to mount you among his collection. Controlling people, in particular, don't advertise their OC traits; they take pains to hide them. So how do you find him out? You could try to get him drunk; alcohol is like truth serum. Controlling people get mean when they're drunk. If he gets mean, then you know. Try to eat off his plate. But then, he doesn't like to get drunk: to get drunk is to lose control. (He doesn't mind if *you* get drunk. Then he can say, "You know, you really shouldn't drink so much.")

You can check his family tree. OC traits are highly heritable, so you might learn a lot if you get to know the fellow's mother and father and brothers and sisters. I ought to have told you that earlier, when I mentioned the *why* of OC traits. This is where they come from: we inherit them, hypertrophic cingulum and all, and the unlucky ones among us get them from both sides.

In light of that, it is good to *meet the family*. Of course, by the time he gets around to inviting you to Sunday dinner at the homestead, you will probably already be emotionally embroiled and your affections will likely subdue critical judgment. But keep your head in spite of your heart and *observe*. His father is a pleasant fellow who has a squinting tic and his eyes scrunch closed every few moments as he greets you. His mother makes you take your shoes off before you enter the house. You notice that the magazines are stacked neatly, and if there is a *tchotchke* on one side of a table there is another, identical or complementary to the first, on the other side. Like a little blue Delft boy on one side and a little blue Delft girl on the other, a matador on one end of the mantle and a *toro* on the other, a candlestick here and another one there, all in perfect symmetry. There is a map-cabinet in the living room. "These are all the maps from the trips we have taken," Mother says. "Would you like to see them?" Their itineraries have been traced with highlighters, in different colors if they went by car, train, cruise-ship, ferry, bus, rickshaw, sedan-chair, and so forth. "We like to look at these maps and remember where we were." One memorable trip was to the Cincinnati zoo to see the naked mole rats. "You know, dear, it's the only zoo in the world with naked mole rats." His brother shows you his room, where he has an enormous collection of action figures, from *Star Wars* to WWE, all in their boxes and arranged chronologically. He is 40 years old and works as a security guard at night. During dinner, his sister, who is more skeletal than thin, pokes at a spear of broccoli. Hopefully, grandfather will be there as well. He is a nice old man, neat and clean, and he greets you graciously. You should note that he uses a separate fork for every different thing on his plate. During dinner, he leans to one side and releases a long, loud fart. No one seems to notice. Hardly anyone speaks during dinner. When you help afterwards in the kitchen, Mother says, "Here, I'll load the dishwasher."

On the way back to the City, your boyfriend says, disarmingly, "They're real characters, aren't they?" Your affectionate, benighted self, too polite to agree, releases a chuckle nonetheless. Your natural psychology ought to tell you: *Characters! I'll say. Out of an Alfred Hitchcock movie.*

* * *

Since my preoccupation with OCs and controlling men has become widely known, my mail-bag has been full of letters from women and gay men, asking what they should do about a wrathful, controlling husband, often but not always their own. It could be about a mate who has three graduate degrees but is so obsessed with getting things right that he never gets anything done. In spite of his superlative qualifications, he can't hold a job for longer than six weeks. If my professional opinions were as superficial as my scientific observations, I would suggest, *You need to get outta there.* My experience, however, tells me that definitive solutions are easier to suggest than to execute, especially if he is the kind of man who stands in the doorway and threatens "I will never let you leave me." Even if one does manage to escape, one still has to deal with him over the children. A controlling man can make shared custody as nightmarish as a shared bed.

The clinical method is more efficient when it prevents disease; diagnosis and treatment are expensive and time-consuming. By the same token, it is more difficult to get out of a relationship than to get into one. How, then, to detect the OC before he succeeds in inflicting himself on your life? Looking for minor physical anomalies and neurological soft signs is not the best way; they are non-specific pathology indicators. You have to learn the scientific method that physicians have cultivated over years of study and experience.

* * *

Short of a family tree that ought to be growing in front of a haunted house, how does one discover if a prospective mate, employee or elected official is OC, either a fussy man who will drive everyone crazy, an OC who checks his work so many times it never gets done, or a controlling, wrathful man? Or a man with social anxiety who is just looking for someone to latch onto? There are questionnaires one can use, but they are clumsy to apply on a speed-dating expedition, and if you ask a job applicant to take one he will only complain to the Employment Commission. You can take a blind risk or rely on the intuitions that emerge from your exquisite sensitivity to his brain fields. Social networking sites enable one to see his face, or hers, but how much can you tell from a face?

Our verbal, conceptual hemisphere is preoccupied with the overt characteristics that people have. It has been more or less obsessed, for thousands of years, with superficial differences in terms of tribe, race, sect and custom. People are fat, skinny or well-built; *that's* what makes them different. They have high IQs or low IQs, high-pitched squeaky voices or the mellifluous baritone of Charles Boyer. They count the stairs in even numbers when they go up and odd numbers when they go down. My patient today told me that she couldn't stand the sound of other people eating. "Misophonia," I said, and she said, "I know, I found it on the internet."

Usually, however, our verbal and conceptual faculties are sensitive only to superficial differences, like one's race or sect, or how loudly one chews one's food. Our native appreciation of individual differences, in the social/emotional brain, is more precious and fundamental. We must have an instinct that tells us whether we like someone or not, whether someone will be your friend or not, and whether you will pair off and share your lives. Our sensitivity to such things occurs in a part of the brain that is not well connected to the language centers of the dominant hemisphere. We express it, usually, as a feeling. *I don't know. We just clicked.* The language hemisphere doesn't "click" but the word is meaningful because it captures something more cogent than words.

* * *

All the sensitivity in the world, however, won't do much good if you don't know what you're looking for. Without a vocabulary, one is left with a vague sense of unease or curiosity. It is my purpose to elevate your sensitivities, those vague feelings that emerge, and to give them a vocabulary.

A good psychiatrist can attach words to sensitivities and feelings that are hard to define. But are they the right words? That depends on the concept behind them. If you don't know that something exists it is hard to find it, no matter how hard you look. For example, before you began reading this estimable book, you knew that OCD was something that existed. Now you know that OC is something that exists, too, and because you do, you are going to start seeing it everywhere. Before you are done, you will also have learned that obsessive self-monitoring exists, and compulsive-impulsivity and hysterical self-absorption. SA, too. You will start finding them, too, and in all the wrong places.

The signs of OC are not easily found if one doesn't look for them. They require sensitivity, not to what someone says, but to how they say it; not to what they do, but to the brain fields they exude as they do it. But it is also necessary to understand what they are, and especially what OC is. The method is oblique. It doesn't require a calibrated anthropometric instrument, but a way to turn one's sensitivities into observations and one's observations into words. And at every step an additional measure of simplification is applied. *I have abduced, Risteard, that I need to find another boyfriend.*

15

An Active Mind Is
Its Own Reward

Children are not just small adults. Adults, however, are big children. Was it Nietzsche who said, "The difference between men and boys is the price of their toys," or was it Liberace? Anyway, the nice thing about studying children is observing the gradual unfolding of personhood, from its earliest adumbrations in little babies, through the fascinating transformations of childhood and adolescence, which carry on for thirty years or so. One marvels at the unfolding of the mature adult personality, even if it is the kind of person one can't stand. I'm sorry, but thinking about Nietzsche always puts me in a droll mood. "In every man, a child is hidden that wants to play."

Certain traits are seen more clearly in children than adults, but are not unique to them. A child's high energy and low inhibition reveals flagrancies that mature women usually confine to their book group and mature men to evenings at the Legion Hut. Children, though, are so transparent that their traits can be measured, recorded, analyzed and abduced until a mental light bulb flips on. Right now, the light bulb shining inside my head warns me to clear up a misimpression. For example, that *disproportionate mental exertions* and *disproportionate expansion of the analytical mind* are the essence of OC.[1]

---

1   That *disproportionate mental exertions* and *disproportionate expansion of the analytical mind* are the essence of OC. I don't remember saying any such thing. First,

It is true that many OCs are given to mental exertions that are out of proportion to the requirements of the task at hand. Intrusive analytical minds can tangle themselves up, and usually do. Cingula may be hyperactive and insulae hypersensitive, and they respond by raining down effusions of top-down control. All that is true, but when one looks at children, something more essential becomes apparent: the origins of such anomalies, their earliest adumbrations, and how they are transformed. They arise from a child's active mind; if anything is, an *active mind* is the essence of OC. We know that some minds are more active than others, although even children who seem dull may have minds that are more active than we think.

An active mind is endowed with intelligence and sensitivity. It is a high-energy spirit that resides in neural networks that are unusually complex and well-connected. They form and un-form with celerity. They generate oscillations that are coherent and many more that are not. Whether incoherent networks are the occasion of anxiety, or fertile ground for exploration, is the difference between a good OC and an unhappy one.

The activity in active brains is not only fast, complex and far-reaching, it is also efficient. The most complex networks can be constructed with ease. They may lead nowhere; they may double back upon themselves and clog one's loops; or they may open new and even more complex networks. Such activities are usually distracting. The issue is, whether you mind.

An active mind stays active even as it eats less glucose, burns less oxygen and generates less friction and heat. But it may generate more heat and friction than is good for it; and in that way, some children grow up to be unhappy OCs or angry ones. This can happen if one part is exercised at the expense of others. It turns into a muscle-bound bully. We're not sure where that proclivity

---

I don't use the word "disproportionate"; I make a point of never uttering words that have five syllables. The disproportionate idea is borrowed from writers more lexical than me. Second, disproportionate to what, or to whom? This is not a place for derogatory comparisons. If it were, I would say that adults are disproportionate children.

comes from. Perhaps one is born with a shortage of a particular molecule, with pathways that amplify negative events, or with error messages that are pronounced with intensity. Events like that cause more friction than a sensitive mind can accommodate. Such being the case, a child develops habits, enduring patterns of behavior, to deal with them. One's enduring orientation comes to reflect the misbehavior of molecules, pathways or parts. Brains, like people, can learn bad habits. Forks in one's neural pathways—the ones in the amygdala, the basal ganglia and the thalamus—can grow accustomed to amplifying negative signals and suppressing positive ones. (Molecules can do the same.) A set-point, high or low, is probably something one is born with, but it gets higher if the life of a child is suffused with loving-kindness, or lowered by serial encounters with creeps.

From time to time, the most efficient mind will generate heat and friction. It's how 80 or 90 percent of us have an *occasional* obsession, or a compulsion. Admit it, all of you are fussy about something. Even my Uncle Bruno was fussy about noise in the house when he was trying to take a nap, which he did every day, after breakfast.

* * *

Then, there is the tribe of happy OCs. Their active minds are always thinking, perhaps a bit too much, but their thoughts don't harbor anxiety or ire. They may have hyperactive cingula, but the message conveyed is *This is not quite right. Let's check it out.* Their sensitive perceptual apparatus enlarges the beauty and mysteries of life. One assumes their parts, pathways and molecules have a positive bias. They may get stuck on Coco-Pops, but there's nothing in Creation that's not worth lingering over, at least for a little while.

In Chapter 12, I shared a helpful lesson for minimizing thermal distress to the brain. I suggested that one should hover between default mode and task-positivity. It was my pseudo-neurological way to advise balance between one's computations and their meaning. Our new tribe of OCs doesn't need such lessons, although you may think they do. *His head is in the clouds*, more than one parent has said to me. A cloud, indeed. They do enjoy something numinous, as their minds skip happily from logic to fantasy and back again. The task-positive? There are so many fascinating things to do, to read about, to ponder. The default mode network? It's a resting-place but also a special source of energy. The Play of Musement is electrifying.

Imagine an active mind, inner-reflecting, and her teacher, boss or boyfriend asks a question. It may be the occasion of momentary embarrassment, but: "I was thinking." The teacher, boss or boyfriend demurs. "No, you weren't, Dia. You were daydreaming." To an active mind, daydreams are Deep Thought. Her imaginings are absorbing as they skip to computation mode and dissipate, if not for want of meaning then for lack of any conceivable logic. Then her computations skip to default mode and dissipate, if not for want of logic then for lack of any possible meaning. Such dissipations aren't wasted. In brain, energy is created but it is never lost. What seem idle thoughts to the philistines are really the fodder of creativity. Creation happens when intuition and computations find synchrony. They can only do that after countless networks of activity have formed and un-formed, each one leaving a small residue of possibility. Finally, a coherent signal will emerge. Or maybe it only seems to be coherent. *This is not quite right. What does that mean?*

The very traits in brain that make one OC might also make one's mental life rich and endlessly rewarding. One's psychology is built of signals that are habitually augmented and others that are habitually suppressed. Our new tribe has the right habits. I have seen it most clearly in certain children: the children whom I think of as *innocents*.

Innocents

The problem of an active mind may be a problem for a child, because it takes a while to get it under control. They get into trouble for their unbridled enthusiasms. They are identified by the authorities and trundled off to a professional evaluation. The mental health professional with whom their parents consult is hardly likely to diagnose a surfeit of *joie de vivre*. No, the child is likely to be called hyperactive, or ADD. If the child seems to be a bit awkward, socially, then he or she is "on the spectrum"—that is, autistic.

ADD and the autism spectrum are the Procrustean beds of child psychiatry. We have plenty of patients in our clinics who fit into those beds quite comfortably—not too short to be stretched or too long to be amputated—but the children in this chapter are different. They are excited, exuberant and exhilarated at how rich and full the world is, how many things there are to do, to see, to learn about. They tend to be high-energy kids, which is a thoroughly good thing to be, as long as one's values are in the right place. They assume that others are as kind, joyful and sensitive as they themselves; for that reason, they take liberties that aren't always welcomed.

Gavin

Gavin was a healthy ten-year-old and quite smart. He had big eyes and a delicate face, but he was all boy, active, and he loved sports. Not that he was particularly good at any one of them, but he loved them all. It wasn't his clumsy attempts at the game that made him unpopular with the other boys. It was his exuberance, which often showed itself in eruptive remarks and endless chatter, bouncing around in the dugout and giving high-fives to kids who only thought he was weird.

He badly wanted to hang with other kids and was quick to form a club or identify a boy as his best friend. He liked other kids to play the elaborate games he concocted. Before very long, the club would disintegrate and the best friend was no longer a friend at all. So he spent a lot of time by himself or playing with his little sister. He loved to read and he had a little library in his bedroom. At intervals, he would take the books out of the case and organize them in a different way. Before he put them all back he'd get sidetracked by a book he hadn't read for a few months.

He was a very smart little boy but his grades didn't always reflect that. He did well enough in school but he didn't always listen, he made funny remarks and interrupted other children. When something came to mind, he would blurt it out. He was easily distracted, perhaps by another kid or a bird in a tree outside the window, but more often by his fertile imagination. Then he would raise his hand and ask a question that might be incisive in a college seminar but that his fourth-grade teacher thought was a bit weird. "His mind was always busy. His mind seemed to rebel at stagnation. He abhorred the dull routine of existence. He craved mental exaltation. He was in his own atmosphere with the most abstruse cryptogram or the most intricate analysis. At such times, he was the only one in the world."[2]

As you might expect, Gavin was identified as ADD and prescribed Ritalin®. He didn't do well on the medication. He was more subdued in class, but he also seemed depressed. Even without Ritalin® he was prone to moods, usually when he was treated harshly by his erstwhile friends, but the drug only made his moods worse. He was in therapy, too. Although his therapist thought he was a wonderful child, he wondered if Gavin might have a mood disorder. He had periods of exuberant excitement (Gavin, not the therapist), and quiet periods when his mother thought he was depressed. He would lie on his bed and read.

Even when he was very young, he was obviously quite bright and a true original. He would spend hours making original structures out of Legos. He was also sensitive to the feeling of the clothes that he wore. He preferred to wear really old things until they fell apart. He collected things, hated to throw anything away, and was particularly attached to the number 19. His reactions to medication were interesting. When he took Ritalin® he said, "I can't move my

---

2   Arthur Conan Doyle, *The Sign of Four*.

face. I can't say B or F." He worried about the oddest things. A dream he had was: "I'm on a remote, desolate planet, infinitely far away from the Earth, and I don't know how I'm ever going to get back."

Gavin's diagnoses had, at various times, been Asperger's syndrome, ADD and bipolar disorder. I told his parents, who were both academics and sweet, gentle people, that Gavin didn't have a diagnosis at all. He had a few OC traits. His attention would get sidetracked by a new train of thought, and every new thought seemed special to him; but he had problems focusing on what his teachers wanted him to focus on. His real problem was OC, but he was good OC with a special kind of brain. It was a very active brain and it was going to take him a while to learn to control it.

Some kids have brains that are so complicated they take a long time to develop and mature. In the meantime it's difficult for such children to control their impulses—*impetuous* is a better word. They have so much positive energy. Children like that will learn better control, but it takes a while and they will always have an exuberant nature. Gavin's enthusiasms were a function of high energy and a positive disposition. He couldn't always control them, but, hey, he was ten years old. As a result, he suffered disappointments and petty humiliations. When he did his suffering was palpable; he didn't hide his emotions. But he was resilient, and his own active, bountiful brain was capable of salving most wounds.

Before very long, usually in Middle School, kids like Gavin learn to comport themselves more carefully among their peers. They will find their tribe in High School or perhaps in college. Until they do, they will be surrounded by philistines, other children who don't appreciate the odd turns their minds take, the clumsy ways they seek approval or friendship. They get carried away and blurt out clever remarks that strike other children as bizarre.

Gavin was often the scapegoat and the victim of teasing. His father told me, "Gavin asked a little girl at camp if she would be his girlfriend. She was irate. She and the other kids in her circle spent the rest of camp throwing dirt-clods at Gavin." *Good grief*, I thought, *didn't they have counselors at that camp?* I could imagine them, too, throwing dirt-clods at the poor child. Such are the travails of someone who has evolved a bit too far for his conspecifics to appreciate.

The early lives of such exuberants are laden with humiliations like that, but they rise above them. I wanted to tell him: You are a wonderful child and I would be proud if you were my son. In fact, one of my sons was just like you and now he is the sweetest and most intelligent man I know. You are going to be discouraged, from time to time, by people who are too dull to appreciate what an intelligent person you are. You are going to rise above them.

He's only ten, though, and if I told him that he wouldn't remember it. But everything in my manner and prescriptions conveyed the opinion.

In thirty years, Gavin may be a professor of Anglo-Saxon literature or even a neuropsychiatrist. Wherever his path takes him, whatever tribe he finally joins, he will remain exquisitely sensitive to his own feelings and to all the delicate vibrations that suffuse the world of high intelligence. He will always be an OC.

Ditzy Blondes

If I were interested in eponymous fame, it wouldn't be for a new type. It would be for a new spectrum: one that included fussy men and women, exuberant children and Ditzy Blondes. I would include them in the spectrum of *innocents*.

Here is a clinical pearl. A woman comes to the clinic because she thinks she is ADD. She probably has a good job, a husband and small children. For a woman in those circumstances not to get distracted is a small miracle, but she is worried because her husband thinks she is scatter-brained. The question to ask is, Has anyone ever called you a "ditzy blonde"? Just yesterday, one said, "My father used to." In the event, a sensitive mental health professional should say, If more people in the world were like you, it would be a much better place.

Ditziness is not an established dimension. I'm quite sure it wasn't one of those 17,953 adjectives the psychologist pulled out of Webster's *Dictionary* in 1925. "Dizzy" probably was, although it didn't make the cut. A "dizzy blonde" was a "dumb broad" in 1950s lingo, *à la* Bensonhurst and Las Vegas. An "old pitsy" is a fuss-pot.[3] Hence, the origin of "ditzy," a syncretism that refers to someone who is fussy but a bit silly about it. You see, I know a lot about Ditzy Blondes, and not because my sister is one, nor my wife. C & F are both blondes, as their hairdressers will attest, but ditzy they are not. Well, not *that* ditzy…

You know by now that I don't believe in stereotypes any more than I do in types, but there are patients who come to the clinic for an ADD evaluation who put *themselves* into the category: "My boyfriend calls me a ditzy blonde." She meant that she was scatter-brained—she had been that way since she was little and now, grown woman that she was, it was getting in the way. *What she ought to get*, I think to myself, *is a new boyfriend.* Unless he, like your author, loves Ditzy Blondes (DBs).

It's not the blonde part that gets in the way. Surveys on the two continents where blondes are prevalent consistently show that popularity, success, happiness and wealth are visited upon blondes, especially blonde *women*. It is clearly a social effect; most blondes on any continent aren't that way, genetically; blondeness, in most cases, is an acquired characteristic. Nor is *ditziness* more common in congenital blondes or secondary blondes than in women who aren't blonde at all. My oldest daughter, for example, is a DB, but she is from China, and although her hair is occasionally tinged with shades of lavender, it is mostly black. Why, then, do we insist on using the term *ditzy blonde* rather than *ditzy women* or *ditzy persons whatever their self-selected gender*? It's an easy question. It's like, "Why do people like to tell blonde jokes?" Easy. They're jealous.

Better to ask, *Is ditziness more common in women than in men?* The answer is yes, and brain science tells us why.

* * *

---

3   *Pitsy* means "small" in Yiddish, but in Brooklyn it came to mean "fussy."

Back to the patient who told me her father called her a DB. This patient, DB#1, had always been a bit disorganized, but she managed well enough in school and in the small offices where she worked. Her responsibilities were manageable. It was only when she climbed the ladder to a newly created position at a nearby institution that she felt scattered and disorganized to a fault.

Her examination was perfectly normal, of course. She did well on all our tests. The only problem she had was slow mental processing speed, evident on the symbol-digit coding test of the CNT, a computerized nerocognitive test we use in the clinic (www.atonc.com). We gave her a small dose of Ritalin®, and she returned to the office an hour later and reported that she felt more focused. On the CNT, her processing speed normalized. We gave her a prescription, and I am sure that she will return to the halls of academe with the focus and efficiency of a cyborg.

Another patient, DB#2, was clever and well spoken but so scattered and disorganized that she couldn't keep up with the simple chores of an office assistant. But she was as smart as the Reese Witherspoon character in *Legally Blonde*. She scored higher on our computerized IQ tests (the TGMA, or Test of General Mental Ability (www.atonc.com)) than almost anyone who had ever taken the tests, but her processing speed was slow, too, and she did poorly on a test of sustained attention, the continuous performance test. She, too, felt like a *new woman* after we had given her one of our fabulous drugs. So what is a DB? She's ADD, right?

Are Ditzy Blondes ADD?

DB#2 was probably ADD, based on her tests and her school history. DB#1 also had problems with focus and concentration and was easily distracted. Was she ADD, too? Yes, and no. I think she *acquired* ADD. DB#2, on the other hand, was *congenitally* ADD; she had been that way all her life. Both, however, were a bit anxious about their performance in the world of adult responsibility. This gives us an important clue as to what a DB really is and also how some people, especially women, can acquire ADD.

Research on girls with ADD show that they tend to be under-active and inhibited; they don't have behavior problems, and although they struggle in school they are seldom referred for diagnosis and treatment. DBs are *not* under-active and inhibited. They have problems with attention and distractibility, too, but they tend to be impetuous and disinhibited. They don't usually have problems in school because they do OK in structured situations. In school, all they have to do is what they sense the teachers expect. Even if they're not smart, DBs are **context-sensitive**. That means that they are keenly attentive to other people, and can usually figure out what the teacher requires in order that they get a good grade.

Yet when they come to us as women, their usual complaint is, "I think I'm ADD." No, they're not. The odd thing is, they are *reflective*. We usually think that DBs are clueless, but that is only an illusion. They may seem ditzy or scatter-brained, but that's only an outward sign. It isn't necessarily what is going on inside their heads. What, then, is going on inside? (If anything. Ha ha.)

In unfamiliar situations, the so-called DB tends to *reflect*. That may seem paradoxical, but we know all about paradoxes now and we also know how too much thinking can clog parts of one's head. Like any context-sensitive organism, the DB responds to events with a keen eye, taking in all the details, and pondering. That, by the way, is why her processing speed seems slow. She is thinking hard, and cogitation is always slow work. It may take her a while to decide, for example, what the fellow sitting next to her is driving at.

She is also sensitive to what he might be feeling. She knows that what she perceives is not necessarily what is going on inside his head. So she runs through the possibilities. *He seems to like me*, she thinks. *Is that why he put his hand on my knee?* Her active mind runs through the alternatives: *Perhaps he is cold, or lonely, or maybe he is just trying to be nice.* Reflecting deeply on the possibilities, her spirit of ineffable sweetness gives him the benefit of the doubt and her slow mental processing delays the appropriate action step.

A non-DB would say right off, "Buzz off, creep," but the DB, after some moments, says, "Excuse me, I have to go to the bathroom." If she's not a smart DB, it may take a while longer before she gets around to it.

The *reflective* Ditzy Blonde sounds like a contradiction in terms. It weakens the hypothesis that DBs are ADD; in fact, most are OC. Naturalists have observed that the traits of high arousal, context-sensitivity and reflectiveness often run together. The fact is well-established in studies of passerine birds and certain types of monkey, and I have found it to be true of human beings as well. Animals with a high-arousal set-point tend to be acutely attentive to their surroundings and to the things that happen, but they respond slowly and only after a period of contemplation. DBs, as a group, have a high-arousal set-point, they are more sensitive to events in their environment, and their minds work overtime as they ponder. Noting the blank expression on their faces as they do, one is tempted to think, *She is clueless*.

DBs are thought to be ADD because they are impulsive and disinhibited sometimes. I think it's a mischaracterization. They are lively and charming, joyful and ebullient. They are also vivacious. It just happens that a lively, vivacious blonde is more likely to attract attention than all the bays, chestnuts, roans and duns in the room. People tend to underestimate the DB's ebullitions.

Are Ditzy Blondes anxious?

The second most common diagnosis inflicted on DBs is anxiety. They do tend to worry, but they don't usually have an anxiety disorder. You have to understand what makes them worry. Remember the line, *her spirit of ineffable sweetness*? It doesn't have anything to do with an anxiety disorder or even with ADD, but rather, this: *They are anxious to do good*.

Women who assign themselves to the category of DBs worry that they may have an anxiety disorder just as they worry that they may have ADD. It's usually not the case. If DBs worry or if they get distracted, it is usually because of their surfeit of *kindness*. If a DB laughs at your stupid joke, she's being kind. She might even laugh loudly, and since hardly anyone even sniggers at the lame jokes you tell, you assume she must be dumb, or clueless. What that says about *you* is more interesting. The world does regard a DB with ridicule, but it is a measure of the world's deficiency, not hers.

Anxious to please: what a thing to hold against someone. In fact, it is related to DBs' context-sensitivity. DBs are perceptive of what other people are thinking and feeling and their first impulse is to respond sympathetically. You can even say that they are *impulsively empathic*. And if they seem disinhibited, it is because they feel comfortable in social intercourse. They assume that others are as sweet and well-meaning as they themselves are. Of course, most *others* are no such thing and the consequences of the erroneous assumption may be regrettable. Be that as it may, like most good OCs, DBs tend to be resilient and optimistic. The unfortunate events of Friday night need not re-occur on Saturday.

DBs may not be anxious but they are *worriers*. It is a function of their reflective, caring disposition. What do they worry about? They worry about doing right by the people they are with. They really *care* about you. They feel compelled to laugh at your feeble jokes, worrying that no one else will. They are reluctant to tell you to buzz off, as a less-kind woman would do, and for that you think she must be clueless. What does that say about you?

DBs are wide-open, in spite of their worries, but they aren't uptight. But because they are so successfully expressive of emotion, and because their emotional lives are so rich and full, they seem to attract uptight, controlling men. The latter view them as complementary to their own bleak emotional lives. Controlling men see them as likely victims. *She is so bright and lively*, the controlling man says. *I love it. Now let me crush her spirit.*

There are many reasons why DBs worry. If one really perceives what is going on, if one reflects on it and considers all the possibilities, and if one's abiding concern is how one's conspecifics feel, it's not only going to be distracting but also the cause for worry. *I worry,* she says, *that my (controlling, wrathful) husband is disappointed with me. I must resolve to do better.*

To that end, she seeks the advice of another (controlling) man, who like her husband is also threatened by her unbridled sweetness and good cheer. He is a physician who writes her a benzo in self-defense. As it happens, such drugs have decidedly negative effects. DBs are not good candidates for benzodiazepines like Xanax® or Valium®. *If Dr. N prescribed it for me, it must be something that will be good for me.* If a little is good for her, a bit more may be better. DBs, like all good girls, are respectful towards authority, which is why so many of them wind up with controlling husbands and/or drug habits.

The life-course of Ditzy Blondes

What are their worries about? It's interesting; it has to do with their ineffable sweetness. They are so eager to do right, to be kind and generous, to think well of everyone they meet, they worry that they may not live up to the attendant responsibilities. It makes them scattered and disorganized, sometimes. This is why their condition may not come to clinical attention until they are older, especially after they have a career and a family.

DBs can keep up well enough with the circumscribed duties of school. They are often quite good at school, which only makes their conspecifics more jealous. They also thrive in the superficial world of young adult life, because they are promiscuous with their kindness. Because they are vivacious and, well, *blonde*, they attract a good deal of positive attention. ADD girls who are quiet and inhibited are usually socially awkward, but our DBs, ADD or not, are extroverts, open to experience and facile in most situations because of their positive energy and their high capacity for involvement.

It's *involvement*, though, that gets a DB in trouble. In the first instance, it's the men she chooses to involve herself with: most often controlling, wrathful men, but also the full range of no-goodniks: men who are projects, wrecks, jerks, self-centered dolts or psychopaths. DBs express the weaknesses that all women share: a surfeit of trust and empathy; a tendency to assume that men and women mean the same things simply because they seem to speak the same language; and the determination to make the best of situations that a less trusting and empathic soul would consider hopeless. Only they express those supposed weaknesses to a greater degree.

The second instance is no less challenging. It is the accumulation of responsibilities that come with career and family. This brings us to one of the fundamental differences between men and women: what they think responsibility is. To a man, it's a function of being true to himself, an expression of what he deems his inner genius. Essentially, responsibility to a man is doing what he wants to do. To a woman, it is what responsibility *really* is: taking on all of the burdens that come one's way, and taking them on seriously and with good cheer. Women on the job are pretty much the same as women at home: *If I don't do it, that indolent clot sure won't.*

Are there Ditzy Blonde males?

I have known guys who seem to be clueless but are really quite smart. They seem clumsy in social situations because of their exuberance and positive energy. There certainly are men who are absent-minded and seem disorganized. Guys, for example, who never finish the things they start.

Are they *ditzy*, though? No, of course not, any more than men can be "bimbos" or "dizzy blondes." Those kinds of demeaning words are reserved for the weaker sex because men have to reassure themselves that they *are* weaker. Not that men are resistant to pejorative adjectives and nouns. No woman, for example, is ever a *jerk, creep, wreck* or *project.* Pejorative adjectives are sexually dimorphic, appropriate to one or the other gender but rarely to both.

If ditziness means vivacity, good humor, innocent charm and a caring, trusting disposition coupled with exquisite sensitivity to others' feelings, a willingness to take on more responsibilities than she ought to, and an abiding belief that men, too, are caring and trustworthy beings, then I can say with confidence that there are no ditzy males. No ditzy *straight* guys, anyway.

Maybe it does have to do with hormones, or *harmones*, as the ladies in my mother's bridge club used to say, fanning themselves mightily. Perhaps, one day, we should examine what hormones do to a person's brain, or alternatively what brain does to one's hormones, but it is a subject of devilish complexity.

Persecution

Why do we laugh at OC? Think about it. OCD is the only mental illness that is a reliable source of mirth. Fussy men and women, not to mention Ditzy Blondes, are true innocents. When human beings encounter an innocent, having learned nothing from what they did to Socrates, Jesus and Billy Budd, their first thought is: persecute. Fussy men and women, exuberant children and Ditzy Blondes exist to be teased. It's not so bad as hemlock, a cross or gibbet, but the rationale is the same.

An active mind may be its own reward, but it may also be a problem, and not only for children. It is confusing to less active minds. Thus discomfited, the error messages they generate are less encouraging. They say, *Something is wrong here. Get rid of it.* Or, *Change it.*

Teasing is an effective form of social control. Among friends and in families it is one way to shape the behavior of someone who deviates from the local norm. Improperly done, teasing is cruel, but whether harsh or not, it is an effective form of behavior modification, and it's something that all the social animals do. I suppose it's one of those noisome traits we inherited from our four-legged ancestors. Deviation from the norms of the herd is potentially dangerous, and animals deal with it summarily. Older siblings tease younger ones, parents tease their children and children tease parents. Friends tease each other. They do it in a gentle, playful way. It's fun to say to a good friend, *OMG, where did you get that tie?*, but it's not OK to say that to a stranger on the elevator. One doesn't tease someone who has a real weakness. That's sadistic, cruel and stupid. A good teaser *wants* to be teased back.

Fussy men and women, therefore, with their serious pre-occupations, seem to be threatening to the social order, which for most of us is careless and sloppy. Innocents threaten our hard-earned discovery that the world is not trustworthy, that life is a zero-sum game and that people are out to exploit one another. Someone who is blissfully unaware of such enduring truths but none the worse for it forces us to confront the bleakness of our own psychology, our own gloomy expectations and default modes riven with anxiety.

In the face of the seeming perfection of an active mind, philistines feel only tension that must be released, somehow. They usually just make a joke of it, although I have known some who throw dirt-clods. The rabble feel compelled to react with antipathy. *Someone who is neat and tidy. Ugh! Someone who is kind and thinks well of others. Double ugh! Someone whose thoughts are as broad as Nature... I've run out of ughs!* In fact, teasing is often a compulsion, especially among children. Like the boy in school who said, "Carrot-top, Carrot-top," whenever he saw Anne Shirley in the morning. Gilbert was only a child and didn't understand that teasing has proper rules. One only teases someone with whom one is close; it must be done in a good-natured way; and one has to be prepared to be teased back.

We react sharply to fussy men and women because they take things so seriously. They are always thinking. When you say, "Marcia, you're so OCD about loading the dishwasher," she is likely to explain precisely why she loads the dishwasher as she does. Having read thus far, you now know to say, "Marcia, you're so OC," and you can observe her response with clinical understanding. She doesn't take it as an insult or an assault on her way of doing things but as an opportunity to share her well-considered rationale. "You should alternate the big dishes with small ones on the lower rack, so the big ones will get more spray. The small ones need less spray, you see. See how I do it? Here. Try it yourself..."

One never teases an angry, controlling man. It will make him mad. One teases innocents, and their OC traits are easy targets. They never feel put upon and seldom complain. When they do complain, it is in a good-hearted way, accompanied by a sub-audible sigh. One of my best friends actually used to say "Sigh," at times, usually after I had committed some minor solecism.

Fussy men and women and Ditzy Blondes are true innocents who believe in the importance of what seem to others the most trivial things. They have exquisite attention for details. Their conscientiousness makes them stand out. Philistines want to modify their behavior, make them less conscientious, less attentive, dull-witted, just as the philistines are themselves. Yet a good OC will rise above the rabble. Marcia's mental exertions are the occasion of fun. Her concern is doing right and preventing untoward outcomes, like the damage that will ensue when a plastic container is placed on the bottom rack. Teasing, to her, is a didactic opportunity. "A dishwasher will heat water to between 55 and 75 degrees Celsius. That won't melt your plastics, but it may well distort the shape and you won't be able to fit the top back on."

People tease fussy men and women because they seem to have come from another planet. In fact, they *live* in another planet. It is the rich and enticing domain of their fertile minds. They don't necessarily tease back, but they smile at the joke. A good OC thinks, *This is what they do, this strange breed of unenlightened souls. But I love them anyway.* Such thoughts are deep within innocents' psyches and drive their good feelings; they won't be aware of them before the age of 60 or so.

16
The OC Loop or OC Circuit

Thus far, I have shared pithy anecdotes and helpful advice, for which I am sure you are grateful. The world-wide popularity of this OC book is attributable, doubtless, to the self-improvements it has wrought among long-suffering OCs and their longer-suffering associates. But now, it's time to get serious. What has gone before, I assure you, is fluff compared to the Deep Thought in the next few chapters.

* * *

The cerebral cortex grew out of the structures of the lower brain, especially the basal ganglia and the thalamus, but the new layers that formed were organized differently and they also operate differently. Connecting the new layers, which evolved rather quickly, to older, established systems was an engineering problem of no small magnitude, but the solution was to simplify. Cortical regions would be connected to the subcortical structures directly beneath by loops.

A **loop** is a neural circuit that connects brain part A to B, B to C and C to A. They are comparatively simple circuits that move neural signals from a subcortical region to a cortical region and then back again. Signals in the loop are modified at the **nodes**, the brain parts they connect. Some loops have two nodes and most have more than two, but the principle is the same: a signal vibrates around the loop, absorbing inputs from each node. The signal is modified by new inputs at every node, as it continues around the loop until all the inputs are synchronized (or integrated, entrained or bound). The result is a brain field capable of accomplishing something. It might be an action step, like raising one's heart rate or making one scratch on a place that itches. The brain field might also generate an experience of some sort—that is, something of which one is aware, like a thought or a feeling. However, we are not aware of most of the brain fields roiling about beneath the surface of our heads.

There are many such loops, but one in particular is relevant to OC: the **lateral orbital-striatal loop** (LOS loop). In 1987, Baxter and his colleagues reported that the LOS was particularly active in patients with OCD (Baxter *et al.*, 1987).

> The most widely accepted model of OCD proposes that abnormalities of corticostriatal circuits, involving the orbito-frontal cortex (OFC), anterior cingulate cortex (ACC), thalamus and striatum, play an important role in its pathophysiology. (Spalletta *et al.*, 2014)

The **LOS loop**, also known as the **OC loop**, has three nodes: A is the orbito-frontal cortex (OFC), B is the caudate nucleus in the basal ganglia, and C is the thalamus. You need to know about this loop.

The prefrontal cortex

The **frontal lobes** are the largest chunk of brain we have (Figure 16.1). Open your hands, and put the heels of each hand over your eyes. It's easier if you put the heel of your right hand over your right eye, and the left over the other, but you can do it either way. Then lay your hands on your head. Beneath them are the right and left frontal lobes.

The **prefrontal cortex** (PFC) is the rostral (front) two-thirds of the frontal lobes. The latter third of the frontal lobe is concerned with the organization of voluntary movements, but the front two-thirds is occupied by a wide range of disparate functions, including expressive language in **Broca's area**. It is called the *prefrontal* cortex because it sits in front of the premotor strip and the motor strip.

The many functions of the prefrontal cortex are contained in the theory that it integrates perceptions, memories, thoughts and feelings in order to direct and regulate behavior; the so-called **central executive** lives there. In broader perspective, its purpose is self-regulation: the ability to control one's impulses, to delay gratification, and to exercise critical judgment about one's thinking, feeling and doing. It is also involved in moral judgment, one's sense of oneself and of others, and also the regulation of emotion, the autonomic nervous system, the endocrine glands and one's physiology in general.

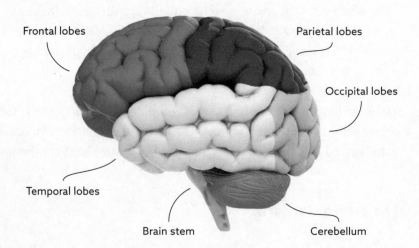

Figure 16.1 The cerebral cortex

I can tell you all you need to know about the anatomy of the frontal lobes if you find a grapefruit and cut it into quarters. Take two of the quarters and lay them together, flat side down, on your desk. What you have before you is a hemisphere; in brain lingo, the two quarters are the right and left *hemispheres*, although really they are just *quadraspheres*. Then move the two quarters apart slightly, an eighth of an inch or so. The gap between the two quarters is the central **commissure**, which separates right brain from left brain. The round yellow skin of the grapefruit is the lateral surface (the side) and the dorsal surface (*dorsum* = "back") of the cerebral cortex; together these form the *dorso-lateral surface* or the *convexity*. This is the **neocortex**, the most recent brain part to have evolved and the seat of the analytical-theoretical mind, and it's not much thicker than the skin of a grapefruit. The front half of the two grapefruit quarters are the frontal lobes, and the front half of them is the PFC.

Now look closely at the grapefruit. It has two additional surfaces: the *ventro-medial surfaces*, phylogenetically much older than the dorso-lateral surface. One is the flat side on the desk; that is the bottom or "ventral" surface of the prefrontal cortex. (*Ventrum* means "belly.") The sides of the two grapefruit quarters on the inside and almost touching are the medial surface. If the grapefruit were a more accurate rendition of the hemispheres, there would be yellow skin on the ventral and medial surfaces also, because they, too, are covered by the same sheet of cortical neurons as the dorso-lateral surface. Now eat the grapefruit and clean up the mess. There is nothing quite so delicious as a sweet, juicy grapefruit.

* * *

The anatomy is important because it captures one of the themes of the book. The evolution of the prefrontal cortex is from ventro-medial to dorso-lateral. That is, it grew from the bottom up and from the inside out. The sequence reflects the evolution of thought:

- From medial to lateral, that is inside to out: from one's personal and intimate perspectives to governance by rules and understanding categories.
- Ventral to dorsal, bottom to top: from embodied experience to abstract representations.

The evolution of our way of thinking, therefore, began with personal, emotional, social and embodied experiences. The ventro-medial prefrontal cortex is an extrusion of one's social/emotional brain.

As the neocortex expanded radially, thinking developed increasing capacity for abstract representations.

There is no dividing line between medial and lateral or between ventral and dorsal. The functions, like the anatomy, merge one into the other. The lateral prefrontal cortex occupies itself with abstract thinking, the generation of rules and categories and inhibitory control, the typical functions of the analytical mind. The dorsal-lateral surface of the PFC is the abode of our highest mental faculties; hence the expression "higher cortical functions." As one moves down towards the bottom of the lateral PFC, those functions grow increasingly more pertinent to one's social and personal circumstances. Put your finger in the middle of your forehead at the hairline. Then move it down towards the temple. If your finger were inside your head, it would be moving along the lateral surface of the PFC, from the dorsal-lateral PFC to the ventral-lateral PFC.

This is how the cortex is organized in general, and in the frontal lobes in particular: the lateral surfaces are farther from the inner dwelling places of the social/emotional brain, the habit system and the thalamus. They are newer in evolutionary terms, higher in terms of phylogenesis, and more or less unique to humans. They are more abstract and less *embodied*. Some people like them that way.

The ventral-medial prefrontal cortex feeds into the OC loop. It is usually called the **orbito-frontal cortex** (OFC) because it lies just above one's eye-sockets. The OFC is one of the nodes of the OC loop and feeds it with all its capacity for social cognition and emotional regulation. It also receives the signals of abstract thought, planning, self-correction and inhibition from the dorsal and lateral surfaces. It's a lot of stuff to feed a loop, and if it goes wrong from time to time we shouldn't be surprised.

The basal ganglia

The habit system or the habit brain resides in the **basal ganglia** (BG), a second node of the LOS loop. The BG are a small brain in their own right, centrally located below the cerebral hemispheres.

Small mammals, birds and reptiles do perfectly well without any cerebral cortex at all, or a very small one, relying almost entirely on their subcortex. With little more than BG and a thalamus, they can integrate emotional states, motivation and memory to generate effective behavior. Their thalamus takes care of all the sensory inputs to the central nervous system, while the BG takes care of all the output functions that involve movement.

Nature established the basic structure of the basal ganglia in the reptiles. Since both birds and mammals evolved from reptiles, there was a fork in the evolutionary road when birds elected simply to pile on additional ganglia in their BG. The mammals, consigned to a terrestrial existence, had to expand the thin layer of nervous tissue that surrounded their BG, and, over the years, that mushroomed into the cerebral cortex. The birds, it seems, took the easy way out, presumably because they could solve a lot of problems just by flying away. Mammals, living in a more dangerous environment with limited escape routes, had to rely on their wits. It is surprising that birds are as intelligent as they are because they don't have much of a cerebral cortex, so there must be a kind of intelligence built into one's BG. But, then, birds aren't that smart. My Aunt Christina used to tease my sisters about their boyfriends. *He's a real bird*, she would say. She wasn't suggesting that the fellow was smart.

The structure of the nerve cells in the basal ganglia and thalamus is unique. The cells are highly organized, but folded among themselves like a nest of caterpillars. MacLean has suggested that these long, folded cords of cells were designed to generate an internal picture of three-dimensional space, which may explain why birds have more facility in three-dimensional space than mammals do (MacLean, 1990). The extraordinary agility of birds in flight requires large BG relative to the size of the rest of their brains. But whether one flies around or just trundles along on the surface of the Earth, the principle is the same. The BG is a processing unit, not just a switch. It is a motor output unit, but it coordinates sensory input, memory and motivation in the expression of behavior, just as the prefrontal cortex does, but *without the distraction of abstract representations.*

The basal ganglia are another node in the OC loop. They operate nicely with a minimum of top-down control, and it is dangerous to infuse them with an excess of direction. Doing so can foul the BG and send signals down the wrong forks. The BG operate quickly and efficiently when called upon to perform familiar, overlearned tasks. When they receive directions that are ambiguous or ambivalent, they are prone to misbehave. When damaged or confused, they will generate stereotyped or repetitive behaviors.

The thalamus

A third node of the OC loop is the **thalamus**, whose central location deep in the brain is captured by its name, which means "inner chamber." It is the gathering place for virtually all of the information that comes in from one's soma and from the outside world, before it is conveyed to the cerebral cortex. It is not just a relay station for sensory data to the cerebrum. It has many functions, as the basal ganglia do. It receives modulatory input from brain areas involved in memory, attention and arousal, and uses the input to process the sensory data it receives (Saalmann and Kastner, 2009). A lot of information-processing goes on in the thalamus; nervous signals are integrated and coordinated before they are sent on. It is a little brain of its own as well; along with the insula, it is the nexus of the somatic brain.

The LOS or OC loop

With their caterpillar-nest of neurons, the basal ganglia and the thalamus process neural signals in their own particular way. The OC loop, therefore, like all the other loops that connect the cortex and the subcortex, is responsible for synchronizing signals that have different qualities. The orbito-frontal cortex, basal ganglia and thalamus, the three nodes of the OC loop, are themselves integrating signals arriving from elsewhere in the neocortex, the hippocampus and amygdala, the cingulum and the insula. Such loops are said to be **convergence zones**. Not only are signals arriving from many different places, but the signals themselves are constantly changing. I warned that you needed to know about loops, if only to avoid their baleful residues.

The OC loop has three nodes, each of which is richly endowed with connections to virtually all the other parts of brain. It is a central player in perception, action, and the motivators of action. It synchronizes the regulation of behavior. Two of the nodes in the LOS are very old in terms of phylogenesis; small mammals, even reptiles, have basal ganglia and thalami that are not very different from our own. In the small animals and even in human children, mental activities that occupy almost all of an adult's cerebral cortex are well served by those subcortical nuclei. Yet they have arranged to come together with a small sliver of the prefrontal cortex, its ventral and medial surfaces, to form a loop. And not just any loop. Here is a loop that captures *disproportionate mental exertions*, which can tangle thoughts and obscure vision. Something about the loop allows exhausting repetitions to take the place of proper action. It lets thought and actions fuse, as if the thinking of a thing were the same as doing it, as if supposing a thing were the same as if it were there. *Gad, my hands are filthy.*

The orbito-frontal cortex is a component of the social/emotional brain. The basal ganglia are the habit system, and the thalamus is part of the somatic brain. The OC loop strives to maintain a balance between them all. To that end, it resonates with energy from many different parts of brain. In its ideal state, the OC loop allows thought and action to proceed. In the OC state, the process is belabored, and you can guess why, I bet.

The OC loop has to work harder in patients with OCD. When OCD patients are compared to healthy controls, its pattern of activation is abnormal; paradoxically, the orbito-frontal cortex is smaller in OCD patients. That is interesting; the OFC, a part of brain that is central to behavioral and emotional regulation and that ordinarily does it in an effortless way, is puny among patients with OCD. The good news is that when OCD patients are treated with an effective drug, the activity of the OC loop seems to normalize, although their OFC doesn't get any bigger (Menzies *et al.*, 2008; Saxena *et al.*, 1999).

What does it all mean?

What do loops have to do with OC? An attentive student would say that in pathological cases it reverberates wildly, the unhappy victim of neural oscillations that refuse to be synchronized and to form a coherent field. If her professor were a Gestalt psychologist, she would give her two marks for the right answer. If the professor were a classical neurologist, she would give her only one mark for being metaphorical, or none at all if she thought the student was being mystical. If she were indeed a mystic (the student, not the neurologist), I myself would give her three marks, because what happens in the life of an oscillating loop is like a spirit: it is alive but immaterial, a ring of neural energy, and it exists to guide one's motivated behavior. Also, it has a mind of its own.

The world of spirits and brain fields may be immaterial, but they are not unmeasurable. The measure is indirect; functional imaging indicates increased activity in this super-circuit of interacting loops, and newer kinds of functional imaging can define their patterns of connectivity. The structures of the OC circuit, therefore, are hyperactive. Why so? Presumably because they are trying to synchronize a neural network that, in OC, is hard to synchronize.

Why does the OC circuit find it hard to synchronize? Well, it doesn't, not always. It may simply generate a motor action plan that helps to set things right. The plan may be irrelevant, like tapping one's inflated cheek eight times, but it relaxes the loop. An OC finds balance in her life and synchrony in her oscillating neural assemblies by organizing the towels in the linen closet, just so; or by flicking his fingers on the wall as he walks down the corridor;

or as he gives his hands a good wash with Neutrogena soap. Thus, one famous theory of OCD: a dyssynchronous neural assembly makes one anxious, but the anxiety is dispelled by exercising a compulsive behavior. Its repetitive nature, presumably, regularizes the dyssynchronies. In severe cases of OCD, the dyssynchrony must be interminable because no amount of compulsive behavior helps it to calm down. Those are patients who require the most heroic treatments, even deep brain stimulation or cingulotomy, an operation that cuts off one's internal error detector. In the case of ordinary, garden-variety OCs like you and me, the dyssynchrony can be dispelled by pursuing our favorite hobby and then having a nice lie-down.

What causes dyssynchrony in the first place? Well, it could come from anywhere. In Batman's case, it was the indelible memory of those awful bats in the cave. The memory of violent bats is an entrenched and toxic memory in the poor fellow's mind, a spirit that flies out of his memory banks and disrupts his motivational repertoire. *I must fight crime*, he thinks, a motivation with its source in another toxic memory from his beleaguered past. Rather than joining the police force, however, or becoming a prosecutor or a crime-scene investigator, as most normal people might do, or even just setting up a Neighborhood Watch, he feels compelled to behave like a bat. His primal obsession, you could say, is satisfied by a counter-phobic compulsion. Something like that.

Loop dyssynchronies are not, by themselves, pathological. Dyssynchronies occur all the time in all of us. The process of disequilibration/stabilization in neural networks is what mental activity *is*. To illustrate, another of our pithy vignettes.

Sheila

A, Sheila's orbito-frontal cortex, comes up with a bright idea that has emotional salience. She feels like working out. B, in her basal ganglia, can generate motor patterns so that her legs and arms can move up and down or whatever, more or less automatically; C, in her thalamus, lets her know when she's getting tired because it receives sensory input from her arms and legs; C tells A, therefore, that it's time to stop. A, however, in the form of Sheila's determination, will not permit synchronization to occur by giving up easily. Oscillations arrive from other sources and they generate the memory of Xavier, her personal trainer, who is known to say: "No pain, no gain." Xavier is wildly handsome but is not known for the originality of his heartening remarks. The synchrony that forms in Sheila's convergence zone, then, originates in many brain parts, but the most important contributor to the energy of the loop are Xavier's words. Sheila persists in her efforts, suppressing the experience of pain and fatigue. Her OC loop keeps vibrating in harmony until the buzzer sounds, she collapses, smiles, drinks some water and retires to the smoothie bar. Then she texts her boyfriend, Risteard: "Where r u?"

It's important to appreciate that Sheila's determination in working out does not involve running around the loop like a rat in a maze. The whole loop lights up all at once. The activation of a functional loop in the brain is virtually simultaneous at all points. The circuit is an oscillating mass of neuronal connections, a harmony that arises around a particular event—*It's workout time!*—with countless millions of neurons participating as if they were instruments in an orchestra. They are playing, not in sequence, like "Row, row, row your boat," but *all together*. They try to stay in harmony, but tiny dyssynchronies occur all the time: *My legs are really hurting*, Sheila notices, but then the thought of Xavier recruits additional mental energy and her oscillating neural assemblies come back in synch.

The nodes of the OC loop receive inputs from all over the brain and send outputs to all of them as well, but those inputs and outputs aren't like little messages sent hither and thither through pneumatic tubes. Other parts of brain suddenly join the symphony, as if they belonged there, and almost instantaneously. This is one of the problems that has arisen, in fact, when brain researchers try to describe the OC loop. They keep discovering other parts of brain that are inserting their brain fields into it: the parietal lobes, the cingulum, the hippocampus and the amygdala, and so on. Brain scientists have also discovered other cortical-striatal loops. Even if they are aren't structurally connected, the intensity of the event recruits their inputs as well.

It gets better. Sheila may be diligent about her workout routine, even a bit obsessive, but as she executes the same motor programs in precisely the same way, as she does every Monday, Wednesday and Thursday, her mind is filled with different thoughts and feelings. The loop is always different because it has so many inputs and outputs, so many sub-loops. It is impossible for the symphony to sound the same every time it's played. Sheila knows her pre-Socratics: *You never enter the same river twice.*

Within the nodes of the OC loop, and even in the affiliated structures, there are those forks in the road. During the process of integrating inputs from multiple sources, the forks can direct them in one way or another. The basal ganglia, for example, have two different outputs to the thalamus. The "direct circuit" is activating, whereas the "indirect circuit" is inhibitory. Whether an input goes into the direct or indirect pathway influences the activity of the entire loop; and one can only assume that there is more than one fork in the knotlike masses of the BG and the thalamus. Which fork does a particular event take? It depends. On one particular day, Sheila's output may favor the direct path: her exercise is furious and unrestrained, and she emerges with a feeling of exhilaration. On another day, it favors the indirect path, and her endeavors are languid and she feels exhausted.

One theory of OCD is that the condition favors the direct, excitatory pathway. As an event transpires, additional inputs from around the brain are integrated into the event, and are amplified. The brain fields generated in the loop persist in a prolonged, dyssynchronous state.

Risteard

Picture poor Risteard, Sheila's boyfriend, who was supposed to meet her at spinning class. As he was about to leave his apartment, he experienced this: *My hands feel dirty*. The feeling was amplified by a series of excitatory forks in the pathways of his OC loop. He ought to remember that he had just washed his hands five minutes ago. He should recall what his therapist said: "This feeling is just your hand-washing compulsion. Deal with it." His loop, however, is in a state of unrestrained excitement and refuses to synchronize with those sensible inputs. His oscillations grow stronger and generate an irresistible thought: *My hands still feel dirty. I must have missed a spot*; and then, the appropriate action step: *Where the hell is the Neutrogena soap?* Later, he texts Sheila: "Can't meet you. Too much work." It's true. It's hard work to contend with the dyssynchronous loops and it has left him feeling exhausted.

We have all of us had the feeling that our hands are dirty, even when they're not. How such feelings are amplified or inhibited is governed by different tracks within the OC circuit, among other things. Risteard, however, is reassured by Sheila's text: "That's OK. I'm exhausted 2." As it happens, Xavier is in the smoothie bar 2.

* * *

Dyssynchronies occur all the time in all of us, but the OCs among us have a bit more, and OCDs, like Risteard, a lot more. Activity in the LOS loop is virtually continuous, because the loop itself has an essential function. It integrates sensory data from the thalamus, feeds it into a central processing unit in the orbito-frontal cortex (which integrates the data with one's cognitive motivation and emotional state), and transfers the data to the basal ganglia, where the appropriate output is generated. In Risteard's case, it means that his feeling of slimy hands is constant as well.

Neural networks strive to maintain a state of equilibrium, and sometimes equilibrium can only be achieved by adding other networks to the endeavor. Since they all communicate by producing electromagnetic fields, it is appropriate to describe their equilibrium as a state of synchrony, resonance or harmony. On the other hand, disequilibrium or dyssynchrony within a neural network is a perfectly normal event. It occurs whenever one is confronted with a novel or challenging event, or when one is trying to solve a problem or to be creative. Mental work is no less than the behavior of neural networks as they try to recruit additional neural resources to synchronize properly. We experience that as solving a problem.

You have had this experience, I'm sure: *I know this fellow, I remember his face—now what the devil is his name?* A disequilibrium has arisen at that very moment between one's facial memory, which is quite powerful, and one's memory for names, which is notoriously weak, especially after age 40. Those two neural networks, facial memory and memory for names, can re-equilibrate themselves quite easily in a healthy young mind, recruiting a few additional resources to recover the poor fellow's name. At that point, *when the Gestalt is completed, the field comes into equilibrium.*

If you are past 40, you may have noticed that it's not quite so easy to recruit those additional resources. The fellow's name will only come to mind several minutes after he's gone on his way, or perhaps the next day. *By gad, it was Joseph Tarantino!* Ageing does something to the speed and flexibility with which one can recruit additional neural resources, and brain ageing, sad to say, begins in the fifth decade of life. That does not mean that old people live in a constant state of disequilibrium, but their preference for control over openness to experience and for comfort over adventure, and their vulnerability to dysnomia,[1] reflects the slowing and reduced power of their oscillating neural assemblies. They prefer to

---

1   Dysnomia is word-finding difficulty, a universal problem that begins in one's 40s and grows increasingly bothersome as one ages. It is an example of "benign senescence" and has no pathological significance.

maintain them in nice little grooves. Old people are not so badly off, though, as individuals who live in a *constant* state of mental disequilibrium: the mentally ill. The discomfort you experienced in failing to recall Joseph's name and in bumbling through an embarrassed conversation is only a small drop of unpleasantness compared to the flood experienced by someone like Risteard, who would be obsessed for days over that fellow's name. *Was it Joseph Tarantino or Richard Escobales? By gad, my hands are filthy!*

Constraint satisfaction

I try to bring models of neural structure and function to life, not only by describing brain regions as if they were grapefruit or homunculi, but by bridging what we know about brain function to what we know about human activity. For example, all this oscillating-loop business. There *is* an LOS loop, and it *does* show aberrant activity in patients with OCD. It *does* try to accommodate inputs from various sources, and in the case of OC, input from the analytical mind *does* tend to overwhelm inputs from other sources. There *is* an error detector in one's cingulum, and for one reason or the other, OCs do tend to amplify the problem. When you think about it, it's simply amazing.

It's not inappropriate to make the characters in this loop story behave like homunculi and homunculae, because they all come into it with minds of their own. The OC loop is one convergence zone where inputs are synchronized in order to generate actions and experiences; the brain has many loops doing similar things nearby with different purposes. But the lateral orbital-striatal loop is particularly salient to OC.

The OC loop comes alive as neural assemblies generate signals that converge in it and then synchronize within it. The signals are different when they arrive at the loop, but after a few turns around, they equilibrate, come into balance and generate a single, coherent brain field, which is close to something that we *experience*—a perception, a thought, a feeling or an action. If the entering signals are balanced to begin with, they don't take very long to synchronize, and one's thoughts and actions flow smoothly and efficiently. If they aren't so balanced to begin with, it takes them longer to synchronize. They have to take a lot of turns around the loop, the cingulum has to keep sending them back for another turn, and the loop keeps reverberating. As it does so, it picks up additional inputs; from A's memory banks, the time when B loaded the dishwasher in the wrong way and the damn machine broke; from his emotional brain, the valence of hard-to-control rage. In A's OC circuit, the loops are so active as they try to achieve a balance while dissonant inputs accrue that it becomes more like a treadmill than a generator of experience. He is not likely to break, but he may say something harsh. "Here. *I'll* load the dishwasher!" He's loading the dishwasher *at* you.

* * *

The OC loop tries to attain a state of **parallel constraint satisfaction**, to re-use the phrase from computer science. In that field, it refers to the problem of integrating the actions of competing algorithms. Now, I am never one to compare brains to digital computers, but in this case the term is appropriate because it is used in artificial intelligence research—that is, in trying to model computers after the human brain. Parallel constraint satisfaction, though, is not just what brains and computers do. Most people execute parallel constraint satisfaction processes so often they hardly ever think about it. We do it quite naturally. It's not only our brains that believe in parallel constraint satisfaction: we do too.

Parallel constraint satisfaction simply means that two algorithms, two oscillating neural assemblies, or two people, can operate successfully together if each respects the constraints imposed by the other. It is the essence of a successful reciprocal relationship. It is something like mutuality or compromise.

A brain model only makes sense to me if it resembles something that human beings do, and what we do all the time is live and work in parallel with other human beings, contending with constraints on our behavior imposed by having to work and live in parallel with other human beings. To that end, we have evolved a high degree of social cooperation, comparable only to organisms like bees and naked mole rats who manage the trick only by being clones. Humans are not clones, and each individual brings a mind of his or her own to the story. You might say that each of us oscillates at his or her own frequency. How, then, do we manage to get along so famously?

Think of human beings as if they were brains. One's central executive comes up with a really bright idea; well, is it a hare-brained scheme or a really good plan? The bright idea is this: *We are going to eat more steamed vegetables for a change.* It is a good idea, but it has to be reconciled with constraints imposed by other parts of the system. The habit system has certain constraints: *I don't know how to cook steamed vegetables.* Her husband's somatic brain has them, too: *I been working all day. I need a big dinner.* His emotional brain: *What the hell is this crap?* Her emotional brain: *Good grief. A bunch of kale costs $3.98 and it boils down to this?* The reverberating loop that is the life of Roy and Debbie together jangles around a few turns until the constraints are all satisfied and a coherent signal emerges: *Let's send out for pizza.*

Everything we do is bounded by constraints, which must always be respected even if they sometimes have to be defied. The life of an OCD patient is not *bounded* but *confined* by constraints, because they can never be satisfied. Nor will his or her error detector allow them to be defied.

When one is exercising vigorously, a constraint will be imposed by one of the inputs to one of those loops. The somatic brain oscillates at a frequency that conveys pain and fatigue in the thigh muscles. Sheila's tired legs are a constraint she has to respect. There are competing inputs, however, and they, too, impose constraints. Her analytical brain calculates her relative standing in spinning class: *Dead last.* Sheila's emotional brain generates this constraint: *I'm not going to let that fat cow Doreen beat me.* Those competing strengths can't be reconciled; she appreciates the problem, but it is a fork in the road, and she has to choose one or the other. Like a rational economic animal, she recognizes that the cost of losing the contest is greater than the cost of tired legs. The analytical mind is good for some things, especially when one's autobiographical self is at stake. A coherent signal emerges: *Go, girl.*

One's habit system wants to keep on doing what it knows best how to do. Konrad, a world-class animal biologist, for example, likes to travel to and from Vienna by different routes. Today, however, his wife called and imposed a constraint. She asked him to pick up her laundry from the cleaner's. This, however, entails driving home the same way he came into town. There are competing constraints, therefore, from his habit system and from his wife, Gretl, who is as close to a central executive as most men ever have. Maybe he can drive home, back out of the driveway, dash to the cleaner's and come home. That would satisfy *both* constraints, but it would take a lot of time.

The lives of oscillating neural assemblies communicate effectively when they are entrained, vibrating in synchrony like Konrad and Gretl during their long and happy lives together. Konrad may have been a bit OC, but he didn't have a mental disorder and he was the antithesis of a controlling, wrathful man. He had no difficulty, therefore, in resolving the problem of competing constraints, and so—like Sheila—he ignored one and satisfied the other. Sheila and Konrad were both able to suppress their error detectors in the service of a meritorious goal.

Risteard, on the other hand, was paralyzed by competing constraints. He found the soap and gave his hands a good long wash. Then he took a shower, but before he left the bathroom to put on his pajamas, he gave his hands one more wash because he had touched the taps. He brushed his teeth, put the toothbrush back into its antiseptic solution, washed his hands one last time, and went to bed.

Parallel constraints are what one's brain has to put up with, and we do too. Constraints in the brain are competitions among the activities of multiple minds. They can be reconciled, but some, inevitably, must be suppressed. Constraints are guidelines; but to the OC, they are immutable laws.

17

Aspergerites

The balance among one's multiple minds may be skewed in different ways. In OC, it is the analytical-theoretical mind that dominates events inside the head. There is always a hyperactive cingulum delivering the message *Something is wrong here*. Sometimes there is a hyperactive insula that causes unusual reactions to sensory events. Sometimes the social/emotional brain is feeble or virtually impotent. That may explain the tribe of OCs who are almost *autistic*.

Alexithymia

Self-awareness shouldn't be hard, but for some it is. For example, there are those with **alexithymia**. Their application for federal recognition as a tribe has been held up by the usual bureaucratic infighting and resistance from other tribes, notably the Aspergerites. The alexithymics insist that they are a legitimate tribe because, in contrast with the Aspergerites, they have a clear sense of *I* and *Thou*. They have their own kind of brain fault: they have difficulty identifying their feelings, expressing them, or even knowing that they have them. They have little difficulty with thoughts, as long as they are abstract or utilitarian, but they are "impoverished in their capacity for introspection or imagination" (Krystal, 1998).

Alexithymics have social deficits, ranging from the profound to the simply boring, in contrast to the Aspergerites, who are usually interesting, if peculiar. The psychiatrist Henry Krystal, described his alexithymic patients as "dull, mundane, unimaginative, utilitarian, and [given to] sequential recitation of concrete facts... [There is an] absence of the human quality [which] contributes to making these patients' thoughts 'operative' or 'thing orientated'" (Krystal, 1998). The appropriate question, of course, is what Krystal's patients thought of *him*. Also, how he felt about going to work in the morning.

Alexithymic patients seem dull, colorless or boring even if they are intellectual and clever (Taylor, 1984). Many such people find success and happiness in technical fields like engineering or IT, where a utilitarian style of thinking is useful. They don't realize they are happy, and that is just as well, because reflecting on one's emotional state can be distracting when one is trying to work.

Alexithymics, though, are a dying race. They are gradually being absorbed by the much bigger tribe of Aspergerites—that is, the people with **Asperger's syndrome**—even as the Aspergerites themselves have been reassigned by the Indian Bureau to the "Autism Spectrum Disorder." The psychiatric categories, you see, are modeled on brain itself: they are made by distributed networks of learned men and women oscillating for a while over a particular problem, like how to pigeonhole yet one more unfortunate collection of their conspecifics. They recruit data from parallel networks, make what seem to them to be necessary changes, and then oscillate away to make mischief somewhere else.

Asperger's syndrome

Since "Asperger's disorder" has been expunged from the latest DSM, we can assume that the copyright has expired and one is free to use the term as one chooses. The Aspergerites have been quick to take advantage. On their websites and in their chatrooms they gather in open defiance of DSM criteria and refer to themselves as "Aspies." I prefer "Aspergerites," which is less warm and fuzzy but more appropriate to the tone of this book. I would never call them "analytical mindists" or "intellectualists," although they are afflicted by the systematizing and utilitarian energies of the analytical mind; they have little interest in imposing such ways of thinking on others. They tend to be shy, not controlling, and content in the exercise of logic and reason.

I would never suggest that every towering intellect is detached from or insensitive to their emotional lives or those of others, even if many of them are. Some are Aspergerites, others are just OC, although sometimes it's hard to tell the difference. A more common reason why most Great Brains are oblivious is that they are content in their active minds. They aren't necessarily unempathic: they just don't notice the comings and goings of other human beings. You might say that they are preoccupied, like absent-minded professors.

I have known more than a few fellows like that. A Great Brain such as Dr. Heinrich Klüver, for example, spent his later years squirreled away in the lab, never receiving visitors. He was hard at work, one presumes; although we don't know, because shortly before he retired a plumbing leak destroyed most of his papers. If one happened into his inner sanctum—before the flood, anyway—he could be a cordial colleague, although after you came in he locked the door.

If you're married to such a man, you may have noticed that it's not easy to get his attention, although the kids can, or the dog. My wife sometimes comes into the library and says, "I'm running away with the milkman," but she's just kidding, of course. Just another example of the hilarity that suffuses our happy home. She has learned to find fulfillment in the children, her busy restaurant and her personal trainer, Xavier.

Most of the Great Brains of history were not Aspergites but some were certifiable cases of Asperger's syndrome, obsessive-compulsive disorder, Tourette's syndrome or alexithymia, or all of the above at the same time. Newton and Einstein, for example, are thought to have had Asperger's syndrome. Granted, the diagnoses were made by people who didn't know them personally and never had the chance to give them a psychological test. Nevertheless, the interpersonal peculiarities of those two men are compelling. Einstein was a nonverbal child, dreamy and solitary, and when he started to talk he was echolalic, repeating what he had just heard before he responded. He continued to do so as an adult. His personal life was a hash, too.

Einstein was a creature of habit, and his best friend during the years in Princeton was the mathematician Kurt Godel, who himself was given to persistent, low-level insanity (the radiators in his house, he thought, emitted toxic gas, so he kept them turned off). Godel, too, was a creature of habit, and he called for Einstein every morning at 11 o'clock. Whatever the weather, they walked together to the Institute. If only we knew what they talked about, walking that mile to Fuld Hall. "Well, Kurt, have you got those radiators fixed?" "Not yet, Al, but, say, do you know you've been wearing that same sweatshirt for two weeks now?"

Newton was an odd character, careless in his dress like Einstein, and singularly incapable of forming close friendships. He is said to have been "morbidly secretive and suspicious" (James, 2003).

The prolific inventor Nikola Tesla, who claimed to have been celibate and whose life history reveals numerous autistic traits, once said:

> I do not think there is any thrill that can go through the human heart like that felt by the inventor as he sees some creation of the brain unfolding to success... Such emotions make a man forget food, sleep, friends, love, everything... I do not think you can name many great inventions that have been made by married men. (Pickover, 1998)

Henry Cavendish, an English scientist of extraordinary accomplishment, was a perfectionist in the pursuit of his work and also painfully shy. He was said to consider himself as a solitary being and unfit for society. "He probably uttered fewer words in the course of his life than any man who lived to fourscore years, not at all excepting the monks of La Trappe" (James, 2003).

Paul Dirac, one of the architects of quantum mechanics, was also taciturn to a fault, but "He would emit unusual vocalizations, a shrill cry he uttered as he shuffled quickly from room to room, seeming to be annoyed if looked at" (James, 2003).

Irène Joliot-Curie, elder daughter of Marie and Pierre Curie, is a good example of the consequences of assortative mating. Both of her parents were shy, and her mother was a bit eccentric, to say the least. Irène herself had great difficulty greeting and dealing with strangers, was "Rather awkward in her movements," and was "by nature very reserved" (James, 2003). She had difficulty making friends. She never acquired the art of casual conversation and was remarkably insensitive. If there's a Mead-hall in Asgard for warriors who die with a slide rule in their hand or an unsolved formula on the mind, it can't be a lively place—but, then, neither were our faculty parties at the Brain Research Institute.

Einstein once said:

I do not socialize because social encounters would distract me from my work and I really only live for that, and it would shorten even further my very limited lifespan. (James, 2004)

Einstein thought that social intercourse would simply crowd his capacity for deep thought, and who am I to disagree with Einstein? Theoretically, the mental energy that would ordinarily be devoted to social cognition is, in such men and women, entirely subsumed by their extraordinary powers of abstract thought. Hence the idea that the empathic brain and analytical intelligence are competitive, and that to be good in one necessarily entails weakness in the other. It's not something I just made up: Einstein did. Or maybe Newton.

* * *

Like many people who are OC, Aspergerites usually have intelligent brains. Sometimes they are superior; and sometimes, like Einstein and Newton, they are sublime. Mozart was not an Aspergerite. His tics, coprolalia (scatological language) and repetitive behaviors are suggestive of OC and Tourette's syndrome. The vast majority of such patients do not have the complete syndrome, and Mozart didn't either.

Some autistic **savants** have fabulous talents, like perfect pitch or calendrical skills—"What day of the week was August 3, 1492?" There are also **hyperlexics**, who can read a page in 8 seconds and recall its content perfectly well, and **mnemonists**, like the young man who memorized *The Rise and Fall of the Roman Empire* and could recite it forwards and backwards (Down, 1887). Others have prodigious sensory or perceptual abilities. Savants are fascinating, especially to neurologists, because prodigious skills have been known to arise following brain injuries or strokes, and even during the early stages of frontotemporal dementia; and to psychologists who propose that savant skills can be cultivated in "neurotypical" adults. Naturally, there have been theories or conjectures, at least, none of which have been successful, although all of them have an element in common: one part of brain—one complex functional unit—can achieve primacy at the expense of some others. Mozart, I suppose, won his radiant musicality at the expense of money-management skills.

Autism and Asperger's syndrome

At about the same time that Leo Kanner, a child psychiatrist at Johns Hopkins, described the first cases of "Autistic disturbances of affective contact" (Kanner, 1968), an Austrian pediatrician, Hans Asperger, wrote his graduate thesis on "'Autistic psychopathy' in childhood" (Asperger, 1944). That both authors chose the same adjective was a happy accident, because Baltimore and Vienna were at war at the time, and the two men did not communicate until much later. Autism is a venerable psychiatric term that means "a loss of contact, a retirement into self and a disregard of the outside world," and it had previously been applied to patients with schizophrenia. Neither Kanner nor Asperger thought that their cases were schizophrenic, but they were struck by their deficits in social relating—even during infancy, some autistic infants resist "molding" contentedly in their parents' arms—and by the intense, circumscribed and unusual interests they had, especially for inanimate objects and for patterns.

It wasn't until many years later that psychiatrists in North America and Britain learned of Asperger's work. They agreed that Asperger's syndrome (AS) was in the autism family, but they weren't quite sure whether it was the same as "high-functioning autism" (HFA)—that is, autistic individuals with normal intelligence. Whether it is or isn't has been the occasion of innumerable arguments, the likes of which the reader has come to expect from learned psychiatrists. Some respected psychiatrists believe that HFA and AS are different conditions, albeit both on the **autism spectrum**.

In common clinical usage, Asperger's syndrome is a mild form of autism. The term is usually applied to people who are socially clumsy, rather than unrelated, as an autistic person is; to someone who has difficulty in reading the emotional state of another person, but only because he doesn't care to notice; who is empathic, but only when he is reminded to be; and whose thinking is utilitarian or operational and deeply engaged in special, arcane interests, but not preoccupied with meaningless rituals and repetitive behaviors, as autistic people are. In the new terminology, an Asperger's patient will be someone on the mild side of the autistic spectrum.

In his seminal paper, Hans Asperger wrote:

> A good professional attitude involves single-mindedness as well as a decision to give up a large number of other interests. Many people find this a very unpleasant decision. Quite a number of young people choose the wrong job because, being equally talented in different areas, they cannot muster the dedication to focus on a single career. With the autistic individual the matter is entirely different. With collected energy and obvious confidence and, yes, with a blinkered attitude towards life's rich

rewards, they go their own way, the way in which their talents have directed them since childhood.

It seems that for success in science or art a dash of autism is essential. For success the necessary ingredients may be an ability to turn away from the everyday world, from the simple practical, an ability to rethink a subject with originality so as to create in new untrodden ways, with all abilities canalised into the one speciality. (Asperger, 1944)

The next time you visit your doctor and he seems to be brusque and doesn't make good eye contact, if he seems to be a bit socially awkward and incapable of sympathy, let alone empathy, remember this: "A good professional attitude involves single-mindedness as well as a decision to give up a large number of other interests." Medicine, I think, like a good many other highly competitive fields, is increasingly laden with men and women who were content to spend the four best years of their lives, the varsity debauch, taking the most difficult courses and single-mindedly pursuing a GPA higher than 3.85. This is as it should be, I suppose; one doesn't want a degenerate or a wanton as one's doctor. In evolutionary terms, however, this kind of selection pressure leads to a degree of homogeneity in the profession, selecting for men and women who are a bit on the OC/SA side. Does this account for the problems that have arisen in the practice of medicine: the focus on procedures rather than people; the preoccupation with details rather than the broad picture; and a medical edifice that is so perfectly regulated and complex that no one, not even national governments, can afford to pay for it? Probably not; such changes are inevitable as a field matures, acquires new technologies and a bureaucratic superstructure, and as the bureaucratic superstructure then takes over. But the perfectionistic men and women who fill its highest places are not likely candidates to perceive what the problem is, let alone to change it.

For the record, the Dustin Hoffman character in *Rain Man* was a high-functioning autist, a social and emotional isolate, but he was also a savant: that is, a Great Brain in narrow confines. The Great Detective, however, was an Aspergerite, disinterested in matters social and emotional, but able to understand them well enough when he had to. In the field of detection, one needs to understand the wellsprings of human nature even if one doesn't share them. If Holmes were an HFA, he might be adept at uncovering the obscurest clues but Dr. Watson would have to solve the crime.

Alexithymia, Aspergerism and high-functioning autism are categories, but arguments over what they are and how they relate to one another have been so rancorous and unproductive that the authorities have consigned them all to a spectrum. The spectrum theory is that alexithymia, Aspergerism and high-functioning autism are different in some respects but similar in some fundamental way that has yet to be uncovered. There are plenty of theories. Simon Baron-Cohen, a psychologist at Cambridge (and a cousin of Sacha Baron-Cohen, the comic), proposed that autism is an extreme manifestation of "male psychology." It is only one of many theories that try to explain that condition, each less probable than others previously expounded. I, for one, prefer to associate male psychology with penile readiness, if anything; hardly a trait to characterize any of the gentlemen described above.

The autism epidemic

Is there an autism epidemic? There is evidence to that effect. Studies done before 1985 cited autism rates of 4 to 5 per 10,000 children; recent data in Sweden show a prevalence of autism and related conditions at 71 per 10,000; and in the USA, the figure is 67 per 10,000 children. The idea that the disorder is increasing in the world originated with a Swedish child psychiatrist, Christopher Gillberg, who reported that the rate had increased thirty times from 1980 to 1988 in the city of Göteborg, where he worked (Gillberg, Steffenburg, and Schaumann, 1991). Gillberg is a serious researcher and was only making the point that autism wasn't as rare as clinicians had once thought and that, when they were properly instructed, they made more accurate diagnoses.

As a result of Gillberg's work and that of many other autism researchers a generation ago, autism became more than a curiosity among the child psychiatrists. Since then, psychologists, social workers and teachers are routinely drilled on the subject, advocacy groups have arisen around the world, and special programs in schools have been developed for autistic children. All that has been a good thing, no doubt, although it's regrettable that corresponding efforts have not been made with equal vigor on behalf of children with run-of-the-mill developmental disabilities or emotional problems who aren't autistic. In order to take advantage of such programs, it's not surprising that clinicians bend over backwards to denote a child as autistic or "on the autism spectrum."

In spite of an obvious explanation, the wrong message has taken hold and the autism epidemic has become an article of faith. Social critics and others of that ilk have cited the predictable explanations, such as vaccination, toxic chemicals in the environment, infertility treatments and induced labor. In other words, Modern Society. The original theory of autism was that it was caused by "refrigerator mothers." There is something about autism that just invites ideological divagations. There isn't an autism epidemic. *There's an epidemic of OC.*

"Any truth is better than indefinite doubt"[1]

Now, autism is not OCD and OC is not Aspergerism, but they are close relations and have a lot in common. As we shall see, the brains of autists and Aspergerites are similar to those of OCs and SAs. But we don't want to get ahead of ourselves. Our method, you may have noticed, is "to reason backward from effects to causes."[2]

---

1   Arthur Conan Doyle, "The Yellow Face" (*The Memoirs of Sherlock Holmes*).
2   Arthur Conan Doyle, "The Adventure of the Cardboard Box" (*His Last Bow*).

The defining properties of autism are (1) persistent deficits in social communication and social interaction and (2) restricted, repetitive patterns of behavior, interests or activities. The defining properties of OC are (1) restricted, repetitive patterns of behavior, interests, activities or thought (2) that affect social, emotional, occupational and recreational behavior. The defining properties of social anxiety are (1) fears that arise in social, occupational and recreational endeavors with unfamiliar people (2) that lead them to lead restricted lives. It is easy to tell them apart in a strong light, but harder at dusk.

OC and Aspergerism are similar on an overt level:

- Studies of autistic individuals have shown a high rate of OC symptoms, repetitive behaviors, rituals, tics and stereotypies. Those are said to be different from compulsions, but I'm not so sure.
- Unusual sensory reactions are common to both species. Young OC patients, like autistic patients, react to the labels on the inside of T-shirts, the elastic in shorts, the seams in socks, the texture of fabrics and food.
- Autistic people are preoccupied with routines and sameness in their environment. One can even say that they are obsessed with sameness. Going to the store or to school, one must always follow the same route. Going back home does not have to be by a different route: it needs to be the same way. I suppose that is one way to distinguish an Aspergerite from an OC.
- They will keep their special things just so on their desk, line things up, and order them by color or shape. If something is out of order, they will notice it immediately and promptly correct it. They are quite rigid in their ways, and also in their thinking. Cognitive rigidity is the inability to accommodate one's thinking to environmental feedback or to the exigencies of a novel situation. "They" might equally refer to an autistic person or to an OC.

- The families of autistic patients almost invariably include a number of individuals who are OC. Conversely, genetic studies of OCD patients show high numbers of relatives with autistic traits. There is also a genetic association between OCD and social anxiety (Samuels *et al.*, 2014).

Whether the resemblance between autism and OC is superficial or fundamental, the treatments overlap to a remarkable degree. Among physicians who treat numbers of autistic people, as we do, a serotonergic (such as an SSRI) antidepressant is one of the first medication treatments brought to bear and is usually helpful; in autistic children, we also use $alpha_2$ agonists like guanfacine, which is also effective for OC symptoms and tics. The clinical response to these agents is like that of OCD patients: rituals and compulsive behaviors are reduced; anxiety, depression and emotional instability are alleviated; the harsh intensity of interpersonal reactions is diminished; and positive elements, like attention, productivity and communication, are increased. Aggression and self-injurious behavior may also decrease.

The autism spectrum is like the OCD spectrum I described in Chapter 3. On the basis of the evidence cited above, we *abduce* that there is a common deficit in brain activity among individuals whose overt characteristics may be quite different. Precisely what that deficit is remains an open question.

18
Theory of Autism

In 1888, two British surgeons, Sanger Brown and E. A. Schafer, studied monkeys by performing lesions—that is, cutting out selected parts of their brains. Their goal was to define the cerebral localization of sensory systems (Brown and Schafer, 1888). They failed to appreciate the importance of what they had found, which is why it is called "the Klüver-Bucy syndrome" rather than "the Brown-Schafer syndrome."

Brown and Schafer described the monkeys with lesioned brains. Monkey #6 was a "fine, large, active Rhesus monkey" who had first his right and then his left temporal lobe removed. The monkey had been "very wild and even fierce, assaulting any person who teased or tried to handle him." After the operation he became placid and indifferent. When a "strange Monkey, wild and savage, was placed in the common cage…our Monkey immediately began to investigate the new comer, but his attentions were repulsed, and a fight resulted, in which he was being considerably worsted." The authors remarked that the "memory and intelligence [of Monkey #6] seemed deficient" because before very long he set about investigating the wild and savage monkey again. The outcome of his second investigation was not described, but one can only imagine.

Monkey #6 had some other peculiar behaviors:

He no longer seemed to understand the meaning of sounds, sights, and other impressions that reached him. Every object with which he came into contact, even those with which he was previously most familiar, appeared strange and were investigated with curiosity. Everything he endeavored to feel, taste, and smell and to carefully examine from every point of view. Food was devoured greedily, the head being dipped into the dish, instead of the food being conveyed to the mouth by the hands in the way usual with monkeys.

Brown and Schafer didn't make too much of all this. Monkey #6 made a nice recovery, they said, and before long he was behaving like every other monkey in the common cage. This led them to conclude that there wasn't much function localized in the temporal lobes at all, let alone anything that had to do with sensory processing. They were wrong, of course, but in their day there weren't very good ways to examine the psychology of monkeys. Nor were there psychologists about who were interested in trying. For that reason, brain scientists in the 19th century and the first half of the 20th tended to assume that vast expanses of the cerebral hemispheres didn't do very much.

* * *

Much changed when a psychologist, Heinrich Klüver, took to studying animal psychology in earnest. Klüver was a German psychologist who emigrated to the USA in 1923. He spent a year at Stanford, then he went to the University of Minnesota and finally to the University of Chicago; in the latter two places he became a good friend of Karl Lashley. He was young then and hadn't yet taken to locking himself, alone, in his lab.

Klüver's first interest was memory, and in particular **eidetic imagery**: the ability to retain an accurate, detailed visual image of a complex scene or pattern, to envision an exact copy of the original sensory experience. This, he said, was "first among the true advances in psychology in the last decade" (Nahm and Pribram, 1998).

To advance his study of eidetic memory, Klüver developed an interest in the peyote cults of the Southwestern Indians; the active drug in peyote, mescaline, produces vivid visual hallucinations. He was the Carlos Castaneda of his day. "With the aid of an assistant in a laboratory setting at the University of Minnesota around 1924, he ingested mescal buttons and compulsively documented the nature of his own experiences during intoxicated states" (Nahm and Pribram, 1998). Before long he moved on to primates, and developed tests for them to do after he had given them mescal and other psychoactive drugs. Then his friend Lashley taught him the technique of lesion analysis.

For a good reason that we won't go into now, Klüver decided that mescaline might exert its effects on the temporal lobes. He convinced a neurosurgeon, Paul Bucy, to perform temporal-lobe resections, which were beyond his skills as a lesionist.

> On the afternoon of December 7, 1936, Dr. Bucy removed a large portion of the left temporal lobe in the aggressive adult female Rhesus monkey named "Aurora." This monkey had been an experimental subject of Prof. George W. Bartelmes, but due to its viciousness was offered to Klüver who was recognized for his monkey handling skills. As recounted by Bucy, on the morning after the left temporal lobe was removed, Klüver called him on the phone and exclaimed, "What did you do to my monkey?" Hastening to the laboratory, Bucy saw that this preoperatively aggressive monkey had by all accounts become "tame." It was unbelievable. This formerly vicious, unmanageable beast was indeed tame. (Nahm and Pribram, 1998)

The characteristics of Aurora and a number of similarly lesioned monkeys have since been known as the **Klüver-Bucy syndrome** (KBS). They had these characteristics:

Emotional placidity or indifference—KBS monkeys lose their instinctive fear of snakes.

Psychic blindness—"The monkey seemed just as eager to examine the tongue of a hissing snake, the mouth of a cat, a wire cage, or a wagon as a piece of food" (Klüver and Bucy, 1937). The salience of an object is lost.

Hypermetamorphosis—Repetitive and persistent handling of objects. The monkeys were "stimulus-bound": anything that crossed their field of vision seemed to require their full attention.

Hyperorality—The monkeys evaluated everything around them by putting it into their mouths.

Hypersexuality—Increased manipulation of the genitals and compulsive, "omnisexual" behavior.

Klüver and Bucy reasoned that damage to the temporal lobes had disrupted the processes by which the meaning of a sensory event is appreciated. Between the stimulus and the response lay an essential psychological process: the ability to perceive an event in a way that makes sense. It is in the medial structures of the temporal lobes that a Gestalt slots into place. The KBS experiment has been repeated many times, and the syndrome also occurs in humans with severe traumatic brain injuries or temporal-lobe (limbic) encephalitis. When such tragedies occur in children, the children are quite autistic and have severe intellectual disabilities. Symptoms like those of the KBS also occur in patients with frontotemporal dementia: emotional shallowness, social avoidance, perseverative self-stimulation, disinhibition, inappropriate exploratory behavior and even hypersexuality (Tang-Wai *et al.*, 2002). Subsequent research has identified the source of all these problems: it is our friend the amygdala, which has a key role in perceptual processing; that is, in making sense of data that arrives on multiple sensory channels.

* * *

Destroying both amygdalae (one has one on each side) disables an animal from forming **cross-modal associations** among sensory data. Information received on one sensory channel doesn't synch with information received on the others. What something looks like can't be integrated with what it feels like, tastes, sounds or smells like. One can only imagine how confusing this must be. In monkeys, amygdalar lesions blind them to the meaning of their perceptions. Give the monkey an object, it doesn't matter what, and he touches it over and over again, he puts it to his mouth and may even try to have sex with it. The object excites excruciating feelings of doubt and uncertainty, and he relies on his most primitive senses to alleviate the problem. Autistic children may do something similar, and the term for it is **near-receptor preference**. One's near receptors—taste, touch and smell—are phylogenetically much older than vision and hearing and require fewer neural connections in the brain. As a consequence, autistic children are given to repetitive touching, smelling and tasting, whatever the object happens to be. It's as if they're responding to uncertainty with compulsive behavior. Little babies also do something similar. They are much more sensitive to taste, touch and smell, and as soon as they can manipulate objects they bring them to their mouths. (Small babies also show psychic blindness: they aren't even afraid of spiders or snakes, or strangers.)

Hypermetamorphosis and hyperorality are ways for an organism—a lesioned monkey or a little baby—to strengthen a percept that is normally reinforced by the integration of parallel sensory inputs. The result of a Klüver-Bucy lesion is cross-modal failure; the animal can't grasp the wider meaning of an object or an event because he is deprived of all the salient data. KBS monkeys can stimulate one sensory channel at a time, but the stimulus, unsupported by information from other sources, fades from their working memory soon after it has been formed. So, they do the same thing again, and again.

* * *

Klüver's work was the first systematic investigation of what the amygdala was there for. He never referred to it as an "emotional processer"; only later was it known that the amygdala participated in social and emotional regulation. The principle, however, is the same. Social and emotional processing—understanding people, what they are up to and how they feel—entails associating data from multiple sources, not only from the words they say but also from their tone of voice, their gestures and facial expressions, and the vibrations they exude. The data are picked up by more than one sensory channel and integrated with memory and intuition. Meaning and affect are thus conjoined by means that are neither verbal nor abstract.

Cross-modal integration is essential to social relating and it happens in most mammals the same way. In one experiment, a horse (A) was made to watch a member of his herd (B) led before him and then hidden behind a barrier. Then, the whinnies of an unknown horse were played over the loudspeaker. This incongruency between what he saw and heard caused no little dismay to horse A, who dealt with the matter in the most emphatic way. He sought horse B assiduously—*Was that really horse B I saw?*, we can imagine him saying to himself (Proops, McComb, and Reby, 2009). Recognizing one's familiars, it seems, entails knowing them in many dimensions, and that's probably what makes them familiar.

The Klüver-Bucy operation has even more devastating effects if the experimental animal is lesioned in infancy. The surgery is an approximation of what may happen in utero or at the time of birth to make someone autistic; they are unable to activate the amygdala in social situations, even in intense circumstances. Animals deprived of an amygdala at the time of birth evade contact with their conspecifics. They respond repetitively when posed with a problem, unable to resolve the persistent doubt that accompanies all their perceptions. They focus their attention on a particular part, a niggling detail, and are never able to generate the meaning that only emerges when parts are appreciated as a whole. They make inappropriate responses to social cues (Gualtieri, 2002).

* * *

The theme should be familiar by now: parts of brain can be disconnected, or weakly connected. They are disabled from making the necessary contributions to neural circuits, and some kind of imbalance ensues. In autism a central fault is weakness in integrating information arriving on multiple channels. It has a particular effect on social and emotional processing.

The problem must be dealt with. A weakness in one component of brain always generates changes in others. Brain compensates as best it can. Aspergerites, we assume, like OCs, have circumscribed weaknesses. They also have ample resources to make effective compensations; for example, "Activation of the error monitoring system triggers an intensification in top-down control by the cerebral cortex" (Botvinick *et al.*, 2001). Such compensations don't make them whole, but they are able to get by and sometimes they prosper. Einstein did, and Tesla and Newton. Godel, on the other hand, was a suicide.

* * *

The problem that most autistic children have is that their weaknesses are more diffuse. The congenital insults that damaged the inner surface of the temporal lobes have likely damaged other parts. Their compensations are less effective. They retire into autistic isolation. Aberrant neural signals excite unusual activity in the basal ganglia and they engage in repetitive, stereotypical behaviors. Their perceptual apparatus is impaired and they respond to sensations in unusual ways. Their experience of pain and reward can be disrupted and with baneful consequences.

Thoughts arising in an unusual context

Aspergerism and OC are examples of an excess of analysis overshadowing social and emotional arenas. If meaning fails to arise in parts of brain that are dedicated to provide just that, or if those parts attach too much meaning to the most obscure sensation, there is only one thing for the neocortex to do: *figure it out*. And quite literally, with *figures*: numbers, symbols, mathematical operations and logical sequences. We have observed, therefore, that the cognitive style of the Aspergerite is utilitarian or operational, and prone to deep engagement in special, sometimes arcane, interests. Aspergerites are as well endowed in analytical intelligence as they are impoverished in social communication. What lends meaning to their lives is abstract thought, the geometric, mathematical regularity of their thinking. They are unable to synchronize the feeble, irregular rhythms of their social/emotional brains with the potent, regular rhythms of their analytical minds.

In such circumstances, this happens: thoughts arise in unusual contexts. Isaac Newton, for example, came up with the unusual idea that planetary bodies could affect one another, at a distance, and with mathematical regularity. To Aristotle, an apple falling from a tree was simply acting out its meaning. It was heavy, and heavy things fall to the Earth. That's the *meaning* of heavy. But Newton found meaning somewhere else, in symbols.

* * *

Newton, apparently, was struck by the fact that the apple fell *perpendicularly* to the Earth. Now, you've probably seen something falling to the Earth—if not an apple then something else, like the freshly-baked strawberry shortcake you were carrying to the picnic table. It isn't likely you noticed it fell *perpendicularly*. You probably dealt with the event in a less abstract way.

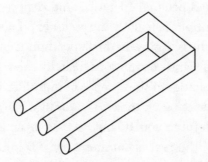

Figure 18.1 An ambiguous figure

Thoughts and actions that arise in an unusual context, like Newton's, are not always successful. In certain psychological tests, autistic people are better at perceiving the details of a problem than its Gestalt. This trait is captured by the theory of **weak central coherence**: autistic people have a detail-focused cognitive style that makes it hard for them to extract global form or meaning (Happé and Frith, 2006). In common language, they don't see the forest for the trees.

One's brain is normally equipped to integrate its locally oriented processing units in order to generate a Gestalt, a coherent whole. It is synchronization, when perceptions, memories, intuitions and feelings are bound together in order to generate meaning. The cognitive style of the Aspergerite, the high-functioning autist, is different: it is an information-processing bias that favors part or detail processing over processing wholes or meaning. What matters are small things, not how they fit together or what their significance might be. An autistic person has no difficulty at all with Figure 18.1 above. For the rest of us, it is impossible; the Gestalt simply won't slot into place. If, however, you found the illusion quite normal, complete this sentence: "You can go hunting with a knife and...." If you say "a fork," you were responding to "local coherence." If your answer is "kill a hawg," you appreciate the global coherence of the sentence.

The cognitive style of weak central coherence is not simply being "detail-oriented." It's attending to detail to the exclusion of the big picture, and it's not peculiar to autists and Aspergerites. Obsessive slowness, for example, is usually the result of pondering details and forgetting deadlines. A moralistic disposition is preoccupied with adherence to rules and conventions, usually their smallest codicils and usually in defiance of the essence of morality. The Rabbi Hillel, it is said, was able to teach the entire Torah while standing on one leg: "What is hateful to you, do not do to your neighbor. That's the whole Torah. All the rest is commentary" (Talmud Shabbat 31a). Details of procedure are emphasized by some, even when those details thwart the proper course of morality, justice or effective governance.

The Russian neuropsychologist Alexander Luria spent his early years in the Central Asian republics studying the psychology of illiterate people. He was interested in their capacity for abstract thought, among other things. He asked an illiterate peasant to describe a tree. "Why should I describe a tree? Everyone knows what a tree is. There's a lot of trees around here" (Gleick, 2011). The meaning of a tree, to the peasant, wasn't something to abstract. A tree was just there, and if an apple fell out of it, well, that's what apples do. You ought to pick them first, so you can eat them before the bugs get to them. Nothing is more delicious than a fresh apple right off the tree.

One's subcortex appreciates the meaning of an apple, and a tree, as they relate to us as links in the great chain of Nature, as habitants of a world that is as marvelous as it is mysterious. This, like the Bushman's, is considered by some to be a *lower form* of thought. One must approach the apple in a systematic way and assign its fall to a category, perpendicularity. That, we are taught, is an act of *reason*, than which there is nothing higher. Now, I have nothing against abstract thought, higher reasoning or indeed mathematical symbols, but one never wants to spend too much time there. In a few minutes I shall be in the garden, where some azalea bushes must be moved to make more room for F's flowers. This will lend meaning to my day.

* * *

Analytical thinking, a penchant for perceiving something in a unique way coupled with a strong desire to figure it out, is characteristic of an active mind. Aspergerites, OCs and alexithymics may have active minds, but they perceive parts to the exclusion of the whole. Analytical thinking may overshadow intuition, especially in Aspergerites, but the two aren't mutually exclusive. Each is better if they hover together. The perpendicular fall of an apple stimulated an intuition in Newton's head. He went on to create a language of sublime abstraction with which to express it. Which was the more important accomplishment? They were both important. Newton can't have been a perfect Aspergerite because he was able to hover between the dorsal networks that generate abstractions and the default networks that generate meaning. Perhaps Great Minds like Newton's are capable of occupying both networks at once. There is a brain part, we have learned, that does that.

The Klüver-Bucy phenomenon is, like every abstraction, only an imperfect model of what happens in the lives of OCs and Aspergerites. No pathological process is surgically precise, and one that extirpated both temporal lobes would necessarily damage other parts of brain as well. Even in the most severely afflicted patients, damage to cross-modal processing is never absolute. The KBS, therefore, is only suggestive. OCs and Aspergerites aren't *unable* to make cross-modal associations; but they do have a relative *weakness* in doing so. Their experience of social and emotional events is not incoherent, just less coherent. In response, they rely on analytical thinking. They look for "alternative strategies for interpreting emotionally evocative encounters":

> High-functioning children with autism were less inclined to organize their emotional accounts in personalized causal-explanatory frameworks and displayed a tendency to describe visually salient elements of experiences seldom observed among comparison children. Findings suggest that children with autism possess less coherent representations of emotional experiences and use alternative strategies for interpreting emotionally evocative encounters. (Losh and Capps, 2006)

One's perceptions, and how one puts them together, are dominant influences on how one thinks, feels and behaves. We have seen the consequences of a hyper-reactive perceptual apparatus. It makes an OC behave in certain ways. A perceptual system that integrates data in untypical ways produces another result. One that never integrates at all... Fortunately, that hardly ever happens. Brain will ultimately find a workaround. That's why Monkey #6 was able, finally, to calm down and rejoin the troop. It's why social relating may be difficult in childhood, but as kids grow up, most of them figure it out.

Folie de doute

There is a theory that uncertainty and doubt drive OC. We can attribute it, in part at least, to the idiosyncrasies of the perceptual system, or rather to its diversity. It's hard to figure why natural selection allowed deviations in such a fundamental function, but there you are. *You're so sensitive, Risteard. You take umbrage at the slightest little things.* His exquisite sensitivity to detail has allowed Risteard to win the confidence of his clients, who entrust him with vast sums. He can perceive the smallest trends in the market before they even begin to trend, but he misinterprets your night out with your friends just because Xavier happened to be there. How different from your last boyfriend, who hardly noticed whether you were there or not. A natural selectionist would suggest that this kind of phenotypic diversity gives Sheila an opportunity to make the right choice on behalf of the future of the race. In my opinion, the right choice is, neither.

If social interactions and families operated on the basis of analysis rather than meaning, the consequences would be stultifying. Families and societies, in contrast to bureaucratic agencies, operate on the basis of shared values and common assumptions—cognitive habits, one might say—that operate automatically and beneath one's conscious horizon. Social cognition is communal, although it may also be sectarian; families, tribes and small groups cultivate their own intimate styles of social perception, judgment and effective action. Analytical thinking, on the other hand, is universal. Its language, mathematics, is symbolic and disembodied.

Social cognition is holistic and impressionistic. Its tools are inference, intuition and counterfactual thinking. It is highly context-dependent and it is also tolerant of paradox and inconsistencies. It evolved among the birds and mammals because it provided a survival advantage in environments where things are always changing, where predictions are only conjectures because perfect knowledge is never available. Analytical thinking is focused and linear. If it can construct a Gestalt at all, it is only by a series of steps and lawful relationships. It seeks patterns and disdains inconsistencies. How tiresome it would be to deconstruct every social event to all of the granular processes operating beneath the surface and to try to reconstruct their meaning from the bottom up.

Bureaucracies are all about process and regulations, not efficient operation or achieving worthwhile goals. To a bureaucracy, following procedures and obeying regulations is a sufficient goal. They go hunting with a knife and a fork. For example, on January 13, 1865, Dostoevsky tells us, Ivan Matveitch, a government clerk, went with his wife to see a crocodile that was being displayed at the Arcade. Tickling the crocodile's nose to see him snort, Ivan Matveitch fell into the animal's jaws and was swallowed whole. His wife, Elena Ivanovna, grasped the situation immediately and demanded that her husband be cut out at once, whereupon ensued a heated argument with the crocodile's owner, who was reluctant to lose his only source of livelihood.

> ...Mein Vater showed crocodile, mein Grossvater showed crocodile, mein Sohn will show crocodile, and I will show crocodile!...[1]

After further discussions proved fruitless, the voice of Ivan Matveitch was heard from within the horrible beast.

> My dear, my advice is to apply direct to the superintendent's office... I am only uneasy as to the view my superiors may take of the incident: for after getting a permit to go abroad I've got into a crocodile, which seems anything but clever.

1　Fyodor Dostoevsky, *The Crocodile*.

As it happens, men's central coherence tends to be weaker than that of women. For example:

Linda and Armand

Linda: "Hello, Armand? It's Linda. I called to tell you there's a dead clown in my bathtub."

Armand: "Really? I wonder what he's doing there?"

L: "He's not doing anything, Armand. He's dead."

A: "Do you know who he is, Linda?"

L: "No, Armand. But I think it's your clown suit. The one you wore last year at Halloween."

A: "No, Linda, it can't be. Last year I was a pirate."

L: "Last year you were a clown, Armand. Why do you always contradict me?"

A: "I don't *always* contradict you, Linda. I try to be affirming. Let's try to stay focused here; I'm quite sure I was a pirate last year."

Granted, such interactions are not likely to occur in the improbable event of a dead clown in one's bathtub, but the anecdote captures the turgidity of one's adventures with bureaucracies of every stripe. Armand is either an Aspergerite or he has something to hide. Ivan Matveitch, by the way, survived the ordeal and became quite famous. Attention to procedure, any bureaucrat will tell you, is the road to success.

Technocrats make decisions based on systematic analysis. Common folk think they are crazy. I know that because my grandfather, Camillo, had a penchant for a type of Sardinian cheese that was cured with the larvae of a certain fly. He was eating it one summer evening in our country house. When my sister, C, saw the worm, she had an hysterical attack. It wasn't the first one she had or the last, so I can't attribute her instability to the worm. Nevertheless, I have since learned that the cheese was banned in Brussels.

I understand that the sequence of the events cited is a bit off, but sometimes one can find meaning by being temporally cross-modal. In contrast, the peculiarities of Aspergerites and OCs are related to difficulties making cross-modal associations of any kind. Details perceived in one mental system fail to connect with details perceived in another. Armand's empathic mind perceived that Linda is upset. His analytical mind, however, perceived that she was wrong about the chronology of his Halloween costumery. Assuming that he is an Aspergerite and not a callous murderer, the latter perception will generate more mental energy and occupy his attention, while her distress (like that of Elena Ivanovna) hardly registers in his active but narrowly focused mind.

19
Six Degrees of Kevin Bacon

OCs and Aspergerites are prone to reverberating loops, to cross-modal associations that get crossed and to output spaces that get clogged. We have attributed the problems, thus far, to problems in brain organization and to imbalances that occur when one brain part is hyperactive and another may not be active enough. We have described networks that generate oscillations, thereby binding other networks into something like an integrated brain field. Electric fields in brain are immaterial, just as gravity is immaterial, but we experience gravity when we find it hard to get up from a comfortable chair or when we drop an egg and it splats on the floor. The egg didn't fall because you are clumsy, it's gravity. We also experience brain fields as thoughts, feelings and actions. When you do something stupid, it's really your brain fields.

The activity in one's brain, for better or worse, is expressed as electric fields, and fields are generated by neural networks. Neural networks are connections among neurons, our tiny brain cells. The connections are the way brain organized itself during the evolution of our race and during the development of every individual. Neurons form anatomical connections that are hard-wired and also functional connections that are not only transient but virtually instantaneous. Every part of brain is connected, directly or indirectly, with every other part.

Clearly, one needs to know about those connections. How

neurons connect to one another is the basis for brain organization and everything else that happens in brain. Such facts are the basis for studies of brain connectivity, or the **connectome**. We have discovered, for example, that the brains of OCs and Aspergerites are similar in the way they are connected, and their connectivity is different from that of people who aren't OC or Aspergerish.

Autistic individuals tend to have bigger heads than "neurotypicals," as those of us who are not autistic are called. I'm not sure whether to take it as a complement or derogation. Be that as it may, we neurotypicals also have fewer neurons. At least half of the neurons we are born with are pruned away during childhood and adolescence, hopefully those that we don't need. In autism, the pruning is less aggressive. The autistic brain has more neurons, especially in the cortex, and many of those neurons are ectopic—that is, ones that migrate to the wrong place. As a result, cortical mini-columns have many more connections. Most connections are local, however, and the connectivity is more complex than it is in normal individuals. This increases the power of local computations, but it interferes with the proper development of higher-level networks. The autistic brain, therefore, has a relative imbalance between short- and long-range connections that favors local computations over global information-processing (Belmonte *et al.*, 2004; Ecker *et al.*, 2013).

In the best of circumstances, high-functioning autists and Aspergerites have an enhanced ability to perform circumscribed mental tasks, like mathematics or visual-spatial relationships. At worst, autistic individuals are content with aimless and repetitive forms of self-stimulation. But even in the best circumstances, they have significant deficits in the ability to perform tasks requiring the integration of information from multiple sources.

The famous Aspergerites were virtuosi of circumscribed information-processing tasks; their local processing capacities were impressive, even transcendent. But their lives were circumscribed. Aspergerism confers an extraordinary capacity to visualize mathematical relationships and to manipulate abstract concepts, but it occurs at a price. The mental energy one might ordinarily devote to emotional resonance and the social harmonic is, in such men and women, entirely subsumed by their extraordinary powers of computation. They were able to perceive things to which we neurotypicals are blind.

At one point I said that autistic people are unable to synchronize the feeble, irregular rhythms of their social/emotional brains with the potent and regular rhythms of their analytical minds. Local networks arranged hierarchically are characteristic of the analytical mind, and they are more highly connected than usual in autistic individuals, Aspergerites and OCs. Their long-range connections, characteristic of the social/emotional brain and with an assortative or dedicated structure, are less well connected.

Default, again

The social/emotional brain is also the default mode network (DMN), the brain's resting place and the site of gentle reflections on oneself and others. The default mode network relates reciprocally with the executive powers of the dorsal attention network, and mental activity is a continual back-and-forth between goal-directed activities and inner reflection. The default mode participates in functions that are disabled in autism: emotional processing, understanding social interactions, personal familiarity, theory of mind and the experience of joint attention. In autistic individuals, the DMN differs from that of normals in size and metabolism, patterns of neuronal growth and the concentration of ectopic neurons. Autistic patients have decreased connectivity and decreased activity in the DMN during the resting state, and the more autistic a patient happens to be, the less connected and less active his DMN is. Not only is the default network less well connected, but in addition its connections show a shift towards randomness. They have the organizational structure typical of the analytical mind (Assaf *et al.*, 2010; Jung *et al.*, 2014).

In Aspergerites, SAs and OCs, the default mode is also notably weak and its inner connections are less well developed. When I have said, at several points, that the analytical mind has a habit of intruding upon the operations of the social/emotional brain, it's another way of describing an unbalanced relationship been strong computation and weak reflection.

In a normal individual, the activity of the default mode network is *negatively correlated* with the activity of the central executive, the dorsal attention network (DAN). When the DAN is active, the DMN is not, and vice versa. The DAN is "task-positive," more active when attention is directed to a particular task; the DMN is less active. The default mode is more active in response to inward processes like autobiographical memory, imagination, daydreaming, and thinking about oneself and others (Stern *et al.*, 2012).

Autistic individuals don't deactivate their DMN when their DAN is active (Kennedy, Redcay, and Courchesne, 2006). The implication is that the ordinary activities that brain pursues in default mode don't happen in autistic people; not only self-referential processing and perspective-taking, but also judgments about other individuals and social situations, moral judgments, emotional processing, relaxation based on body consciousness, and even judgments of pleasantness. What neurotypicals consider to be a normal internal life is different for autistic individuals. Their thoughts are directed instead toward obsessive interests and preoccupations.

Patients with OCD are similar to autistic people in the relationship between the dorsal attention network and the default mode network. In OCD, the normal, reciprocal relationship between the DAN and the DMN is neither normal nor reciprocal. The negative correlations are attenuated; when the DAN is active, the DMN is active too. The intrinsic functional relationships between the two large-scale brain systems are distorted (Zhang *et al.*, 2011). Wandering into the domain of inner reflection should ordinarily be a quiet and restful event: when Aspergerites and OCs venture into that nonverbal world of bodily consciousness, however, they discover a landscape that is bleak and devoid of meaning.

The default mode network is designed to be a resting place. Its connections were formed during the long course of evolution. Its connections are meaningful. There are connections for *sad, happy, afraid, surprised, angry, disgusted*. Some have formed because they promote safety, others for love, and yet others as a resting place for quiet reflection. The connections in the DMN have one essence, though. It is groundedness. The DMN is *embodied*.

The analytical mind is cold and neutral for a purpose. It was formed by the accumulation of modules, connected randomly but reinforced by strict adherence to hierarchical organization. It is a *tabula rasa* designed to accommodate abstractions, which are disembodied events. The analytical mind is never grounded; it moves among the spirits of thought.

When one resides in the pleasant resting place of one's imagination, it all comes together. Coherence isn't just a property of neural networks: it should also characterize a good story, and OC is a very good story. One can envisage in all of this the fact of individual differences: the degree to which neurons proliferate or don't, the degree to which they are pruned or not, the numbers of neurons clustering together to form a small-world network and how many of them are in the wrong place, the clustering coefficient of one's small-world networks, the speed and efficiency of one's long-range networks, and the degree to which functions are reciprocal or mutually intrusive. The extremes are evident in the brains and psychology of patients with autism and OCD. Less extreme, but similar in kind, are the minds of Aspergerites and OCs.

20
Indolent Men

Many people have elements of both OC and SA. Many children who are thought to be autistic or "on the spectrum" grow up to be OCs and/or SAs. The families of autistic children are laden with OCs and SAs. There must be a reason why OC and SA are so close and why both are related to autism. It may have to do with the inherent complexity of social intercourse, how diverse we are in our manner, or relating how we express our emotions. Phenotypic diversity makes us evolvable, but you have to admit it's a pain, sometimes.

Now, what is SA? It stands in relation to social anxiety disorder as OC does to OCD and Aspergerism to autism. Of our three subclinical syndromes, SA is the hardest to identify, especially when the light is dim.

Ethan

One of my patients, a presentable young man named Ethan, had been with his girlfriend for five years, but he didn't know what he was going to do. "I don't know," he said. "I don't know if she's the right one. She wants to get married, but I don't know." He couldn't commit, as they say. I thought he needed a measure of right-thinking: "You don't keep a girlfriend for five years and then wonder whether you should marry." A gentleman lives up to implied commitments. In Brooklyn we say, "S— or get off the pot."

He was foundering, this attractive but altogether indolent young man. He had trained in supply-chain management, but left a good job because he wasn't sure what he wanted to do. He was idle for a while, although he played a lot of golf. He moved from job to job, hardly any that required a college degree. He moved back with his parents. By now he was thirty.

He married the girl, who had a good job. He got a decent job, too, but he tended to get to work late and they let him go. He didn't seem to care. He didn't have much enthusiasm for work, or for anything. He didn't *have* much enthusiasm. His wife, Mila, loved him and now they were married. But he was as indolent as a husband as he had been as a boyfriend.

Through all of this, he would come to see me now and then. At one point, he was convinced that he had ADD. He complained that he couldn't keep his mind focused on anything. I thought he had a bit of depression, what we call anergic or low-energy depression. But antidepressant drugs weren't much help, and neither were ADD drugs. He saw one therapist after another.

His problem wasn't ADD, and it wasn't depression either. He had spent ten years, since he left school, in a kind of haze. His wife came to see me once. She said, "He has so much promise. He's so smart. He is a terrific guy when he's with his friends and we have fun. But he's just not doing anything with his life. He seems determined to be a loser."

Ethan was an *indolent* man, a man who remains at rest unless acted upon by an outside force, and maybe not even then. Indolent men aren't losers; they simply choose not to run the race. They aren't lazy or shiftless, just when it matters. They aren't consumed by hedonic pleasures and epicurean delights, as in *dolce far niente*. They enjoy a good time, but only if it's not too much trouble. They prefer the familiar to the novel, comfort to adventure, observation to active participation. They are a bit on the passive side, but in a gentle, easygoing way; nevertheless, if they are pushed they can be stubborn or even truculent. More likely, if you pressure them, they will wander away. If they obey a natural law, it is the law of inertia.

The indolent man is a problem, but what makes him that way was simply a mystery to me, and when I asked my learned colleagues, they would only suggest...categories! Every one of them, however, proposed a different category, and some of these were so irrelevant that they have been expunged from the DSM. To all the indolent men who have been misdiagnosed, therefore, may I offer this chapter as a belated apology. Hippocrates said, "One's life so short, the craft so long to learn," and he was right. To my ill-treated patients, I say, blame Hippocrates.

* * *

I have met a lot of Ethans along the way. I have wondered, maybe he's not a mental case at all. Maybe he's just *that way*. Maybe he *likes* being lazy and shiftless. Maybe it makes him *happy*. Indolence means something like "not taking the trouble." One has to admit there is something about the hurly-burly of the striving life that makes a sensitive soul content to stand back. Some of them who come to me as patients are teenagers, and the beginnings of the problem are apparent. A boy might be at the top in high school, socially and academically, but he changes when he goes off to college. Others visit when they are older; usually their wives make them come. "He must have ADD," they say, or "I think he's depressed." Sometimes they wonder if he's autistic. There has to be a simple answer, something you can do about it.

What is social anxiety?

We shall entertain the problem of an indolent man in terms of his differential diagnosis. As you might suspect, we shall discover OC on the list. However, we shall also find something on the list that is almost as interesting. It is social anxiety, or SA. What is SA, then?

SA is a constellation of personality traits and cognitive styles that cluster, in pure form, in a relatively small number of people, and in various combinations and permutations in large numbers of people. It is typical of a class of neuropsychiatric conditions that afflict large numbers of people to a mild degree and small numbers of people to a severe degree. As it happens, SA often occurs together with OC, just as Aspergerism and OC often occur together.

* * *

When I began to study the indolent class of patients, utter mysteries that they were, I turned to the medical literature. I discovered that not much consideration has been given to the problem. I searched in vain for a good explanation. There is a clinical condition, for example, the Kleine-Levin syndrome, that mainly affects adolescent males, who sleep all the time—as many as 20 hours per day. When they wake up, their appetites are voracious. They eat much more than adolescent males usually eat, and then they go back to sleep. The Kleine-Levin syndrome is only one of a number of neuropsychiatric conditions associated with hypersomnia, but the indolent man is not a hypersomniac. Most of them like their sleep, but it's usually because inactivity tends to make one drowsy.

There are endocrine disorders that can render one phlegmatic. An article published in 1949 referred to the "natural indolence of persons" (Stevenson, 1949), and I read somewhere that cats are naturally indolent. I was glad to have read that because I always thought they were just cats. For those of us who may not be "naturally indolent," indolence can be promoted by television-viewing (Hu *et al.*, 2003) or by urban design (MacIntyre, MacIver, and Sooman, 1993). However, Dr. Rosanoff suggested that hysterics were indolent, and that was in 1929, before TV became widespread (Rosanoff, 1929).

Finding so little in the medical literature that was pertinent to my patients' plight, I turned, as is my wont, to the Church, which in its long history has had to deal with all the afflictions of the soul, if not the psyche. The parable from Matthew 25 describes the consequences of an indolent soul:

His lord answered and said unto him, Thou wicked and slothful servant, thou knewest that I reap where I sowed not, and gather where I have not strawed. Thou oughtest therefore to have put my money to the exchangers, and then at my coming I should have received mine own with usury. Take therefore the talent from him, and give it unto him which hath ten talents. For unto every one that hath shall be given, and he shall have abundance: but from him that hath not shall be taken away even that which he hath. And cast ye the unprofitable servant into outer darkness: there shall be weeping and gnashing of teeth. (Matthew 25:26–30, KJV)

The Bible has addressed the problem of indolence on many occasions. It advises that sluggish fellows will be poor (Proverbs 6:11), ignorant (Isaiah 56:10), hungry (Proverbs 19:15) and likely to be eaten by lions (Proverbs 22:13), or that their roof will leak (Ecclesiastes 10:18). Bad enough, but not nearly so bad as the outer darkness with weeping and gnashing of teeth. One concludes, therefore, that at the heart of our Judeo-Christian ethic, indolence is a *bad thing*. As opposed to indolence, the Book suggests hard work, learning, an active engagement with the world, and faith that doing so is meaningful. That, I think, is good advice.

Such prescriptions have little effect, though, in the clinic. Anyone who has struggled with an indolent friend, lover or child knows that the solution is not so easy. Suppose the indolent fellow has no fear of being eaten by lions or having a leaky roof, or even of gnashing teeth. Bad as those consequences may seem to you and me, they may not resonate with a man whose motivational sounding-board is stiff and unresponsive.

Acediacs

At one time the Church was exercised over the problem of indolent men. The matter of concern had to do with monks who started off well enough, doing the things that monks are expected to do, but after a while seemed to lose interest. After a few years of chanting at all hours of the day and night, doing penance on behalf of sinners the world over, drinking beer and eating brown bread, some monks just seemed to burn out. They weren't bad fellows; they were just men who "recognize a good, yet who have no motivation for the good" (La Mothe, 2007). One could say that even though they were already monks, *they couldn't commit*. The word for it in Church Latin was *acedia*, but as a category it never caught on. The Fathers and Doctors of the Church knew it was a problem, but they couldn't decide what kind of problem it was: a deadly sin, like sloth, or a morbid state, like depression. Ultimately they just forgot about acedia, which is just as well because we need another deadly sin like a hole in the head.[1]

It's possible that you have an acediac in your life, but hopefully not.

Woman: "Do you love me, Harold?"
Acediac: "Um,... I think so, Marsha."

The philosophers have done little better. Philosophers from Pythagoras to Mahatma Gandhi have been simply dismissive of indolence, posing it in contrast to things effortful and worthwhile, a defensible position if you accept the premise that anything worthwhile has to be effortful. To the Hindus, *Pramada* (negligence or indolence) is simply the worst thing, the root cause of all pains and problems afflicting man. Pramadans are reincarnated as sloths, I suppose. The indolent are also to be found in the fifth circle of Hell, and say: "We were sullen in the sweet air that is gladdened by the sun, bearing in our hearts a sluggish smoke."[2] The existentialists proposed that life was absurd and all striving ultimately meaningless, which qualified at the time as deep insight. Nevertheless, they stayed busy writing books about it. Their advice

---

1   I spoke too soon. Acedia is, in fact, a deadly sin.
2   Dante Alighieri, *Inferno*, Canto VII.

ought to have been "Do nothing" but, for some reason I have never understood, they recommended "Do something." Heck, the Bible tells you that. The existentialists advised that one should make a commitment of some sort, although not to be too committed. The exception to this universal disapproval of the indolent state was René Descartes, who used to stay in bed for hours in the morning, hardly stirring until noon, but presumably deep in thought. If you were René Descartes, you could get away with it.

Motivated people like you and me, as well as the Great Thinkers, don't think much about unmotivated people. They are, well... unmotivated. What more is there to say? They are shiftless, lazy, indolent. Some men are like that, and some women, too; although it's usually the woman who has to get up at night when the baby cries. I think that women are protected from indolence by the fact of squalling babies, who stimulate the secretion of activating neurohumors in their brains. These clever molecules also give rise to a heuristic: *If I don't get up, this lazy clot sure won't.* Men have no such protective humors, so they behave like the majestic lion, just sitting there while the lioness does the work.

* * *

Among the literary masters we find wonderful descriptions of indolent men, but no good explanation of why they are that way and a very bleak view of what becomes of them. In 1859, for example, a Russian writer named Ivan Goncharov published *Oblomov*, a book about an indolent gentleman that the title is named after. Oblomov was only a character in a book, but everyone must have known someone like him because the book was a sensation. **Oblomovism** entered the language—the Russian language, at least—as a special kind of indolence. It was a purposely cultivated idleness that viewed any sort of work or effort as a waste of time, destined to fail and, anyway, beneath the dignity of a pure soul of high rank. Oblomov knew what the trouble was; he even coined the word "Oblomovism" himself. There just wasn't anything he could do about it—or, rather, anything that he wanted to do about it.

With Oblomov, lying in bed was neither a necessity (as in the case of an invalid or of a man who stands badly in need of sleep) nor an accident (as in the case of a man who is feeling worn out) nor a gratification (as in the case of a man who is purely lazy). Rather, it represented his normal condition.

* * *

In 1853, Herman Melville wrote a story, "Bartleby, the Scrivener." A scrivener is a clerk or a copyist, and the narrator of the story engaged Bartleby to be his copyist—he said that Bartleby was "pallidly neat, pitiably respectable, incurably forlorn"! He was a meticulous copyist, but when asked to perform the smallest errand beyond his assigned copying, he'd only say, "I would prefer not to." This he said time and again until it got unnerving. The narrator and the other clerks in the office tried to fathom why he was that way.

> Nothing so aggravates an earnest person as a passive resistance. If the individual so resisted be of a not inhumane temper, and the resisting one perfectly harmless in his passivity; then, in the better moods of the former, he will endeavor charitably to construe to his imagination what proves impossible to be solved by his judgment. Even so, for the most part, I regarded Bartleby and his ways. Poor fellow! thought I, he means no mischief; it is plain he intends no insolence; his aspect sufficiently evinces that his eccentricities are involuntary.
>
> "Bartleby," said I, "when those papers are all copied, I will compare them with you."
>
> "I would prefer not to."
>
> "How? Surely you do not mean to persist in that mulish vagary?"
>
> No answer.

The story captures the frustration and dismay that a well-meaning and active person experiences in the face of indolence and passive resistance. Like Oblomov's friends, the narrator tried to lure

Bartleby out of his ennui, and with the same result. Oblomov died in his bed, and Bartleby just wasted away.

Theoretically, Goncharov's character was a satire on the idle irrelevance of the fading Russian aristocracy, and Melville's Bartleby was a lesson about a sensitive soul in the face of our mortal condition. He had, you see, previously worked at the Dead Letter Office in Washington.

> Dead letters! does it not sound like dead men? Conceive a man by nature and misfortune prone to a pallid hopelessness, can any business seem more fitted to heighten it than that of continually handling these dead letters and assorting them for the flames? For by the cart-load they are annually burned. Sometimes from out the folded paper the pale clerk takes a ring:—the finger it was meant for, perhaps, moulders in the grave; a bank-note sent in swiftest charity:—he whom it would relieve, nor eats nor hungers any more; pardon for those who died despairing; hope for those who died unhoping; good tidings for those who died stifled by unrelieved calamities. On errands of life, these letters speed to death.
>
> Ah Bartleby! Ah humanity!

I don't know. The morals of the stories may well be as described, but the explanations for indolence are limited to two alternatives. Re Oblomov: "Rather, it represented his normal condition." As for Bartleby, one of the other clerks said: "I think, sir, he's a little luny." The literary masters have thus captured the range of human conditions that account for a life of passivity and indolence. In a certain number of men, it is their normal condition. In others, well, there is something wrong with their brains.

* * *

My grandmother never read the great novelists, but if she had, she would have recognized them as adepts of natural psychology. They examine a problem that all of us know from painful experience:

an indolent man, a man endowed with all the gifts but he would prefer not to take the trouble, and they expand on the theme in their literary way. Her experience with indolent men was less literary and more immediate. One of her sons, my Uncle Bruno, carried indolence to the level of High Art. She appreciated that he was a sensitive soul oppressed by the striving life, so she let him sleep, at least until it was time to get up, have a bite to eat and go hang out with his idle friends. His idyll should have ended when my grandfather, intolerant of lazy souls whether sensitive or not, threw him out of the house and told him to fend for himself. As it happened, he fended himself into a position with like-minded souls at the local Democratic club that just happened to be associated with a sinecure in the City government. His position as an "inspector" allowed him to spend a few hours every day dunning local merchants for contributions, a portion of which he was expected to turn over to the club. I don't think he ever really did any real work, but he retired a wealthy man and with a disability pension to boot. Indolence was his normal condition and it served him well. My grandmother used to say "You never know," and she was right.

There were other indolent characters in her life, one being her gardener Pasquale, a countryman of my grandfather who had arrived in America quite by accident. He was a simple soul and never would have found America on his own. He probably joined a team of immigrants in his usual passive way, probably just carrying their trunks from Abruzzi to Naples, and he must have forgotten to get off the boat. When he got to New York, he probably thought it was just another part of Italy, and our part of Brooklyn might just as well have been. My grandfather was compelled to put him up because he was a *paesano* and had nowhere else to go, so Pasquale lived in a small room in the basement of the house on 86th Street.

Pasquale had a special affection for my grandmother and he worked for her, tilling the garden or cutting down an occasional tree, but he could only do one thing at a time, and even then in his own good time. The only pay he required for his occasional exertions was a small room and food to eat and tobacco for his pipe. If he had a few pennies left over when he bought tobacco, he would buy candy and throw it on the sidewalk for the children to pick up and eat as if they were little birds. In the winter he stayed in his room in the basement and smoked his pipe; in the summer he sat in the garden and smoked. Most of the time, though, he would sit in the kitchen as my grandmother worked, listening to her stories. He would run the odd errand, but if you sent him too far he might forget his way home. The police would bring him back and Grandmother would give them something to eat and a glass of wine.

One day I asked Grandmother if there was something wrong with Pasquale, sitting as he did smoking a pipe all day and just staring off into the garden, and she told me that there was something wrong with his brain. When he was a little boy, she said, he had been kicked in the head by a donkey. That, at the age of ten, was my introduction to functional neuroanatomy. Herman Melville suggested that an indolent man might be a *sensitif*, driven mad in a quiet and retiring way by the failure of good intentions and despair at time's impatience. My grandmother had a simpler explanation: Pasquale had been kicked in the head by a donkey. "What about Uncle Bruno?" I asked her. "He is as lazy as sin. Did he also get kicked in the head by a donkey?" I was an insolent kid, but Grandmother indulged me. She said, "No, child. Your uncle, he's just lazy."

On such foundations I gradually learned the clinical method. Every human frailty has a cause, but it may not be what you think it is. Every human behavior has a cause that is in one's brain or genes or perhaps somewhere else. There's a reason for everything; it just may not be a good one.

Initiative

The human condition is not a pathological event but it, too, is amenable to the clinical method. That is because the clinical method operates on many different levels. So does **pathophysiology**, which is a medical term that means simply this: how the system works, and what it does when something causes it to go wrong. Since organisms are complex systems, how they work and how they go wrong occurs on many different levels. The differential diagnosis of a given symptom, therefore, has to be appreciated on different levels of meaning. For example, consider a patient who has difficulty breathing. The underlying condition may be systemic (the patient may have heart failure); infectious (the patient may have pneumonia); neoplastic (like lymphoma); environmental (like silicosis); or genetic (as in cystic fibrosis). The patient may have a psychiatric disorder, like panic attacks. Or he may not have a medical problem at all, but be hysterical or just faking to get out of work. The underlying pathophysiology—that is, *what is really wrong with the guy*—can occur on many different levels and often more than one, operating together.

Thus also human traits, which are not necessarily pathological, but which are operations that occur on different levels of psychology and physiology. The same untoward trait can arise from disruptions in different functional systems and often more than one at the same time. When one tries to understand a condition like indolence, for example, one can't rely on a single explanation.

However, if there were a single psychological function that spoke to the problem of indolence, it would be **initiative**. "Initiative" is a technical word, but it means the same thing in everyday life that it does in neuropsychology. It refers to *motivation*, *self-direction*, *creative behavior*, and *taking an active role in the events of one's life*. It is the motivation to generate energy and to commit it to some kind of meaningful action. Technically, it is an **executive function**, one of the psychological functions that are associated with the prefrontal cortex. The so-called executive functions are what make us effective; they include motivation, planning, cognitive flexibility and critical analysis. Initiative is a higher function: it involves creative imagination, planning, harnessing one's energy and getting on with it.

The converse of initiative is avoidance. One avoids venturing forth, getting out of bed in time to get to work, desisting from a videogame to go to class, going to a party, keeping one's appointment with a therapist. SAs are notable for avoiding strangers, but avoidance is a much broader affliction. One demurs from new and better ways to do something, from a more enlightened way of thinking, from looking at things with a new perspective. If initiative is normal physiology, avoidance is pathophysiology.

With respect to Ethan, my Uncle Bruno, Oblomov, Bartleby and even Meursault—a particularly indolent fellow in Camus' *L'étranger*—they all had problems with initiative. Ethan, like them, just wouldn't get going. Unlike them, he was motivated to do better; he just avoided the measures he had to take. My uncle was also motivated, but only to do well for himself. Work was to be avoided. He controlled the tradesmen on his personal segment of Avenue U, and without much effort on his part, they made generous contributions to the Democratic club, some of which actually found their way *to* the club. His spirit of initiative was confined to a domain he could control.

Ethan

Ethan had done well enough as long as he was with his peers. He made good marks in high school, because he was smart and he came from a good background. He never exerted himself very much, except perhaps in golf. He got through college without troubling himself much and he got a good job, mainly because of family connections. But then things started to unravel. The job wasn't boring, it just didn't interest him. He didn't do badly at the job, he just didn't do well. He didn't have strong feelings about the job one way or another. He just felt there was something else out there that he ought to be doing. Of course, he had no idea of what that might be, and he made no effort to find out. He left the job and went back to his home town. He liked hanging out with his old friends.

He stayed with Mila, and when she asked him he told her that he loved her. But most of the time, he felt they were just drifting. He had that same vague feeling that there was something else over the horizon, something that he ought to be doing, someone else who was better suited for him to be with. It wasn't a feeling that bothered him enough to do anything about it. It never led to the urge to get up and see what or who there was on the other side of the horizon.

His prevailing emotion was diffidence. Like Bartleby, when his family, his girlfriend or I suggested an active role to follow, his response was an empty expression that as much as said, *I would prefer not to*. Perhaps he considered work or effort to be a waste of time, destined to fail and beneath the dignity of a pure soul of high rank. Technically, he had a problem with initiative: at school, at work and in his love-life.

A problem in exercising *initiative* is *avoidance*. It has to do with the **frontal convexity**, the dorsal and lateral surfaces of the prefrontal cortex. The pathophysiology of avoidance and indolence reside in brain systems that govern initiative and motivation.

The lateral convexity occupies a large, exposed position and is particularly vulnerable to certain kinds of injury, as when someone gets hit in the front of the head with a hockey-puck or a baseball bat, or sustains a shrapnel injury, or is kicked in the head by a donkey. I have seen a good number of people with such injuries. They make excellent recoveries, considering the ferocity of the trauma they had. They can walk and talk, dress and look after themselves, and they do OK on many of the cognitive tests that we give them. But then they reach a certain level—a plateau, we call it—and they can't get beyond it. They can dress themselves, but they wear the same dumpy clothes every day. They are inattentive to stains on their clothes or to missing buttons. They can bathe and shave and brush their teeth, if you remind them to. They can live in their own apartment, so long as you help them clean up. They can even work at simple jobs, if you make sure they get there when they're supposed to. After a while, they'll drift away, or get fired, not because they're doing badly but because they're not doing well.

David

One of my frontal-lobe patients, David, made a nice recovery and was ready to go out on his own. He bought a store with the settlement money the insurance company gave him. It was a little country store with cans on the shelves, a cooler with drinks, and a freezer with milk and ice-cream but no beer. He didn't bother to get a license to sell beer. It was too much trouble.

Unfortunately, the store was so far out in the country that hardly anyone ever came by. He hardly sold anything. The cans on the shelves got dusty. He had a TV in the store, and he liked to sit in his chair behind the counter watching TV. A few old men from the neighborhood would drop by for a Pepsi and chat for a bit, and my patient was content with that. The tradesmen got tired of taking back the expired milk and then they stopped bringing him new goods because he couldn't pay what he owed them. After a few months, all that was left in the store were the dusty cans. He even ran out of Pepsi. Finally, he lost the store for taxes. It wasn't a tragic ending, at least for him. He didn't seem to mind. He just couldn't muster the energy to experience a strong emotion about anything.

The function you can serve in the life of such a person, if you're a relation or what we call in the trade a mentor or a coach, is to behave as if you were the patient's missing frontal lobes. A mentor provides direction, makes plans, troubleshoots and anticipates problems—all of the psychological functions that we call "executive" and that most of us are capable of performing on our own. A patient with an injury to the frontal convexity retains all of the mechanical functions of a normal human being. His apparatus can function well enough. What he lacks is the ability to direct the apparatus in an effective way.

Such patients are neither zombies nor automata, but their emotional life is limited. They smile but seldom laugh, they are agreeable but not empathic, they can get with a woman but love is beyond them. They seem sad, but that is a feeling we infer about what seems to us a bleak and empty life. The patient doesn't think his life is bleak or empty. In his own way he is happy.

Such patients have a peculiar attractiveness that comes, I think, from their gentle, unassertive manner and their seeming pliability. But they aren't pliable if someone tries to make them do something that might breach their avoidant shell. In the face of a real challenge, an opportunity to move beyond the predictable life they have settled into, they can be remarkably stubborn, even mulish. They refuse to budge. They won't say no. They might say "I would prefer not to," but they usually say nothing at all; they just don't move. For some reason, they always cultivate rescue fantasies in their therapists and friends, especially women, but the fantasies never come true.

The differential diagnosis

We return to Ethan, an indolent soul, and just beneath his forehead, in the lateral convexity of his frontal lobes, there is an assembly of neural connections resonating quietly. Since it behaves as if it has a life of its own, we can think of it as a spirit, and its job is to generate effective action. The spirit behind Ethan's forehead, for reasons that are obscure to us, was in an indolent state. What could be wrong?

Perhaps it is just a youthful sprite, content with the idle passing of a calm but pleasing day, untroubled by the thought that youth will pass on and someday all its energy will be shackled to someone else's will. Perhaps it is a troubled spirit, confused, perplexed even, and distracted from seeing the main course. Perhaps it is oppressed by the burden of sad memories and a world that seems bleak and gray. Maybe it's just a lazy spirit. It is hard to know.

I wouldn't like to be accused of saying that there really are little spirits inside your head, although psychiatrists have said sillier things. What I call "a spirit," neuroscientists call an "oscillating cell assembly," but I think the word "spirit" is closer to the disembodied event that really transpires. It is just as well to refer to an oscillating neural assembly mediating executive functions as if it were a spirit, because it does behave as if it has a life of its own. It is a delicate spirit that feeds on the music generated by lesser spirits deeper in the brain. It relies on them to join the chorus at just the right times and to strike just the right notes. But it is a very sensitive spirit, and when they don't strike the right notes it may retire to a quiet state of indolence. Then it goes into a sulk. It takes a bit of doing before it is induced to lead the chorus again.

If, then, we were to define the pathophysiology of something like indolence, the best we could do is to bridge the chasm with a bit of a metaphor. Thus, a spirit of initiative, like every other event that occurs in brain, is a function of nerve cell assemblies operating in conjunction, in harmony or not. Under ordinary circumstances, initiative is a brain field that mobilizes one towards commitment and meaningful behavior. Neural systems, comprised of innumerable little things, sing together like cheerful spirits and make joyful music. Or not, as the case may be. A dissonant chorus is the source of our lapses and imperfections. One can even imagine a phenotypic variant who can't even carry a tune.

You have a husband, then, or a sibling or a child, who has all the right qualities but who never manages to put it together and make something of himself. *What is really wrong with the guy?* Thus we arrive at the third stage of the clinical method, the differential diagnosis: all the pathological events that could possibly account for the problem of an indolent man.

An existential crisis

The first category is a common problem in our clinics. The patients are usually adolescents who find themselves immersed in existential crisis. For their own reasons, they wear black clothes and take pains to make themselves unattractive, which usually isn't very hard. They are often smart kids from good families, but school holds no interest for them and commitment is, to their thinking, absurd. Their parents usually bring them to the clinic because the parents think they are depressed; and they are, if nihilism can be considered a form of depression. One such young man said to me: "We are specks of dust on a small ball of rock, orbiting a minor star in the outer spiral arm of a minor galaxy. The universe is cold and meaningless and you and I are, too." Nihilism, he thought, and the company of like-minded friends, was the only appropriate response. "What does it matter?" I should be flattered to be a party on his cold and dusty rock, but I have heard this line so many times before. It is an adolescent conceit, although similar ideas are sometimes expressed by patients who are severely depressed or psychotic, and at other times by Great Thinkers. In such cases it has to be taken quite seriously. In the case at hand, however, one has to restrain oneself from saying, *If I hear that stupid speck-of-dust thing one more time I'm going to scream.* There are treatments we can apply in such cases. They aren't particularly effective, but they don't do any harm and they keep a lid on things until the kid gets over it.

When we think of an existential crisis, we picture it happening in the shabby black clothes of a young Emo with scars on her wrists, various piercings and tattoos, and a fondness for espresso; or in the sullen appearance of a disappointed intellectual, sullen in the sweet air and bearing in his heart a sluggish smoke. *Who am I? Why am I here? Does it even matter?* It strikes us a new thing, but I assure you there have been such types down through the ages.

> When I consider the short duration of my life, swallowed up in the eternity before and after, the little space which I fill and even can see, engulfed in the infinite immensity of spaces of which I am ignorant and which know me not, I am frightened and am astonished at being here rather than there; for there is no reason why here rather than there, why now rather than then.[3]

---

3   Blaise Pascal, *Pensées* 205.

A creative illness

One must address such broodings respectfully, especially in the clinic, but without forgetting that in the great circle of experience deep thought merges first with the fatuous and finally with *morosité*. My friend, Miles, called me once. I asked where he had been because it had been a long time since I had heard from him.

> ### Miles
>
> "*I was in a rut,*" he told me. "*I had to get away and think about things.*" Miles had been working at the museum and his special area of interest was a type of clam whose mating behavior defied all of the usual rules. I won't distract you with details about the clam, but I thought that maybe *Miles's* mating behavior was going through one of its periodic dry spells. "It sounds as if you were depressed again," I said. Miles was prone to feeling blue.
>
> "*Not at all,*" he said. "*It was a crise spirituel. I was feeling down but I think it was a creative illness. You're a psychiatrist. You should know about this. It happened to Freud and to Carl Jung. I took a leave of absence and traveled in Anatolia. I didn't even think about those damn clams. But I tell you what. When I got back, I knew exactly what those little buggers were up to.*"

A creative illness is another one of those existential crises, during which one feels swallowed up by the enormity of time and space. One's soul, like a shaman's, "ventures into a spirit world on a long and perilous path of initiatory conquests and moments of illumination. Dragons have now to be slain and surprising barriers passed—again, again, and again. Meanwhile there will be a multitude of preliminary victories, unretainable ecstasies, and momentary glimpses of the wonderful land" (Campbell, 2004). Out of such an event may come, Who knows?, something sublime and unique, perhaps a deep insight, the solution to a famous paradox or a song to capture the hearts of men and women all over the world. Spiritual paralysis, therefore, might be the prelude to something.

Sigmund Freud and Carl Jung are said to have experienced creative illnesses during their early careers, when they struggled with inner turmoil and various psychosomatic symptoms, all the while nurturing the great ideas that changed psychiatry—for better or worse, depending on your point of view. During those periods, although they kept to themselves a lot, they continued to work in the clinic and raised large families, so it can't have been all that bad. I have little doubt that sensitive, introspective people may occasionally need to be left to themselves, if only to get their creative juices flowing again. I advise leaving them be. But don't believe them when they start talking about dragons.

Transient episodes of torpor

Transient episodes of torpor, creative distraction or existential crisis are not clinical concerns as long as they don't happen too often or last too long. Most of our teenaged nihilists come out of it. Extravagant displays of sullenness during one's adolescent years do not necessarily indicate a bad prognosis.

Sometimes one discovers that one is in a rut. Such occurrences are like transient paralysis in one's spirit of initiative, but sooner or later it comes alive again. It is understandable to be impatient with such a person. *Do something. Make a decision.* Mila once considered throwing a bucket of water over Ethan's head.

Ethan

The essence of initiative is an active engagement with the world and faith that so doing is important. Ethan was engaged, but in a sluggish sort of way. Some would say he was in a rut, but that would imply that all he needed to do was get out of the rut and trundle on down the road. Mila had the idea that being married, having real responsibility, would get him out of his rut.

It was an understandable mistake. There seems to be something about a young man in the throes of a spiritual crisis that excites this reaction: just shake him by his shoulders and say, "Get a grip, man." And love, as we know, can make a perfectly ordinary girl think that she is capable of extraordinary works: *I can do it. No one else has been able to do it, but I can.* But Ethan was not having a spiritual crisis, and he didn't want saving. He was having indolence, the opposite of initiative, and indolence is not so easily deterred. Metaphorically speaking, it has a life of its own.

An existential crisis, as in "To be or not to be," is not Deep Thought but the analytical mind caught up in its own divagations. Bartleby and Oblomov were what you might call *existential heroes*. They perceived the meaninglessness of existence and made their decision, as Meursault did in the novel by Camus.

> Before the night sky alive with signs and stars I opened myself to the tender indifference of the world. To find it so like myself, indeed, so brotherly, I felt that I had been and that I was happy still.[4]

One might argue that the indolent man is at home, even happy, with the tender indifference of the world. If that is true, then subjecting him to a differential diagnosis is only presumptuous.

Psychiatry to the rescue

Psychiatrists know a lot about indolence, as you might expect from a profession that makes its living sitting down. We know that there is a form of schizophrenia that tends to emerge in adolescence but is

---

4   Albert Camus, *L'étranger.*

not associated with overt psychosis, like delusions or hallucinations. Patients with this indolent form of schizophrenia are given to odd but not psychotic behavior and gradually lose their ability to function in society. They are socially avoidant and sometimes a bit paranoid. Strikingly, they lose their initiative and even their volition, the desire to do anything at all. What occurs over the years is gradual "social impoverishment," and they become self-absorbed, idle and aimless.

Certain forms of depression are also associated with deficits in initiative and motivated behavior, and some depressed patients also show abnormal oscillations in frontal-lobe activity (Cho, Konecky, and Carter, 2006). When we perform a PET scan, for example, in patients with depression, we can measure the metabolic activity of different areas of the brain. Depressed patients have less metabolic activity in the lateral convexity. The cells there are burning less glucose; they are under-nourished, as it were, even starving, and this accounts for patients' lassitude and withdrawal, their exquisite sensitivity to pain, their feelings of helplessness and oppression. There is even a form of depression that is not associated with sadness or the experience of feeling depressed at all, but with low energy and lack of initiative and motivation. Such patients are not necessarily sad. They can still experience pleasure and positive emotional events, although they do so passively and without the usual intensity. In such patients, initiative, not mood, is the main target of the depressive process.

It is possible that Bartleby had a form of depression or even simple schizophrenia, originating as we are told from his untoward experiences in the Dead Letter Office. We should be grateful, therefore, for advances in trade unionism and occupational health that have made such outcomes rare to non-existent in today's postal worker. Where would literature be, on the other hand, if Bartleby had retired to Florida on a disability pension? We might find him playing golf or watching the dog races with other disabled civil servants. What if Hannibal Lecter had been treated with an antipsychotic drug, if cars had had airbags in the days of Camus, or if Nietzsche had had the benefit of a course of intramuscular penicillin? Such thoughts shake my conviction from time to time when I treat a patient, but not to the point of existential crisis, thankfully.

The spirits of initiative and motivation that occupy the prefrontal cortex can be compromised, obviously, if that area is damaged in some way. For Pasquale, indolence was a function of his frontal-lobe lesion, acquired from the donkey. There are many things that can go wrong with those spirits. Hypofrontality, reduced metabolism in the PFC, is almost universal in PET scan studies of patients with various psychiatric disorders.

What, then, has the clinical method gained us thus far? Indolence: one or another of the hypersomnias, the consequence of TV or urban planning, a deadly sin or not, and the natural inclination of persons and cats. A frontal-lobe lesion or frontal lobes compromised when one is upset or feeling unwell, sad, sleep-deprived, unfit, or burned out by too much cortisol. One form of schizophrenia and another form of depression. Is that all?

Differential diagnosis, continued

There are individuals for whom doing it right is of such vital importance that they never get it done at all. We have met their cousins before: the gentle, fussy man who does it right all the time and inspires the rest of us to be more tidy; and the controlling man, who is so afraid it won't get done right he frightens everyone else into getting it done wrong. He seethes with rage as he does it himself; usually just to make things worse. And then there is this third class of men with OC traits, who account for a good part of the indolence afflicting the world. They are so preoccupied with getting it right that they never get it done at all. They care too much, you can say.

Such men may be given to *checking*. The report is never quite right. It just needs one more going-over, and so it sits, in a great pile of other reports that also need one more going-over. There they will all remain, like letters in the Dead Letter Office. Others are given to *procrastination*, the thief of time. Their initiative is such a precious thing, it must be held in reserve, until just the right moment, at which time the perfect report will spring forth, full-formed like Athena from the brow of Zeus.

And then there are men who have what we call "obsessive slowness." A fellow gets so tangled up in his ruminations that he can't get from point A to point B. He can't even get to point A. His life is the paradox of Zeno. Every step has to be contemplated, tried and checked, and then tried and checked again. But every step is composed of two half-steps, and so he contemplates the first of those; and that, too, is really two quarter-steps, and the first of those...*ad infinitum*. This type of obsessive man is an enduring tragedy, because he is often quite intelligent and well educated; people like him do well in school, at least the better schools where people tend to be highly regarded for their unproductive ruminations. They respond to the structure of school, a regular staircase of achievement with every step marked by an exact number, or even better, an *acronym*.

I have told you of doctors who were brilliant diagnosticians, kind and sensitive clinicians, but who could never get their notes done. You would be amazed at the barriers such men erect against getting their reports written, their phone calls answered or their files returned to where they should be. But there you will find them, their nose in a book, their office cluttered with reports to be written, phone messages to return, files that the nurses have been looking for weeks. Neuropsychiatry, my field, must have more than a small share of these types, aswarm as it is with earnest but mildly obsessional scholars. *I shall master the intricacies of the human brain*, they say to themselves. *First, I shall study neurology. Then, I will study psychiatry.* It sounds good, doesn't it, but it's really like the man who wears a belt *and* suspenders. If you try hard to be a neurologist *and* a psychiatrist, you probably won't do either particularly well. Too much learning, sometimes, makes one a bit stupid, and such fellows just get tangled up in the intricacies of their own minds. As Einstein said, "There is too much education altogether."[5] Dealing with such a fellow, as I have on more than one occasion, one feels inclined to pour a bucket of cold water over his head.

There are other types to mention: the fellow who is a perfectionist, as in "the perfect is the enemy of the good." Infestations of this type occur in large corporations, universities and other bureaucracies. Each participant contributes a small measure of *This is not quite right* to whatever project he or she is involved with, until the whole thing just collapses under the weight of accumulated perfection. It is the particular curse of an aggregation of critical minds, each inciting another to a state of reflective torpor. Any institution, even the most dynamic, can be intelligenced into such a state.

Ethan's indolence was, in part, the consequence of his broodings. *The world is not perfect, the meaning of my life is not clearly apparent, the striving life is absurd, and the people who believe otherwise are only fools.* An intellectual living on the Upper West Side, entertaining the same nocive thoughts, would likely write a screed on *An Epidemic of Imperfection in America* and influence cultural discourse for years. Such men and women are hardly shy about exhibiting their emptiness in the cloak of high ideals. Their obsession with controlling ideas gives the illusion of active engagement with the world. Intellectualizing is a way of *avoiding* engagement.

Ethan's inclination was not to engage the world but to avoid it. My uncle, whose inclinations were not dissimilar, slept through the parts he didn't like. But Ethan was a gentle soul, content to live in a small, congenial world that may not have been profitable but was at least predictable. His self-absorption was not self-indulgent, self-important or even particularly reflective. His obsession with control was confined to his immediate neighborhood.

Ethan had a very common problem, one that is frequently overlooked, even by acute psychiatrists, and hardly known to

---

5   Albert Einstein, *The World as I See It*, 1935.

anybody else. He had a combination of two very common problems: social anxiety and OC. Though both were in small doses, together they led to a controlling state of lassitude. This was his problem. He had an active mind. It was so active that he was absorbed—not so often by brooding, although he would brood from time to time—but by his active mind. It was so absorbing he could spend all his time there. He would forget to notice there was anything else.

A controlling state of lassitude

One doesn't ordinarily associate anxiety with indolence. Nervousness, hyperactive fussiness, an excess of vigilance, hyperventilation, hysterical over-reactions, attacks of panic, incessant ruminations about what might happen if... Those are the overt manifestations of anxiety that everyone recognizes. They are examples of how some people *express* the feeling of anxiety. The more insidious expressions of anxiety are fatigue and weakness, substance abuse, low self-confidence, fantasy, slowness, lack of initiative, indolence and avoidance. In the first list, we can identify the proverbial *plea for help*. In the second, a *plea to be left alone*. Both, in fact, are attempts to control...what? Probably, anxiety.

If anyone doubts that anxiety is an inescapable element of the human condition—the non-psychopathic human condition, that is—just look at how every child is, at one time or another, thus afflicted. Perhaps you remember the bedtime rituals you had to endure with child #1 because he was afraid of the dark; child #2 had no such problems at night, but when you dropped her off at the day-care center or at kindergarten she dissolved into tears and clutched your skirts as if she were drowning. Anxiety is almost universal in children—and in grown-ups, too, but adults learn to hide it.

Separation anxiety is what we call that day-care drop-off problem; it is very common and usually has no pathological significance over the long term. There is, however, an adult variant of the condition, and most adults with **social anxiety disorder**

had problems with separation anxiety as children. In contrast to conditioned fears—anxieties that arise, like taste aversion, phobias and PTSD—separation anxiety and its adult form, social anxiety, are built-in. In that way, it resembles OC. They are both highly heritable conditions, and, for some reason, they frequently occur together. Social anxiety is pertinent to the subject of indolence because adults learn to hide it by being passive and avoidant. They also learn to hide their passive, avoidant dispositions.

Individuals with social anxiety don't necessarily seem shy and they aren't given to attacks of nervousness. Their condition may be manifest only as a lack of confidence, a reluctance to venture forth from a comfortable, familiar routine. This may be manifest as indolence and a lack of initiative. Paradoxically, however, a comfortable routine may be a very busy life. This is why SA is so difficult to detect in some people. A man's occupation can be a very effective hiding-place. This doesn't mean that every workaholic is down deep inside a shy person. But SA is one of the pathological conditions that lead some people to invest an inordinate amount of mental energy into one small component of their lives, to the exclusion of others, and at the expense of living a balanced, harmonious life.

Dennis

Dennis came to see me because his memory was getting bad. He was 47 years old but his mother had had Alzheimer's disease and he was worried. Actually, *he* wasn't worried, but his wife was. She didn't know if he had early Alzheimer's or not, but she knew something was wrong. When we tested him, however, his memory was quite good, and all his other cognitive tests as well. He was doing well enough in his job. He was a financial analyst for an insurance company, perhaps a bit beneath what he might have been expected to achieve with his MBA, but he was perfectly content with his little cubicle and a day full of numbers to analyze.

But he was forgetful, mainly at home, and his wife told me it was driving her crazy. He would lose the keys, forget to pick her up, come home late on an evening when they had to go out. "And you know what else drives me crazy," she said. "He talks baby talk." She imitated the way he used to talk, different ways, like characters from cartoons, and she said that he did it when she took him out with other people. "Once we were out with another couple to dinner. While we were talking, he was coloring. He found a coloring book that one of their kids had left in the dining room and he was coloring in it. While we were supposed to be talking to this other couple. He acts like a child."

The fellow was cheerful enough, and was quite agreeable during our long and arduous evaluation. But there was a certain tension behind his smiles and nervous laugh. Then we discovered that he had a long history of shyness and avoidant behavior, something that he always managed to cover up or keep in check. Then we discovered a number of relations he had, an uncle who had been a lawyer but lived alone in a cabin in the woods and never saw anyone, and a cousin who was another solitary. Dennis wasn't nearly so bad as his uncle or his cousin, but they all had social anxiety. His wife, who was a teacher, wondered whether he had Asperger's syndrome. She had been with him for 21 years, enduring his childish behavior. She appreciated how well he got on with their children and their little friends, but after 21 years, she was beginning to wonder.

There are particular occupations that appeal to individuals with SA. Not only solitary positions that don't require a lot of contact with the public but also social occupations that entail constant contact with a different kind of public, that is people who are *different* from the index case. Have you ever wondered why pediatricians and child psychiatrists are so gentle and self-effacing? It's their charm and makes them good at what they do. Schoolteachers are the same way. As a group, though, they are a shy bunch, and their social lives are with family, with close neighbors and at church. In the course of their work, their contacts with others are close, even intimate, but also controlled and predictable. They love *children*. They aren't so comfortable with the children's parents.

I have observed, during my career in medicine and food-service (my wife owns a restaurant, remember?), that many people who work in the medical field or in restaurants have high levels of SA. Why, then, do they choose careers that put them in constant contact with strange new people? It is, I think, an interesting example of counter-phobic behavior. People who are socially anxious *like* social contact, as long as it doesn't make them feel anxious, which usually means close friends and family. It can also mean interactions that are highly structured and stereotyped, like an MD and a patient, or a waiter and a customer. They are both occupations characterized by extreme busyness—rushing from one patient to another or from one table to another. What is possible amidst the hubbub, however, is little more than superficial, targeted interactions that exact nothing in the way of emotional energy. Busyness is an excellent shell to construct around one's anxieties. *Beware the barrenness of a busy life*.

The next time, then, that you have difficulty talking with your child's teacher, or your physician speaks abruptly and avoids eye contact, or your waiter is condescending, or the cute girl you try to meet just walks away, remember this: they're just shy. Poor things.

Patients with social anxiety disorder are sometimes so impaired that they can't even venture out of the house, or they lose their jobs because of their difficulty in getting along with other people. More commonly, people with social anxiety are hard workers, conscientious and compliant. They prefer, however, to keep their horizons narrow. That means they prefer routines and highly structured jobs. Although they may be intelligent and conscientious, they don't care to advance their prospects. Staying in a routine, low-level job is perfectly okay with them, even if they don't make much money.

Anxiety in general and SA in particular are enervating

experiences. They are feelings that erode one's confidence. Some people deal with anxiety by staying busy, but many more are inclined to inaction, fatigue, avoidance or indolence. SA will sometimes lead a person to strive against his or her timidity and to accomplish worthwhile things. But SA is sometimes too strong to overcome and leads to indolence.

What is common to all forms of anxiety is avoidant behavior. A girl with a phobia for escalators takes pains to avoid escalators. Patients with agoraphobia avoid crowded places, and patients with SA avoid people they don't know very well. Patients given to panic attacks develop anticipatory anxiety and restrict their activities to avoid having a panic attack. Generalized-anxiety patients have anxiety that is pervasive. Their burden of perpetual worry is enervating; fatigue is a common symptom and it prevents them from doing anything. The anxiety disorders all sap one's energy and initiative. Anxiety leads to avoidance, and avoidance is the commonest clinical explanation for indolence.

A rather definitive form of social avoidance is alcoholism and substance abuse. People who are socially anxious tend to over-use alcohol and to rely on other intoxicating substances. Physicians and restaurant people are, of course, two of the highest drug-using occupations. The cannabis gang at your local high school is loaded with socially awkward kids. "Misfits" is an old word for them. A good number of the adolescent nihilists I have met are shy kids, and cannabis is rife in that group, too.

Discussing addiction with an adolescent who is a chronic daily user or with a closet alcoholic is a revealing experience. One is tempted to say, *It's just a crutch*. It is, I suppose, but it is more like their shield, their protective coloration and their most reliable friend. It is no accident that the pharmacology of alcohol is almost identical to that of the benzodiazepines, the Valium-like drugs, and that cannabis is a very effective short-term anxiolytic, too. They facilitate avoidance, whether one seeks to escape one's inner demons or the oppressive demands of one's immediate society. The two are usually the same, anyway. The paradox of alcohol and cannabis as anxiolytics, however, is that they increase one's anxiety over the long-run. Seeking constant escape only makes one more fearful. Avoidance narrows the space of what is familiar, and, as time goes by, larger and larger swathes of the world become foreign and frightful.

Social anxiety is a constellation of personality traits and cognitive styles that cluster, in pure form in a relatively small number of people, and in various combinations and permutations in large numbers of people. It is typical of a class of neuropsychiatric conditions that afflict large numbers of people to a mild degree and small numbers of people to a severe degree. SA, like OC, is extremely common, but it is different from OC in the ways people manage to hide it. The fellow who feels oppressed by the rapacity of his social class, the delicate soul quietly napping in the grass, the existential hero who has discovered that it's all absurd and the lazy, shiftless guy who is waiting for the world to come to him are probably all really, terribly shy.

You must agree that there is an indisputable elegance to the clinical method. It takes one to places one never might have imagined. Your shiftless, lazy boyfriend, the surly adolescent who is a chronic daily cannabis user, your workaholic ex who stayed late at the office and came home drunk most nights—they are all really, terribly shy!

Resistance

There was outrage when psychiatrists decided to include social anxiety disorder in the psychlopedia. *It is a conspiracy*, the critics wrote. *It's just shyness. Why, everybody is a bit shy. The psychiatric association and the drug companies are in conspiracy*, they said, *to invent diseases and to sell drugs*. Not to say that some psychiatrists and drug companies don't conspire now and again, or that the latter don't like to sell drugs and the former to prescribe them, but I only wish that social anxiety *were* a corporate conspiracy. True, in mild forms it is quite common, but social anxiety *disorder* is one of the more debilitating mental illnesses.

I have had social anxiety patients who have chosen to live like hermits, in spite of a keen mind and a professional degree. There are some who are so fearful they become paranoid.

Marvis

One young woman we knew, Marvis, was a classmate of my wife. She was a cheerful young woman, amiable among her close friends, but she was always shy and she never went out. During college she lived with a family and enjoyed taking care of their young children. She was always more comfortable among children.

I saw her again thirty years later when she brought her son to see me. She had had a short and tortured marriage to a man who could never understand her, but at least she got a son. Her son's problems were minor and were easily dealt with. He had a minor learning disability. As I got to know him, I saw that he was devoted to his mother, and was probably the only person in the world who understood her. But she was a mess. She had bounced from one job to another—she was a brilliant woman with excellent credentials—but she was increasingly paranoid with every passing year. She finally lost her license for falsifying prescriptions for amphetamines; she took massive doses. She was so afraid of other people, it was the only way she could muster the courage to face a day at work. The amphetamines, of course, just increased her paranoia.

Social anxiety disorder, untreated, will grow over the years, and some patients get quite bad, reclusive, solitary or paranoid. But don't make me take precious space to convince you. "You must come round to my view, for otherwise I shall keep on piling fact upon fact on you, until your reason breaks down under them and acknowledges me to be right."[6] Besides, the matter before us is SA, not social anxiety disorder. SA is a mild condition: the way some people are. It occurs in men and women, and most of the time; its expression just might be a lack of initiative and settling for a quiet, avoidant existence. That's not a *bad thing*. But SA, unrecognized, can grow as the years pass, amplified by the rigidity and cognitive weakness that accompany ageing. Or is it like this? SA, unrecognized and never dealt with, can hasten the rigidity and cognitive weakness that accompany ageing.

Shy trees

Science has studied social anxiety from every perspective. Animals are shy, or not, depending on the animal; the individual animal, that is. Among the pumpkinseed sunfish, for example, the qualities of boldness and shyness can be measured and they seem to be normally distributed within the school of sunfish. What one does, if one is interested in sunfish, is to put a juicy morsel near the fish. Some of the pumpkinseed sunfish will immediately approach the bait; they are the bold ones, or early adopters. Most of the others hold back. Then a few more approach the bait, then more and more of them; some sunfish, the same ones every time, hold back—they are the last to approach the bait. Those are the shy sunfish. If one were so inclined, a normal curve could be drawn that described the trait of boldness-shyness in pumpkinseed sunfish.

There are penguins who stand on the edge of the ice, a whole line of them, peering into the water and wondering if there is a leopard seal lurking below. There is only one way to find out. Finally, a bold penguin jumps in, followed by the kind-of-bold penguins, and then, finally, the shy ones. If you chart the number of penguins jumping into the water against the time they spend standing on the ice, you would probably generate a normal curve. If none of the penguins

---

6   Arthur Conan Doyle, "The Red-headed League" (*The Adventures of Sherlock Holmes*).

jump in, one of the penguins will sneak behind the line and push one of the other penguins in. That only happens, however, if all the bold penguins have on earlier occasions been eaten by leopard seals.

There is even shyness among trees. Some species are hesitant to touch the tips of their canopies to the canopies of other trees. Other trees have no such inhibitions. Shyness/boldness, therefore, is a natural trait that arose as we evolved from trees, and it exists along a continuum, from very bold to very shy. People who are pathologically bold we describe as "intrusive" or "manic." People who are pathologically shy have social anxiety disorder.

It sounds very reasonable and straightforward, but Darwin, who was a bit shy himself (not to mention a world-class OC), had particular difficulty explaining it. For some reason, he was preoccupied with blushing, which is something that shy people do, and he said that it was "the most peculiar and the most human of all expressions." He took pains to discover that shyness and blushing were found in all the races and nations of men, and said that "Almost everyone is extremely nervous when first addressing a public assembly, and most men remain so throughout their lives." Then he told the story of a man who was pathologically shy. It should be entitled "Only in England":

> I will give an instance of the extreme disturbance of mind to which some sensitive men are liable... A small dinner-party was given in honour of an extremely shy man, who, when he rose to return thanks, rehearsed the speech, which he had evidently learnt by heart, in absolute silence, and did not utter a single word; but he acted as if he were speaking with much emphasis. His friends, perceiving how the case stood, loudly applauded the imaginary bursts of eloquence, whenever his gestures indicated a pause, and the man never discovered that he had remained the whole time completely silent. On the contrary, he afterwards remarked to my friend, with much satisfaction, that he thought he had succeeded uncommonly well.[7]

---

7   Charles Darwin, *The Expression of the Emotions in Man and Animals*, 1872.

The next time you are nervous about a PowerPoint presentation you have to give to a bevy of executives from Canada who have just bought your company, consider this possibility: this could happen to you. You may go through all the motions and gestures, in perfect synch with your slides, but never uttering a sound. Since the executives are Canadians, when your gestures indicate the end of the presentation, they will applaud politely.

Shy people are much less shy or not shy at all among people they know well. Among their familiars they can be perfectly natural, jolly even. In fact, if you loosen them up, they can sometimes get disinhibited and do something inappropriate. That is one of the differences between patients with social anxiety disorder and those with Asperger's syndrome, a form of autism. Social intercourse is very important to people with social anxiety and their social skills are often quite good. Their skills and intentions are overwhelmed by anxiety, however, when they venture forth among strangers. It is then that they seem to be awkward. Patients with Asperger's, on the other hand, don't care very much about society and are awkward or inappropriate when they have anything at all to do with people, even people they know well.

Because shyness disappears when shy people are among their intimates, Drs. Maner and Kenrick proposed that hominids, in the State of Nature, experienced no shyness at all, because they lived in small bands with hominids they had known all their lives. Modern living, on the other hand, is burdened by social intercourse with hominids who are utter strangers and likely to remain so even after you've slept with them. This, according to Maner and Kenrick, is what makes people shy.

I'm not so sure, because if that were true we'd never have evolved. Even in the old days, it would sometimes happen that one little band of hominids would bump into another. When they did, they would hang out together for a while, tell stories and find wives for their boys and husbands for their girls. They would exchange boys and girls and say "Good-bye, see you soon," resting content that their genes had been dispersed and that the next stage of evolution—

prehensile thumbs, perhaps—was not far off. I have no doubt that while they were doing all this, some among them, like penguins and pumpkinfish, would be bold and forward, and others shy and demure. There is no way to prove this, of course, but if it weren't true I would be surprised.

On the other hand, support for Maner and Kenrick's theory is based on observations that social anxiety is more common in urban populations than in rural, and that university students, who spend their days among strangers, have high rates of the condition. Perhaps so, but SA is common enough among rural folk, which may be why they have stayed in the countryside. Further, I would caution researchers not to draw too many conclusions based on university students. If a lot of them are SA, it may be because even more are OC (80 percent, remember?), and the two conditions frequently co-occur.

I think there is something missing from the theories of social anxiety. Shyness is a kind of anxiety that occurs in many people when they feel they are on display before people they don't know. The most common manifestation of shyness relates to public speaking, as with Darwin's friend, the extremely shy man. Almost all of us can relate to feeling shy in such circumstances, but that is only one component of social anxiety.

The central element of SA is hypersensitivity to novel, unfamiliar events—which is, after all, what strangers are. People who are socially anxious are cheerful and talkative among their family and lifelong friends. After work, after church, or during a party their spouse has dragged them to, their only desire is to *get the hell away and go home*. They can stay around among foreigners—that is, anyone who is not family or a lifelong friend—but only as long as they absolutely have to. The best thing about a party is driving home. You never know what is going to happen at a party if you stay too long.

The first signs of social anxiety may occur when one takes a child to day care. It is more commonly met with when a student changes schools and leaves his or her crowd of familiars. Going off to college is a terrible transition for a child who is SA, even if most of the other kids there are socially anxious, too. Many if not most of the kids who crash and burn during their first year at college are SA.

The gravitational pull of the familiar

SA deserves a physical theory, not an evolutionary one. Inertia is a possibility, but I prefer the law of gravity. Gravity, or something like it, plays a more important role in the lives of human beings than we realize. Psychological gravity is the lure of the familiar, the well known, the predictable; it's what we prefer. Finding comfort in the familiar is not necessarily a bad thing, either. "Familiar" is the same word, etymologically, as "family," and they both derive from the Indo-European word that means "house" or "home." One can imagine a writer, relieved of her social burdens at a publisher's party, enjoying a long sigh of relief once home. In her small office, surrounded by familiar pictures on the wall and mementoes of youthful travels, her imagination wanders to far-distant places peopled with strange and unpredictable characters. I am never surprised when writers complain that social anxiety is a made-up thing. I think they protest too much.

There are trade-offs to make for having an active mind, for perceiving events in ways that others don't and perhaps a bit more intensely. Sensitivity is good for one's imagination, fantasies and dreams, even if the real world feels less secure. One's preferred state is time alone, or spent quietly with one's best friend. One's mind ventures forth, but it does so best from a secure home base.

I don't suggest that gravity is the basis for SA, but that every organism experiences the tug of the familiar. There is something called **homeostasis**, a biological process that maintains an organism's physiological functions within circumscribed limits. On the level of psychology, one can call it equanimity, or balance. It conveys order to one's existence and the sense of perceived control. An SA preserves balance through avoidance, but his or her avoidance can take many unusual and even paradoxical forms. The OC, also, tries to maintain his or her balance in unusual and paradoxical ways. Both are seeking balance, as all the rest of us do.

21
Zero Point Zero

The essence of SA is sensitivity to novel, unfamiliar events. OC is also a sensitive state, but *what to* varies. Both are characteristics of an active mind, which is a kinder and more accurate way to refer to *disproportionate mental exertions.* It's not surprising, therefore, that both OC and SA frequently occur in university students.

Carlisle

Carlisle was a student at the college in our town, but he and his parents came to the clinic from their home in Wilmington. Carlisle was a good kid, polite and respectful, handsome and smart. He had just flunked out.

His High School career wasn't notable. He had good grades and nice friends. Then, during his senior year, he had his first episode of depression. It was a nasty depression. He stayed in his room and slept a lot. He didn't do much schoolwork and avoided his friends. He missed a lot of school.

Although his grades weren't good that year, he made it into our excellent school by virtue of his earlier performance and high SAT scores. He saw a psychiatrist in Wilmington, got the obligatory SSRI, and began to see a therapist. He recovered from his depression, came to Chapel Hill and continued treatment here.

His first semester GPA was 1.2; shocking news that he didn't share with his parents or his therapist. Nevertheless, he continued treatment, although what they talked about, I have no idea. His second semester GPA was…1.2. He was put out on academic suspension.

It wasn't that the poor kid was a partier. He didn't smoke pot. He wasn't depressed again. Why did he do so poorly? Neither his psychiatrist nor his therapist asked why, because *he didn't tell them*. Nor did he tell his parents.

Why did he do poorly? Well, for one, he didn't go to class. In the mornings he found it more agreeable to sleep in. He had afternoon classes, too, but he wasn't inclined to go to class in the afternoon. What he did all day was not much. He watched movies and played videogames, by himself. His roommate had left school early in the year and Carlisle holed up in his room, idle and alone. It's remarkable he got a 1.2. He should have got *zero point zero*.

Carlisle had a few OC "soft signs"—he had a strong preference for even numbers and he could never throw anything away. Those were petty annoyances, however, compared to his debilitating problem, *avoidance*: extreme reluctance to confront events, people and reality in general. Avoidance is a frequent indicator of social anxiety, and there is even a category called *avoidant personality disorder*. It's not an easy diagnosis to make in young adolescents, because they spend their lives in the company of familiar friends and schoolmates. Carlisle had gone to elite academies and had the same classmates from K to grade 12. Changing schools, especially the prospect of going off to college, elicited his first overt symptoms of avoidance. When he could delay the inevitable no longer, he crashed. A substantial number of the kids who crash and burn during their first year in college have SA traits. They seem okay in High School, but their symptoms may arise before they go off to college, as the great unknown looms.

Carlisle lied to his parents—"Yes, I'm working on it"—and to his therapists—"Things are going well at school"—but it wasn't deceitfulness. He preferred not to confront the truth at this particular moment. "Did you tell your therapist you never went to class, or your psychiatrist?" It was an obvious question. He said, "Yes, I did, I remember that I did," but he was hesitant in his answer because he knew I knew the truth. I told him that I didn't believe him, that he wasn't telling the truth. He started to cry.

Now, I don't *try* to make my patients cry and I'm not usually so blunt, but avoidance—inertia—is such a formidable problem that it sometimes has to be confronted directly. You can visit all the therapists you want and take every one of the psychotropic drugs, but if no one addresses what your problem really is, no treatment is going to work.

We usually associate social anxiety with extreme shyness, and Carlisle had been a shy little boy. But he was perfectly comfortable in his home-town stomping-grounds. Patients with social anxiety are, paradoxically, extremely social when they are among familiars and sometimes exuberantly so. In this regard, they are different from Aspergerites, whose profound deficits in social communication extend even to close family members.

Many individuals with social anxiety traits, paradoxically, have very good social skills. They are quite keen at reading other people, having learned to do so, I suppose, out of self-defense. Carlisle, for example, was polite and well spoken; he had learned to be gracious with strangers. He had a veneer of social acuity but it was his polite way of keeping people at their proper distance.

Not every SA has OC traits, although most of them do. It's not a surprise. OC and SA are at the root of most of the anxiety patients experience, and anxiety often has an obsessive quality— ruminative worry, brooding, intrusive thoughts. Patients with SA traits know how to avoid overt expressions of anxiety, just as they avoid confrontations and most things that are uncomfortable. Every infant is given to stranger anxiety,[1] most young children

---

1   The exceptions: autistic infants and babies who have been abused.

have separation anxiety and the trait of social anxiety is almost as common in adults as OC is. An SA preserves balance through avoidance, but his avoidance can take many unusual and even paradoxical forms. The OC, also, tries to maintain his or her balance in unusual and paradoxical ways.

Anxiety and depression

SAs avoid unpleasant feelings. They channel their mental energy into additional increments of avoidance. The OC trait directs one's mental energy into endless cycles of rumination or repetitive behaviors. SAs and OCs both try to exercise control by ordering their lives just so.

The difference between OC or SA traits and OCD or social anxiety disorder is quantitative: how intense the symptoms are and the degree to which they interfere with one's life. But what determines *that*? Many things, I'm sure, and maybe someday I'll have a chance to tell you. One clue is that social anxiety, obsessions and compulsions are more common in children and young people than they are in adults, and more troublesome. "No doctor, my daughter doesn't count, but when I was young I would count the steps, by twos. When I went up I would count even numbers and going down I'd count 1–3–5–7–9."

I asked a woman if her daughter was shy. Of course she wasn't; she spent her life with family and friends. But the woman said, "I was terribly shy in High School. In college, I had two good friends and then I met my husband. Since I've been working, though, I had to get over it." There's something about being an adult that confers a measure of confidence, or at least *perceived* confidence. Having a job and family doesn't afford much time for petty anxieties and there are plenty or real things to worry about—"Much is gained by transforming your neurotic misery into common unhappiness."[2]

Avoidance and obsession are not the most adaptive traits

---

2   Sigmund Freud, *Studies in Hysteria* (paraphrased).

and most of us learn to give them up, just as a child learns that Aunt Filomena isn't so bad after all and that day care can be fun. "Maladaptive," to a psychiatrist, means that a behavioral pattern is likely to get one into trouble. For many people with SA or OC traits, the trouble may come at work or school or in one's relationships, and the consequence may be depression or attacks of anxiety. In Colin's case, his controlling disposition made him intolerant and angry. He would get furious, and a couple of psychiatrists who saw him decided he must be bipolar.

Mood and anxiety disorders are usually the expression of something else. There are some, like manic-depression, that are the product of one's genes, but most cases of emotional instability, depression and anxiety are the consequence of maladaptive patterns of behavior and emotional responding, and two common sources are OC and SA traits. So, you may go to a doctor and say, "I feel depressed." In the few minutes he or she has to spend with you, it is determined that your problem is: *Depression!* Well, duh.

Anything you say will be held against you

There have been a series of laws and regulations promulgated by the OCs who govern our lives, to the effect that patients are entitled to confidentiality in matters related to their health and medical care. They are contained in the Health Insurance Portability and Accountability Act of 1996, affectionately known as HIPAA, pronounced *hip-uh*. It protects one's *right to privacy*. According to HIPAA, a physician can't discuss an 18-year-old's medical diagnosis with his parents without his permission. Of course, the rules don't interfere with an insurance company requiring the physician to transmit the patient's *entire medical record* to Heaven knows whom, probably some gnome in the bowels of the Blue Cross building. "Hey, Marvin, come here, look at this one. What a dork. Let's put this on the internet."

Similar rules prevent colleges from notifying parents that their child's GPA is *zero point zero*, although they have no qualms about sending them a tuition bill that is the price of a brand-new Harley-Davidson. Yet anyone who shops at a supermarket—"Do you have our Food King Preferred Customer Card?"—should know that their most intimate purchases are living forever somewhere in cyberspace. Be that as it may, you have a right to privacy.

Passive resistance to hip-uh isn't our intention, but almost all of our patients are accompanied by someone in the family, and we routinely tell them something like this: *If your wife calls with a question, we will answer her* and *If you are concerned about how your husband is doing, we expect you to be in touch*. We also communicate, with discretion, with the parents of our college-student patients. I have sent five children off to college. If you have sent even one, you know how anxious one is about their health and safety and also their productivity, and you wouldn't mind a phone call from the Dean when your child has "missed every class for the past month." In that spirit, we let kids know we will communicate with their parents if we think it's important. We know how to be discreet. Professional discretion isn't something hip-uh understands—or OCs, either.

When parents come with more than one child, we usually have them all in the room at least for part of the interview and examination. Sometimes, two of the children are patients and we try to see them together. So, we saw Matt and Russell, who were brothers. They were both ADD. At least they thought they were, and their mother, who was an endocrinologist, thought so too. They were both straight-A students in High School, but they insisted that they were easily distracted and it took them too long to get their work done. They had both been taking Ritalin® for a long time and in rather high doses. They all thought that this was a perfectly sound arrangement. Having just moved to Chapel Hill from New Jersey, they expected me to carry on the treatment. They had been diagnosed, after all, at the New York University Hospital, and by an ADD specialist, no less. Both boys, like their Mom, were a bit intense, and they all had many of the soft signs of OC.

We gave the boys a urine drug screen, something we always do when adolescents come for an evaluation. They were both positive for stimulants, of course. Matt, the older boy, also tested positive for benzodiazepines, opiates and THC. Now, finding THC in a 16-year-old's urine calls for discretion. I talk to the boy by himself, inquire after his habits, and advise him to test negative when he comes back in four weeks. Otherwise, it will be a matter to share with his parents. A boy who is a poly-substance-abuser is another matter entirely, and the issue has to be addressed sooner rather than later.

Matt was a compulsive drug-user. He smoked cannabis almost every day and on weekends he used any pill his friends would share with him. Apparently, his friends had a lot of pills to share. Ritalin® cleared his mind from the effects of the previous day's drugs.[3]

Russell's drug screen was clear. He never used drugs, although he knew about his brother's habits. His obsession was with success. His parents were both professionals, but his mother had gone to medical school and his father to law school at their respective state universities. Russell had his sights set on Princeton. For Princeton, he believed, a GPA of 4.0 was insufficient. He needed a 6.0. He couldn't manage that without a lot of Ritalin®. "It's because I'm ADD," he said.

Many OCs think they're ADD, as we shall see. Many of them do have problems with focus and attention, distracted, as they are, by their obsession with being perfect and their compulsion to succeed. Now, I have nothing against success, but perseverance is not always well served by an OC disposition.

Compulsive drug-taking

Are all Ivy League types OC? My only direct experience was at Columbia when I was too young and ignorant to notice, but the

---

3   There are some parts of the USA where recreational marijuana is legal, at least if one is 18 or older. It's not a good idea to combine cannabis with a stimulant drug. It's like taking an upper in the morning and a downer at night. Teenagers and young adults who say they are ADD should always be screened for other drugs.

number of my classmates who were uptight was memorable. I suppose I was, too. Uptight, that is, not memorable. I have had more than a few young patients who went off to such colleges. All of them had come to see me when they were in High School and they thought they were ADD. One would expect ADD children to be hauled into the clinic by their frustrated parents and at the urging of their teachers, but there are some children, adolescents mostly, who *want* to be evaluated for ADD. Most of them are OCs.

One I remember quite well; even when she was in High School, she was so intense that she sucked the air out of the room. She was a brilliant student, but utterly intolerant of any view of history or politics that wasn't her own. Of course, they weren't her own at all, but straight party-line, so I don't have to tell you what they were. Her favorite word was "stupid," usually preceded by a vulgar participle, and she applied it to most of the writers, historical figures and statesmen I admire. In spite of our differences, we got along famously. She regarded me with fascination, as someone might regard a colorful beetle.

Erin had a GPA of 5.0, in spite of smoking cannabis every day. She was no more ADD than I was. I didn't give her a prescription, but we had the most interesting conversations. I advised her not to smoke so much pot. Then she went off to one of those colleges that you can't get into unless you're OC *and* take massive doses of amphetamine.

I met Erin again a couple of years later, when she got depressed. At college, she had used drugs compulsively, cannabis every day and every pill she could find. Even, on a few occasions, intravenous heroin. She continued to get high marks, but towards the end of her second year she crashed.

Compulsive drug-taking: isn't all substance abuse compulsive? Not necessarily. OCs like Erin and Matt had a particular flaw that made them vulnerable to cannabis and other drugs whose mental effects are intense and come on quickly. They were obsessed with their mental state—what we call **obsessive self-monitoring**. It is a common form of self-absorption, similar to the ways in which some

OBSESSIVE COMPULSIONS

people may be obsessed with their appearance or their health, but this obsession is about one's inner state. Think of what happens when you can't sleep. You lie in bed and you can't turn your mind away from the fact that sleep doesn't come. It's one of those normal obsessions, hopefully short-lived, but it feels like forever. Imagine, then, having a mind continuously turned to whether you are focused or distracted, whether you are happy or not, whether your energy level is high or low. It's mental hypochondria.

Drugs like alcohol, cannabis, Xanax®, opiates and stimulants confer momentary relief from the doubt and anxiety that accompanies obsessive self-monitoring. They give the user control over an internal state that is never quite right. They also reinforce the user's preoccupation with his or her mental state. Drugs can condition a patient to be even more self-absorbed.

Young people are particularly vulnerable to compulsive drug-taking. Self-absorption is one of the normal obsessions of adolescence. Kids can get away with it, or at least some of them can, because of the resilience of their brains. In young people, the effects of such drugs are short-lived; and if they persist into the next day, one can always take an Adderall®. Young people aren't as prone to the ill-effects. Over the long run, however, drug-taking will usually have a negative effect. Depression, irritability, mood swings and loss of initiative are some consequences of compulsive using.

When Erin went back to college, she stayed away from most drugs and pursued her studies with assiduity. She met a fellow whose early career was similar to her own and they calmed down together. In graduate school she devoted herself to research. She won a Fulbright to study something like gender roles in the South American labor movement. She was just as ardent in advancing her opinions—and they are her own, now—and she is still intolerant of fools. I haven't heard from her for a while, but I am told she has become prominent in her field.

Compulsive drug-use is interesting because it is different from the destructive drug-taking or drinking that degrades the lives of some men and women so horribly. Compulsive drug-takers are often able to sustain a high level of performance in spite of their habits. The same week I met Matt and Russell, I met a man, Brian, who had been an addict all his life. He had grown up in an abusive home with two addict parents. He got away during High School and graduated on his own. By then, however, he was smoking cannabis every day. He supported himself by working in construction for several years, but he continued to do drugs—any drug he could get, but he preferred pain pills. Yet he was able to support himself, to marry and raise a child, and to attend college to get a nursing degree.

He did well at work and would usually rise to an administrative post, although he continued to use opiates, alcohol and other drugs. Then he lost his wife and daughter. Periodically he lost his job and sometimes his nursing license. Then he'd recover, straighten out, and go back to work. The pattern repeated itself until he was in his mid-fifties.

When I saw him, he was remarried and had been clean for five years. His wife was worried, though, that his brain was deteriorating: he couldn't remember very well and was disorganized. He worked for her as an assistant and she would cover his mistakes.

She brought him to us for a cognitive evaluation. She thought all those drugs had fried his brain. The evaluation showed that he was quite bright and his memory was fine. He had significant problems with attention, though. If his cognitive deficits were the result of drug use, drinking or depression, we would have seen a different pattern of cognitive impairment.

He was ADD. He had been ADD as a child but was smart enough to do well in school. He also used his drugs of choice in an optimal way, taking stimulants when he had to study, opiates after work, and alcohol or cannabis when he had to sleep. He could monitor his mental state quite intelligently, although, as with Erin, drugs ultimately had an unhappy effect. A lot of drug-users come to us, or their parents bring them, and say that they are "self-treating," but that's usually nonsense. In Brian's case, it was true. He had ADD and OC traits. He knew his mental state was off and he was compulsive about making it right. He just went to the wrong drugstore.

There are trade-offs to make if you have an active mind. You can think about it too much. You can feed it drugs to see what happens. You can make it perform disproportionate exertions. Or, you can stay in bed, content with what it does as you surf the internet. Right before you is life, the Universe, everything. We neurotypicals might think of drugs or indolence in terms of avoidance. That's not what it feels like to an active mind that prefers not to be bothered by the kind of people who ask stupid questions.

22

An Active Mind Can Be Distracting

OCs can be measured by how much insight or self-perspective they have. Some can't imagine that they have a problem: "I ain't mad. I wouldn't be mad if you wasn't so stupid." Others have an inkling they are different but, so what? "Maybe I *am* fussy. I like things clean and tidy." Yet others know exactly what is wrong: "I have ADD, Dr. Gualtieri, and my usual dose of amphetamine just isn't working as well as it used to." That his daily dose of amphetamine is enough to take a trucker from Miami to Tacoma doesn't strike him as irregular.

OCs, for reasons I shall try to explain, *like* ADD. There is something about ADD that appeals to them, whether they are OCD, controlling or just fussy. Several things, actually:

- OCs often have problems with productivity. They can get embroiled in petty details or fret over the imperfections in their work. That being the case, it is hard to get anything finished.
- Others have problems with initiation. It's hard for them to get started. A project is looming; one simply has to lean into the task. Once started, the work will flow. Getting started, however, is the problem. It's inertia, as if one's feet, or mind, were made of lead. It's why so many OCs are procrastinators.

- One may be trying to work but intrusive, anxiety-provoking thoughts keep getting in the way. They make it hard to keep on task. *OMG, how will I ever get this important task done?* Then, worrying that one may have intrusive, anxiety-provoking thoughts becomes an intrusive, anxiety-provoking thought.
- OCs tend to be obsessive in monitoring their mental and/ or physical state. It's hard to stay focused when one is continually distracted by this thought: *I can't focus.* And this one: *My usual dose of amphetamine is no longer sufficient!*
- Yet other OCs have what is known as *obsessive slowness.* For reasons listed above and a few others, they do things slowly. It's not that they move or talk slowly, it's that every task and every component of every task, every sub-component and every sub-sub-component has to be dealt with. Carefully. Precisely. Check it again. It takes time.

Two former colleagues exemplified these problems. One would take *more than a day* to evaluate a single patient. There was the patient's routine history and physical, which took a couple of hours. Then he would review the patient's test results, and those would give pause. Then he had to look something up in one of the heavy textbooks he kept in his office. This led to more tests, another interview with the patient, discussions with a family member, and then back to the books. It was a trial for the poor, elderly patients, who weren't allowed to leave the clinic until 6 or 7.

Another ex-colleague was so obsessive that he could barely complete his daily notes, let alone a patient's report. If he ever completed one, it might be a marvel of clarity and clinical analysis. Alternatively, it was a jumble of disconnected facts—you never knew what you were going to get. Whichever, it took a long time to get it, and usually you got nothing at all.

He used to hoard charts in his office so that he could finish his notes and write his reports. "Where is so-and-so's chart?" the techs would ask. "Oh, it must be in Dr. T's office." There it was, among the stacks of charts awaiting notes and reports. We assigned him a personal nurse to keep up with his notes and to return charts to their proper place. He began to hoard his charts at home.

It is possible that the electronic medical record will obviate such events. If a physician doesn't complete his note, the automatic medical record simply carries over the note from the previous medical visit, changing only the date and the patient's vital signs. No kidding.

Absent IT, one can always resort to psycho-stimulant medications. "I notice," our OC physician told me, "that when I take twice my usual dose of dextro-amphetamine I do better keeping up with my notes."

OCs and stimulant drugs

I don't know if OCs like being ADD so much as they like amphetamines. Pretending to be ADD is a way to pretend one isn't OC, but most OCs don't know they're OC. It's obvious why they like stimulants. Low doses of amphetamine help with focus and distractibility, speed up one's slow processing speed, and help with initiation, perseverance and productivity. Stimulants are safe drugs, as long as one keeps to low doses, and they are usually more effective than any of the other stimulants out there: caffeine, nicotine, alcohol, betel-nut, ginseng, qat or high doses of sugar. Amphetamines are about as stimulating as a good, strong physical workout, but one doesn't sweat so much. Besides, who has time for a good, strong physical workout, except people who are compulsive exercisers? And they may like stimulants to improve their focus as they work out.

If amphetamines are so safe and effective, why not take one? What's wrong with being a bit zippier and a bit more productive? There's nothing wrong with stimulants. They have been around since the 1930s, and we pharmacologists know everything we need to know about them. There's nothing wrong with stimulants, except some of the people who take them.

* * *

Stimulants are appealing to many different kinds of people. Patients with manic-depression have notable problems with attention and they like to take stimulants. It's not a good idea because stimulants can make them manic, but some of them like that. Sociopaths like stimulants because they can sell them. Druggies like to grind them up and snort them—that is, if they can't get their hands on crack cocaine or methamphetamine. Idle layabouts like stimulants because these help them to focus—on watching TV, for example. Nothing is worse than a short attention span when one is trying to watch TV.

Should OCs stay away from stimulant drugs? It depends. With appropriate supervision, patients with cognitive difficulties, slow processing speed, inattention, distractibility and disinhibition can profit from low doses of amphetamine or methylphenidate, regardless of their diagnosis and whether or not they are OC. Such treatment can even have a learning effect, which is why we give them to patients who have had strokes or brain injuries. Even patients who are not recovering from a cerebral insult may benefit from learning what their weaknesses are, by experiencing a different way to be. After a year or two, they can manage on their own.

There are special risks, however, to giving stimulants to OCs. When one takes a stimulant, it confers a boost of energy and a bit more focus and concentration. The drug does that whether or not one is ADD, and it can do it even if one's attention problems are caused by anxiety, obsessive ruminating, chronic hypomania or daily doses of cannabis. ("It's the only thing that helps me go to sleep," the patient says, referring to cannabis. He needs cannabis to sleep because he's taking so much amphetamine.)

One problem is that the effects of stimulants are noticeable; they are "on-off" drugs. That means that the patient experiences the positive effects of the drug when it is acting and then the negative effects of the drug as it wears off. The danger of giving a stimulant to an OC is that the drug is *conditioning* him to monitor his internal state, thus aggravating the problem of obsessive self-monitoring. The patient was already prone to ruminating over perceived deficits;

the stimulant effect gives him one more thing to obsess over. He is led to brood over the effects of drug withdrawal: *This ADD is killing me. I don't have enough Adderall!* He tells his doctor just that and gets a higher dose to take.

Which leads to a second problem. Small doses of stimulants are quite effective at improving cognitive performance. Higher doses have the opposite effect. Taking a higher dose, the patient experiences more cognitive scatter than he had before he started. His reaction? *I don't have enough Adderall.* Finally, he is taking enough amphetamines to fuel a trucker driving from Halifax to Tijuana, but he still wants more. At this point his family doc gets nervous and sends the fellow to our clinic. After our usual evaluation, we tell the patient that he is on an amphetamine treadmill, that his problem is OC, not ADD, and that he needs to get off the stuff. Typically, at this point the patient becomes quite irate and looks for another psychiatrist.

It is odd practice to treat obsessions with drugs that simply increase the patient's proneness to obsess, or to treat a cognitive disorder with a drug that can impair one's cognition, but the ADD industry wouldn't thrive as it does if it didn't play such tricks. Physicians who make their patients worse are held in high esteem as long as they make them feel better for a while, and as long as they prescribe a higher dose next time.

Today I saw a 58-year-old man in the clinic, an engineer who is successful in an obscure but lucrative IT field. He is OC and SA, but his overt problem is depression, which his wife attributed to a "mid-life crisis." Aside from the fact that there is no such thing, his depression was the typical kind of demoralization we see in people who have been struggling with OC and SA too long without knowing what was bringing them down. It was also an anergic—low-energy—kind of depression and hadn't responded to the usual antidepressant drugs, or to psychotherapy. When we tested him, we discovered a slow processing speed and inattention. He responded nicely to a low dose of methylphenidate. Was he ADD? Well, it depends whom you ask. He was ADD as long as one remembers that ADD is a fuzzy set "with a continuum of grades of membership."

What, then, is ADD? It's the attention deficit disorder. What, then, is ADHD? It's the attention deficit/hyperactivity disorder and pretty much the same thing. ADD is easier to say. I never like to say Aitch—do you?

OK. Now, what is attention?

What is attention?

Everyone knows what attention is, William James said.

> It is the taking possession by the mind, in clear and vivid form, of one out of what seem several simultaneously possible objects or trains of thought. Focalization, concentration of consciousness are of its essence. It implies withdrawal from some things in order to deal effectively with others, and is a condition which has a real opposite, in the confused, dazed, scatter-brained state which in French is called *distraction*, and *Zerstreutheit* in German. (James, 1890)

If someone is *zerstreut*, that means he or she has ADD. There ought to be a spotlight in the person's brain to illuminate what is important and immediate, but it's not working right. The muscle that directs her or his mental activity is weak. The envelope within which active awareness stays active is busted. I don't have to give you any more metaphors, because everyone knows what *attention* is.

In fact, we already know that attention is brain's solution to the problem of a **limited input space**. Active awareness is a processing bottleneck. At a point in time, only so much signal can get through to conscious awareness. This is the function of attention; it converts sensation into perception, brings memories to mind and gives favored thoughts a moment in the limelight. It is the interface between awareness and all the other cognitive functions, including memory, processing and movement. Occupying the position it does, it's no surprise when one's attention is distracted by events inside or outside one's body.

We also know that selective attention is a regulatory function, but that it is as fragile as the frontal lobes it lives in. So, you don't have to be ADD to be muddle-headed. You might just be stressed, sad, sleep-deprived or physically unfit, or perhaps you drink too much or smoke too much cannabis. Ageing affects one's *Zerstreutheit*, and so do all the conditions that cause accelerated ageing, such as drinking, smoking, high blood pressure, high cholesterol, diabetes and obesity. There is no mental disorder that doesn't compromise one's attention; being sick does too, and so do pain and discomfort. So does thinking too much about one's attention.

Problems with focus, attention and distractibility are almost universal and so are problems with productivity, initiation and procrastination. When we give the NeuroPsych Questionnaire (NPQ) to perfectly normal people, they invariably describe mild problems in attention, memory and fatigue. See for yourself; the NPQ is at www.atonc.com. Apparently, no one thinks that his or her attention is good enough, or his or her energy level. That must be why more than 80 percent of people in the USA consume pharmacological doses of stimulating beverages every day.

It's not easy to make the diagnosis of attention deficit disorder when virtually everybody feels they don't focus quite well enough or that they are easily distracted, but psychiatrists have risen to the challenge. To qualify for the diagnosis, one fills in a rating scale, a brief questionnaire that is the equivalent of writing 25 times *I have problems sustaining my attention*. To validate the diagnosis, someone who knows you has to fill out the same questionnaire. About you, of course, not about themselves; although they probably think they have attention problems too. Finally, the clinician has to rule out every other possible cause of attention dysfunction, a tall order because just about anything can lead to problems with focus and attention.

What, then, is ADD? It's not what you think it is. The ADD movement has it a bit wrong, too. Think of OC. OC is not OCD. SA is not social anxiety disorder, and Aspergerism is not autism. If patients and physicians were more honest about ADD, they would acknowledge it as a *problem*, not a mental disorder. ADD is a relative weakness in selective or sustained attention; relative, that is, to the task it is put to. OC stands in relation to OCD as ADD stands in relation to...what?

An oblique history of ADD

The story begins in 1935, when Charles Bradley, a child psychiatrist at the Emma Pendleton Bradley Home in Rhode Island, discovered that children with a wide range of psychiatric conditions improved when they were treated with Benzedrine, an amphetamine. Bradley's patients were a diverse group of children with behavior disorders, emotional problems and psychosis. Even allowing for the diagnostic imprecision of the day, Bradley's observations indicated that the effects of amphetamine were virtually universal; that is, they were not limited to any single category of patient. In those days, "psychotic" children were mostly autistic, and they responded as well as the kids with emotional or behavioral problems. Bradley's findings were entirely serendipitous, but his work was the first successful application of a modern psychopharmaceutical. It took psychiatrists twenty years to appreciate the importance of his discovery.

Why did Bradley give Benzedrine to children in the first place? In 1935, Benzedrine sulfate was a new drug that a pharmaceutical firm, Smith, Kline and French (SK&F), wanted to market to doctors. SK&F provided a free drug supply to any interested doctor in order to explore lucrative possibilities such as "adrenaline-like effects" on respiration and stimulating effects on brain function. SK&F hoped to focus on the drug's use for mental enhancement (Strohl, 2011).

While Bradley was consulting at the Bradley Home (it was

named after a remote cousin), he agreed to do a Benzedrine study for SK&F. At the time, it was routine to do pneumoencephalograms on the children at the Home. Pneumoencephalograms are an ancient version of CT scanning that involved performing a lumbar puncture (LP) and injecting air into the cerebrospinal space. Most patients developed a headache following the procedure, and Bradley wondered whether a stimulant drug would increase their blood pressure, thereby causing the choroid plexus to secrete cerebrospinal fluid at a greater rate and alleviating the post-LP headache. Benzedrine didn't do very much for the headache, but teachers at the hospital school observed that children who had taken the drug performed much better in the classroom. The children called Benzedrine their "math pill" (Gross, 1995).

Stimulant treatment was one of those special events in the history of medicine—like quinine, colchicine, reserpine and digitalis—when a successful treatment was discovered long before physicians had any idea what it was they were treating. Bradley had stumbled across a relatively non-specific treatment that happened to improve attention and impulse control in children with a variety of different problems. He never reconciled his discovery with the work of other physicians who were beginning to conceptualize an entity they called **Minimal Brain Damage** or **MBD**.

* * *

The story has a second beginning. A German neuropsychiatrist, Kurt Goldstein, worked in a hospital for First World War veterans who had had brain injuries. Duly recording their focal deficits, he was more struck by their personality changes. Although some were placid and apathetic, others seemed to have a general loss of inhibitory control. They tended to be restless, irritable, inattentive and distractible. Then Goldstein moved to the United States, where his writings were influential and he was held in high esteem. In 1939, Werner and Strauss observed that many of the mentally retarded children under their care displayed traits similar to Goldstein's brain-injured veterans. In 1947, Strauss and Lehtinen published an influential book on the "brain-injured child" that described symptoms with inattention and poor impulse control.

The 1940s and 1950s were a productive era for developmental medicine. Pediatricians and neurologists observed that symptoms of restlessness, inattention, impulsivity and excitability occurred in some children who were *not* mentally retarded and who had not had overt brain injuries. Because the clinical symptoms were so similar, it was assumed that they, too, must have some underlying encephalopathy. They did not have focal abnormalities on the neurological examination, but they did have minor physical anomalies and soft signs of neurological dysfunction. They did not have global intellectual impairments, or focal impairments like amnesia or aphasia, but they were prone to various learning problems, like dyslexia. The term "Minimal Brain Damage" (or "MBD") was coined.

During the 1950s and early 1960s, MBD was conceptualized as a clinical entity composed of three overlapping pathological conditions: the hyperkinetic syndrome (inattention and hyperactivity), specific learning disabilities and developmental language disorder. A child with MBD might have one or two or all three. Then the name of the condition was changed to "Minimal Brain Dysfunction"—an early nod to political correctness, but also reflective of the observation that overt cerebral insult was a relevant factor in only a small number of cases. Finally, the circle was closed, and in the late 1950s the therapeutic benefits of amphetamine began to be linked, specifically, to children with MBD (Clements and Peters, 1962). The MBD label was thought to be a "wastebasket hypothesis," however, and "Hyperactivity" and "Childhood Hyperkinesis" were adopted in its place.

Diagnosis and treatment thus found each other. The relatively non-specific nature of the stimulant response that Bradley had observed and that medicine had ignored for twenty years gave way to a more discriminated understanding of which children ought to be treated with stimulant drugs. The myth of the "paradoxical response" was soon to follow; that hyperactive kids would calm down when treated with a stimulant, while everyone else would just get hyped up. In a triumph of circular reasoning, clinicians even came to believe that a positive behavioral response to stimulants affirmed the diagnosis of Childhood Hyperactivity.

During the 1970s the modern view of Attention Deficit/ Hyperactivity Disorder (ADHD) developed, largely as the result of Virginia Douglas' work in Montreal. Hyperactivity and impulsiveness, the central issues for many years, were considered to be only a part of a syndrome, whose main element was a relative weakness in attention. Not only was inattention more salient to understanding the disorder, but it embraced a much larger group of children, and could be applied to an even larger population of adolescents and adults.

The DSM-III and the DSM-IV both centered the problem of ADD on the issue of "investment, organization and maintenance of attention and effort." What had been a neurobehavioral syndrome related to neurological insult was now a precisely defined concept of neurocognitive impairment. The center was clear and indisputable; but the boundaries of the condition were set to expand. During the 1970s the non-amphetamine psychostimulant methylphenidate (Ritalin®), the tricyclic antidepressant imipramine and the antipsychotic drug thioridazine (Mellaril®) were aggressively promoted for kids with ADD. Before long, the boundaries of the condition would include as "patients" people who would never have come to the attention of Bradley or Douglas or Strauss, let alone Goldstein: intelligent and well-behaved people who had relatively mild problems with inattention and who underachieved at school or at work.

Slowly but surely, the diagnosis grew in popularity. Schoolchildren who were not hyperactive at all were said to have "attention deficit disorder" or ADD. During the 1970s, the prescription of stimulant medications to schoolchildren increased by a factor of three (Safer and Krager, 1983). In 1988, Safer and Krager announced "a consistent doubling of the rate of medication treatment for hyperactive/inattentive students every four to seven years," and in 1987, no fewer than 6 percent of all public elementary school students in Baltimore County were receiving such treatment. In a few more years, the practice had spread to the secondary schools, and girls began to be treated in ever-greater numbers (Safer and Krager, 1994). By 1996, it was estimated that 1.5 million American children aged 5 to 18, about 3 percent of American youths, were taking methylphenidate (Safer, Zito, and Fine, 1996). The most recent data, from a cross-sectional study of more than 3000 schoolchildren in the USA, indicated a prevalence rate of 8.7 percent, which translates to 2.4 million schoolchildren in the USA. Nevertheless, fewer than half of children who meet DSM criteria are treated for ADD with medication (Froehlich *et al.*, 2007). The reported prevalence of ADD is likely to excite a sense of urgency among the converted and skepticism among the dubious. ADD is a good example of a medical diagnosis whose prevalence grew as soon as people realized it was there.

Sometime in the 1980s, ADD became a movement. History repeats itself, it seems, first as tragedy and then as a movement. Stimulant use among adults has increased even faster than in children—between 2002 and 2009, for example, the diagnosis increased by 40 percent per year (Knight *et al.*, 2014; Montejano *et al.*, 2011). About 10 percent of American college students use stimulant drugs obtained informally, and stimulant use increases, not surprisingly, towards the end of the term, just before and during exams (Burgard *et al.*, 2013).

It's easy for kids to buy or borrow Adderall® from a friend, but it's not much harder to get a prescription. What qualifies for the "diagnosis" of ADD in most clinics, as long he doesn't appear to be manic or otherwise crazed, is that an individual complains of inattention, distractibility or problems with productivity. In other words, if someone *thinks* he is ADD then, by gad, he must be.

This is a common scenario: someone, likely an OC, visits his physician. "I have problems with focus and I think I have ADD." The physician asks if he has difficulties at school. "No, I make straight As, but I always have to work harder than anybody else." The physician gives the patient an ADD "rating scale"—a list of questions that ask, in several different ways, whether the patient thinks he has problems with attention. If the patient says "Yes, a severe problem" to enough of these questions—a foregone conclusion, because he came in because he thinks that he has problems with attention—then, sure enough, he's ADD and he walks out with a prescription for amphetamine. This is the sum and total of the diagnostic process in most clinics (although not ours). It is an efficient method, to be sure, to reduce one's analysis of a case to adding up a patient's scores on a questionnaire and to remove reason and accountability from the process, but it doesn't always lead to good results.

The ADD diagnosis has cachet. Colleges, graduate programs and test operators such as the College Board are petitioned to make accommodations that are deemed to be medically necessary. Grown-ups, for no better reason than they think they have it, are not shy about visiting a family doc, announcing that they are ADD, and requesting amphetamines. It is no small measure of how things have changed that today they usually get what they ask for. In some "health systems," if you can believe it, doctors get bonuses on the basis of patient satisfaction. "I asked that doctor to refill my prescriptions for amphetamines and Oxy-Contin and to sign my disability papers, but he wouldn't. I'm dissatisfied."

What, if anything, is ADD?

ADD is one of those mental conditions, like autism, that is enjoying an epidemic. Narcissism is another one, you may have noticed. The unparalleled success of this book, in fact, will undoubtedly lead to an explosive epidemic of OC that the authorities will be hard put to contain.

There *are* some mental disorders that behave like epidemics, but ADD, autism and OC are not among them. Substance abuse is a good example. When a new drug arrives, it spreads from hosts to contacts until the vulnerable population becomes saturated. Then it fades. Adolescent suicide can be a particularly nasty epidemic. Hysteria may spread among schoolchildren who all fall ill, in short order, with an imaginary illness. Within the OC family, eating disorders can spread, especially among young female athletes and dancers. Compulsive exercising is a bit like an epidemic, but it's not *that* bad, as long as one is reconciled to serial hip and knee replacements beginning at age 50.

It is facile to suggest that ADD is no more than an historical curiosity or an intellectual fraud. Its current popularity is probably over-done, but only a troglodyte would maintain that the condition doesn't exist, that it shouldn't be diagnosed from time to time or that successful treatment is illusory. That said, there is an elephant's graveyard of psychiatric "disorders" that were once fashionable and are now forgotten. ADD may have to endure a few more name changes, but it's not likely to be consigned to the dustbin of diagnostic history. It is three generations old, and has earned respectability in spite of its advocates.

What, exactly, is ADD? It's a relevant question, because with a few modifications it is the answer to a different question: What is OC?

ADD is a constellation of personality traits and cognitive styles that cluster, in pure form, in a relatively small number of people, and in various combinations and permutations in large numbers of people. It is typical of a class of neuropsychiatric conditions that afflict large numbers of people to a mild degree and small numbers of people to a severe degree.

The symptoms of ADD are *non-specific*. Inattention and restlessness can occur in a host of other conditions, including psychotic disorders, mood disorders, anxiety disorders, personality disorders and developmental disorders. The proper diagnosis of ADD requires the clinician to *exclude* other conditions. One is not always able to do that with confidence.

The symptoms of ADD are very *common*. In one survey, mothers rated half of the boys as overactive. In others, teachers rated

75 percent of the dull children as inattentive, and 30–50 percent of the brighter children (Lapouse and Monk, 1958; Wortis, 1984). Having taught schoolchildren myself, I think the numbers are underestimates.

ADD is a relative weakness of the regulatory apparatus of the brain, in particular systems that mediate executive control and error detection. These systems are closely identified with the prefrontal cortex, but also reside in the basal ganglia, the thalamus and the cingulum. Their regulatory/executive functions govern the ability to regulate attention, behavior and emotional responding. Although they are important functions, they are vulnerable to disruption by an individual's physical or emotional state.

The complexity of the brain's regulatory apparatus makes it unlikely that its formation and maturation is under the control of a single gene. This is consistent with observations that ADD traits are inherited, but not by means of single genes. Like many dimensional disorders, it is the consequence of multiple genes operating in concert. Like most personality traits and cognitive styles, ADD runs in families and tends to persist over the life span, albeit in modified form. Like most developmental weaknesses, people learn to adjust to it, more or less.

ADD is a developmental disorder related to something called *dysmaturation*. It just means a delay in the development of a particular function in an otherwise normal individual: in the case of ADD, this function is cognitive self-regulation; in AD*H*D, it is cognitive and behavioral self-regulation. They are both frontal-lobe functions, and the maturation of the prefrontal cortex is a long and arduous process. Not all of us manage it at the same rate. Boys, for example, manage it more slowly than girls do. A human's frontal lobes aren't fully *myelinated* and functional until the fifth decade of life (Yakovlev, 1962). It is ironic that frontal-lobe maturation is not complete until core rot has already begun in the white matter and the lower brain regions.

ADD, like OC, is dimensional. Its clinical presentation is *variable*. Some ADD kids were hyperactive *in utero*, and some are said to have "run since they learned to walk." Others are not hyperactive or impulsive at all, but only inattentive and distractible. Hyperactive kids may turn into lazy, inert adolescents. Girls with ADD are often shy and self-effacing. Some ADD patients are referred by their pre-school teachers; others are diagnosed only in college or graduate school. Like the learning disabilities, ADD occupies a spectrum of severity, and the outcomes for persons who are mildly or severely afflicted are quite different.

OC is to OCD as ADD is to...MBD

OC is a benign manifestation of OCD. ADD is equally remote from its progenitor, what used to be called MBD, or Minimal Brain Damage. We need to revisit MBD, because it tells us a lot about that cliff-edge. Also, the converse of a cliff-edge, although I have no idea what we could call that.

There is a small group of ADD patients, mostly children, whose symptoms are *pervasive*—that is, present in all situations. Most such children have additional developmental or neurological problems. Their symptoms are less amenable to drug treatment or to behavioral programming, and one cannot be nearly so sanguine about the outcome. In adult life they often have serious mental problems. Such children have MBD.

MBD may indeed be a "wastebasket," but *atypical brain development* and *minor neurological dysfunction* are real problems. They describe a vexing issue in child psychiatry: the co-occurrence of developmental disorders (Kaplan, Dewey, Crawford, and Wilson, 2001). Most developmental disabilities are not very specific, and the brain dysfunction that underlies them tends to be diffuse rather than localized. Problems like dyslexia, developmental coordination disorder and ADD usually reflect diffuse pathology, and this has been labeled "minor neurological dysfunction" or "deficits in attention, motor control and perception." Atypical brain development can express itself in different ways: delays in fine or gross motor coordination, in language, reading, or math, in attention, or in regulating one's behavioral or emotional reactions. The pattern of deficits is quite variable and most children have delays in more than one area. Within a family, one child may be dyslexic, another ADD, and a third may have several disabilities. One is unable to distinguish one disability from the other on the basis of neurological or genetic information. Minor physical anomalies and neurological soft signs are more likely to occur, in higher numbers, in children with severe disabilities.

A persistent weakness, even a severe one, may not be handicapping. One of my friends is an invasive cardiologist and his credentials are impeccable. There is no one I would rather have shoving a catheter into one of my coronary arteries, although I hope it doesn't happen anytime soon. One day, he confided, *"I have never read a book in my life."* Nevertheless, he got through university and postgraduate training with high marks and is a successful physician. He can read well enough to catch the gist. His excellent memory and high intelligence do the rest. If they are not as well-endowed as my cardiologist friend, MBD kids have serious problems when they grow up. They are more likely to be unemployed, mentally ill or in prison. They are more prone to drug problems.

MBD is a *quantitative* condition. The pathology is diffuse, its neurology is non-focal, and multiple genes contribute to it. In addition to not-so-good genes it may be caused by intrauterine and neonatal insults, such as neonatal sepsis, meningitis, hypoxic-ischemic encephalopathy, neonatal jaundice, low birth weight, neonatal tetanus or congenital infections (cytomegalovirus, toxoplasma, syphilis, rubella and HIV). A more general factor is **obstetrical suboptimality**. This refers to certain maternal problems, which range from relative infertility, minor bleeding and hyperemesis to catastrophic events.

What occurs in the face of untoward obstetrical events and in the presence of neurological soft signs or MPAs is called the **continuum of casualty**, ranging from the most severe disabilities, like mental handicap, cerebral palsy, autism or epilepsy, to comparatively minor problems, like learning disability, developmental coordination disorder, ADD, behavior problems or Aspergerism. MBD is a spot on the continuum. The principle is that brain development is vulnerable to insult. The severity of the insult, or the number of co-occurring insults, determines the severity of the disorder. The mathematical relationship is exponential rather than linear. A child can develop normally if she has to deal with one or two insults, but with every additional one, the risk of a poor outcome increases exponentially.

As it happens, children with disabilities are more vulnerable to the effects of a poor early childhood environment and benefit more from a good one. Parents who are disadvantaged by virtue of poverty or ignorance are less likely to receive good prenatal and postnatal care. Parents who are disadvantaged by virtue of not-so-good genes are likely to transmit them to their kids. In either instance, the child's postnatal environment may be suboptimal or downright damaging. If anything, the problem has grown more acute in developed societies, even those that are highly egalitarian and take child welfare seriously. Even within those societies, there are small groups whose culture prevents them from taking advantage of available resources. The combination of bad culture and bad genes is hard for a child to overcome. It is a tragedy that modern societies need to address, but few, if any, have done so.

The number of adverse circumstances a child is born with and into has a statistical association with poor outcomes. Statistics, however, are not destiny; you know how I feel about counting (although polite people do keep the volume knob on an even number). MBD is a serious problem, but with a little bit of help delivered at the right time, it's amazing how children can overcome the consequences of genes and culture.

The continuum of casualty relates developmental pathologies to the number and severity of adverse circumstances affecting both the fetus and the child. Early insults have an exponential effect. Most children can overcome a single disadvantage, whether it is biological or social. Two such disadvantages raise the risk of a bad outcome by a factor of four; three, by a factor of nine; and so on. There is no better indicator of the resilience of our species than that many children are able to overcome the disadvantage of five, six or seven insults.

Fortunately, most of us living in modern, developed societies are blessed with the opposite: children who are conceived and born and who develop in circumstances of optimality, or super-optimality, with many more than seven advantages. If anything, this should make us more attentive to the needs of families and children who have to struggle. On that note, we shall return to ADD and OC.

ADD traits and OC traits

There's not an epidemic of ADD, but there is a rising tide of individuals who want to be prescribed psychostimulant drugs, because, like hysterical schoolchildren who believe they are sick, they are convinced that *something is wrong here*. It sounds as though their cingulum may be working overtime. Someone ought to tell them that ADD patients have cingula that are rather torpid, but that would only spoil the fun. About half of the children who are evaluated at our clinics for ADD have OC and/or SA traits. More than half of our adult patients who think they are ADD are OCs.

ADD and OC are both constellations of personality traits and cognitive styles that cluster in severe forms in a relatively small number of people, and in mild forms in a great number of people. They quietly meld into the common, day-to-day weaknesses that everybody has. That's what makes the ADD industry so gratifying: the best patients to treat are people who aren't sick at all.

One's ability to sustain focus on a dull, boring task is a *state*— try to do it when you're tired or worried about something. It is also a *trait*. Some people have laser-like attention spans and are utterly resistant to distractions; others among us can be distracted by the least little thing. Also, what is a "dull, boring task" to A may be intensely absorbing to B. Unfortunately, the work in most classrooms and offices is dull and boring, not only to all the As but also to a lot of the Bs.

ADD and OC are opposites with only the appearance of similarity. ADD is a flaccid attentional muscle and OC is an attentional muscle that has been exercised too much. ADD is a weak central executive; in the OCs, the central executive is intrusive and controlling. The similarities between ADD and OC are superficial, but their differences are essential.

What are these differences?

- On a cognitive level, ADDs are distracted by events going on in the outside world. OCs are distracted by events going on inside their heads.

- On a behavioral level, ADDs tend to be disinhibited or wide-open. OCs are usually uptight. ADDs are resilient; bad experiences hurt for a while, then roll off their backs. OCs tend to brood. OCs never forget; ADDs forget all the time.

- On an interactional level, ADDs are stimulating but exhausting. OCs are secure and predictable but boring.

- At the level of elementary neurobiology, ADD is a brain problem with central regulation; that is, *not enough*. OC is also a problem with brain regulation, but *too much*.

- ADD and OC are both identified with the prefrontal cortex, but also reside in the basal ganglia, the thalamus and the cingulum. In ADD, the network is not active enough. In OC, it is too active.

- For example, take the cingulum. The front part of the cingulum is involved with error detection and performance-monitoring, and also with the regulation of attention and emotion. OCs have an overactive cingulum, whereas ADD patients have a cingulum that is less active in performance-monitoring and error-processing.[1] The OCs, therefore, have

---

1   The cingulum is the major white-matter pathway connecting to the cingulate cortex, whose anterior portion is an area that has repeatedly been implicated as abnormal

a brain region that is overly sensitive to things that are not quite right, while the cingulum of ADD patients lets it all just go by (Brem *et al.*, 2014).

Neuropsychological studies of ADD and OCD patients show that both conditions are associated with deficits in sustained attention: that is, inattention to dull, boring tasks (e.g., the test of response inhibition, the continuous performance task at www.atonc.com). The attentional problems of the OCD patients, however, have been described as an *epiphenomenon* caused by the overflow of intrusive thoughts. The cognitive deficits in OCD patients "result from an attempt to gain control over automatic processes in order to reduce impulsive behavior and lapses of attention. This leads them to over-utilize their cognitive resources, which, paradoxically, diminishes effective control." Obsessive thoughts overflow and cause an overload on the executive system (Abramovitch, Dar, Hermesh, and Schweiger, 2012).

OC does not necessarily need to be treated, any more than ADD does. As time goes by, most people learn to manage their weakness in their own way. The most effective treatment is to know what one's weakness is and to devise effective strategies for dealing with it. There are kinds of psychotherapy that do just that.

Where we live

Confusion between OC and Attention Deficit Disorder is a familiar story in my neck of the woods. Where we live, F and I and the children, is a pleasant and unassuming part of the world that local boosters have given the unlikely name, "The Research Triangle." Why anyone would think a triangle is an appealing place to live

---

in ADHD, in terms of smaller volumes, slower rate of thinning in adolescence, decreased activity on task-based functional MRIs, and decreased functional connectivity. The cingulum has been found to have diffusion abnormalities in ADHD adults (Cooper, Thapar, and Jones, 2015).

has always been a mystery to me, but the lure of geometry seems to have attracted a unique concentration of highly educated and mostly fussy people. We have, for better or worse, more PhDs and MDs as a proportion of the population than any other place in the world, except maybe Los Alamos, without the mountains or plutonium. It is a dubious honor, if you ask me, and it is reflected in the reliably wrongheaded way the population votes at election time.

What qualifies your writer as an advanced expert on the topic of OC is the fact that OC traits tend to gravitate towards the PhDs and the MDs of the world, as if these traits were viral parasites that attached themselves to genes for academic achievement. I suppose it is more accurate to say that people with OC traits tend to gravitate to the fields of engineering, science and medicine, especially those who like to spend their lives doing research—which is, after all, simply an exercise in reducing all of Creation to numbers. As you know, OCs love to count, and Heaven knows we have counters around here. *Count it! And if you can't count it, then it doesn't exist.* That is the motto of the purveyors of Evidence-Based Medicine: *If a treatment hasn't been published many times over, then you shouldn't do it.* They aren't troubled by the fact that most medical treatments haven't been subjected to prospective, multi-center, double-blind studies; nor by the astonishing fact that there is a 50:50 chance that the next such study will contradict the one before. Beyond the medical schools, we have numbers of research facilities, including one run by the Environmental Protection Agency (EPA). The EPA's motto is, *If you can count it, it must be dangerous.* Having a surfeit of such characters in our neighborhood—fussy men and women in great numbers, counters and checkers galore—our clinics have a steady flow of customers, and for that we are grateful.

* * *

There is something else about ADD and OC that is more important than careless taxonomy or the dictatorship of the numerariat. It may be best observed in communities like ours. It is the set of problems that active minds fall into.

Active minds are notable in children, but they are found as often in adults who, for better or worse, remain child-like throughout their lives. Their mental exertions seem disproportionate, especially to the *hoi polloi*, but these exertions are proportionate to these people's intelligence and sensitivity. Every mind is always active, but active minds are thinking with speed and efficiency. We have already met some of the problems that active minds may have. They may seem slow, but only because they are making so many connections. Some people have analytical minds that are too intrusive. Others, an indolent tribe, embrace fantasy in default mode and prefer to stay there. The trick, if you have such a mind, is to learn the art of hovering. The analytical mind performs the necessary calculations and informs; the empathic mind conveys meaning.

The Great Detective said, "My mind is like a racing engine, tearing itself to pieces because it is not connected up with the work for which it was built."[2] It is the literary cliché, that high intelligence and exquisite sensitivity have to be attached to someone who is vulnerable, eccentric or borderline certifiable. It is a truism that such minds must be active. Such a mind is especially active in default mode, as it reflects. That's where intuitions are born. You may have solved a vexing problem while you were doing a mindless task, like tilling the garden or folding the laundry, or when you were asleep. If you did, it is your active mind, which is never mindless.

The analytical mind is capable of fabulous computations, but it flourishes in short bursts and then it likes to rest. True, there are people or individuals with laser-like focus who can sustain prolonged states of awareness in the nether regions of the neocortex, especially when they are taking high doses of amphetamine. It may be necessary to do that, in some occupations at least. Aspergerites even like it there. It is not, however, a creative space. Creativity does require organization, flexibility, planning and self-correction, but it also needs something else that doesn't happen

---

2   Arthur Conan Doyle, "The Man with the Twisted Lip" (*The Adventures of Sherlock Holmes*).

by local computations. It needs the long-range connections that lend resonance to disparate thoughts and that can find meaning in what seems meaningless. Imagination is the highest form of intelligence.

You can imagine that a racing-engine kind of mind—especially one that prefers to hover—requires special controls. An active mind is constantly opening new networks, most forming as functional, not anatomical, networks. They are transient networks, stimulated by a perception or a memory. They lend novelty to perception and call forth memories that aren't usually associated. It's common to experience such associations when we dream. Most dreams are incoherent; brain has a use even for incoherence. In dreaming, one is consolidating the memories of the day. How they fit with all the others in our memory banks—which new ones must be kept and which old ones degraded—is a creative exercise. If an active mind seems dreamy, it is doing the same. It is relating its sharp thoughts and sensitive experiences to hosts of others in its past. Activity like this is fertile ground for creativity.

Every perception and thought involves a conjuring of memories and passages through forks in neural pathways that amplify this and inhibit that. Every coherent mental signal is a change in the vibrations of the network for selective attention, the dorsal attention network. In an active mind, new perspectives arise, and then others. Every thought changes the behavior of many other networks and even the content of one's memory. Every moment in conscious awareness, even a silly or outrageous one, endows the mind not only with a new present but also with a new history. Active minds do this with speed and efficiency, but they do need a nice lie-down now and then.

But not more amphetamine. Psychostimulant drugs are very good at controlling the controller—the central executive—but, as you know now, that is only one among many controllers in brain. Every brain part is controlled by all the others, and obeys their constraints. Brain functions in dynamic balance between hierarchical and distributed control, between modularity and integration, and between organization and autonomy. You never control an active mind: you only try to balance it.

An active mind is not necessarily intelligent, in the conventional sense, although it usually is. Active minds are excited, exuberant and exhilarated at how rich and full the world is, how many things there are to do, to see, to learn about. They are full of energy. They trust their perceptions. They don't experience doubt as much as curiosity. They are sensitive and react acutely to sensory events, but the forks in their neural networks are inclined to amplify the positive. They are trusting, sometimes to a fault, but also resilient. They may be given to preoccupations and intense absorption with arcane matters, and they may have a clumsy way with their companions. Their computations are often distracted by frequent sojourns in the Play of Musement. What absorbs them is not what they are doing but how it exercises their fertile minds.

I meet active minds most often in children, the innocents in Chapter 15. An active mind can be a problem for a child—it takes a while for someone to learn to harness all of an active mind's energies. They may not manage it until they are old and have accumulated enough perspectives to appreciate what their minds have been up to for all that time, and why it led to so many misunderstandings. As children they may get into trouble for their unbridled enthusiasms, but this can also happen even to grown-ups. I know of one man who was banished for stretching the rules of normal fan behavior, and another who was castigated by his wife for communicating in faux sign language on the elevator. Even the Banana-Man— immortalized, I hope, in these pages—must have raised doubts among close friends.

Children, however, enjoy the dubious privilege of being "identified" and trundled off to mental health professionals. There is no diagnostic category for a surfeit of *joie de vivre*. No, the child is likely to be called hyperactive, or ADD. If he or she happens to be a bit awkward socially, then he or she is "on the spectrum." It is possible that such a child's cingulum is too active, or the insula, but errors detected aren't the occasion of dismay: they are an opportunity to discover a correction. It's even possible that their OC loops reverberate wildly from time to time, for example around the number four, to which all numbers can be reduced, in English anyway.

Is it a tragedy if some well-meaning health care professional prescribes a stimulant for such a person? No, no more than it would have been to fix Kurt Godel's radiators, to get Albert to wear a nice new polo shirt or to give Hamlet a serotonin reuptake inhibitor. Active minds have their own trajectories and it takes more than five, six or seven disadvantages to change them.

23

The Narcissism Epidemic

There is one more tribe of OCs whose problem deserves our attention. Their problem is obsessive self-regard. Their capacity for self-referential processing is as excessive as their capacity for perspective-taking is deficient. We have already met two other, related tribes. One believes that they alone get things right. Rather than taking advantage of their unique wisdom to make a killing on the stock-market or at the dog-races, they prefer to dwell on how stupid everyone else is. The other tribe is given to obsessive self-monitoring. Some of them use drugs compulsively, others are hypochondriacs, and still others worry so much about being sick that they make themselves sick. Both typify the problems that beset people who are self-absorbed. If I were given to fantasy, I would suggest that this must have happened when the two bands bumped into each other on the primordial African savannah. They would have hung out together for a while, told stories and found wives for their boys and husbands for their girls. They would have exchanged boys and girls and said "Good-bye, see you soon," confident that their genes would be conjoined and that the next stage of evolution would soon arrive. And it did: a whole new tribe, whose self-regard grew to unimagined heights. The new tribe was grandiose, self-centered and unempathic. Paleo-anthropologists know them as narcissists, but they think of themselves as The Great Men.

Everyone knows what **narcissism** is, and that's a problem. It's the reason pop psychology is self-defeating. By the time an idea in psychology has become popular, it has usually outlived its clinical usefulness. When headlines and book titles appear to this effect— *America is suffering from an epidemic of narcissism*—one can be sure that the term has lost whatever small meaning it may once have had (Twenge and Campbell, 2009). Almost a thousand books and articles have been published on the subject of narcissism in recent years, and hardly any of us are the better for it. "My ex-husband is a real narcissist," you say. Well, too bad, next time marry a Canadian.

The American Psychiatric Association was tempted to eliminate the Narcissistic Personality Disorder from the latest version of its diagnostic manual. I suppose that if we all have it, one can't call it a disorder anymore. Maybe it's pathological *not* to be a narcissist, at least in America. Or maybe it was meant to be a nasty swipe at all those narcissists out there: "Hello-oh. We're taking you out of the DSM!"

This time, psychiatrists aren't the bad guys. What began as a rather obscure notion, bequeathed by a 19th-century sexologist, Havelock Ellis, erupted into a pseudo-science before psychiatric researchers had a chance to discover whether there really *was* such a thing. As a result, every self-centered dolt had a syndrome to call himself. I don't think so. "My ex-husband is a narcissist," you say? Hardly. He might be selfish, of course, or a braggart or an exhibitionist—or maybe he's just a psychopath.

The first egotist

Everyone knows what narcissism is, in a muddled sort of way, but not even Ovid got it right. In fact, it's not even clear what Narcissus did or why he did it.

Narcissus on the grassie verdure lyes:
But whilst within the chrystal fount he tries

To quench his heat, he feels new heats arise.
For as his own bright image he survey'd,
He fell in love with the fantastick shade;
And o'er the fair resemblance hung unmov'd,
Nor knew, fond youth! it was himself he lov'd.[1]

In the myth there is a girl, Echo, who is a "wood nymph" (whatever that is). She is in love with Narcissus. Narcissus, as it turns out, is a man so stupid that he can't recognize his own reflection in a pond, so he's an unlikely boyfriend. Despite this, not only Echo but a bunch of other "Naiads" and "Dryads" regretted the poor fool's death:

For him the Naiads and the Dryads mourn,
Whom the sad Echo answers in her turn;
And now the sister-nymphs prepare his urn:
When, looking for his corps, they only found
A rising stalk, with yellow blossoms crown'd.

A rising stalk with yellow blossoms: the narcissus flower. Well, the flower, a kind of daffodil, wasn't named after that silly fellow at all. It has a particularly noxious bulb which is toxic if consumed. It contains alkaloids, most notably lycorine, which is why the daffodils in one's yard are mostly safe from squirrels but tulip bulbs aren't. The plant is named after *narke*, which means (in Greek) "numbness," "deadness," or "torpor." (Hence, *narcotic* drug.) From that comes Narcissus' name and the flower. The etymological lesson is that self-absorption is intoxicating. Or better, it's deadening. Too much self-referential processing, the *I* without the *Thou*, is not a good thing.

Finally, and for sake of completeness, it isn't clear whether Narcissus was running away from Echo or from a guy (they were Greeks, remember); or whether he was really in love with his identical twin sister (really?); or whether he killed himself with a

---

[1]   Ovid, *Metamorphoses*, Book 3.

sword, as opposed to killing himself by staring into a pool of water. There are several versions of the myth, all equally improbable.

On the basis of this flimsy tale, Havelock Ellis coined the term "narcissism" to refer to a form of self-love: "the emblem of the absorbed self-love of youths and maidens who had not yet reached the stage of falling in love with another person of the opposite sex" (Ellis, 1937). The term, if not its limited meaning, was adopted by Freud and a number of his followers and eventually grew to embrace "All human efforts, and man's most sublime aspirations... brought within the Narcissistic sphere."[2] A concept that embraces everything, I'm afraid, touches nothing and is bereft of meaning.

The culture of *The Culture of Narcissism*

It wasn't bereft of meaning to Christopher Lasch, a respected historian and social critic who wrote a bestseller in 1979 called *The Culture of Narcissism*. Lasch, it has been said, "looked at the American and found him peering into a mirror, anxiously rating the figure staring back at him and wondering how to combat the inexplicable emptiness he felt" (Rosen, 2005). As a result, Americans had "retreated to purely personal preoccupations," mostly involving the maintenance of good health or the spiritual growth of the self. Those, he thought, were *bad things*.

Lasch placed the blame on "quite specific changes in our society and culture—from bureaucracy, the proliferation of images, therapeutic ideologies, the rationalization of the inner life, the cult of consumption, and in the last analysis from changes in family life and from changing patterns of socialization." The extremes of individualism and secularism freed people from the restrictive confines of family, religious, social and political obligation, and left them preoccupied with nothing more than their own empty selves. Lasch, contrarian that he was, thought that the restrictive confines of family, religious, social and political obligation were good for you, as was working on a farm or in a factory—though

---

2   Havelock Ellis, *Psychoanalytic Review XIV*, April 1927.

not, presumably, in IT, fashion modeling or the movies, or perhaps even as a social critic. What was bad for you included: a fear of commitment and lasting relationships, the youth culture and dread of ageing, boundless admiration for fame and celebrity, the motion-picture industry and television, the emergence of the information age, psychotherapy and the "therapeutic mindset." These and other factors produced the "narcissistic personality of our time... [someone who] depends on others to validate his self-esteem...[and who] cannot live without an admiring audience."

The cognitive distortions implicit in this kind of social criticism are all too apparent: filtering (picking out a few unpleasant details and dwelling on those that are consistent with one's opinions), overgeneralization, catastrophizing, polarized thinking, global labeling... Cognitive distortions are common to all of us, but to some of us, like social critics, more common than to others. I, for one, don't really know what "the American" sees when he looks in the mirror; I know what I look for, and it mainly has to do with spots I may have missed when shaving. I have had the privilege of getting to know a number of Americans along the way, and I don't remember any of them confiding in me the "emptiness of his own self" or any such thing. You could say it is a bit grandiose to suggest one's own insight is so cogent that one can perceive visions of the self that hardly anybody else can see. A natural psychologist has a different vision of what one sees in the mirror:

There! Now that looks really good!

Or:

OMG! I've got to do something about that!

Or, most often:

Well, it could be better, but it's pretty good considering all it's been through.

Formerly known as Narcissistic Personality Disorder

> The fuzziness of the term reflects the complexity of the
> concepts, while the persistence of the term reflects their central
> importance... At the same time, we remain with more ambiguity
> than is desirable or useful. (Cooper, 1984)

Lasch borrowed his definition of narcissism from Freud: the
grandiose self-image of a narcissist is an escape from repressed rage
and self-hatred, usually having to do with something that Mom did
or didn't do. Deprived of maternal affection, the narcissist uses other
people as objects for his gratification, demeaning them while craving
their love and approval. He is unable to identify with the feelings
or needs of other people and is exploitative in his relationships.
He is arrogant and haughty, grandiose or exhibitionistic, devoid of
empathy and given only to superficial relationships, usually with
hangers-on or hero-worshippers.

The narcissistic personality disorder, defined by its four key
attributes—grandiosity, the need for admiration, exploitation,
and lack of empathy—is said to occur in 6.2 percent of Americans
(7.7 percent of men, 4.8 percent of women), at least according
to one well-regarded epidemiological study published in 2008
(Stinson *et al.*, 2008). Prevalence rates for the condition in other
studies range from 0.0 percent to 14.7 percent; I know of no other
psychiatric disorder that is said by some to be non-existent, yet
by others to afflict one in seven adults. Two reasons why the
Psychiatric Association wanted to abandon the diagnosis are the
paucity of reliable research on the matter and the dubious quality
of the research that *has* been reported. If the diagnosis had been
expunged when the new diagnostic manual was published, all those
grandiose, exploitative and unempathic people would have had to
find something else to call themselves. In kindness, the Psychiatric
Association left them in.

What would Sam Vankin have done? He is an Israeli stockbroker
who was a self-made millionaire in his mid-twenties, "heavily into

group sex and voyeurism" and his "moods swung between attacks of rage and obsequiousness." "I was borderline schizoid, but the most dominant (personality disorder) was NPD," he says. "It was a relief to know what I had." Naturally, he wrote a book about it, *Malignant Self-Love*; "You see, I have leveraged my narcissism: I have lived on the proceeds of my book for 15 years. What would I have been without my illness? Another businessman?" (All quotes from Tempany, 2010.)

Much is made of the narcissism of entrepreneurs, politicians, Wall Street *wunderkinder*, IT geniuses and the like. There is nothing, I suppose, like billions of dollars or an admiring crowd of fanatics to stroke one's ego, and it is natural to be a bit self-centered when one is, after all, at the center of things.

Kets deVries argued that most CEOs exhibit narcissistic tendencies. He wrote that "a solid dose of narcissism is a prerequisite for anyone who hopes to rise to the top of an organization." In many companies, competition for appointment as CEO is an intense battle, and "perhaps individuals with strong narcissistic personality features are more willing to undertake the arduous process of attaining [such] a position of power" (deVries and Miller, 1985). This view is supported by Lubit, who claimed that "certain personality traits commonly but not exclusively found in destructive narcissism help superior people to rise within management structures... [Such traits include]...high levels of expressed self-confidence, magnetic enthusiasm, and unrelenting drive to attain prestige and power" (Lubit, 2002). Pech and Slade argue that narcissists "covet higher managerial positions" and that they can satisfy their covetousness and acquire power by legitimate means through a capacity to conform "to the demands of the organization's rituals and routines" (Pech and Slade, 2007).

The problem is that narcissism, a pseudo-scientific word, has been appropriated by social critics to lend a veneer to human traits that have been known for a long time under different but perfectly good names. A natural psychologist might prefer "self-confidence" or "drive" or "ambition" or "high energy" to describe the positive attributes of CEOs who are supposed to be narcissists, and "self-centered," "ruthless," "cold-blooded" or "heartless" for their negative characteristics. There are also a lot of perfectly good psychiatric diagnoses to apply to patients who are grandiose, exploitative and suchlike. Patients who are manic may believe that they have super-powers or even that they are divine. Psychopaths are perfect combinations of self-centered grandiosity and a lack of empathy for other people. Pathological self-absorption is often found in patients who are addicted to drugs or who have histrionic or OC personalities.

Three men in recent history are invariably proposed as "malignant narcissists": Hitler, Stalin and Mao Tse-Tung. The idea is that all three were "great men" because of their extraordinary visions and their will to make those real. They were malignant, however, because their visions were fantastical and their will resulted in the deaths of countless millions. No one can argue against their malignancy. Eric Fromm referred to them as the "quintessence of evil" (Fromm, 1964), although I prefer to think of them merely as monsters. They may have shared the narcissistic triad of grandiosity, a need for adulation and a lack of empathy, but their more salient qualities, from a historical perspective, were sadism, paranoia and a controlling disposition. In Hitler's case, these may have been the effects of neurotoxic gas during the First World War and neurotoxic drugs during his later life; and all three were subject to the intoxication that comes with unlimited power.

The "cult of celebrity" is supposed to be a driver of narcissism in modern society, but in such cases it is an acquired characteristic. It is easy to be grandiose when one has been hugely successful, especially when success brings the company of flatterers and sycophants and when wealth shelters a person from critical commentary. The words "exhibitionism" and "vainglory" usually apply to such characters, although many are simply *poseurs*. To pose as a narcissist is a good way for a celebrity of small talent to attract attention—or to have become a famous celebrity in the first place.

The most telling problem with narcissists is how rarely they can be found in the pages of great literature, except in fairy tales. More than one psychiatrist has suggested that the evil queen in *Snow White* and Cinderella's cruel stepmother were narcissists. The observation may have a germ of truth, but I don't think it advances either our understanding of narcissism or our appreciation of the fairy tales. In popular stories and in a lot of the movies my daughters used to like, a character with an inflated ego is brought back to earth and is grateful for it, or else he dies, to no one's regret. But those, too, are morality tales. It isn't easy to find embodiments of the syndrome in serious literature,[3] because narcissists are just not very interesting. They are childish characters, one-dimensional, annoying when you are forced to pay attention to them, and best avoided if you can.

More letters from my mail-bag
My boyfriend is a braggart and seems conceited and self-important.
I have no doubt that he is. I'm not sure that an additional increment of psychologizing is going to enhance your appreciation of the fellow. Perhaps you can find another boyfriend.

I met a man on the internet dating service and all he can do is talk about himself.
The poor fellow just may be nervous, or perhaps his social skills are a bit weak. Pragmatics, by the way, is a technical term that describes the appropriate division of conversational activity between two persons. On your internet profile, specify that you prefer someone with good pragmatics.

---

3   Emma Woodhouse and Captain Ahab have been described as narcissists by literary critics, but I don't think so. Stephan Daedalus is an egoist, I think, not a narcissist. There is a difference between egotism, which is an inflated view of oneself, and egoism, which is the tendency to perceive and consider events in terms of oneself and one's own interests. Narcissists are braggarts or exhibitionists. Egoists may even be quite diffident, but are equally self-absorbed.

My husband cares more about his boyish games than he does about me or the family.

Hopefully, his boyish games don't cost a lot of money. If so, you are probably lucky to have him out of the house.

My husband actually believes that he is an undiscovered genius. He won't hold a job very long because he is always jumping from one hare-brained scheme to another. He thinks he is going to be the next internet billionaire.

He may well be, you never know. Freud's wife had no patience for psycho-analysis, Karl Marx's wife thought socialism was a joke, and Darwin's wife was a churchgoing woman who believed in the literal truth of Genesis. On the other hand, uxorial disapproval is no guarantee of great success.

When I try to load the dishwasher, my boyfriend gets mad at me. He says, "Here. I'll load the dishwasher." Then he does. I feel like he's loading the dishwasher at me.

My mail-bag is full of letters and cards from women and gay men whose mates are self-centered, if not grandiose, and unempathic, if not abrasive or exploitative. They all ask, "Is he a narcissist?" To which I respond, "Who knows?" Some of these letters might be pranks, I think. But they give me some good lines.

Nature's plan for narcissists

Narcissists are usually annoying (*socially abrasive*), but when they have to, they can turn on the charm. Controlling men are like that, too. Neither are *socially inept*, as men or women with Asperger's are. Psychopaths are charming, but they are *antisocial*. In our clinics, we also encounter patients who are *hypersocial, asocial, socially anxious, socially disinhibited, dyssocial, unsocialized* or *socially inappropriate.* All of these terms refer to afflictions of the social brain, affecting one or another of its operations. I find that interesting. Most social animals have social faculties with a less expansive phenotypic space, but among the humans the opposite has been the case. Every imaginable variant of social dysfunction is found somewhere in our race, in individuals and sometimes in whole tribes. This extravagant display of social diversity, I suppose, gives evolution an opportunity to exercise considered judgment on behalf of one trait and not another.

How evolution does that, we all know, is natural selection, a general process that rewards fitness. The primary agents of natural selection are said to be chance and differential mortality, but neither explains where narcissists come from. It's hard to believe that narcissism was an accidental point mutation because no other human trait is. Nor is it likely that egocentricity, group sex or voyeurism might promote one's reproductive fitness. But then, I know little of such things. I have observed that narcissists don't have trouble attracting girlfriends for activities that are less anomalous and more likely of issue. If there is a tribe of unbridled egocentrics in the world, there must also be a sub-tribe of sycophants, hangers-on and hero-worshippers whose perspective-taking is as warped as the narcissists' self-appraisal.

Natural selection was extended to include sexual selection; that males exist in order to express their genotype, for better or worse, and that females exist to choose the ones they like. However, Darwin himself struggled with the problem of elaborate display. He knew nothing of narcissists, but he was troubled by the peacock, whose tail is attractive, indeed, but as likely to attract predators as cute peahens. "The sight of a feather in a peacock's tail, whenever I gaze at it, makes me sick," he said.[4] Darwin, of course, was a sensitive soul.

Fisher, his student, explained the value of extravagant display. The evolution of odd mating preferences is self-reinforcing because

---

4   Charles Darwin, Letter to Asa Gray, April 3, 1860.

the offspring of such matings inherit two characteristics: the capacity for elaborate sexual ornamentation from the father and a preference for same from the mother. The traits are mutually reinforcing and grow stronger in succeeding generations. The process is successful because excessive ornamentation indicates the individual's underlying fitness: he has sufficient resources to waste some on mere display. Ultimately, animals that are given to extravagant display speciate. They hang together, exclude their non-ornamented and non-preferring relatives, and by the process of sexual isolation and phenotypic divergence eventually form a new species. Their erstwhile conspecifics, I imagine, are just as happy to see them go.

Sexual selection is a special case of natural selection that rewards extravagant reproductive display in the service of reproductive fitness. The narcissist, therefore, can afford his elaborate displays; because he has so many robust good qualities, he is irresistible. Perhaps that explains our antipathy to the poor narcissist. We are just those erstwhile conspecifics who have a sexual isolation problem. Are we afraid we'll be left behind? Maybe we already have been.

Neither natural selection, red in tooth and claw, nor sexual selection can explain the evolution of narcissists. If sexual selection were operating in the case of narcissism, it would only amplify their traits in the population gene pool. In that case one would have to admit that Lasch, Twenge and Campbell and Vankin were right, and I am not inclined to do that. Yes, elaborate sexual display and other forms of conspicuous consumption are still with us, but they are an evolutionary dead-end, best illustrated by unimportant characters like peacocks, gambusia fish and the preposterous Irish elk. My theory is that narcissists evolved, like Irish elk, to serve as a warning to others.

Theories based on a semi-mechanical approach to mate selection don't have much relevance to humans, and one reason is that the males and females of our species are both choosers. The bases of human mating choices have been studied in depth. They have little to do with elaborate display, but rather with social virtues: honesty, kindness, generosity, good humor. This fact illuminates the ultimate form of natural selection as it occurs among human beings: **social selection**. As humans evolved, they appear to have cultivated value-sets that reflect what made them evolve: social cooperation, effective communication and intelligence. It's a feed-forward process; as societies evolved, those values affect the mating choices of men and women to a greater degree, and supplant dead-end selection pressures like race, sect, caste and propinquity. The values inherent in social cooperation and intelligence militate against extravagant display. They explain the antipathy with which most of us greet the boastful, uninsightful behavior of the narcissist.

Every student knows perfectly well how social selection works, because it's evident in the behavior of schoolchildren from about the third grade. It begins with the expression of disapproval to children with undesirable traits. Some children form in-groups and outsiders are excluded. This is cruel, we grown-ups think, and small-minded. If an outsider is bullied or dealt with harshly by a teacher, the other kids smirk. A child's tolerance of differences and capacity for empathy are circumscribed; that is a *bad thing* and we counsel children against it. It is only natural for children to behave that way, however, because their parents do, too, in their own ways. It is in our nature to exclude individuals of whom we disapprove, and most of us disapprove of those who are obsessively self-absorbed. We are fortunate indeed that the characters schoolchildren spurn these days are not defined in terms of disability, race, religion or sexual preference; but spurning outsiders will never disappear as long as the criterion is socially disquieting behavior.

Social pressure is no less than a force for evolution. The human genome generates an expansive phenotypic space within which many different kinds of traits arise. Phenotypic diversity is something the human species is good at, especially in the social and emotional domains. It's what makes social selection possible.

Social selection in evolution has cultivated the important trait of social cooperation, which entails, among other things, kindness, tolerance, generosity and good humor. During the span of an individual's life, social pressures promote the same goals. We want our fellow humans to cultivate certain traits and to suppress others. We start doing it, in clumsy ways, when we are very young. We continue to do it after we grow up, and we hardly ever stop.

The goal of social disapproval is not mortal punishment, but rather just a bit of self-improvement. Social selection is not the agent of differential mortality, as is survival of the fittest, but it has relevance to mate selection and can thus change the racial genome. Like teasing, it exerts social pressures in order to shape the behavior of one's errant conspecifics. Such pressures are quite effective at influencing behavior. They can even affect one's genes, or at least how they are expressed. So, we disapprove of a narcissistic friend. We prefer him to be less boastful, to be more realistic about his qualities and to take responsibility for his mistakes. We don't want to tame his self-confidence and ebullience, but we would like him to be more generous in his attributions and more gracious in response to constructive criticism. Perhaps, as Havelock Ellis said, narcissism is a developmental stage, but adolescents quickly learn that neither affection nor admiration are won by obsessive self-absorption.

Social pressures may seem outdated and oppressive in societies devoted to individual self-expression; that was a point that Lasch himself made. One can object to his argument because social pressures are often exercised in unfortunate directions: to diminish the lives of unbelievers, for example, or to encourage wanton and immoderate behavior, or to violate ethical standards in order to make a lot of money. The list of reprehensible behaviors that can be excited by social influences is virtually endless. If such negative influences were the only kinds of pressures to which humans were exposed, the evolution of our race would be decidedly retrograde. Social pressures, however, are much more likely to be directed in favor of tolerance, kindness, moderation and honesty.

Social pressures are usually applied, for example, on behalf of the trait of **modesty** and against the trait of **self-enhancement**, the latter referring not to self-improvement but rather to what narcissists do. This we know from psychological investigations that show the social benefits of modesty. Modest individuals make favorable impressions. They are regarded as better-adjusted socially, more likeable, more reliable, more honest and more authentic. We like people better when they take responsibility for failure—sincere responsibility—rather than blaming other people. Modest people are not likely to be exploitative, angry, hostile or aggressive. They have lower rates of depression, more life satisfaction and greater vitality. They score better on measures of agreeableness, empathy, affiliation and intimacy. They know how to experience gratitude, appreciation and forgiveness. They have closer relationships and experience greater well-being when they are with their friends. They are less likely to engage in dangerous behaviors. Self-enhancers, on the other hand, are prone to vengefulness and rumination. They do risky things like drinking from a stranger's water bottle, engaging in unprotected sex, sunbathing for long periods of time, obsessing over their weight, and consuming illicit drugs, although not necessarily all at the same time (Sedikides, Gregg, and Hart, 2007).

Finally, modest people are much more likely to be accurate in their self-perception than narcissists are. The narcissist's "self-delusions" are deeply held and resistant to correction, even in the face of overwhelming evidence. They continually overestimate their abilities, distort their past behaviors, and hold overly positive views of their personalities, even when self-enhancement puts them at social risk (Vazire and Funder, 2006). Such faulty thinking has been likened to a cognitive disability of the social brain (Morf and Rhodewalt, 2001). Those of us who have been shaped into states of tolerance and empathy should regard them with kindness. Mostly, though, we just can't stand them. We're not just being uncharitable; blame evolution.

Not-so-pathological self-absorption

Narcissism isn't an epidemic, but the issues Christopher Lasch raised may have more significance than his popularizers might lead you to believe. His hypothesis would be more cogent if he had compared self-absorption to a small tumor growing in a segment of society. Think of it as a tribe arising in our midst. They are full of themselves, even grandiose, but their self-perceptions are *accurate*. Call it a form of narcissism if you like, but this new tribe is too clever to be boastful and too confident to be unempathic. It didn't arise from the chance meeting of fictitious tribes but by the deliberate association of serial generations of clever, task-positive people. Suppose there were such a tribe, not distracted by "thoughts as broad as Nature" but rewarded at every step for the flexibility of their analytical minds, at the same time lacking nothing in social acuity. Could we say that their self-regard was excessive or obsessive? It wouldn't cause distress. They would be happy to venture into the autobiographical notebook in their default mode. When they did, the risk is they would discover, as Zaphod did,[5] that they are really terrific and great guys. Common sense reminds one that Zaphod isn't quite the great guy he thinks he is. But as Lasch said, "common sense, the traditional wisdom and folkways of the community, is an obstacle to progress and enlightenment."

I often tell my children that they are blessed to live in a society that doesn't limit friendships according to race, religion or background. They will have to read this book to learn that they and their peers will be afflicted by an unintended consequence: assortative mating on the basis of intelligence and personality traits. For those on the right side of the Gaussian curve in both dimensions, it will be a blessing indeed.

Or will it? Lasch said, "Every age develops its own peculiar forms of pathology, which express in exaggerated form its underlying character structure." The risk of the coming age is to engender, in a fortunate few, a character structure that is not overtly pathological yet is subject to different faults. They have active minds, these wonder-children, but an active mind is not without its perils.

SA is one of those faults, and it isn't confined to indolent souls.

---

5   See Douglas Adams, *The Restaurant at the End of the Universe*.

It occurs in the very best people, even those whose social skills are exemplary. SA is a special kind of sensitivity, to the ambiguities and disappointments that occur in the company of people who are not one's intimates. It breeds intolerance; in patients, it can lead to paranoia. One expects those born into social and genetic privilege to be endowed with the gifts of openness and self-assurance. That isn't always the case. A protected life may well be intolerant of ambiguity and unpredictability, let alone the irrational, which governs social interactions more than we think. Nor does success always lead to openness: it is equally likely to induce a preoccupation with privacy. One is entitled to safety and comfort in exchange for a life well lived. One can be narcotized by the specialness of one's position.

OC is a second fault, but not in the form of odd preoccupations or eccentric habits. It may show itself in the unhappy state of obsessive self-absorption.

It's not hard to be self-absorbed if one has been successful from day care through the Ivy League, and thence in careers in finance, consulting, academia or government. An intelligent mind is *entitled* to such success. It attracts the company, not of sycophants or hangers-on, but of amusing and like-minded people. There they live, well-regarded by friends and acquaintances in privileged communities, well-shielded from disgruntled Morlocks like you and me. The disproportionate evolution of brain is more disproportionate in some than others, and the consequence is not necessarily narcissism but self-absorption.

Doing everything right justly increases one's self-regard; self-esteem, self-love and self-reflection are positive qualities. Psychologists have examined all of those "self-" characteristics, and also self-awareness, self-understanding, self-rumination, self-focused attention and self-consciousness, both public and private. They agree that self-love is an essential component of a healthy personality. Self-reflection is a neutral term that indicates that one is interested in what's going on inside one's head. It may refer to peaceful stays in default mode, gently pondering one's past and future and what they mean. Or it may mean rumination, or self-absorption, which is never peaceful or gentle. It is linked to anxiety, depression and neuroticism. It may be motivated by perceived threats or it may concoct them by reflecting too much. To someone who is obsessed with doing everything right, the idea that he or she just might do something wrong can only be threatening. Better, then, to check one more time (Harrington and Loffredo, 2010; Joireman, Parrott, and Hammersla, 2002; Trapnell and Campbell, 1999).

24
OC and the Future of the Race

There isn't an epidemic of narcissism, or of autism, or of ADD. There may be an over-supply of people who think they are, or who want to be, but that's another story. It is entirely possible, however, that there is an excess of OCs, at least in certain quarters; too many analytical, hyper-rational brains in the bodies of individuals absorbed by their work. They like to take psychostimulants so that they can be *more* absorbed in their work. If people think there is more autism around, it may just be Aspergerism, an infestation of systematizers. If they worry that Americans, looking in the mirror, will fall in love with themselves, I can assure them that the self-absorbed are too clever to fall for that one. Nevertheless, it's not unreasonable to fear that the empathic mind has reached its evolutionary limit at the very time that the analytical, systematizing brain, inflated by silicon and complex financial instruments, is taking on new, invigorated life. I have no way to know if that might be the case. My powers of observation are less than keen and grow more so (i.e., more less-than-keen) as the years pass. My skills as a futurist, however, are as weak as they have ever been.

Nevertheless, if such were the case, it would be a nice way to end our investigations. We shall therefore pretend that there *is* an epidemic of OC looming. A more highly evolved and complex brain is upon us, not just *in silico* but *in vivo*. The rational utopias envisioned by Plato, St. Thomas More and Aldous Huxley are on the near horizon. I'm getting off the bus at the next Indian reservation.

People get smarter

The human race is getting smarter, and not just because we have instant access to the internet. It has been going on for almost a century and perhaps longer, although the collection of hard data began in 1932. That was when psychologists began using IQ tests routinely, in schools and when young men were inducted into the military. Before long they noticed that each successive wave of recruits did better on IQ tests. Studies in schoolchildren, especially in the British Isles, extended the observation. It was quite a surprise, too, because the prevailing view among psychologists eighty years ago was that the human race was getting dumber. It was the era of eugenics, and psychologists, like Dr. Popenoe, believed that "the less intelligent must have a higher average rate of reproduction" (Lynn and Hampson, 1986). When the precise opposite was observed, they were at a loss. They were the men who believed in Social Darwinism: that human societies could only advance by survival of the fittest; that social programs, like special classes for children with autism, led to retrograde evolution and racial corruption.

The fact that such men are virtually extinct should be proof enough that human evolution is advancing in a positive direction, but there are plenty of additional data. The phenomenon of rising IQ scores has been replicated many times and in nations on every continent. The IQ tests that psychologists use have to be re-standardized every ten years because children are getting smarter. This is the **Flynn effect**, first described in the 1940s but eponymously associated with James Flynn, a psychologist in New Zealand. He wrote:

> Every Stanford-Binet and Wechsler standardization sample
> from 1932 to 1978 established norms of a higher standard than

its predecessor. The obvious interpretation of this pattern is that representative samples of Americans did better and better on IQ tests over a period of 46 years, the total gain amounting to a rise in mean IQ of 13.8 points. (Flynn, 1984)

A similar observation was made at the same time by Richard Lynn, a psychologist in Northern Ireland, who was happy to refute earlier concerns by psychologists that the average intelligence of Britain, the USA and other developed countries was going down. In fact, people everywhere are getting smarter, at least in terms of their scores on intelligence tests, and by an average of 3 points per decade.

In contrast to the autism epidemic, the secular change in intelligence is real, but its cause is a matter of speculation. There are probably several contributing factors. One is radio, cinema and TV. Banal as they are, they convey an extraordinary volume of basic knowledge and expanded vocabulary. They expose audiences to different cultures and ways of thinking. It is probably one of the causes of rising IQ scores; if so, think of the effect that smartphones and the internet are having.

Lynn suspected that the increase was related to advances in health and nutrition, which is always a safe bet. Flynn suggested that the way people think is actually changing: we are more likely to be analytical or scientific in our mode of thought. To illustrate, there is a component of several IQ tests, the similarities test: how are these items similar? Show a potato, a knife and a bunch of kale to an undergraduate, and she will (hopefully) choose the potato and the kale because they are both vegetables. Show them to a Bushman, and he will choose the potato and the knife. "Why?" you ask him. It's because he can take the knife and cut up the potato to cook. That makes sense, but it isn't a *categorical* similarity, which is what the test is looking for. Now ask the Bushman how a fool might relate the objects, and he will select the potato and the kale. He is being a bit concrete, that Bushman, but the idea of grouping things by virtue of their Linnaean category isn't meaningful to him. So, to the Bushman, the undergraduate is a fool. But is she smarter? Yes, and in this sense. She has no difficulty understanding the rationale of the Bushman's selection; one presumes she knows that one can cut a potato with a knife, but she also knows that that isn't the point of the question. The point of the question is to abstract a specific relationship between two of the three items, but the Bushman, even if he is a clever fellow, has a hard time grasping her abstract style of thought. Her thinking, therefore, *incorporates* his and is therefore more cogent. IQ tests, even nonverbal tests, reward her way of thinking and penalize his. Flynn is right, I think. The modern mind is increasingly analytical because that is the way we are taught in school and that is what we learn from radio, TV and the movies. We have learned that abstract associations are not only meaningful but useful.[1]

Another explanation for the increase in IQ is **heterosis**, which means the same as *hybrid vigor* or *heterozygote advantage*. It goes like this: the 20th century saw the movement of populations away from small villages where people chose their mates from a limited gene pool. When large numbers of people moved to cities, they found mates if not with good genes then at least with better genes than there were back in Frosolone.

An example of heterosis is what happened when vast hordes of immigrants came to the US at the end of the 19th century, mostly from shtetls in eastern Europe and the peasant villages of southern Italy. They were, in their day, the worst brood-stock one could imagine. The eugenicists proved it by administering IQ tests to the huddled masses when they landed. The immigrants tended to score in the 70s, the borderline mentally retarded range, a frightening bit of data that led to the belief that Jews and Italians would only corrupt the American gene pool. Gould proposed that this pseudo-science was what led to restrictive immigration laws passed in the 1920s, although I suspect that the odd customs and unruly behavior of the immigrants also had something to do with it. Even the largest

---

1   There is a perfectly delicious recipe that one can make with potatoes and kale, but you do need a knife and you have to look it up on the internet.

and most welcoming nations become surfeited with new arrivals after a while. They like to take a rest and digest what they just took in before returning to the banquet of humanity.

Nevertheless, those intellectually compromised immigrants managed to thrive in spite of their supposed limitations; IQ tests didn't measure their native intelligence, let alone their cultural cohesion. They settled in, most of them I think in my old neighborhood in Brooklyn or in the Jewish neighborhood on the other side of McDonald Avenue. Their children ate better and went to school. The kids went to school and to the movies, and they listened to the radio. They also happened to be products of exogamous matings between different shtetls and different provinces in the south of Italy. Their grandchildren went to college, and there they mated extra-exogamously with girls from Minnesota and boys from Kansas. There are a lot of reasons why their descendants got so much smarter so soon, but I think exogamy and heterosis were part of it.

There are several contributing factors to account for the secular increase in IQ, including the ones I just listed. Recall the factors that contribute to MBD, especially a bad outcome for an MBD child: not-so-good genes, intrauterine and neonatal insults, obstetrical suboptimality, poverty, ignorance and not-so-good cultures, neglect and abuse, poor schools, and the expectation of failure. Compare their unhappy state to children born in modern, developed societies, blessed with the fruits of assortative mating, optimal medical care, nurturing environments, excellent schools, and an extraordinary degree of positive stimulation. Most of them have brains that are well equipped to take advantage. They are conceived, they are born and they develop in circumstances of super-optimality. *It is my observation* that they are smarter than ever.

If the secular increase in IQ is the result of environmental events or heterosis, we should expect the population increase in intelligence eventually to bump up against the limits of our phenotypic space. In Norway, for example, military recruits are given the equivalent of an IQ test. For many years, their scores kept going up, just as they did in other countries. Then, during the 1990s, Norwegian recruits stopped getting smarter. They had reached a plateau, presumably the genetic limits of their intellectual potential (Sundet, Barlaug, and Torjussen, 2004). Of course, they're all still Norwegians. They need to import some Italians and Jews.

The limits of our phenotypic space are determined by one's genome; and that, we are taught, is fixed. In fact, there is reason to believe that the genetic limits of our intellectual potential are expanding, and not just by the admixture of foreign genes. There is a new understanding of genetics that has gone well beyond Gregor Mendel and the Modern Synthesis that merged Mendelian genetics with Darwinian selection. We now know that genes can change within a generation or two, and even within one's own lifetime. Humans, alone among the animals, possess a dynamic genome that mutates by fast operations, like genetic transformations and inherited epigenetic change. The most mutable genes happen to be those related to brain development. Brain evolution might well be happening right now, before our very eyes.

We have evolved real fast

It's not my custom to give too much credit to human beings, but if we're good at anything, it's evolving. The appropriate term is **evolvability**. If anything, we are evolvable.

Human beings and chimpanzees shared a common ancestor about 5–6 million years ago, and then we went our separate ways. Our evolutionary lineage may have begun with the australopithecines, a successful species that lived in Africa 3–5 million years ago. The most famous australopithecine was Lucy, whose fossilized skeleton was discovered in Ethiopia in 1974. From that skeleton, and also from some fossilized footprints, anthropologists concluded that Lucy walked upright. However, she had the cranial capacity of a chimpanzee, about 400 cubic centimeters. We can't be sure, but we think that Lucy and her kind gave rise to the genus *Homo* about

2 million years ago. That is our genus, of course, but it also includes several species of proto-humans called hominids. The first hominid was **Homo habilis**, whose brain volume was about 750 cc. Then there was **Homo erectus**, whose brain volume was about 900 cc, and then **Homo sapiens**, whose brain tips the scales at about 1600 cc. H sapiens appeared about 200,000 years ago and managed to get around pretty well. As the hominid brain grew in size, the hominids themselves grew larger, although the size differential between males and females decreased. Hominids became fully bipedal and developed complex social structures, language, sophisticated tools, swell clothes and, *mirabile dictu*, monogamous pair-bonding strategies.

The study of hominid evolution no longer relies on fossils. It is possible to time the occurrence of genetic changes. We know of several such changes since our species appeared. Gene mutations associated with speech, language and brain growth occurred about 100,000 years ago (Corballis, 2004; Enard, Przeworski, *et al.*, 2002). About 50,000 years ago, humans carrying those new genes spread out of Africa and summarily replaced all previous hominid migrants, including colonies of *Homo* who had migrated earlier (Semino *et al.*, 2000; Tang, 2006; Underhill *et al.*, 2000). We think that fully modern languages were formed around 40,000 years ago, at the same time as a sudden, marked improvement in stone tool technology (Krantz, 1980). At the same time, we see the first representational art, for example in the caves at Lascaux. Around that time, the dead were buried with ritual and surrounded with objects that may have symbolized their lives or that they might have needed in the afterlife. Human beings, *H. sapiens sapiens* by now, were developing the capacity for abstract thought. Then another genetic mutation arose, only about 5800 years ago, and has since swept to high frequency (Mekel-Bobrov *et al.*, 2005). This mutation is simultaneous with what is called the Paleolithic revolution, the development of agriculture, cities and literacy. Two of the most recent such mutations, in Microcephalin and ASPM (the abnormal spindle-like microcephaly-associated gene), both have a very young genetic signature; they may still be evolving in *H. sapiens sapiens* (Tang, 2006).

Those, however, are only point mutations—changes in one of the base pairs in a coding segment of one's DNA (i.e., a gene). The problem of relating the Modern Synthesis to human evolution is that our genome remains quite similar to those of the gorilla, the chimpanzee and the orangutan. We share no less than 98.5 percent homology with the higher apes at the DNA level and 99.4 percent identity at functionally important regions (Wildman *et al.*, 2003). Recent research, however, has revealed more genetic dissimilarity between humans and the great apes than anticipated simply on the basis of chromosome analysis. The areas of dissimilarity, however, are not in the genes themselves but in the mechanisms that govern how genes are expressed: the real divisor between humans and chimpanzees is **gene expression**.

During hominid evolution, mechanisms of gene expression have been elaborated to an extraordinary degree, and this is especially true of genes that govern brain development (Chimpanzee Sequencing and Analysis Consortium, 2005; Dorus *et al.*, 2004; Enard, Khaitovich, *et al.*, 2002; Gommans, Mullen, and Maas, 2009). In fact, almost all of the genetic differences between humans and other primates are a result of changes in the way genes express themselves (Jauch *et al.*, 1992; Yunis and Prakash, 1982). The accelerated pace of human evolution cannot be attributed to point mutations, which occur at a sluggish rate, but is probably a function of mechanisms like **genomic rearrangements**, which are dynamic in their capacity to generate human **genetic variation** from one generation to the next (Lupski, 2007; Morrow, 2010). In humans, there is more **non-coding DNA** than in other primates; these non-coding regions affect gene expression. They are also unstable and tend to generate new mutations, like copy number variants—changes that occur quite frequently and that account for the striking differences that sometimes exist between parents and their offspring. The unstable, non-coding regions of DNA have been called "gene nurseries for genomic innovation" (Bailey and Eichler, 2006; Feder, 2007; Nahon, 2003).

Hominid evolution is mainly about brain evolution. It has little to do with genes, but a lot to do with genomic mutability. It has to do with the expansion of non-coding regions of DNA, the instability that occurs in such areas, the emergence of new patterns of gene expression, and thence the capacity to generate an extraordinary degree of phenotypic diversity.

Human evolution did not only serve the purpose of adaptation to specific niches, in the way that Darwin's finches adapted to different islands on the Galapagos. During hominid evolution, brain and behavior were at issue, not the color of one's feathers or the shape of one's beak. Feathers and beaks allow a bird to *adapt*; brain and behavior allow humans to *be adaptable*. The widest range of phenotypic variation occurs in matters that have to do with brain function. They are the four functions that distinguish human brain from all others: *cooperative socialization, abstract intelligence, effective communication* and *fine motor dexterity*.

The growth of brain size by a factor of four over two million years or so was an impressive achievement because evolution doesn't usually happen so fast; we are the benefactors of what they call **runaway evolution** (Willis, 1993). It was impressive also because there were so many biological constraints against it happening, like the size of a female's pelvic outlet, which could only accommodate the birth of infants who were several months premature in comparison with other primate babies. A large brain was metabolically hyperactive, and in particular the neocortex. Greater amounts of nourishing food, especially animal protein and fat, were needed to stay alive. It required a lot of work on our part, or our hominid ancestors'. That all this happened was by virtue of a remarkable technological achievement: the way our hominid ancestors decided to organize their little societies. It was our first and arguably our most important technological achievement. The evolution of intelligence was nothing less than a triumph of social organization over the limitations imposed by biology. Think of it as an achievement of the empathic mind.

We are riders on an evolutionary trajectory that is accelerating at an exponential rate, and it has been for some time. It is possible that we have reached the omega point beyond which no further changes are possible. If that is so, one would have to explain why; and I can't think of a good answer, except maybe that we're getting too fat. It is far more likely that brain evolution still has a way to go—a good thing, if you ask me.

We are still evolving, aren't we?

The evidence is mounting that development along our evolutionary line is accelerating. One finds many fabulous things when examining human DNA with instruments that didn't exist twenty years ago, and among them are the fingerprints of accelerated evolution. When a gene mutates and forms a new allele, it carries a mark of sorts, a span of DNA right next to the gene known as a **linkage disequilibrium** (LD). An LD is a block of hundreds or thousands of base pairs, right next to the new allele. As the new allele persists during succeeding generations, its LD decays and grows progressively shorter. By measuring the length of those LDs, therefore, one can calculate whether a mutation occurred recently or long ago, and also how many new alleles have occurred at different points in time.

When Eric Wang and Robert Moyzis at UC-Irvine applied the study of linkage disequilibria to the human genome, they found not only that the formation of new alleles in the human genome is ongoing but also that the formation of new, mutated genes has accelerated during the last 40,000 years. Further, the number of such genetic changes is particularly high in humans in comparison with chimpanzees, suggesting that we are evolving faster than they are. In fact, the number of recently evolved alleles in the human genome is comparable only to the number of mutations in the maize plant; not necessarily a flattering comparison until one considers that maize has been the target of intensive selection by human farmers for 10,000 years (Wang, Kodama, Baldi, and Moyzis, 2006). Not only are we evolving, but we are evolving as fast as corn.

There is a term for the sort of genetic change that occurs from one generation to the next and that leads to phenotypic changes in just a few years or decades: **microevolution**. It is continually reported in modern humans. In isolated populations, for example in Quebec and Finland, parish records going back for centuries indicate changes in human fertility, in particular in the age of a woman's first reproduction (the AFR). Over a 140-year period, for example, Quebecois living on the Ile aux Coudres in the St. Lawrence River lowered their AFR from 26 years to 22. Not only did their AFR go down, but this was a heritable trait and could be related to other measures of genetic fitness (Courtiol *et al.*, 2012; Milot *et al.*, 2011). Similar events have been observed in Framingham, the town west of Boston that has been the subject of the longest-running reality show in medical history. In Framingham, researchers have documented additional evidence of recent evolutionary changes. The daughters and granddaughters of the original Framinghamites have lower blood pressure and cholesterol levels. They also tend to have their first child earlier than their mothers did. The Framingham researchers insist that they had nothing to do with any of these occurrences, and that they have uncovered clear evidence of Darwinian selection at work right there, on the south side of the Mass Pike. They also aver, on the basis of their data, that they can make "predictions about our future evolution." Their prediction, though, is a bit of an anticlimax. The future women of Framingham are going to be shorter and stouter (Byars, Ewbank, Govindaraju, and Stearns, 2010).

I'm not sure what the Darwinian advantage is of being short and stout. Even having one's first baby at an earlier age may seem a dubious advantage, but to a biologist it indicates improved fertility, improved fitness and the likelihood of greater evolutionary success. Selection also likes more babies because more babies mean more phenotypic diversity. It likes an expanded population, too, because that expands the field of eligibles, just as internet dating services do. More people mean more new adaptive mutations: with more individuals there are more new mutations; and as the population grows, the likelihood of new, beneficial mutations increases as well (Hawks *et al.*, 2007). Of course, it also means more mutations that are *not* so adaptive, and we have met some of those in these pages.

Thus we discover changes in the human phenotype, especially over the past century, and also in our genotype. Humans—except in Framingham—are growing taller. The rate at which children grow and mature sexually is increasing. Head circumferences are getting larger (Mingroni, 2004).

> The platonic, essentialist view that *Homo sapiens*, once formed, remains the same biological entity throughout the centuries is patently incorrect…changes in human genes and phenotypes from generation to generation do occur. (Ruhli and Henneberg, 2013)

Some people argue against continuing evolution, contending that humans have only improved their ecological flexibility by virtue of social and cultural adaptations, just as Flynn and Lyn explain the increase in IQ scores in terms of social and cultural improvements. It's only half true, however, because social and cultural improvements have eliminated one of the *constraints* on evolution. Advances in food production, sanitation and medical care have largely eliminated mortality among young people. Before 1850, even in rich countries, more than half of the babies born would die before they reached maturity. Now, more than 90 percent survive and enjoy the opportunity to participate in the reproduction of the next generation. Therefore, natural selection by **differential mortality**—the survival of the fittest—has become virtually irrelevant. In terms of differential mortality, the laws of natural selection have been relaxed, if not repealed. This was the reason why eugenicists were afraid of the rise of a degenerate race.

The eugenic argument is wrong because relaxing one selection pressure—differential mortality—allows other pressures to exert greater influence. Natural selection by survival of the fittest had terrific difficulty in explaining the extravagant sexual ornamentation of certain species, like the peacock. It wasn't differential mortality that accounts for elaborate display, Fisher explained, but sexual selection, which represented a different kind of pressure. Then a new selection pressure became important during the evolution of the hominids. Among the humans, **social selection** has been the driving force and has exerted pressures on behalf of the traits of social cooperation, analytical intelligence and effective communication. Perhaps fine motor coordination, too, because you have to keyboard faster if you want a good date.

Assuming that there is only one kind of selective process in evolution is like assuming that genes have only one way to mutate or only one way to express themselves. Those are mechanistic constructions and fundamentally at odds with biology, which is all about flexibility. A single-minded evolutionary force, such as a sluggish genome, is not likely to generate complex, adaptable organisms. Nor will it generate complex, adaptable organs, such as brains and hands, within those organisms. There are many different kinds of selection pressures; the virtual elimination of differential mortality and selection for secondary sexual characteristics merely opens an opportunity window for new selection pressures.

In brain, for example, there is yet another form of selection pressure: selection based on use. Protein-coding genes provide the scaffolding upon which brain in constructed. The activity of protein-coding genes is reflected in the size of the cortical sheet, its infoldings, and the general coordinates according to which neurons migrate during development. Looking more closely at what happens as brain develops, one finds that the connections that neurons make with one another are under very loose genetic control. Neurons grow axons and dendrites, and connections form with other neurons; but this activity is stimulated by electrical and chemical signals from other neurons. Such signals excite genes within each neuron to guide growth and development according to usage patterns (Krubitzer and Kaas, 2005; Krubitzer and Kahn, 2003). **Selection by usage** reflects an efficient way to deal with the problem of getting a vast array of neurons to achieve good functional integration. They complement one another with maximum flexibility and minimum design information by responding to patterns of use (Deacon, 2010). An extraordinarily healthy infant brain is more than ready to stimulate the connections among neurons and even how neurons express their genes.

Natural selection by survival of the fittest is red in tooth and claw. There are other ways for selection to operate, less morbid than differential mortality and less extravagant than sexual selection. Selection is not just one process, but an array of processes—processes that operate differently at different levels and in response to different pressures. It operates very slowly at the level of point mutations that affect survival, and it operates very quickly in terms of brain plasticity in response to use patterns. Social selection probably began slowly but accelerated among the primates and then achieved runaway status among the hominids. It has generated a human society that is ever more numerous and complex, more diverse, and free to relax the old rules and cultivate new ones. An ever more dynamic genome is equipped to respond. The question is, what will the new rules be?

The future of the race

We animals never allow our friends to make fools of themselves beyond a certain limit.[2]

When you opened this book about errant OCs, you may not have bargained for predictions about humanity's future. But: "As Cuvier could correctly describe a whole animal by the contemplation of a single bone, so the observer who has thoroughly understood one link in a series of incidents should be able to accurately state all the other ones, both before and after."[3]

2   Kenneth Grahame, *The Wind in the Willows*.
3   Arthur Conan Doyle, "The Five Orange Pips" (*The Adventures of Sherlock Holmes*).

Thus far, social selection has favored the traits of social cooperation, analytical intelligence and effective communication, and they appear to have evolved together. The question, now, is whether they will continue to evolve together, or whether one or the other—the empathic mind or the analytical brain—may have reached the limits of its phenotypic space. Theoretically, genetic changes will change the dimensions of that space, but there may be limits. Humans are getting taller, but one doesn't envision that process going on forever. Air travel would be even less agreeable. On the other hand, brain-power is less constrained than height, which has to contend not only with gravity and low doorways but also with the rickety architecture of the human spine. Nevertheless, I am quite sure our descendants will not be short and stout.

Does brain evolution have any constraints at all? Granted, Norwegians have got to a place where they just can't get any smarter, but it is always a mistake to generalize from Nordic tribes. They have made progress, granted, during the thousand years since their ancestors wreaked wanton violence on the civilized people of Europe. They have even achieved a level of smug global happiness, rivaled only, perhaps, by Canadians. Even if their phenotypic space is constrained with respect to analytical intelligence, perhaps they can make up for it in other ways, for example by cultivating a new cuisine or creative new approaches to detective fiction. The rest of us have a long way to go before we reach the limits of our brain-power, but which will it be? Will it be the cool, analytical mind of the systematizers? Or the empathic mind of loving-kindness and compassion?

The analytical mind is ensconced in the cerebral cortex with a modern, flexible matrix design that is capable of endless plasticity. It gives rise to oscillations that reorient thought and action with only the tiniest changes in frequency. It has a way of thinking with universal appeal, free of the prejudices that divide nations. True, it is slow and burns a lot of fuel, but those are only opportunities for an improved version. Brain cases may be getting smaller, but probably only because neural connections are getting more efficient.

Technically minded men and women have guaranteed our safety, comforts and opportunities for pleasures, high and low. We have no reason to believe that they are going to stop. There seem to be no barriers to the potential of the analytical mind, inured as it is to primitive experiences like meaning, happiness, love and sexuality.

Or will it be the empathic brain, whose foundation is an emotional sounding board, prone to disruption by viruses and hypoxic events? The social brain is a complex instrument that does its best atop an antiquated, hierarchical organization of nuclei scattered about the limbic cortex and the brain stem. The social brain, for all its sophistication, is still largely dependent on a reward system that has changed very little from that in our ancestors, the rats. Yet it, too, has good talking-points, like love and happiness, which are not only limitless but infinite—a fine distinction, perhaps, but not without meaning. Meaning, too, is an advantage that the empathic brain confers. The analytical brain, on the other hand, has trouble with things like *meaning*.

> The more the universe seems comprehensible, the more it also seems pointless. (Weinberg, 1994)

The analytical brains among us are not readily given to such moments of frankness. It is not the kind of admission one would make in the introduction to a grant proposal. *We propose to tear up a 17-mile circle in the countryside of France and Switzerland, just outside Geneva. We want to bury ten thousand magnets 300 feet beneath the surface of the Earth. Once we've done that, we shall supercool the magnets to 1.9 degrees Kelvin and accelerate protons around the circle at heretofore unattainable levels of energy. This promises to be one more utterly pointless experiment that no other physicist has yet had the chutzpah to propose to you ignorant baboons. Don't ask how much it will cost, by the way. If you have to worry how much a particle accelerator costs, you can't afford it. Anyway, remember that:*

Any mingling of knowledge with values is unlawful, forbidden. (Monod, 1971)

Advocates for the analytical brain counter that we have only begun to tap its potential. They are right, of course. Digital watches and transistor radios can probably be made much smaller, there are ever more complex financial instruments to devise, more regulations to promulgate, and more pointless information to glean from the early moments of the universe. Once knowledge is unmoored from values, it can accumulate at an ever-faster rate and that is a *good thing*. We may not know what any of it means, of course, but *hey*— we can always dig up those magnets in Geneva and put in colder ones. Anyway, with the extraordinary expansion of channels of communication and information exchange, there is nothing we are going to need so much as information to exchange. And the last thing we want to do is mingle that surfeit of information with *values*, which are of dubious value anyway and only tend to make people uncomfortable.

The problem with evolvability

The problem with evolvability is this: we may be evolving, but we're not sure where we're going with it. Perhaps I can help, or the theory of OC can. Stripped to its essentials, OC is an excess of mental energy that finds its outlet in thoughts and actions. They be weird or hilarious, disturbing or comforting, avoidant or exuberant, enervating or highly productive. Depending, I suppose, on those forks in one's neural pathways, the oscillations in one part of brain may overwhelm the others and one's disposition may be, at heart, riven with anxiety or good cheer. Wherever your OC traits may carry you, they are the expressions of a complex brain and an active mind.

Social selection seems to prefer active minds, but not all the traits that sometime accompany them; Aspergerism, for example, or ruminative anxiety, avoidance or indolence, or an angry, controlling disposition. If your neural oscillations are bound in the service of meaningless gestures or efforts that are degrading or painful to conspecifics, you may not get very many dates, especially since the other sex is getting smarter, too. There are too many examples in recent history and today's news to indicate that the tribe of unhappy OCs is not extinct, but there is nothing about bad OC that confers reproductive fitness. We can only hope that unhappy OCs are a dying breed.

Then there are the happy OCs. Their odd thoughts and behaviors capture something rich and creative about the evolving brain. They are children who are smarter than they used to be, and even grown-ups who are micro-evolving as we speak. You can tell that they are from the effusion of kindness, tolerance and generosity that simply drips like catarrh from their psyche. Even their weaknesses speak to a higher level of engagement with the world and the people in it. They may experience disconnects and frequent embarrassments, especially when they are young, and girls have been known to throw dirt-clods at them. They are only silly little girls, though; just the growth pains that a new and wonderful brain must endure. Active minds can be distracted by their wealth of connections and by networks that skip happily among so many processors. They take time to drink in a world that is rich and full beyond measure. Sooner or later, A will discover that there is nothing fuller or richer than B. When he finds someone as sweet and well-meaning as he, you can imagine what their little a's, b's and c's will be like.

* * *

Phenotypic diversity is a term from evolutionary biology. Selection likes to have a diverse pool to select from, and we evolvable humans have been doing our best to provide it with an Olympic-sized pool of diverse specimens. Some people think selection plucks them out at random.

> Pure chance, absolutely free but blind, is at the very root of
> the stupendous edifice of evolution; this central concept of

modern biology is no longer one among other possible or even conceivable hypotheses. It is the sole conceivable hypothesis, the only one that squares with observed and tested fact...man knows at last that he is alone in the universe's unfeeling immensity, out of which he emerged only by chance. (Monod, 1971)

The theory is that we humans are the product of random mutations, genetic drift and the accidental success of a small band of hominids who managed somehow to stay a step ahead of perilous droughts and advancing glaciers. They won out only because they were nastier than the other hominid groups in the neighborhood. Heck, it's not just a theory, it's "the sole conceivable hypothesis." I think the Great Detective had the right idea:

What object is served by this circle of misery and violence and fear? It must tend to some end, or else our universe is ruled by chance, which is unthinkable.[4]

Most of us don't think much about evolution, let alone evolving, but that doesn't bother me. Our native overconfidence and sense of perceived control would only recoil at the idea that pure chance and nothing else governs the destiny of our race. Rather, most of us regard Nature as a beneficent figure. It is a sound and agreeable image, built up over the years from our devoted pets, those delightful wildlife movies we watch on TV, tramping around with the kids at a National Park, or growing flowers or a tomato plant on the fire escape. Perhaps it is an illusion. Nature and Her handmaiden, evolution, may well be impersonal forces that have done no more than embody the laws of physics and chemistry within the membranes of organisms. That evolution accomplished this by blind chance is not an idea that can be affirmed or falsified, but it's not outlandish. If that is the way it happened, then chance has succeeded in creating a thing of marvel and beauty beyond anything

---

4 Arthur Conan Doyle, "The Adventure of the Cardboard Box" (*His Last Bow*).

that exists in the realms of physics or chemistry. That would take some explaining. If chance governed the universe, I think it would be stranger than it is and, I venture to say, not nearly so marvelous. Nature is lawful; if it weren't, science would be impossible.

A lawful universe is not uniform or even orderly, but coherent and most of the time harmonious, like a thousand voices singing a beautiful chorus but with each voice slightly out of tune. They balance out, those voices. It is true that some things seem to happen by chance, like A who met B at choir practice. That A connected with B, however, was not chance, but a *probability*. That is how the laws of Nature manifest themselves in the universe, just as they do in our lives: by probabilities.

Chance events, like the throw of dice, obey the laws of probability; but probability is not pure chance. Probability in Nature is historical; what is likely to happen depends on what happened before. We know that from how Nature behaves when She stumbles on a good idea, like lipid bilayers or the base pairs in DNA. She tends to hold onto the idea; it's the principle of evolutionary conservation. Not only does Nature hold onto good ideas, but She also has a way of putting them to marvelous new uses. The discovery of a useful design increases the probability that new and better designs will arise. And in every evolutionary lineage, improved designs engender new and better ways for organisms to interact with their environment and with each other.

Brains must have seemed a great idea to Nature, because she made so many of them. Brains have elaborated the ways in which organisms interact with their environment and with each other. One organism with which I am familiar is notable for its facility in both endeavors; it even has parts in its brain that do both in different ways and from different perspectives. It is probable that Nature found two of those parts to be especially good ideas, because She has been building them both up at a fast rate and, by gad, She's still at it.

They may be building up at a disproportionate rate, the analytical brain and the empathic mind. Perhaps they are in competition, but

I don't think that's probable. The social/emotional brain has come up with some excellent ways for humans to get along with their conspecifics. Empathy, for one, not to mention kindness, tolerance, generosity or love. Not to mention the great good times we have on Saturday night with our sweetie. Evolution tends to conserve good designs and I can't think of any that are better.

The analytical brain is a terrific design, too, and I'm sure Nature will conserve that one as well, and even elaborate it in beneficent ways. Someday, the analytical mind will solve some of the problems that continue to vex us, like losing the key one needs to open a can of anchovies, what to do about books that are too heavy to carry when we take a long trip, and a way to get from the East to the West side on the subway. I probably won't be around to enjoy the fruits of its future successes, but I have secreted an extra anchovy-can key in a secret place in case it takes too long.

My credentials as a futurist may be dubious. I tend to speak from the perspective of a cheerful disposition, the consequence of high doses of antidepressant and mood-stabilizing drugs and 120 vitamins and supplements taken intravenously so that my body can absorb them better. I speak with confidence, in spite of days spent among people whose brains are riven by conflict, imbalance and unhappiness. I'm not referring only to the members of my immediate family, but also to my patients. In meeting those people, I have observed that bad OC is not a good thing. It's not good to have or to be around, it's not good for the human race, and I would be surprised if Nature wanted to conserve it.

Good OCs? You betcha, Nature will hold onto them. Fussy men and women, Ditzy Blondes, Great Detectives and Great Brains, children with active minds, and grown-ups with the active minds of children—they are all terrific ideas and evolution deserves a lot of credit. When more people in the world are like them, it will be a much better place.

Analytical and empathic brains working in synchrony is one of Nature's best designs. The latter may be prone to impetuous leaps of faith and the former to the nether reaches of self-absorption; those are not necessarily exceptions because they happen so often, but it's not unfair to consider them aberrations. In any case, we are just at the beta-testing stage. Less-than-evolved as we are, we still have our natural psychology, which understands the absurd lengths to which we can carry our proclivities and does its best to rein them in. "Do as you will," the Badger might have said, "as long as you don't make a fool of yourself too often." Badgers are fussy animals, and natural psychology can be fussy, too, but I am confident that it will help us choose a good way to evolve. The end-point may seem pointless to some, but we shall gather nonetheless for Sunday dinner, drink red wine with our macaroni, and express value-judgments—saints and sinners together, in kind, tolerant and generous ways. The human species will even be able to adapt to pointlessness and absurdity. We have had a lot of experience with it.

References

There is more to say about OC than a single book can contain. The interested reader, or one who is baffled by some of the author's obscure references and peculiar theories, can read further here: www.atonc.com/blog

Introduction

Apter, A., Fallon Jr., T. J., King, R. A., Ratzoni, G., Zohar, A. H., Binder, M., ... Cohen, D. J. (1996) 'Obsessive-compulsive characteristics: from symptoms to syndrome.' *Journal of the American Academy of Child and Adolescent Psychiatry 35*, 7, 907–912. https://doi.org/10.1097/00004583-199607000-00016.

Fineberg, N. A., Hengartner, M. P., Bergbaum, C. E., Gale, T. M., Gamma, A., Ajdacic-Gross, V., ... Angst, J. (2013) 'A prospective population-based cohort study of the prevalence, incidence and impact of obsessive-compulsive symptomatology.' *International Journal of Psychiatry in Clinical Practice 17*, 3, 170–178. https://doi.org/10.3109/13651501.2012.755206.

Fullana, M., Mataix-Cols, D., Caspi, A., Harrington, H., Grisham, J. R., Moffitt, T. E., and Poulton, R. (2009) 'Obsessions and compulsions in the community: prevalence, interference, help-seeking, developmental stability, and co-occurring psychiatric conditions.' *American Journal of Psychiatry 166*, 3, 329–336. https://doi.org/10.1176/appi.ajp.2008.08071006.

Fullana, M., Vilagut, G., Rojas-Farreras, S., Mataix-Cols, D., de Graaf, R., Demyttenaere, K., ... Alonso, J. (2010) 'Obsessive-compulsive symptom dimensions in the general population: results from an epidemiological study in six European countries.' *Journal of Affective Disorders 124*, 3, 291–299. https://doi.org/10.1016/j.jad.2009.11.020.

Hollander, E., Kim, S., Khanna, S., and Pallanti, S. (2007) 'Obsessive-compulsive disorder and obsessive-compulsive spectrum disorders: diagnostic and dimensional issues.' *CNS Spectrums 12*, S3, 5–13. https://doi.org/10.1017/S1092852900002467.

Miller, E. S., Hoxha, D., Wisner, K. L., and Gossett, D. R. (2015) 'Obsessions and compulsions in postpartum women without obsessive compulsive disorder.' *Journal of Women's Health (2002) 24*, 10, 825–830. https://doi.org/10.1089/jwh.2014.5063.

Muris, P., Merckelbach, H., and Clavan, M. (1997) 'Abnormal and normal compulsions.' *Behaviour Research and Therapy 35*, 3, 249–252.

Okasha, A., Ragheb, K., Attia, A. H., Seif el Dawla, A., Okasha, T., and Ismail, R. (2001) 'Prevalence of obsessive compulsive symptoms (OCS) in a sample of Egyptian adolescents.' *L'Encéphale 27*, 1, 8–14.

Pallanti, S. (2008) 'Transcultural observations of obsessive-compulsive disorder.' *The American Journal of Psychiatry 165*, 2, 169–170. https://doi.org/10.1176/appi. ajp.2007.07111815.

Park, L. S., Burton, C. L., Dupuis, A., Shan, J., Storch, E. A., Crosbie, J., ... Arnold, P. D. (2016) 'The Toronto Obsessive-Compulsive Scale: psychometrics of a dimensional measure of obsessive-compulsive traits.' *Journal of the American Academy of Child and Adolescent Psychiatry 55*, 4, 310–318.e4. https://doi.org/10.1016/j.jaac.2016.01.008.

Rachman, S., and de Silva, P. (1978) 'Abnormal and normal obsessions.' *Behaviour Research and Therapy 16*, 4, 233–248. https://doi.org/10.1016/0005-7967(78)90022-0.

Salkovskis, P. M., and Harrison, J. (1984) 'Abnormal and normal obsessions—a replication.' *Behaviour Research and Therapy 22*, 5, 549–552. https://doi. org/10.1016/0005-7967(84)90057-3.

Chapter 2

APA (2000) *Diagnostic and Statistical Manual of Mental Disorders, Fourth Edition, Text Revision (DSM-IV-TR)*. Arlington, Virginia: American Psychiatric Press.

APA (2013) *Diagnostic and Statistical Manual of Mental Disorders, Fifth Edition (DSM-5)*. Arlington, Virginia: American Psychiatric Press.

Miller, E. S., Hoxha, D., Wisner, K. L., and Gossett, D. R. (2015) 'Obsessions and compulsions in postpartum women without obsessive compulsive disorder.' *Journal of Women's Health 24*, 10, 825–830.

Monod, J. (1971) *Chance and Necessity: Essay on the Natural Philosophy of Modern Biology*. New York: Vintage.

Semendeferi, K., Armstrong, E., Schleicher, A., Zilles, K., and Van Hoesen, G. W. (2001) 'Prefrontal cortex in humans and apes: a comparative study of area 10.' *American Journal of Physical Anthropology 114*, 3, 224–241.

Uhde, T., and Nemiah, J. (1989) *Comprehensive Textbook of Psychiatry*. Baltimore: Williams & Wilkins.

van den Hout, M., and Kindt, M. (2003) 'Repeated checking causes memory distrust.' *Behaviour Research and Therapy 41*, 3, 301–316.

Chapter 3

Allen, A., King, A., and Hollander, E. (2003) 'Obsessive-compulsive spectrum disorders.' *Dialogues in Clinical Neuroscience 5*, 3, 259–271.

Chapter 4

Allemand, M., Zimprich, D., and Martin, M. (2008) 'Long-term correlated change in personality traits in old age.' *Psychology and Aging 23*, 3, 545–557.

Allport, G., and Odbert, H. (1936) *Trait Names: A Psycho-Lexical Study.* Princeton, NJ: Psychological Review Company.

Bleidorn, W., Kandler, C., Riemann, R., Spinath, F. M., and Angleitner, A. (2009) 'Patterns and sources of adult personality development: growth curve analyses of the NEO PI-R scales in a longitudinal twin study.' *Journal of Personality and Social Psychology 97*, 1, 142–155.

Bouchard Jr., T. J., and McGue, M. (2003) 'Genetic and environmental influences on human psychological differences.' *Journal of Neurobiology 54*, 1, 4–45.

Costa, P. T., and McCrae, R. R. (1994) 'Set like plaster: evidence for the stability of adult personality.' In *Can Personality Change?* (pp.21–40). Washington, D.C.: American Psychological Association.

Cundiff, J. M., Smith, T. W., and Frandsen, C. A. (2012) 'Incremental validity of spouse ratings versus self-reports of personality as predictors of marital quality and behavior during marital conflict.' *Psychological Assessment 24*, 3, 676–684.

Fowler, J. H., Settle, J. E., and Christakis, N. A. (2011) 'Correlated genotypes in friendship networks.' *Proceedings of the National Academy of Sciences of the United States of America 108*, 5, 1993–1997.

Garcia, J. R., MacKillop, J., Aller, E. L., Merriwether, A. M., Wilson, D. S., and Lum, J. K. (2010) 'Associations between dopamine D4 receptor gene variation with both infidelity and sexual promiscuity.' *PLoS ONE 5*, 11, e14162.

Gaunt, R. (2006) 'Couple similarity and marital satisfaction: are similar spouses happier?' *Journal of Personality 74*, 5, 1401–1420.

Gruzelier, J. H. (2006) 'Frontal functions, connectivity and neural efficiency underpinning hypnosis and hypnotic susceptibility.' *Contemporary Hypnosis 23*, 1, 15–32.

Munafò, M. R., Clark, T., and Flint, J. (2004) 'Does measurement instrument moderate the association between the serotonin transporter gene and anxiety-related personality traits? A meta-analysis.' *Molecular Psychiatry 10*, 4, 415–419.

O'Rourke, N., Claxton, A., Chou, P. H. B., Smith, J. Z., and Hadjistavropoulos, T. (2011) 'Personality trait levels within older couples and between-spouse trait differences as predictors of marital satisfaction.' *Aging and Mental Health 15*, 3, 344–353.

Pelham, B. W., Mirenberg, M. C., and Jones, J. T. (2002) 'Why Susie sells seashells by the seashore: implicit egotism and major life decisions.' *Journal of Personality and Social Psychology 82*, 4, 469–487.

Rantanen, J., Metsäpelto, R.-L., Feldt, T., Pulkkinen, L., and Kokko, K. (2007) 'Long-term stability in the Big Five personality traits in adulthood.' *Scandinavian Journal of Psychology 48*, 6, 511–518.

Sen, S., Burmeister, M., and Ghosh, D. (2004) 'Meta-analysis of the association between a serotonin transporter promoter polymorphism (5-HTTLPR) and anxiety-related personality traits.' *American Journal of Medical Genetics 127B*, 1, 85–89.

Shiota, M. N., and Levenson, R. W. (2007) 'Birds of a feather don't always fly farthest: similarity in Big Five personality predicts more negative marital satisfaction trajectories in long-term marriages.' *Psychology and Aging 22*, 4, 666–675.

Small, B. J., Hertzog, C., Hultsch, D. F., Dixon, R. A., and Victoria Longitudinal Study (2003) 'Stability and change in adult personality over 6 years: findings from the Victoria Longitudinal Study.' *The Journals of Gerontology: Series B, Psychological Sciences and Social Sciences 58*, 3, P166–P176.

Srivastava, S., John, O. P., Gosling, S. D., and Potter, J. (2003) 'Development of personality in early and middle adulthood: set like plaster or persistent change?' *Journal of Personality and Social Psychology 84*, 5, 1041–1053.

Zion, I. Z. B., Tessler, R., Cohen, L., Lerer, E., Raz, Y., Bachner-Melman, R., ... Ebstein, R. P. (2006) 'Polymorphisms in the dopamine D4 receptor gene (DRD4) contribute to individual differences in human sexual behavior: desire, arousal and sexual function.' *Molecular Psychiatry 11*, 8, 782–786.

Chapter 5

Ahmari, S. E., Risbrough, V. B., Geyer, M. A., and Simpson, H. B. (2012) 'Impaired sensorimotor gating in unmedicated adults with obsessive-compulsive disorder.' *Neuropsychopharmacology 37*, 5, 1216–1223. https://doi.org/10.1038/npp.2011.308.

Ardila, A., and Rosselli, M. (2002) 'Acalculia and dyscalculia.' *Neuropsychology Review 12*, 4, 179–231.

Childe, G. (1936) *Man Makes Himself.* London: Watts.

Curr, E. M. (1887) *The Australian Race: Its Origins, Languages, Customs, Place of Landing in Australia and the Routes by Which It Spread Itself over that Continent.* Melbourne: John Farnes, Govt. Printer; London: Trübner, 1886–1887.

Dehaene, S., Spelke, E., Pinel, P., Stanescu, R., and Tsivkin, S. (1999) 'Sources of mathematical thinking: behavioral and brain-imaging evidence.' *Science 284*, 5416, 970–974. https://doi.org/10.1126/science.284.5416.970.

d'Errico, F., Zilhão, J., Julien, M., Baffier, D., and Pelegrin, J. (1998) 'Neanderthal acculturation in Western Europe? A critical review of the evidence and its interpretation.' *Current Anthropology 39*, S1–S44.

Donald, M. (1991) *Origins of the Modern Mind: Three Stages in the Evolution of Culture and Cognition.* Cambridge, MA: Harvard University Press.

Drucker, P. F. (1995) *People and Performance: The Best of Peter Drucker on Management.* London: Routledge.

Gainotti, G. (2014) 'Why are the right and left hemisphere conceptual representations different?' *Behavioural Neurology 2014.* https://doi.org/10.1155/2014/603134.

Halberda, J., Mazzocco, M. M., and Feigenson, L. (2008) 'Individual differences in non-verbal number acuity correlate with maths achievement.' *Nature 455*, 7213, 665.

Hurford, J. R. (1999) *The Evolution of Culture.* Edinburgh: Edinburgh University Press.

Paivio, A. (2007) *Mind and Its Evolution: A Dual Coding Theoretical Approach.* New York: Lawrence Erlbaum.

Piazza, M., and Izard, V. (2009) 'How humans count: numerosity and the parietal cortex.' *The Neuroscientist 15*, 3, 261–273. https://doi.org/10.1177/1073858409333073.

Trewavas, A. (2002) 'Plant intelligence: mindless mastery.' *Nature 415*, 6874, 841.

Wang, Y. (2012) 'In search of denotational mathematics: novel mathematical means for contemporary intelligence, brain, and knowledge sciences.' *Journal of Advanced Mathematics and Applications 1*, 1, 4–26. https://doi.org/10.1166/jama.2012.1002.

Weinberg, S. (1994) *Dreams of a Final Theory: The Search for the Fundamental Laws of Nature*. New York: Vintage Books.

Chapter 6

Evans, A. H., Kettlewell, J., McGregor, S., Kotschet, K., Griffiths, R. I., and Horne, M. (2014) 'A conditioned response as a measure of impulsive-compulsive behaviours in Parkinson's disease.' *PLoS ONE 9*, 2.

Kandel, E. R., Schwartz, J. H., and Jessell, T. M. (2000) *Principles of Neural Science, Fourth Edition*. New York: McGraw-Hill.

Lorenz, K. (1966) *On Aggression*. London: Methuen & Co.

Rauch, S. L., Savage, C. R., Alpert, N. M., Dougherty, D., Kendrick, A., Curran, T., … Jenike, M. A. (1997) 'Probing striatal function in obsessive-compulsive disorder: a PET study of implicit sequence learning.' *The Journal of Neuropsychiatry and Clinical Neurosciences 9*, 4, 568–573.

Chapter 7

Maltby, N., Tolin, D. F., Worhunsky, P., O'Keefe, T. M., and Kiehl, K. A. (2005) 'Dysfunctional action monitoring hyperactivates frontal-striatal circuits in obsessive-compulsive disorder: an event-related fMRI study.' *NeuroImage 24*, 2, 495–503.

Modirrousta, M., and Fellows, L. K. (2008) 'Dorsal medial prefrontal cortex plays a necessary role in rapid error prediction in humans.' *Journal of Neuroscience 28*, 51, 14000–14005.

Vogt, B. A. (2016) 'Midcingulate cortex: structure, connections, homologies, functions and diseases.' *Journal of Chemical Neuroanatomy 74*, 28–46.

Chapter 8

Aron, E. N., Aron, A., and Jagiellowicz, J. (2012) 'Sensory processing sensitivity: a review in the light of the evolution of biological responsivity.' *Personality and Social Psychology Review 16*, 3, 262–282.

Craig, A. D. (2003) 'Interoception: the sense of the physiological condition of the body.' *Current Opinion in Neurobiology 13*, 4, 500–505.

Curtis, V. A. (2007) 'Dirt, disgust and disease: a natural history of hygiene.' *Journal of Epidemiology and Community Health 61*, 8, 660–664.

Douglas, M. (1966) *Purity & Danger*. London: Routledge Press.

Flynn, F. G. (1999) 'Anatomy of the insula functional and clinical correlates.' *Aphasiology 13*, 1, 55–78.

Freud, S. (1955) *The Sense of Symptoms* (Vol. 16). London: Hogarth Press.

Gu, X., Hof, P. R., Friston, K. J., and Fan, J. (2013) 'Anterior insular cortex and emotional awareness.' *The Journal of Comparative Neurology 521*, 15, 3371–3388.

Hartmann, A. S., Becker, A. E., Hampton, C., and Bryant-Waugh, R. (2012) 'Pica and rumination disorder in *DSM-5.' Psychiatric Annals 42*, 11, 426–430.

Okada, H., Kuhn, C., Feillet, H., and Bach, J.-F. (2010) 'The "hygiene hypothesis" for autoimmune and allergic diseases: an update.' *Clinical and Experimental Immunology 160*, 1, 1–9.

Olatunji, B. O., and Sawchuk, C. N. (2005) 'Disgust: characteristic features, social manifestations, and clinical implications.' *Journal of Social and Clinical Psychology 24*, 7, 932–962.

Rozin, P., and Fallon, A. E. (1987) 'A perspective on disgust.' *Psychological Review 94*, 1, 23.

Sartre, J.-P. (1969) *Being and Nothingness: An Essay on Phenomenological Ontology.* London: Routledge Press.

Strachan, D. P. (1989) 'Hay fever, hygiene, and household size.' *BMJ (Clinical Research Ed.) 299*, 6710, 1259–1260.

Taylor, K. S., Seminowicz, D. A., and Davis, K. D. (2009) 'Two systems of resting state connectivity between the insula and cingulate cortex.' *Human Brain Mapping 30*, 9, 2731–2745.

Terasawa, Y., Shibata, M., Moriguchi, Y., and Umeda, S. (2013) 'Anterior insular cortex mediates bodily sensibility and social anxiety.' *Social Cognitive and Affective Neuroscience 8*, 3, 259–266.

Voigt, C. C., Capps, K. A., Dechmann, D. K. N., Michener, R. H., and Kunz, T. H. (2008) 'Nutrition or detoxification: why bats visit mineral licks of the Amazonian rainforest.' *PLoS ONE 3*, 4, e2011.

Wolf, M., van Doorn, G. S., and Weissing, F. J. (2008) 'Evolutionary emergence of responsive and unresponsive personalities.' *Proceedings of the National Academy of Sciences of the United States of America 105*, 41, 15825–15830.

Woolley, J., Strobl, E. V., Sturm, V. E., Shany-Ur, T., Poorzand, P., Grossman, S., ... Rankin, K. P. (2015) 'Impaired recognition and regulation of disgust is associated with distinct but partially overlapping patterns of decreased gray matter volume in the ventroanterior insula.' *Biological Psychiatry 78*, 7, 505–514.

Chapter 9

Blackstone, W. (1765–1769) *Commentaries on the Laws of England.* Oxford: Clarendon Press.

Bolte, A., and Goschke, T. (2005) 'On the speed of intuition: intuitive judgments of semantic coherence under different response deadlines.' *Memory and Cognition 33*, 7, 1248–1255.

Carson, D. (2009) 'The abduction of Sherlock Holmes.' *International Journal of Police Science and Management 11*, 2, 193–202.

Dar, R. (2004) 'Elucidating the mechanism of uncertainty and doubt in obsessive-compulsive checkers.' *Journal of Behavior Therapy and Experimental Psychiatry 35*, 2, 153–163.

Gant, S. G. (1916) *Constipation, Obstipation and Intestinal Stasis (Autointoxication).* New York: W. B. Saunders.

Masley, S. C., Masley, L. V., and Gualtieri, C. T. (2012) 'Effect of mercury levels and seafood intake on cognitive function in middle-aged adults.' *Integrative Medicine* 11, 3, 32–39.

Mayo, E. (1952) *The Psychology of Pierre Janet*. London: Routledge and Kegan Paul.

Nestadt, G., Kamath, V., Maher, B. S., Krasnow, J., Nestadt, P., Wang, Y., … Samuels, J. (2016) 'Doubt and the decision-making process in obsessive-compulsive disorder.' *Medical Hypotheses 96*, 1–4.

Peirce, C. (1931) *Lectures on Pragmatism* (Vol. 1). Cambridge, MA: Harvard University Press.

Popper, K. R. (1996) *In Search of a Better World: Lectures and Essays from Thirty Years*. Hove: Psychology Press.

Poulin-Dubois, D., Brooker, I., and Chow, V. (2009) 'The developmental origins of naïve psychology in infancy.' *Advances in Child Development and Behavior 37*, 55–104.

Rapoport, J. L. (1991) *The Boy Who Couldn't Stop Washing: The Experience and Treatment of Obsessive-Compulsive Disorder*. London: Penguin.

Shapiro, D. (1965) *Neurotic Styles*. New York: Basic Books.

Sodre, I. (1994) 'Obsessional certainty versus obsessional doubt: from two to three.' *Psychoanalytic Inquiry 14*, 3, 379–392.

Valle, G., Carmignani, M., Stanislao, M., Facciorusso, A., and Volpe, A. R. (2012) 'Mithridates VI Eupator of Pontus and mithridatism.' *Allergy 67*, 1, 138–139.

Volz, K. G., and von Cramon, D. Y. (2006) 'What neuroscience can tell about intuitive processes in the context of perceptual discovery.' *Journal of Cognitive Neuroscience 18*, 12, 2077–2087.

Whorton, J. C. (2000) *Inner Hygiene: Constipation and the Pursuit of Health in Modern Society*. New York: Oxford University Press.

Chapter 10

Averill, J. R. (1983) 'Studies on anger and aggression: implications for theories of emotion.' *American Psychologist 38*, 11, 1145.

Bandura, A. (1977) 'Self-efficacy: toward a unifying theory of behavioral change.' *Psychological Review 84*, 2, 191.

Botvinick, M., Braver, T., Barch, D., Carter, C., and Cohen, J. (2001) 'Evaluating the demand for control: anterior cingulate cortex and conflict monitoring.' *Psychological Review 108*, 3, 624–652.

Brune, M. (2006) 'The evolutionary psychology of obsessive-compulsive disorder: the role of cognitive metarepresentation.' *Perspectives in Biology and Medicine 49*, 3, 317–329.

Heckhausen, J., and Schulz, R. (1995) 'A life-span theory of control.' *Psychological Review 102*, 2, 284–304.

Ortony, A., Clore, G., and Collins, A. (1988) *The Cognitive Structure of Emotions*. Cambridge: Cambridge University Press.

Power, M., and Dalgleish, T. (1997) *Cognition and Emotion: From Order to Disorder*. Hove: Psychology Press.

Rothbaum, F., Weisz, J., and Snyder, S. (1982) 'Changing the world and changing the self: a two stage process of perceived control.' *Journal of Personality and Social Psychology 42*, 5–37.

Skinner, E. (1996) 'A guide to constructs of control.' *Journal of Personality and Social Psychology 71*, 549–570.

Woody, E. Z., and Szechtman, H. (2011) 'Adaptation to potential threat: the evolution, neurobiology, and psychopathology of the security motivation system.' *Neuroscience and Biobehavioral Reviews 35*, 4, 1019–1033.

Chapter 11

Adolphs, R. (2010) 'What does the amygdala contribute to social cognition?' *Annals of the New York Academy of Sciences 1191*, 42–61.

Bishop, S. J., Duncan, J., and Lawrence, A. D. (2004) 'State anxiety modulation of the amygdala response to unattended threat-related stimuli.' *The Journal of Neuroscience 24*, 46, 10364–10368.

Breggin, P. R. (1974) 'Psychosurgery for political purposes.' *Duquesne Law Review 13*, 841.

Mark, V., and Ervin, F. (1967) 'Role of brain disease in riots and urban violence.' *The Journal of the American Medical Association 201*, 217.

Mark, V., and Ervin, F. (1970) *Violence and the Brain.* New York: Harper & Row.

Murray, E. A. (2007) 'The amygdala, reward and emotion.' *Trends in Cognitive Sciences 11*, 11, 489–497.

Pickens, C. L., Golden, S. A., Adams-Deutsch, T., Nair, S. G., and Shaham, Y. (2009) 'Long-lasting incubation of conditioned fear in rats.' *Biological Psychiatry 65*, 10, 881–886.

Quirk, G. J. (2004) 'Learning not to fear, faster.' *Learning and Memory 11*, 2, 125–126. https://doi.org/10.1101/lm.75404.

Siever, L. J. (2008) 'Neurobiology of aggression and violence.' *The American Journal of Psychiatry 165*, 4, 429–442.

Swanson, L. W., and Petrovich, G. D. (1998) 'What is the amygdala?' *Trends in Neurosciences 21*, 8, 323–331.

Zald, D. H. (2003) 'The human amygdala and the emotional evaluation of sensory stimuli.' *Brain Research Reviews 41*, 1, 88–123.

Chapter 12

Batson, C. (1990) 'How social an animal? The human capacity for caring.' *American Psychologist 45*, 336–346.

Broyd, S. J., Demanuele, C., Debener, S., Helps, S. K., James, C. J., and Sonuga-Barke, E. J. S. (2009) 'Default-mode brain dysfunction in mental disorders: a systematic review.' *Neuroscience and Biobehavioral Reviews 33*, 3, 279–296.

Buckner, R. L., Andrews-Hanna, J. R., and Schacter, D. L. (2008) 'The brain's default network: anatomy, function, and relevance to disease.' *Annals of the New York Academy of Sciences 1124*, 1–38.

Cilliers, P. (1998) *Complexity and Postmodernism: Understanding Complex Systems*. London: Routledge.

Dosenbach, N. U. F., Fair, D. A., Miezin, F. M., Cohen, A. L., Wenger, K. K., Dosenbach, R. A. T., ... Petersen, S. E. (2007) 'Distinct brain networks for adaptive and stable task control in humans.' *Proceedings of the National Academy of Sciences of the United States of America 104*, 26, 11073.

Hou, J., Song, L., Zhang, W., Wu, W., Wang, J., Zhou, D., ... Li, H. (2013) 'Morphologic and functional connectivity alterations of corticostriatal and default mode network in treatment-naïve patients with obsessive-compulsive disorder.' *PloS One 8*, 12, e83931.

Ingvar, D. H. (1979) '"Hyperfrontal" distribution of the cerebral grey matter flow in resting wakefulness; on the functional anatomy of the conscious state.' *Acta Neurologica Scandinavica 60*, 1, 12–25.

Peirce, C. S. (1931) *Lectures on Pragmatism. The Collected Papers: Pragmatism and Pragmaticism*. Cambridge, MA: Harvard University Press.

Peterson, A., Thome, J., Frewen, P., and Lanius, R. A. (2014) 'Resting-state neuroimaging studies: a new way of identifying differences and similarities among the anxiety disorders?' *Canadian Journal of Psychiatry/Revue Canadienne de Psychiatrie 59*, 6, 294–300.

Raichle, M. E. (2010) 'Two views of brain function.' *Trends in Cognitive Sciences 14*, 4, 180–190.

Spreng, R. N., Stevens, W. D., Chamberlain, J. P., Gilmore, A. W., and Schacter, D. L. (2010) 'Default network activity, coupled with the frontoparietal control network, supports goal-directed cognition.' *NeuroImage 53*, 1, 303–317.

Yerys, B. E., Gordon, E. M., Abrams, D. N., Satterthwaite, T. D., Weinblatt, R., Jankowski, K. F., ... Vaidya, C. J. (2015) 'Default mode network segregation and social deficits in autism spectrum disorder: evidence from non-medicated children.' *NeuroImage. Clinical 9*, 223–232.

Chapter 13

Freeman, P. J. (2009) *Wit in English*. Bloomington, IN: Xlibris Corporation.

Rapoport, J. (1991) *The Boy Who Couldn't Stop Washing: The Experience and Treatment of Obsessive-Compulsive Disorder*. New York: Dutton Books.

Chapter 14

Zadeh, L. A. (1965) 'Fuzzy sets.' *Information and Control 8*, 3, 338–353.

Chapter 16

Baxter, L. R., Phelps, M. E., Mazziotta, J. C., Guze, B. H., Schwartz, J. M., and Selin, C. E. (1987) 'Local cerebral glucose metabolic rates in obsessive-compulsive disorder: a comparison with rates in unipolar depression and in normal controls.' *Archives of General Psychiatry 44*, 3, 211–218.

MacLean, P. D. (1990) *The Triune Brain in Evolution: Role in Paleocerebral Functions.* Berlin: Springer Science & Business Media.

Menzies, L., Chamberlain, S. R., Laird, A. R., Thelen, S. M., Sahakian, B. J., and Bullmore, E. T. (2008) 'Integrating evidence from neuroimaging and neuropsychological studies of obsessive-compulsive disorder: the orbitofronto-striatal model revisited.' *Neuroscience and Biobehavioral Reviews 32*, 3, 525–549.

Saalmann, Y. B., and Kastner, S. (2009) 'Gain control in the visual thalamus during perception and cognition.' *Current Opinion in Neurobiology 19*, 4, 408–414.

Saxena, S., Brody, A. L., Maidment, K. M., Dunkin, J. J., Colgan, M., Alborzian, S., ... Baxter Jr., L. R. (1999) 'Localized orbitofrontal and subcortical metabolic changes and predictors of response to paroxetine treatment in obsessive-compulsive disorder.' *Neuropsychopharmacology 21*, 6, 683–693.

Spalletta, G., Piras, F., Fagioli, S., Caltagirone, C., and Piras, F. (2014) 'Brain microstructural changes and cognitive correlates in patients with pure obsessive compulsive disorder.' *Brain and Behavior 4*, 2, 261–277.

Chapter 17

Asperger, H. (1944) 'Die "Autistischen Psychopathien" im Kindesalter.' *Archiv fur Psychiatrie und Nervenkrankeiten 1117*, 76–136.

Down, J. L. (1887) 'Lettsomian lectures on some of the mental affections of childhood and youth.' *British Medical Journal 1*, 1360, 149–151.

Gillberg, C., Steffenburg, S., and Schaumann, H. (1991) 'Is autism more common now than ten years ago?' *British Journal of Psychiatry 158*, 403–409.

James, I. (2003) 'Singular scientists.' *Journal of the Royal Society of Medicine 96*, 1, 36–39.

James, I. (2004) *Remarkable Physicists: From Galileo to Yukawa.* Cambridge: Cambridge University Press.

Kanner, L. (1968) 'Autistic disturbances of affective contact.' *Acta Paedopsychiatrica 35*, 4, 100–136.

Krystal, H. (1998) *Integration and Self-Healing: Affect-Trauma—Alexithymia.* New Jersey: Lawrence Erlbaum Associates.

Pickover, C. (1998) *Strange Brains and Genius: The Secret Lives of Eccentric Scientists and Madmen.* New York and London: Plenum.

Samuels, J., Shugart, Y. Y., Wang, Y., Grados, M. A., Bienvenu, O. J., Pinto, A., ... Nestadt, G. (2014) 'Clinical correlates and genetic linkage of social and communication difficulties in families with obsessive-compulsive disorder: results from the OCD collaborative genetics study.' *American Journal of Medical Genetics—Neuropsychiatric Genetics 165*, 4, 326–336.

Taylor, G. J. (1984) 'Psychotherapy with the boring patient.' *Canadian Journal of Psychiatry/Revue Canadienne de Psychiatrie 29*, 3, 217–222.

Chapter 18

Botvinick, M. M., Braver, T. S., Barch, D. M., Carter, C. S., and Cohen, J. D. (2001) 'Conflict monitoring and cognitive control.' *Psychological Review 108*, 3, 624.

Brown, S., and Schafer, A. (1888) 'An investigation into the functions of the occipital and temporal lobes of the monkey's brain.' *Philosophical Transactions of the Royal Society of London B 179*, 303–327.

Gleick, J. (2011) *The Information: A History, A Theory, A Flood*. New York: Pantheon.

Gualtieri, C. (2002) *Brain Injury and Mental Retardation: Neuropsychiatry and Psychopharmacology*. Philadelphia: Lippincott Williams & Wilkins.

Happé, F., and Frith, U. (2006) 'The weak coherence account: detail-focused cognitive style in autism spectrum disorders.' *Journal of Autism and Developmental Disorders 36*, 1, 5–25.

Klüver H. and Bucy P.C. (1937) 'Psychic blindness and other symptoms following bilateral temporal lobectomy in Rhesus monkeys.' *American Journal of Physiology, 119*, 352–353.

Losh, M., and Capps, L. (2006) 'Understanding of emotional experience in autism: insights from the personal accounts of high-functioning children with autism.' *Developmental Psychology 42*, 5, 809–818.

Nahm, F. K., and Pribram, K. H. (1998) 'Heinrich Klüver: May 25, 1897–February 8, 1979.' *Biographical Memoirs: National Academy of Sciences 73*, 289–305.

Proops, L., McComb, K., and Reby, D. (2009) 'Cross-modal individual recognition in domestic horses (*Equus caballus*).' *Proceedings of the National Academy of Sciences 106*, 3, 947–951.

Tang-Wai, D., Lewis, P., Boeve, B., Hutton, M., Golde, T., Baker, M., ... Petersen, R. (2002) 'Familial frontotemporal dementia associated with a novel presenilin-1 mutation.' *Dementia and Geriatric Cognitive Disorders 14*, 1, 13–21.

Chapter 19

Assaf, M., Jagannathan, K., Calhoun, V. D., Miller, L., Stevens, M. C., Sahl, R., ... Pearlson, G. D. (2010) 'Abnormal functional connectivity of default mode sub-networks in autism spectrum disorder patients.' *NeuroImage 53*, 1, 247–256.

Belmonte, M. K., Allen, G., Beckel-Mitchener, A., Boulanger, L. M., Carper, R. A., and Webb, S. J. (2004) 'Autism and abnormal development of brain connectivity.' *The Journal of Neuroscience 24*, 42, 9228–9231.

Ecker, C., Ronan, L., Feng, Y., Daly, E., Murphy, C., Ginestet, C. E., ... Williams, S. C. (2013) 'Intrinsic gray-matter connectivity of the brain in adults with autism spectrum disorder.' *Proceedings of the National Academy of Sciences of the United States of America 110*, 32, 13222–13227.

Jung, M., Kosaka, H., Saito, D. N., Ishitobi, M., Morita, T., Inohara, K., ... Iidaka, T. (2014) 'Default mode network in young male adults with autism spectrum disorder: relationship with autism spectrum traits.' *Molecular Autism 5*, 35.

Kennedy, D. P., Redcay, E., and Courchesne, E. (2006) 'Failing to deactivate: resting functional abnormalities in autism.' *Proceedings of the National Academy of Sciences of the United States of America 103*, 21, 8275–8280.

Stern, E. R., Fitzgerald, K. D., Welsh, R. C., Abelson, J. L., and Taylor, S. F. (2012) 'Resting-state functional connectivity between fronto-parietal and default mode networks in obsessive-compulsive disorder.' *PLoS ONE* 7, 5, e36356.

Zhang, T., Wang, J., Yang, Y., Wu, Q., Li, B., Chen, L., … Gong, Q. (2011) 'Abnormal small-world architecture of top-down control networks in obsessive-compulsive disorder.' *Journal of Psychiatry and Neuroscience 36*, 1, 23–31.

Chapter 20

Campbell, J. (2004) *The Hero With a Thousand Faces*. Princeton and Oxford: Princeton University Press.

Cho, R. Y., Konecky, R. O., and Carter, C. S. (2006) 'Impairments in frontal cortical gamma synchrony and cognitive control in schizophrenia.' *Proceedings of the National Academy of Sciences of the United States of America 103*, 52, 19878–19883.

Hu, F. B., Li, T. Y., Colditz, G. A., Willett, W. C., and Manson, J. E. (2003) 'Television watching and other sedentary behaviors in relation to risk of obesity and type 2 diabetes mellitus in women.' *The Journal of the American Medical Association 289*, 14, 1785–1791.

LaMothe, R. (2007) 'An analysis of acedia.' *Pastoral Psychology 56*, 1, 15–30.

MacIntyre, S., MacIver, S., and Sooman, A. (1993) 'Area, class and health: should we be focusing on places or people?' *Journal of Social Policy 22*, 2, 213–234.

Rosanoff, A. J. (1929) 'Neuropsychiatry.' *California and Western Medicine 30*, 3, 197.

Stevenson, G. (1949) 'Armchair psychiatry.' *Psychiatric Quarterly 23*, 1, 71–82.

Chapter 22

Abramovitch, A., Dar, R., Hermesh, H., and Schweiger, A. (2012) 'Comparative neuropsychology of adult obsessive-compulsive disorder and attention deficit/ hyperactivity disorder: implications for a novel executive overload model of OCD.' *Journal of Neuropsychology 6*, 2, 161–191.

Brem, S., Grunblatt, E., Drechsler, R., Riederer, P., and Walitza, S. (2014) 'The neurobiological link between OCD and ADHD.' *Attention Deficit and Hyperactivity Disorders 6*, 3, 175–202.

Burgard, D. A., Fuller, R., Becker, B., Ferrell, R., and Dinglasan-Panlilio, M. J. (2013) 'Potential trends in Attention Deficit Hyperactivity Disorder (ADHD) drug use on a college campus: wastewater analysis of amphetamine and ritalinic acid.' *The Science of the Total Environment 450–451*, 242–249.

Clements, S. D., and Peters, J. E. (1962) 'Minimal brain dysfunctions in the school-age child: diagnosis and treatment.' *Archives of General Psychiatry 6*, 3, 185–197.

Cooper, M., Thapar, A., and Jones, D. K. (2015) 'ADHD severity is associated with white matter microstructure in the subgenual cingulum.' *NeuroImage: Clinical 7*, 653–660.

Froehlich, T. E., Lanphear, B. P., Epstein, J. N., Barbaresi, W. J., Katusic, S. K., and Kahn, R. S. (2007) 'Prevalence, recognition, and treatment of attention-deficit/ hyperactivity disorder in a national sample of US children.' *Archives of Pediatrics and Adolescent Medicine 161*, 9, 857–864.

Gross, M. D. (1995) 'Origin of stimulant use for treatment of attention deficit disorder.' *American Journal of Psychiatry 152*, 2, 298–299.

James, W. (1890) *The Principles of Psychology.* New York: Holt & Co.

Kaplan, B. J., Dewey, D. M., Crawford, S. G., and Wilson, B. N. (2001) 'The term comorbidity is of questionable value in reference to developmental disorders data and theory.' *Journal of Learning Disabilities 34*, 6, 555–565.

Knight, T. K., Kawatkar, A., Hodgkins, P., Moss, R., Chu, L.-H., Sikirica, V., … Nichol, M. B. (2014) 'Prevalence and incidence of adult attention deficit/hyperactivity disorder in a large managed care population.' *Current Medical Research and Opinion 30*, 7, 1291–1299.

Lapouse, R., and Monk, M. A. (1958) 'An epidemiologic study of behavior characteristics in children.' *American Journal of Public Health and the Nation's Health 48*, 9, 1134–1144.

Montejano, L., Sasané, R., Hodgkins, P., Russo, L., and Huse, D. (2011) 'Adult ADHD: prevalence of diagnosis in a US population with employer health insurance.' *Current Medical Research and Opinion 27* (suppl. 2), 5–11.

Safer, D. J., and Krager, J. M. (1983) 'Trends in medication treatment of hyperactive school children: results of six biannual surveys.' *Clinical Pediatrics 22*, 7, 500–504.

Safer, D. J., and Krager, J. M. (1988) 'A survey of medication treatment for hyperactive/inattentive students.' *JAMA 260*, 2256–2258.

Safer, D. J., and Krager, J. M. (1994) 'The increased rate of stimulant treatment for hyperactive/inattentive students in secondary schools.' *Pediatrics 94*, 4, 462–464.

Safer, D. J., Zito, J. M., and Fine, E. M. (1996) 'Increased methylphenidate usage for attention deficit disorder in the 1990s.' *Pediatrics 98*, 6, 1084–1088.

Strohl, M. P. (2011) 'Bradley's Benzedrine studies on children with behavioral disorders.' *The Yale Journal of Biology and Medicine 84*, 1, 27–33.

Wortis, J. (1984) 'Restless kids.' *Biological Psychiatry 19*, 8, 1169–1171.

Yakovlev, P. I. (1962) 'Morphological criteria of growth and maturation of the nervous system in man.' *Association for Research in Nervous and Mental Disease 39*, 3–46.

Chapter 23

Cooper, A. (1984) 'Narcissism in normal development.' In *Character Pathology* (pp.39–43). New York: Brunner/Mazel.

deVries, K., and Miller, D. (1985) 'Narcissism and leadership: an object relations perspective.' *Human Relations 38*, 6, 583–601.

Ellis, H. (1937) *Studies in the Psychology of Sex* (3rd ed.). New York: Random House.

Fromm, E. (1964) *The Heart of Man.* New York: Harper & Row.

Harrington, R., and Loffredo, D. A. (2010) 'Insight, rumination, and self-reflection as predictors of well-being.' *The Journal of Psychology 145*, 1, 39–57.

Joireman, J. A., Parrott, L., and Hammersla, J. (2002) 'Empathy and the self-absorption paradox: support for the distinction between self-rumination and self-reflection.' *Self and Identity 1*, 1, 53–65.

Lubit, R. (2002) 'The long-term organizational impact of destructively narcissistic managers.' *Academy of Management Executive 16*, 1, 127–138.

Morf, C. C., and Rhodewalt, F. (2001) 'Expanding the dynamic self-regulatory processing model of narcissism: research directions for the future.' *Psychological Inquiry 12*, 4, 243–251.

Pech, R., and Slade, B. (2007) 'Organisational sociopaths: rarely challenged, often promoted. Why?' *Society and Business Review 2*, 254–269.

Rosen, C. (2005) 'The overpraised American.' *Policy Review*, online.

Sedikides, C., Gregg, A., and Hart, C. (2007) 'The importance of being modest.' In *The Self: Frontiers in Social Psychology* (pp.163–184). New York: Psychology Press.

Stinson, F. S., Dawson, D. A., Goldstein, R. B., Chou, S. P., Huang, B., Smith, S. M., ... Grant, B. F. (2008) 'Prevalence, correlates, disability, and comorbidity of DSM-IV narcissistic personality disorder: results from the Wave 2 National Epidemiologic Survey on Alcohol and Related Conditions.' *The Journal of Clinical Psychiatry 69*, 7, 1033–1045.

Tempany, A. (2010) 'When narcissism becomes pathological.' *Financial Times*, September 3, 2010.

Trapnell, P., and Campbell, J. (1999) 'Private self-consciousness and the five-factor model of personality: distinguishing rumination from reflection.' *Journal of Personality and Social Psychology 76*, 2, 284–304.

Twenge, J., and Campbell, W. (2009) *The Narcissism Epidemic: Living in an Age of Entitlement*. New York: Atria.

Vazire, S., and Funder, D. C. (2006) 'Impulsivity and the self-defeating behavior of narcissists.' *Personality and Social Psychology Review 10*, 2, 154–165.

Chapter 24

Bailey, J. A., and Eichler, E. E. (2006) 'Primate segmental duplications: crucibles of evolution, diversity and disease.' *Nature Reviews: Genetics 7*, 7, 552–564.

Byars, S. G., Ewbank, D., Govindaraju, D. R., and Stearns, S. C. (2010) 'Natural selection in a contemporary human population.' *Proceedings of the National Academy of Sciences 107* (suppl. 1), 1787–1792.

Chimpanzee Sequencing and Analysis Consortium (2005) 'Initial sequence of the chimpanzee genome and comparison with the human genome.' *Nature 437*, 7055, 69–87.

Corballis, M. C. (2004) 'The origins of modernity: was autonomous speech the critical factor?' *Psychological Review 111*, 2, 543–552.

Courtiol, A., Pettay, J. E., Jokela, M., Rotkirch, A., and Lummaa, V. (2012) 'Natural and sexual selection in a monogamous historical human population.' *Proceedings of the National Academy of Sciences of the United States of America 109*, 21, 8044–8049.

Deacon, T. W. (2010) 'A role for relaxed selection in the evolution of the language capacity.' *Proceedings of the National Academy of Sciences of the United States of America 107* (suppl. 2), 9000–9006.

Dorus, S., Vallender, E. J., Evans, P. D., Anderson, J. R., Gilbert, S. L., Mahowald, M., ... Lahn, B. T. (2004) 'Accelerated evolution of nervous system genes in the origin of *Homo sapiens.' Cell 119*, 7, 1027–1040.

Enard, W., Khaitovich, P., Klose, J., Zöllner, S., Heissig, F., Giavalisco, P., ... Pääbo, S. (2002) 'Intra- and interspecific variation in primate gene expression patterns.' *Science (New York, N.Y.) 296*, 5566, 340–343.

Enard, W., Przeworski, M., Fisher, S. E., Lai, C. S. L., Wiebe, V., Kitano, T., ... Pääbo, S. (2002) 'Molecular evolution of FOXP2, a gene involved in speech and language.' *Nature 418*, 6900, 869–872.

Feder, M. E. (2007) 'Evolvability of physiological and biochemical traits: evolutionary mechanisms including and beyond single-nucleotide mutation.' *Journal of Experimental Biology 210*, 9, 1653–1660.

Flynn, J. R. (1984) 'The mean IQ of Americans: massive gains 1932 to 1978.' *Psychological Bulletin 95*, 1, 29.

Gommans, W. M., Mullen, S. P., and Maas, S. (2009) 'RNA editing: a driving force for adaptive evolution?' *BioEssays: News and Reviews in Molecular, Cellular and Developmental Biology 31*, 10, 1137–1145.

Hawks, J., Wang, E. T., Cochran, G. M., Harpending, H. C., and Moyzis, R. K. (2007) 'Recent acceleration of human adaptive evolution.' *Proceedings of the National Academy of Sciences of the United States of America 104*, 52, 20753–20758.

Jauch, A., Wienberg, J., Stanyon, R., Arnold, N., Tofanelli, S., Ishida, T., and Cremer, T. (1992) 'Reconstruction of genomic rearrangements in great apes and gibbons by chromosome painting.' *Proceedings of the National Academy of Sciences of the United States of America 89*, 18, 8611–8615.

Krantz, G. (1980) *Climatic Races and Descent Groups*. Boston: Christopher Publishing House.

Krubitzer, L., and Kaas, J. (2005) 'The evolution of the neocortex in mammals: how is phenotypic diversity generated?' *Current Opinion in Neurobiology 15*, 4, 444–453.

Krubitzer, L., and Kahn, D. M. (2003) 'Nature versus nurture revisited: an old idea with a new twist.' *Progress in Neurobiology 70*, 1, 33–52.

Lupski, J. R. (2007) 'Genomic rearrangements and sporadic disease.' *Nature Genetics 39* (suppl. 7), S43–47.

Lynn, R., and Hampson, S. (1986) 'The rise of national intelligence: evidence from Britain, Japan and the USA.' *Personality and Individual Differences 7*, 1, 23–32.

Mekel-Bobrov, N., Gilbert, S. L., Evans, P. D., Vallender, E. J., Anderson, J. R., Hudson, R. R., ... Lahn, B. T. (2005) 'Ongoing adaptive evolution of ASPM, a brain size determinant in *Homo sapiens.' Science (New York, N.Y.) 309*, 5741, 1720–1722.

Milot, E., Mayer, F. M., Nussey, D. H., Boisvert, M., Pelletier, F., and Reale, D. (2011) 'Evidence for evolution in response to natural selection in a contemporary human population.' *Proceedings of the National Academy of Sciences of the United States of America 108*, 41, 17040–17045.

Mingroni, M. A. (2004) 'The secular rise in IQ: giving heterosis a closer look.' *Intelligence 32*, 1, 65–83.

Monod, J. (1971) *Chance and Necessity: Essay on the Natural Philosophy of Modern Biology*. New York: Vintage.

Morrow, E. M. (2010) 'Genomic copy number variation in disorders of cognitive development.' *Journal of the American Academy of Child and Adolescent Psychiatry* 49, 11, 1091–1104.

Nahon, J.-L. (2003) 'Birth of "human-specific" genes during primate evolution.' *Genetica* 118, 2–3, 193–208.

Ruhli, F. J., and Henneberg, M. (2013) 'New perspectives on evolutionary medicine: the relevance of microevolution for human health and disease.' *BMC Medicine* 11, 115.

Semino, O., Passarino, G., Oefner, P. J., Lin, A. A., Arbuzova, S., Beckman, L. E., … Underhill, P. A. (2000) 'The genetic legacy of Paleolithic *Homo sapiens sapiens* in extant Europeans: a Y chromosome perspective.' *Science (New York, N.Y.)* 290, 5494, 1155–1159.

Sundet, J. M., Barlaug, D. G., and Torjussen, T. M. (2004) 'The end of the Flynn effect? A study of secular trends in mean intelligence test scores of Norwegian conscripts during half a century.' *Intelligence* 32, 4, 349–362.

Tang, B. L. (2006) 'Molecular genetic determinants of human brain size.' *Biochemical and Biophysical Research Communications* 345, 3, 911–916.

Underhill, P. A., Shen, P., Lin, A. A., Jin, L., Passarino, G., Yang, W. H., … Oefner, P. J. (2000) 'Y chromosome sequence variation and the history of human populations.' *Nature Genetics* 26, 3, 358–361.

Wang, E. T., Kodama, G., Baldi, P., and Moyzis, R. K. (2006) 'Global landscape of recent inferred Darwinian selection for *Homo sapiens*.' *Proceedings of the National Academy of Sciences of the United States of America* 103, 1, 135–140.

Weinberg, S. (1994) *Dreams of a Final Theory: The Search for the Fundamental Laws of Nature*. New York: Vintage Books.

Wildman, D. E., Uddin, M., Liu, G., Grossman, L. I., and Goodman, M. (2003) 'Implications of natural selection in shaping 99.4% nonsynonymous DNA identity between humans and chimpanzees: enlarging genus *Homo*.' *Proceedings of the National Academy of Sciences of the United States of America* 100, 12, 7181–7188.

Willis, C. (1993) *The Runaway Brain: The Evolution of Human Uniqueness*. New York: Basic Books.

Yunis, J. J., and Prakash, O. (1982) 'The origin of man: a chromosomal pictorial legacy.' *Science* 215, 4539, 1525–1530.

Subject Index

Author Index